Citrix® MetaFrame®
Access Suite
Advanced Concepts:
The Official Guide

ABOUT THE AUTHORS

Steve Kaplan is the National Director of Enterprise Strategy for Vector ESP, Inc., two-time Partner of the Year for Citrix Systems, as well as the largest independent Microsoft Gold Partner for Enterprise Systems. Kaplan is a Microsoft MVP. Kaplan is widely recognized as one of the originators of the ROI concept for an enterprise Citrix/ Terminal Services deployment, and helped develop the Citrix ACE Cost Analyzer Tool. He has sat on the advisory boards of several industry leaders, including a position on the Microsoft Partner Advisory Council. Kaplan is co-author of *Citrix MetaFrame Access Suite for Windows Server 2003: The Official Guide* (McGraw-Hill/Osborne), and also co-authored the first edition. He has written dozens of articles for various IT-related publications, including the first published article on utilizing Citrix software to facilitate Sarbanes-Oxley compliance. Since 1998, he has traveled around the country preparing ROI analyses for some of the nation's most prominent firms considering access infrastructure deployments. Kaplan holds a BS in business administration from U.C. Berkeley and an MBA from Northwestern's J. L. Kellogg Graduate School of Management.

Tim Reeser is President and cofounder of Engineering Computer Consultants (ECC), Inc. ECC is a Colorado-based Microsoft Gold Partner in Enterprise Systems and a Citrix Platinum partner, and has been providing enterprise security and access solutions for nine years. Tim is co-author of *Citrix MetaFrame Access Suite for Windows Server 2003: The Official Guide*, and has also written for *Windows.NET Magazine* and *Selling NT Solutions Magazine*. Additionally, Tim has been a nationwide speaker at industry events such as Citrix Solutions Summit, Ingram Micro's Venture Tech Network, and various user groups and consortiums. Tim holds a BS in Mechanical Engineering from Colorado State University, and is MCSE and CSA certified.

Alan Wood is a Program Manager and Senior IT Security Engineer with Engineering Computer Consultants. Alan co-authored *Citrix MetaFrame Access Suite for Windows Server 2003: The Official Guide.* In addition to his Microsoft certification, he is a Cisco Certified Network Professional (CCNP) and a Cisco Certified Design Professional (CCDP). Alan has over 25 years experience in designing, operating, maintaining, and troubleshooting IT security, networks, and telecommunications systems, ranging from military infrastructure to campus networks and teletypes to SONET. In the academic realm, he has developed and taught college curriculum for Microsoft Windows NT Network Administration and Telecommunications Systems.

Citrix® MetaFrame® Access Suite Advanced Concepts: The Official Guide

STEVEN **KAPLAN**
TIM **REESER**
ALAN **WOOD**

McGraw-Hill/Osborne

New York   Chicago   San Francisco
Lisbon   London   Madrid   Mexico City   Milan
New Delhi   San Juan   Seoul   Singapore   Sydney   Toronto

McGraw-Hill/Osborne
2100 Powell Street, 10th Floor
Emeryville, California 94608
U.S.A.

To arrange bulk purchase discounts for sales promotions, premiums, or fund-raisers, please contact **McGraw-Hill/Osborne** at the above address. For information on translations or book distributors outside the U.S.A., please see the International Contact Information page immediately following the index of this book.

Citrix® MetaFrame® Access Suite Advanced Concepts: The Official Guide

This book provides a summary of information regarding advanced concepts of the Citrix MetaFrame Access Suite. To further your knowledge, Citrix offers a full curriculum of structured educational opportunities, including instructor-led training through Citrix Authorized Learning Centers, eLearning, and Citrix Certification exams.

For in-depth training on the Citrix MetaFrame Access Suite, or to prepare to earn your Citrix Certified Administrator (CCA), Citrix Certified Enterprise Administrator (CCEA), or Citrix Certified Integration Architect (CCIA), we recommend that you visit www.citrix.com/edu.

1234567890 CUS CUS 01987654

ISBN 0-07-225710-5

Vice President & Group Publisher
Michael Hayes
Vice President & Associate Publisher
Scott Grillo
Editorial Director
Wendy Rinaldi
Project Editors
Kenyon Brown
Patty Mon
Acquisitions Coordinator
Jessica Wilson
Technical Editor
Jennifer Lang

Copy Editors
Linda Marousek
Bart Reed
Proofreader
Linda Medoff
Indexer
Jack Lewis
Composition and Illustration
Apollo Publishing Services
Series Design
Peter F. Hancik
Cover Design
Pattie Lee

This book was composed with Corel VENTURA™ Publisher.

CONTENTS

Part II

MetaFrame Access Suite: Administration, Maintenance, and Troubleshooting

Part III

Appendixes

FOREWORD

What is access? Access is a means to an end—the means of closing the gap that separates ideas, understanding, knowledge, insight, and action. Access facilitates, access informs, access empowers, and access has the ability to transform the way we work, live, play, and learn. From the telegraph, to radio, to television and the Internet, technological evolution over the past 100 years has focused on advancing access to create a world without borders. In today's information economy, access is more relevant than ever. Access creates opportunities for businesses and individuals to communicate and collaborate in ways that drive economic growth and improve the quality of our lives. Access means the ability to communicate wherever, whenever, and on any device—a quick glance at e-mail on a smartphone while rounding the golf course, secure connectivity to vital corporate data from a laptop in a hotel room, real-time patient updates while toting a tablet PC from the operating room to the recovery room. Boundless access transforms work from just being a place into an activity, and is the engine driving the successful twenty-first century enterprise.

In today's increasingly global business climate, competitive advantage pivots on how well companies link access to business strategy. A well thought-out access strategy extends beyond tactical implementations and must relate to the organization as a whole as well as to individual needs for information and collaboration.

Whereas individuals seek accuracy, timeliness, ease of use, and interactivity from their information access environment, companies look for security, control, cost savings, scalability, and ease of administration. Strategically treating access as a foundational element enables organizations to slash operating costs, tightly link global supply chains, unlock new markets, expand global operations, overcome unforeseen obstacles, and generally removes the barriers that separate worker from customer from company. One company has helped drive this vision of access more than any other—Citrix Systems, Inc.

This book is designed to help you plan, deploy, and administer a successful enterprise access strategy using the Citrix MetaFrame Access Suite. Through secure, easy, and instant access to information anytime from anywhere, using any device, your customers can realize the full potential of an on-demand enterprise. The Suite represents the most comprehensive approach to enable flexible, mobile, secure access to even the most widely dispersed enterprises. Nearly 50 million people and more than 120,000 organizations around the world currently rely on this market-proven access philosophy to drive their business forward and sustain competitive advantage.

The authors of this book—Steve Kaplan, Tim Reeser, and Alan Wood—have had something to do with this success, and they are members of a select group of Platinum-level Citrix Solution Advisors. They have contributed to our success and the increasing adoption of the Citrix vision of access infrastructure for the on-demand enterprise with both how-to information and hands-on implementation. In a combination of cutting-edge ideas and market-tested experience, the authors present the very latest on access infrastructure technology, along with best practices based on years of setting up hundreds of Citrix MetaFrame and Microsoft Terminal Server systems. I am grateful to them for their expertise and proud to contribute this forward. I am also very proud of the Citrix Product Development Team for researching, validating, and documenting the contents of this book.

Whereas access infrastructure for the on-demand enterprise simplifies the complexity of information systems, successful implementation requires careful planning and skillful administration. That's what this book is all about, and anyone planning to transform their company into an on-demand enterprise will benefit from reading it.

Russ Naples
Vice President, Product Development
Citrix Systems, Inc.

ACKNOWLEDGMENTS

We would like to thank the following departments within Citrix for their contribution to the content of the book:

▼ Product Development
■ Technical Communication
■ Consulting Services
■ Technical Support
▲ System Engineering

Also a special thanks to the Test Engineering group within Product Development for researching, validating, and documenting the content for this book. Additionally, Jennifer Lang of the Citrix Advanced Access Collateral Team worked many tireless days and weekends writing, coordinating all the Citrix resources, and ensuring content accuracy.

In addition to Citrix's help, Ben Reeser, Engineering Computer Consultants' Lead Support Center Engineer, also provided additional technical verification and support for the Password Manager and Conferencing Manager chapters.

INTRODUCTION

Without any fanfare or special promotion, Citrix's "Advanced Concepts Guide for MetaFrame Presentation Server for Windows Version 3.0" has become the most popular downloaded document from the Citrix support Web site. Savvy Citrix administrators have been garnering valuable information from different versions of this manuscript dating back to early 2001. We have assisted Citrix in expanding and updating their PDF into a comprehensive book encompassing best practices and recommendations for the entire MetaFrame Access Suite.

How This Book Differs from Citrix MetaFrame Access Suite for Windows Server 2003: The Official Guide

Our companion book is written for two audiences: business decision makers who evaluate enterprise IT options, and the IT administrators responsible for implementing and maintaining access infrastructure built on server-based computing. It covers both the technical and business requirements of implementing a Terminal Services/Citrix architecture capable of accommodating thousands of users running their desktop applications from central datacenters. Topics such as Windows Terminal Server 2003, project and organizational management, disaster recovery, and various third-party add-on applications are all discussed at length.

This guide is strictly a technical book focused on the planning, configuration, administration, and troubleshooting of the MetaFrame Access Suite. It provides in-depth analyses of the four MetaFrame Access Suite components: MetaFrame

Presentation Server, MetaFrame Secure Access Manager, MetaFrame Password Manager, and MetaFrame Conferencing Manager. This book is written for experienced IT administrators who want to improve their Citrix environments by incorporating best practices.

How This Book Is Organized

The book is divided into two main parts. Part I covers the concepts, planning, and configuration of the MetaFrame Access Suite. It is designed to assist in the pre-deployment of the different MetaFrame Access Suite components. It contains best practices and explanations of methods used by Citrix engineers in the planning and configuration of these components within different types of environments. Part I also includes a chapter covering security concerns in a MetaFrame Access Suite environment, with a focus on security related to the MetaFrame Access Suite itself.

Part II presents best practices for the administration, maintenance, and troubleshooting of the MetaFrame Access Suite. It is designed to assist in the daily administration and maintenance of Citrix MetaFrame Access Suite products. Part II is targeted to administrators who need to fine-tune their systems as well as troubleshoot issues that arise within the Citrix environment.

Appendix A details error messages, including Independent Management Architecture (IMA) error codes, IMA subsystem tracing, MetaFrame Presentation Server console error codes, Resource Manager billing error codes, and event log warning and error messages intended to help in troubleshooting and resolving problems with MetaFrame Presentation Server.

Appendix B is a table showing all registered Citrix ports.

Appendix C outlines the various files, locations, and registry entries that are added to a system when MetaFrame Presentation Server Client for 32-bit Windows (Program Neighborhood Client), Web Client, and Program Neighborhood Agent are installed onto a client machine.

Appendix D shows the Citrix *e*Labs hardware used for the test cases discussed in this book.

We also include Note, Tip, Important, and Caution elements to supply additional detail to the text. A Note is meant to provide information when the general flow of the discussion is concentrating on a different area or is not as detailed as the Note itself. A Tip is a specific way to do or implement something being discussed. An Important is a specific piece of information that is emphasized in order to catch the reader's attention. A Caution is meant to alert the reader to watch out for a potential problem.

When registry entries are discussed, we have abbreviated the keys to save space. For example, HKEY_LOCAL_MACHINE is abbreviated throughout the text to HKLM.

Throughout the book, we include appropriate references to further documentation that can be accessed from http://support.citrix.com.

Contacting the Authors

We welcome your feedback and will incorporate appropriate suggestions into further releases of the book. You can contact Steve Kaplan at steve.kaplan@vector.com, Tim Reeser at Tim.Reeser@engcc.com, and Alan Wood at Alan.Wood@engcc.com.

PART I

An Introduction to Citrix MetaFrame Access Suite

CHAPTER 1

Introduction to Citrix MetaFrame Access Suite and Components

"On-Demand Enterprise" is becoming a commonplace term in the IT vernacular. The on-demand enterprise gives users access to the information required to build business by providing easy, secure, and instant access to enterprise information and applications from anywhere, using any device or connection.

In addition to providing this ubiquitous access, the on-demand enterprise utilizes an effective access infrastructure strategy which both simplifies IT complexity and strengthens administrative control; access is more efficient, secure, and cost-effective. The Citrix MetaFrame Access Suite offers organizations the easiest and most cost-effective way to provide a single, secure point of access to enterprise applications and information on demand. The suite ensures a consistent user experience anywhere, on any device or connection, while allowing IT staffs to centrally deliver, manage, monitor, and control enterprise resources.

This chapter introduces the Citrix MetaFrame Access Suite and the products of which it is comprised: Citrix MetaFrame Presentation Server, Citrix MetaFrame Secure Access Manager, Citrix MetaFrame Password Manager, and Citrix MetaFrame Conferencing Manager.

THE CITRIX METAFRAME ACCESS SUITE

The Citrix MetaFrame Access Suite is an integrated infrastructure for delivering applications and information resources as IT services to any user regardless of device, connection, or location. Each component product of the MetaFrame Access Suite—MetaFrame Presentation Server, MetaFrame Secure Access Manager, MetaFrame Password Manager, and MetaFrame Conferencing Manager—adds to the technology portfolio in order to solve a myriad of access challenges for an organization. All of the products work together seamlessly to provide a secure, single point of access to enterprise applications and information on-demand, while ensuring a consistent user experience anywhere, anytime, using any device, over any connection.

While not a comprehensive list, the following are some of the benefits provided by the MetaFrame Access Suite component products:

▼ **Citrix MetaFrame Presentation Server**   Lowers the cost of IT and greatly improves scalability, adaptability, and predictability through Application Centralization

■ **Citrix MetaFrame Secure Access Manager**   Enables IT administrators to deliver browser-based access to the entire enterprise and increases productivity with access that is appropriate to user roles

■ **Citrix MetaFrame Password Manager**   Lowers help desk costs, improves security, and simplifies user experience by providing password security and enterprise Single Sign On access to any application or information resource delivered through the MetaFrame Access Suite

▲   **Citrix MetaFrame Conferencing Manager**   Provides intuitive application conferencing to eliminate the geographical distance between team members, thus increasing the productivity of meetings and enabling easy collaboration

CITRIX METAFRAME PRESENTATION SERVER

The foundation for the Citrix MetaFrame Access Suite, the MetaFrame Presentation Server, centralizes applications and their management to enable enterprises to provide users with access to a wide range of applications.

MetaFrame Presentation Server Editions

MetaFrame Presentation Server 3.0 is available in three different editions: Standard, Advanced, and Enterprise.

MetaFrame Presentation Server, Standard Edition

MetaFrame Presentation Server, Standard Edition is the standard version for standalone point solution implementations with 1 server and with 1 to 15 concurrent users. Standard Edition feature highlights include the Web Interface for MetaFrame Presentation Server, user shadowing, the Secure Gateway, Universal Print Driver, client time-zone support, Novell NDS support, client device support, and MetaFrame Presentation Server Client support. Although more than one server can be used with the Standard Edition, it is rare because applications cannot be load-balanced across servers, and any application publishing will have to be done separately on each server with different names.

MetaFrame Presentation Server, Advanced Edition

MetaFrame Presentation Server, Advanced Edition is the advanced version that includes all of the Standard Edition features with the addition of Load Management. This upgrade is designed for use in farms with 2 to 20 servers and 15 to 1,000 concurrent users.

MetaFrame Presentation Server, Enterprise Edition

MetaFrame Presentation Server, Enterprise Edition contains all the features included with the Advanced Edition as well as additional features required for enterprise management. These extended features include Resource Manager, Installation Manager, a plug-in for Microsoft Operations Manager, and Network Manager. Enterprise Edition is designed for 20 or more servers.

Table 1-1 is a comparative matrix of the three different editions and enumerates the feature support available with each edition.

	MetaFrame Presentation Server 3.0, Standard Edition	MetaFrame Presentation Server 3.0, Advanced Edition	MetaFrame Presentation Server 3.0, Enterprise Edition
ENABLING THE GLOBAL ON-DEMAND ENTERPRISE			
Enhanced Connection Policies	x	x	x
Management Console for the MetaFrame Access Suite	x	x	x
Delegated Administration	x	x	x
Increased Large Server Farm Support	x	x	x
Custom Dashboard Views with Active Content			x
Report Center			x
Zone Preference and Failover			x
SMOOTHROAMING: Increasing Productivity Through Reliable Mobile Access			
Dynamic Display Reconfiguration	x	x	x
Workspace Control		x	x
Session Reliability		x	x

Table 1-1.   MetaFrame Presentation Server Feature Grid

	MetaFrame Presentation Server 3.0, Standard Edition	MetaFrame Presentation Server 3.0, Advanced Edition	MetaFrame Presentation Server 3.0, Enterprise Edition
IMPROVING APPLICATION PERFORMANCE			
SpeedScreen Acceleration: Images	x	x	x
SpeedScreen Acceleration: Audio and Video		x	x
SpeedScreen Acceleration: Macromedia Flash		x	x
Web Interface Enhancements	x	x	x
Improved User Login Screens	x	x	x
Microsoft Remote Desktop Client (RDC) Support	x	x	x
Bi-directional Audio		x	x
PROVIDING A SECURE PLATFORM FOR REGULATORY COMPLIANCE			
FIPS-140	x	x	x
Section 508	x	x	x
ON-DEMAND LICENSING			
MetaFrame Access Suite Licensing	x	x	x

Table 1-1.   MetaFrame Presentation Server Feature Grid *(continued)*

	MetaFrame Presentation Server 3.0, Standard Edition	MetaFrame Presentation Server 3.0, Advanced Edition	MetaFrame Presentation Server 3.0, Enterprise Edition
ADVANCED SHADOWING			
Cross-server Shadowing	x	x	x
Many-to-One Shadowing	x	x	x
One-to-Many Shadowing	x	x	x
Shadowing Indicator	x	x	x
Shadowing Taskbar	x	x	x
APPLICATION MANAGEMENT			
Anonymous User Support	x	x	x
Application Publishing	x	x	x
Content Publish	x	x	x
Program Neighborhood	x	x	x
TCP-based Browsing	x	x	x
APPLICATION PACKAGING AND DELIVERY			
Centrally Install and Uninstall Applications			x
Create Logical Server Groups			x
Customizable Project Details			x
Delivery Verification			x
Distribute Service Packs, Updates, and Files			x
MSI Support			x

Table 1-1.   MetaFrame Presentation Server Feature Grid *(continued)*

	MetaFrame Presentation Server 3.0, Standard Edition	MetaFrame Presentation Server 3.0, Advanced Edition	MetaFrame Presentation Server 3.0, Enterprise Edition
Package Applications, Files, and Service Packs			x
Package Inventory			x
Packager Rollback			x
Schedule Package Delivery			x
Server Reboot Support			x
Support for the Unattended Installs			x
CENTRALIZED ADMINISTRATION			
Active Directory Support	x	x	x
Novell NDS Support	x	x	x
User Policies	x	x	x
Administrator Toolbar	x	x	x
Centralized Data Store	x	x	x
Citrix Administrative Accounts	x	x	x
Presentation Server Console	x	x	x
Citrix Web Console	x	x	x
Connection Control		x	x
CPU Prioritization		x	x
Windows Installer Support	x	x	x

Table 1-1.   MetaFrame Presentation Server Feature Grid *(continued)*

	MetaFrame Presentation Server 3.0, Standard Edition	MetaFrame Presentation Server 3.0, Advanced Edition	MetaFrame Presentation Server 3.0, Enterprise Edition
CENTRALIZED LICENSE MANAGEMENT			
Centralized License Activation	x	x	x
Enterprise-wide License Pooling	x	x	x
Plug-and-Play Licensing	x	x	x
CLIENT MANAGEMENT			
Auto-client Update	x	x	x
Business Recovery	x	x	x
ReadyConnect	x	x	x
Web-based Client Installation	x	x	x
NETWORK MANAGEMENT			
Monitor and Manage from Third-party Management Consoles			x
SNMP Monitoring Agent			x
PRINTER MANAGEMENT			
Citrix Universel Print Driver	x	x	x
Printer Auto-creation Log	x	x	x
Printer Driver Access Control	x	x	x
Printer driver replication	x	x	x
Printing bandwidth control	x	x	x

Table 1-1. MetaFrame Presentation Server Feature Grid *(continued)*

	MetaFrame Presentation Server 3.0, Standard Edition	MetaFrame Presentation Server 3.0, Advanced Edition	MetaFrame Presentation Server 3.0, Enterprise Edition
RESOURCE-BASED LOAD-BALANCING			
Instant Load-balancing Feedback		x	x
Load-balancing Reconnect Support		x	x
Schedule Application Availability		x	x
Specify Client IP Range	x	x	
SCALABILITY			
Enterprise-class Scalability	x	x	x
Cross-subnet Administration	x	x	x
SYSTEM MONITORING AND ANALYSIS			
Application Monitoring			x
Customized Reporting			x
Summary Database and Reporting			x
Perform System Capacity Planning			x
Real-time Graphing and Alerting			x
Server Farm Monitoring			x
Track User Access to Applications			x
User-definable Metrics			x
Watcher Window			x
ICA Session Monitoring			x

Table 1-1. MetaFrame Presentation Server Feature Grid *(continued)*

	MetaFrame Presentation Server 3.0, Standard Edition	MetaFrame Presentation Server 3.0, Advanced Edition	MetaFrame Presentation Server 3.0, Enterprise Edition
WEB APPLICATION ACCESS			
Web Interface	x	x	x
Application filtering and caching	x	x	x
Support for MetaFrame Secure Access Manager	x	x	x
Enterprise Services			x
ACCESS TO LOCAL SYSTEM RESOURCES			
Auto-printer Creation	x	x	x
Automatic Drive Redirection	x	x	x
Client Drive Mapping	x	x	x
Clipboard Redirection	x	x	x
COM Port Redirection	x	x	x
PERFORMANCE			
Instant Mouse-click Feedback	x	x	x
Persistent Bitmap Caching	x	x	x
Priority Packet Tagging	x	x	x
SpeedScreen 3	x	x	x
Text-entry Prediction	x	x	x
SEAMLESS USER EXPERIENCE			
High-/True-color Depth and Resolution	x	x	x
16-bit Audio Support	x	x	x

Table 1-1.   MetaFrame Presentation Server Feature Grid *(continued)*

	MetaFrame Presentation Server 3.0, Standard Edition	MetaFrame Presentation Server 3.0, Advanced Edition	MetaFrame Presentation Server 3.0, Enterprise Edition
Application Save Position	x	x	x
Auto-client Reconnect	x	x	x
Client Printer Management utility	x	x	x
Client Time Zone Support	x	x	x
Server-to-Client Content Redirection	x	x	x
Client-to-Server Content Redirection		x	x
Multimonitor Support	x	x	x
Panning and Scaling	x	x	x
Pass-Thru Authentication	x	x	x
Roaming User Reconnect	x	x	x
Seamless Windows	x	x	x
Win16 Multisession Support	x	x	x
UNIVERSAL CONNECTIVITY			
Universal Client Access	x	x	x
Support for Direct Asynch Dial-up	x	x	x
Support for TCP/IP, IPX, SPX, and NetBios	x	x	x
USER COLLABORATION			
Support for MetaFrame Conferencing Manager	x	x	x

Table 1-1.   MetaFrame Presentation Server Feature Grid *(continued)*

	MetaFrame Presentation Server 3.0, Standard Edition	MetaFrame Presentation Server 3.0, Advanced Edition	MetaFrame Presentation Server 3.0, Enterprise Edition
SECURITY			
Secure Gateway	x	x	x
Delegated Administration	x	x	x
SSL 128-bit Encryption	x	x	x
TLS Encryption	x	x	x
Smart Card Support	x	x	x
SecureICA 128-bit Encryption	x	x	x
SOCKS 4 & 5 Support	x	x	x
Ticketing	x	x	x

Table 1-1.   MetaFrame Presentation Server Feature Grid *(continued)*

CITRIX METAFRAME SECURE ACCESS MANAGER

Citrix MetaFrame Secure Access Manager is the most cost-effective way to provide secure remote access over the Web to any enterprise IT resource. MetaFrame Secure Access Manager provides access to client/server, legacy, and UNIX applications deployed on MetaFrame Presentation Server, as well as Internet and intranet sites, streaming media, documents, network file services, and XML-based web services. With a powerful set of easy-to-use wizard-driven configuration tools, IT administrators can enable browser-based access to the IT infrastructure with secure connectivity over the Web.

MetaFrame Secure Access Manager makes any enterprise resource available through a single point of access, securely delivered over the Internet using standards-based security—without the need to configure client-side software. IT administrators simply enable network resources to be presented through MetaFrame Secure Access Manager and then configure access control based on each user's business requirements.

CITRIX METAFRAME PASSWORD MANAGER

Managing passwords can be problematic. Users tend to forget multiple passwords, select easily guessed words for passwords, or store them in insecure places. These problems affect employee productivity, increase support costs, and even threaten system security. Citrix

MetaFrame Password Manager provides password security and Single Sign On access to Windows-, Web-, proprietary-, and host-based applications running in the MetaFrame environment, driving down the costs and confusion in managing multiple passwords while improving network security. Users authenticate once and MetaFrame Password Manager does the rest, monitoring all password-related events and automating end-user tasks, including logon and password changes. MetaFrame Password Manager simplifies computing for the end user, who has just one secure password to log on everywhere. This in turn helps to reduce the cost of supporting password problems and frees IT staff for more strategic projects.

> **NOTE:**   One large financial institution we worked with used to have 20.4% of their help desk calls related to password issues (which is about 5 percentage points below the average). After mandating that users implement complex passwords, the ratio of help-desk related password calls fell by half. Why? There were two reasons. Some users simply gave up trying to access certain applications. The primary reason, though, was that virtually everyone compromised authentication security by keeping a list of their passwords (usually in their upper-right desk drawer or on a sticky note attached to their monitors). Implementing MetaFrame Password Manager enabled them to both virtually eliminate password related help desk requests while significantly improving security.

MetaFrame Password Manager is comprised of three components:

▼ **MetaFrame Password Manager agent**   A 32-bit agent that runs on MetaFrame Presentation Servers or on a local client workstation, the agent acts as an intermediary between users and the applications that require authentication

■ **MetaFrame Password Manager Console**   A centralized management tool to configure the central credential store and control the settings and features that are available to the agent

▲ **Central Credential Store**   The central location where copies of users' credential records and agent settings files are stored. The central credential store is implemented using a shared folder (file synchronization) or Microsoft Active Directory. The agent synchronizes its local store with the central store, allowing users to access and maintain their credentials from any workstation

Once a user has logged in and authenticated to a directory service, the agent intercepts any future password requests with a query, asking if the user would like the password manager to manage this password. If the user answers yes, then the password information is stored in the agent's local store and handed back to the client workstation when the workstation queries for that password again. Depending on configurations in MetaFrame Password Manager Console, the agent's local store can synchronize this new information with a central credential store.

MetaFrame Password Manager enhances security by centralizing security policies, providing an encrypted file for each user's credentials, and allowing IT administrators to automatically generate passwords that are more difficult to crack. They can also change the passwords more frequently.

CITRIX METAFRAME CONFERENCING MANAGER

Presentations and conferencing have evolved from one-way presentation broadcasts and web conferencing to full collaboration and application conferencing. The trend toward "virtual" teams that work together from remote locations and different time zones is expanding because such teams can reduce overhead costs, drive new business, and optimize productivity.

The lack of information and communication systems' flexibility are often obstacles to enabling the on-demand enterprise because remote people cannot securely connect to the business information they need. Citrix MetaFrame Conferencing Manager remedies this by adding intuitive application conferencing to MetaFrame Presentation Server, helping to increase the productivity of meetings and enabling easy collaboration from different geographic locations.

MetaFrame Conferencing Manager integrates three components: a Microsoft Exchange/ Outlook calendar form; a MetaFrame Conferencing Manager interface that initiates, cancels, and manages the users and applications of the conferences; and MetaFrame Presentation Server's session shadowing features. These three components form an intuitive interface by which users create and join a collaborative conference session among multiple people. Teams can share application sessions, work together on documents of all kinds, and conduct online training regardless of the location of individual team members, the access devices, or network connections they're using.

CHAPTER 2

Management Architecture

This chapter covers MetaFrame Presentation Server architecture topics that must be addressed in the planning and pilot phases prior to deploying MetaFrame Presentation Server in the enterprise. The concepts discussed in this chapter include zones, the server farm's data store, the local host cache, bandwidth requirements for Independent Management Architecture (IMA) communication in the server farm, and license server sizing and scalability.

IMA COMPONENTS

Citrix's Independent Management Architecture contains four components: the IMA data store, zone data collectors, local host caches, and the IMA protocol. The IMA data store is responsible for keeping information about generally static farm settings such as published applications, load-balancing parameters, printer options and security. Farm information that changes regularly, such as the number of connected users or which member servers are currently online, is maintained in an in-memory database on each data collector. Each zone in a farm has its own data collector responsible for maintaining the operating information for that zone. Data collectors gather their information through communication with the servers in its zone and then communicate their zone's information to the data collectors in the other zones in the farm. Each server maintains a local database containing a subset of the information in the data store. The IMA protocol is responsible for communications between MetaFrame Presentation Servers and communications between servers and the Presentation Server Console.

UNDERSTANDING ZONES

In a MetaFrame Presentation Server farm, a *zone* is a grouping of MetaFrame Presentation Servers that share a common data collector (a MetaFrame Presentation Server that receives information from all the servers in the zone). Zones in a farm serve two purposes: to collect data from member servers in a hierarchical structure and to efficiently distribute changes to all servers in the farm.

All member servers must belong to a zone. By default, the zone name is the subnet ID on which the member server resides. A zone in a MetaFrame Presentation Server farm elects a Zone Data Collector (ZDC) for the zone if a new server joins the zone, a member server restarts, or the current ZDC becomes unavailable.

The trade-off of adding more zones is the open link (and thus the bandwidth required) to maintain updates between each ZDC so that all updated data can be propagated throughout the farm. During a zone update, the member server will update the ZDC with the requests and the changed data.

Sizing Zones and Data Collectors

Zone Data Collectors are used to keep information within a server farm up-to-date between member servers and other ZDCs. Every server farm has at least one zone that is set up by default. The challenge is to design the right number of zones in a farm so that each ZDC does not get overloaded with traffic from its member servers while at the same time limiting the amount of additional load on the ZDCs and bandwidth required by multiple zones. The interzone traffic should be both minimized and balanced between ZDCs.

The number of zones needed by a farm is dependent on the topology of the site in which the farm is being deployed, the number of users connecting to the farm, the number of simultaneous user logons, the number of published applications with load evaluators attached, and the length of time the average user stays logged on to a session (a single daily session or repeated short sessions), which should be kept to a minimum. The fewer zones a farm has, the more it will scale. The reason is that every time a dynamic event occurs, such as a logon, logoff, or disconnect, an update is sent to the ZDC. The ZDC must then forward the update to all other ZDCs in the farm. This consumes both bandwidth and CPU processing because the other ZDCs must keep up with the events in other zones as well as in their own.

Zones should not always be based on subnets. Zones can scale beyond 500 servers unless other environmental conditions warrant limiting their size. Suppose, for example, that a company has a MetaFrame Presentation Server farm containing 1,000 servers distributed between two distinct data centers which each host 500 servers. In this case, it would be more desirable to create two separate zones of 500 member servers each. In another scenario, this company plans to expand operations to a small, remote site in another location that would house 10 MetaFrame Presentation Servers in the same farm. In this case it would be optimal for the servers in the new location to join one of the original site's zones. The reason is based on the number of events that would flow across the wide area network (WAN). If the new site was placed in its own zone, the data collector for the new zone would receive replicated events from all the other data collectors in the farm. The number of events (logons, logoffs, and so on) coming from the other zones would be in the tens of thousands. On the other hand, the number of events generated by the new zone would be in the hundreds. It is optimal not to replicate the data collector traffic if it is not necessary. Therefore, by consolidating the new site into one of the original zones, the only traffic flowing across the WAN link would be events sent from the new site's member servers to the original site's zone data collector.

ZDC Hardware Configuration

Since the data collectors store all dynamic information in memory, it is important that the ZDC has sufficient RAM to store all of the records. For a farm consisting of 1,000 servers and 10,000 users, the data collector consumes approximately 200MB of memory. Memory usage will vary based on the number of published applications and users in the farm. The CPU plays an important role in determining the number of resolutions the data collector can process in conjunction with managing dynamic information. In general, a fast dual processor server with 1GB of memory makes a good ZDC.

It is important that all data collectors in the farm are sized to accommodate the largest zone. Since data collectors must manage the global state of the farm, they require the same processing capability of the other data collectors in the farm regardless of the size of their particular zone. Likewise if the data collector needs to be dedicated for one zone, all data collectors in the farm should be dedicated for their own zones.

Traffic from a Member Server to a ZDC

During a zone update, the member server will update the data collector with the requests and the changed data. To approximate the number of bytes sent from a single server to the ZDC during a complete update, use the following formulas based on the version and service pack level of MetaFrame XP:

MetaFrame Presentation Server 3.0: Bytes = 4900 + (200*Con) + (100*Discon) + (300*Apps)

MetaFrame XPe / SP3: Bytes = 6300 + (200 * Con) + (100 * Discon) + (150 * Apps)

MetaFrame XPe / SP2: Bytes = 3800 + (600 * Con) + (400 * Discon) + (300 * Apps)

MetaFrame XPe / SP1: Bytes = 3300 + (400 * Con) + (250 * Discon) + (150 * Apps)

MetaFrame XPe: Bytes = 11000 + (1000 * Con) + (600 * Discon) + (350 * Apps)

where

Con = Number of connected sessions

Discon = Number of disconnected sessions

Apps = Number of published applications in the farm

Traffic from a ZDC to a Member Server

In addition to the traffic generated by the member server, a small amount of traffic is also sent from the ZDC to the member server. This traffic accounts for approximately half of the data sent from the member server to the ZDC, so to predict the full bandwidth utilization, multiply the number of bytes from the formula above by 1.5. To approximate the amount of traffic destined for the ZDC, multiply the number of bytes from the above formula by the number of member servers in the zone.

CAUTION: These numbers are an approximation from data gathered in the Citrix eLabs. Actual results may vary.

A full zone transfer, the transmission of all of a zone's information, occurs when a ZDC comes online (for example, reboots or new ZDC added) or when a new ZDC is elected due to ZDC failure detection. To approximate the amount of data sent between two data collectors during full zone transfer, use the following formula:

MetaFrame Presentation Server 3.0 : Bytes = 9530 + (300*Con) + (300*Discon) + (500*Apps)

MetaFrame XPe: / SP3 Bytes = $(7400 + (6.3 * Srv\_Zone)) + (400 * Con) + (200 * Discon) + (300 * Apps)$

MetaFrame XPe: / SP2 Bytes = $17000 + (600 * Con) + (300 * Discon) + (600 * Apps)$

where

Con = Number of connected sessions

$Discon$ = Number of disconnected sessions

$Apps$ = Number of published applications in the farm

Srv_Zone = Number of Servers in the zone

During a zone update, approximately the same amount of data is transmitted between data collectors, so to predict the full bandwidth utilization, be sure to double the bytes from the formula above. To approximate the amount of traffic across all data collector links, multiply the number of bytes obtained from the above formula by the number of data collectors minus 1 in the farm.

Traffic Between Zones

Each ZDC has a connection open to all other data collectors in the farm. This connection is used to immediately relay any changes reported by member servers within its own zone to the data collectors of all other zones. Thus all ZDCs are aware of the server load, licensing, and session information for every server in the farm. The formula for interzone connections is the following:

$N * (N-1) / 2$

where N is the number of zones in the farm.

IMA Ping

If a ZDC doesn't receive communication from a zone member server within the configured time interval, the ZDC pings (IMA Ping) the member server to verify that it is online. The default interval is once a minute. A data collector will also send an IMA Ping to any other data collectors if it has not received any data from the target server within the configured time interval. This interval is configurable by adding the following value to the registry. The interval, in milliseconds, is expressed in hexadecimal (hex) notation.

HKLM\SOFTWARE\Citrix\IMA\Runtime\
KeepAliveInterval (DWORD)

Value: *0xEA60* (60,000 milliseconds default)

In normal operation, data collectors are synchronized through frequent updates. Occasionally, an update sent from one data collector to another data collector can fail. Instead of repeatedly trying to contact a zone that is down or unreachable, a ZDC waits a specified interval before retrying communication. The default wait interval is five minutes. That value is configurable by adding the following value to the registry. The interval, in milliseconds, is expressed in hex notation.

HKLM\SOFTWARE\Citrix\IMA\Runtime
\GatewayValidationInterval (DWORD)

Value: *0x493E0* (300,000 milliseconds)

Configure Data Collectors in Large Zones

The ZDC maintains all load and session information for every server in its zone. By default, a single zone supports 512 member servers in MetaFrame Presentation Server Feature Release 3 and above. Prior to FR3, each zone supported 256 member servers. If a zone contains more than 512 servers, each ZDC and potential ZDC must have a new registry setting. This new setting controls how many open connections to member servers a ZDC can have at one time. We recommend that the registry value be set higher than the number of servers in the zone to prevent the ZDC from constantly destroying and recreating connections in order to stay within the limit. This value is configurable by adding the following value to the registry in hex:

HKLM\SOFTWARE\Citrix\IMA\Runtime\MaxHostAddress
CacheEntries (DWORD)

Value: *0x200* (default 512 entries)

NOTE: If you do not have more than 512 servers in a zone, then increasing this value will not increase the performance of a zone.

Number of Servers in a Zone

A common misconception is that no more than 100 servers should be placed within a zone. The problem with designing too many zones in a large datacenter deployment is that the presence of multiple zones in a single datacenter will cause performance of the farm to decrease. This decrease is due to the fact that ZDCs must keep up with all the information contained within all other ZDCs in the farm. Each time an event occurs, the ZDC must forward this information to all other ZDCs in the farm. This increases the network consumption and the CPU load on the ZDC, as it needs to handle sending and receiving updates for all the events in the farm.

TIP: As a starting point, place 300 servers into a single zone and then monitor the CPU utilization on the ZDC.

THE DATA STORE

The data store provides a repository of persistent farm information for all servers to reference. The data store retains information that does not change frequently, which includes the following:

▼ Published application configurations

■ Server configurations

■ MetaFrame Administrator accounts

■ Trust relationships

▲ Printer configurations

CAUTION: Always maintain a backup of the data store database. If you do not have a backup from which to restore, you must re-create the farm if the MetaFrame database is lost. You cannot re-create the database from an existing farm.

Database Format

With the exception of indexes, all information in the data store is in binary format. No meaningful queries can be executed directly against the data store. Neither MetaFrame administrators nor users should directly query or change information in the data store. Use only IMA-based tools, such as the Presentation Server Console, to access the information in the data store.

CAUTION: Never directly edit any data in the data store database with IBM DB2, Microsoft SQL Server, or Oracle tools. Directly editing the data with one of these tools corrupts the farm database and causes the farm to become unstable or completely unusable.

Data Store Activity

If the data store is available, all servers in the farm query it during startup. The following registry setting determines if IMA requires a connection to the data store to start:

HKLM\SOFTWARE\Citrix\IMA\Runtime\

PSRequired (DWORD)

Value: *0* or *1*

If the value is *0*, IMA can start without a connection to the data store. If the value is *1*, IMA requires a connection to the data store to start. After the first time the IMA service starts successfully, the value is set to *0*.

Local Host Cache and the Data Store Polling Interval

A subset of the information from the data store is stored locally on each MetaFrame Presentation Server. This local copy of data is referred to as the Local Host Cache (LHC). The IMA service attempts to synchronize the LHC with the data store every time the IMA service is started.

Every 30 minutes, IMA will also query the data store to determine if any changes were made since the LHC was last updated. The first LHC polling cycle starts at a random time between x and $2x$, where x is the LHC polling interval. By default, since the LHC polling interval is 30 minutes, the first cycle will start anywhere between 30 minutes and 60 minutes after the IMA starts. The subsequent polling cycles start at 30 minute intervals (there is no randomness). If changes were made since the last query, then each server requests the changes and updates its own LHC. By default, the data store query interval is 30 minutes. However, the query interval is configurable through the following registry key with the value set in hex:

HKLM\SOFTWARE\Citrix\IMA\

DCNChangePollingInterval (DWORD)

Value: *0x1B7740* (default 1,800,000 milliseconds)

The IMA service will need to be restarted for the data store polling interval change to take effect.

For MetaFrame Presentation Server 3.0, it is not necessary to change the polling interval, even for large farms. Polling queries have been optimized in such a way that the amount of information read from the data store during an update is negligible. High amounts of data store activity should not be seen during normal MetaFrame Presentation Server 3.0 farm operations.

Troubleshooting High CPU Usage

With MetaFrame XP (prior to MetaFrame Presentation Server 3.0), maintaining a small number of servers in a farm means that 30-minute queries are not noticeable. As the farm grows in size though, more servers are querying the data store and the response time may increase. This is especially an issue with pre-FR3 farms. In very large farms, an incorrectly sized data store can consume all of its processing time just responding to the periodic polling queries. If the data store experiences high CPU usage when there should not be reads or writes to the data store, it is possible that the data store is not powerful enough to handle a query interval of 30 minutes. In order to determine if the data store query interval causes the high CPU usage on the data store, the query interval can be set to a very large number for testing purposes. If the CPU usage returns to normal with a large query interval, then the data store query interval is likely the cause of the high CPU usage, and will need to be adjusted by trial and error.

In order to troubleshoot high CPU usage, set the polling interval to 60 minutes and then restart all of the servers in the farm. If the data store still experiences constant high

CPU usage, the polling interval should be increased further. If, however, the CPU usage returns to normal, a smaller value should be tested.

Determine the Polling Interval

Ordinarily, when a change is made to the farm it is sent to all servers in the farm. It is possible though that some servers will miss an update due to network problems. In a worst case scenario, any changes to a server will not get propagated to that server until the next data store polling interval. Since the query interval is a backup method to guarantee synchronization if a server missed an event, it should not be set to an abnormally high value. Also, the polling interval does not have to be uniformly applied across all servers. Consider leaving the default polling interval on the data collectors, but increase it on the member severs. For example, if a data store takes 10 seconds to respond to a single polling query, then theoretically that database server could support up to 180 farm servers (6 servers a minute × 30-minute polling interval) in the default configuration before it falls behind servicing incoming requests. If the polling interval on all farm servers was set to 60 minutes, that same database server could respond to 360 farm servers before the requests would overlap.

NOTE: When zone changes are made, such as zone membership or properties of a zone, the servers affected should be rebooted to force the data store update and speed the synchronization process. Due to optimizations in the way the LHC pulls data from the data store in MetaFrame Presentation Server 3.0, normal farm operation should not cause data store CPU spikes.

Data Store Connectivity

For Feature Release 3 and earlier versions of MetaFrame Presentation Server XP, if a member server is unable to contact the data store for 96 hours, licensing stops functioning on the member server and connections are disabled. During the 96-hour grace period, however, users will still be able to log into the farm. Logons are dependent upon dynamic information and thus are handled by a ZDC in the farm; the data store is not accessed during the logon process. This grace period is built into the licensing subsystem for licensing enforcement. After 96 hours, clients will not be able to connect to the farm until the data store is brought back online.

If the data store has been down for more than 96 hours, it is not necessary to rebuild the farm. Once connectivity to the data store is reestablished, the farm will continue to function as it had prior to the data store disconnection regardless of the amount of time the data store had been offline.

NOTE: MetaFrame Presentation Server 3.0 relies on connectivity to the license server. If a MetaFrame Presentation Server 3.0 loses connectivity to the license server, it enters into a 96-hour grace period. During the grace period, the farm is operational. After 96 hours, only one administrator logon is granted and all other connections are denied.

> **Misconception**   "Data collectors are the only servers that communicate with the data store."
>
> **Actual**   IMA on all the servers must be initialized with the same settings regardless of the role of the server. Also, when the Presentation Server Console is opened, it connects to a specified MetaFrame server. This server's IMA service performs all reads and writes to the data store for the Presentation Server Console. Most changes made through the Presentation Server Console are written to the data store.

Refresh the Local Host Cache

If the IMA service is running, but published applications do not appear correctly during ICA Client application browsing, then force a manual refresh of the local host cache by executing **dsmaint refreshlhc** from a command prompt on the affected server. This action forces the local host cache to read all changes immediately from the data store.

A discrepancy in the local host cache occurs only if the IMA service on a server misses a change event and is not synchronized correctly with the data store.

Re-Create the Local Host Cache

The IMA service can fail to start because of a corrupt local host cache.

To re-create the local host cache, run **dsmaint recreatelhc** from a command prompt, which performs three actions:

1. Sets the following value to 1:

     HKLM\Citrix\IMA\Runtime\PSRequired

2. Deletes the existing imalhc.mdb

3. Re-creates an empty imalhc.mdb

When the IMA service is stopped and restarted, the local host cache is repopulated with the data from the data store.

NOTE: The data store server must be available for `dsmaint recreatelhc` to work. If the data store is not available, the IMA service will fail to start.

METAFRAME PRESENTATION SERVER COMMUNICATION BANDWIDTH REQUIREMENTS

The Citrix eLabs used a Microsoft SQL 2000 data store in order to determine bandwidth requirements for normal communication in a MetaFrame Presentation Server environment. This information can be used to determine potential bandwidth requirements for WAN-based farms.

CAUTION: The following results may not hold true for all situations. Recommendations vary based upon how much bandwidth is used by other network applications.

Bandwidth of Server to Data Store Communication

In a single server configuration, the server reads approximately 456KB of data for SP2 servers and 402KB of data for SP3 servers from the data store when it starts. The amount of data read is a function of the number of published applications in the farm and the number of servers in the farm in SP2, but this is no longer the case in SP3.

The amount of data (in kilobytes) read from the data store during startup of MetaFrame Presentation Server 3.0 is approximated by the following formulas:

MetaFrame Presentation Server 3.0: KB Read = $431 + 3.15*(Srvs -1)$

MetaFrame XPe / SP3: KB Read = $402 + 6.82*(Srvs -1)$

MetaFrame XPe / SP2: KB Read = $456 + 22*(Srvs -1) + .0720*Apps$

where

$Srvs$ = Number of servers in the farm

$Apps$ = Number of published applications in the farm

The amount of data read from the data store can require higher bandwidth as the farm size increases and certain actions are executed, especially when several servers are started simultaneously. Most network traffic consists of reads from the database. In the case of high latency or low bandwidth links, Citrix recommends that the data store be replicated across the link(s) [using the built-in replication tools of the database vendor chosen for your data store (such as Microsoft SQL, Oracle, or IBM DB2)]. A replicated data store allows all reads to occur on the network local to the MetaFrame server, resulting in improved farm performance.

If performance across the WAN is an issue, and having a replicated database at each site is cost-prohibitive, analyze the WAN links for alternative solutions. The IMA service start time ranges from a few seconds to several minutes. When the amount of data requested from the data store by the IMA service is greater than the size of the pipe between WAN segments, IMA waits for all of the data, resulting in a longer startup time.

> **TIP:** A third-party solution, such as Packeteer's PacketShaper, can be used to dedicate a specific size pipe for exclusive use by database traffic, thus avoiding network flooding in WAN environments.

When the IMA service takes a long time to start after a restart, an error may display on the server console of the server stating that the IMA service could not be started. The event log may have a message that states that the IMA service hung on starting. These errors are benign. The IMA service starts properly after the requests to the data store are serviced.

Bandwidth of Data Collector Communication

In order to maintain consistent information between zones, data collectors must relay all of their information to all of the other data collectors in the farm.

Table 2-1 illustrates the impact to network traffic by listing the amount of data transmitted for session-based events.

Each time these events occur, the member server sends data to the ZDC, which then sends data to all other ZDCs in the farm.

Table 2-2 illustrates the impact to network traffic by listing the amount of data sent by one ZDC to another when operations are performed by the Presentation Server Console on servers residing in different zones.

> **CAUTION:** Limit the use of zones to avoid the cost associated with the replication of zone data. For more information see the section on Zone Design in Chapter 4.

Application Publishing Bandwidth

The bandwidth consumed when publishing an application varies depending upon the number of servers in the server farm. In general, the amount of bandwidth consumed increases 390 bytes for every additional server in the server farm. Starting a new server generates the most amount of traffic to the other ZDCs. Starting a new server generates about 8.9KB worth of traffic to the ZDC in a default configuration.

IMA Compression

The amount of data transmitted in a typical server-to-server "conversation" can be compressed by as much as 4 to 1 with the IMA compression enabled in MetaFrame Presentation Server XP 1.0, Service Pack 1 and higher. IMA compression does not reduce the

MetaFrame Presentation Server 3.0

Event	Data transmitted (approximate)
Connect	.51KB
Disconnect	.48KB
Reconnect	.47KB
Logoff	.30KB

MetaFrame XPe / SP3

Event	Data transmitted (approximate)
Connect	.86KB
Disconnect	.68KB
Reconnect	.70KB
Logoff	.63KB

MetaFrame XPe / SP2

Event	Data transmitted (approximate)
Connect	1.20KB
Disconnect	1.3KB
Reconnect	1.2KB
Logoff	.65KB

Table 2-1.   Session-Based Events

number of frames transmitted on the network. Instead, IMA compression reduces the size of each frame that is transmitted between MPS servers. IMA compression is enabled by default.

TIP: The Packeteer PacketShaper with PacketWise version 5.02 automatically supports IMA traffic. Other third-party solutions can be configured to recognize IMA traffic by port number.

MetaFrame Presentation Server 3.0

Event	Data transmitted (approximate)
Presentation Server Console server query	.27KB
Application publishing	2.7KB
Changing a zone data collector	12KB

MetaFrame XPe / SP3

Event	Data transmitted (approximate)
Presentation Server Console server query	.53KB
Application publishing	.92KB
Changing a zone data collector	29KB

MetaFrame XPe / SP2

Event	Data transmitted (approximate)
Presentation Server Console server query	.42KB
Application publishing	.75KB
Changing a zone data collector	25KB

Table 2-2.   Management Console-Based Events

Application of IMA Bandwidth Formulas

The formulas presented in this chapter can be applied to determine bandwidth requirements for various scenarios including the initial boot of a MetaFrame farm, idle farm communication, event-based communication, new data collector election, Presentation Server Console communication, and LHC change events.

Initial Boot of a MetaFrame Farm

When a MetaFrame server is booted, it must initialize IMA Service during start up and it must also register with the data collector for the zone in which it resides. Figure 2-1 shows the schematic for an initial boot of a MetaFrame farm. In this example there are only two zones, so the data collector must only replicate the updates it receives from the member servers once to the other data collector. If there were three zones, it would have to replicate the same information twice. This causes higher bandwidth consumption and places a higher load on the data collectors in the farm.

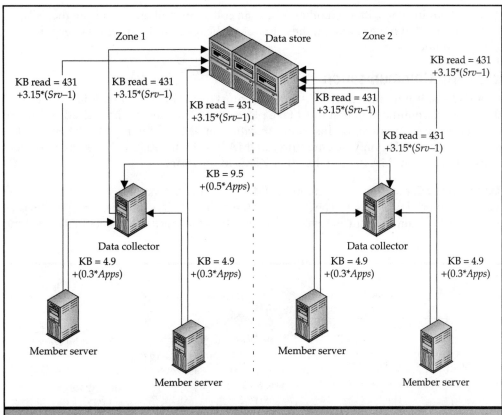

Zone 1   Data store   Zone 2

KB read = 431
+3.15*(Srv–1)

KB read = 431
+3.15*(Srv–1)

KB read = 431
+3.15*(Srv–1)

KB read = 431
+3.15*(Srv–1)'

KB read = 431
+3.15*(Srv–1)

KB read = 431
+3.15*(Srv–1)

KB = 9.5
+(0.5*Apps)'

Data collector   Data collector

KB = 4.9   KB = 4.9   KB = 4.9   KB = 4.9
+(0.3*Apps)   +(0.3*Apps)   +(0.3*Apps)   +(0.3*Apps)

Member server   Member server

Member server   Member server

Figure 2-1.   Initial boot of a MetaFrame farm

Note that license communication is not included in the diagram shown in Figure 2-1. The bandwidth utilized for contacting the license server is covered in the Network Bandwidth section of this chapter.

During the initial boot of a MetaFrame server, communication occurs in the following sequence of events:

1. The IMA Service establishes a connection to the data store for the farm. The IMA Service will then download the information it needs to initialize. It will also make sure the data contained in its LHC is current.

2. After the IMA Service is initialized, the member server will register with the data collector for the zone.

3. Next the data collector will need to relay all of the updated information written by the member servers in the zone to ALL other data collectors in the farm to keep

them in sync with each other. The data collectors will only replicate the *delta,* or items that have changed, they do not replicate all of their tables every time an update is sent.

Idle Farm Communication

There is a small amount of overhead that IMA must use, even if the farm is idle. Figure 2-2 shows the communication that must take place on a farm after it is initialized. There are three primary components of this communication, an IMA coherency check between the member server's LHC and the data store, an IMA Ping by the ZDC to the member servers in its zone, and an IMA Ping to the other ZDCs in the farm.

IMA Coherency Check   Every 30 minutes, IMA performs a coherency check between the member server's Local Host Cache (LHC) and the data store. If neither has changed, this operation only consumes about 200 bytes of bandwidth. If the check determines that something

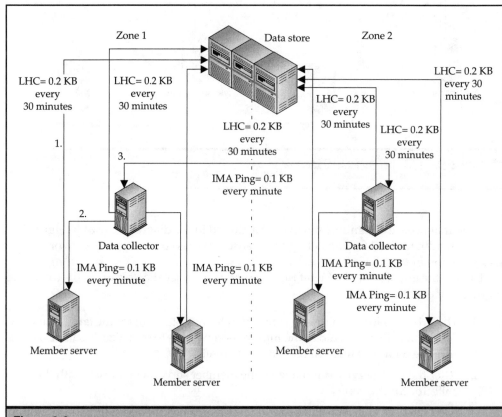

Figure 2-2.   Farm communication

has changed, the member server will search through the various contexts within the data store to determine what has changed in order to update the information in the LHC.

IMA Ping to Member Servers   In order to make sure the MetaFrame servers in its zone are functional and able to contribute to published applications, the data collector will send an IMA Ping to each of the member servers in its zone if it has not received an update from the member server within the last 60 seconds. The data collector will also ask the member server for its server load if it has not received a load update within the past 5 minutes.

IMA Ping to Other ZDCs   As mentioned earlier in this chapter, the data collectors will perform an IMA Ping to the other data collectors in the farm to ensure they are still ZDCs, and to ensure they remain operational if they have not received an update in the last 60 seconds.

Event-Based Communication

Most IMA traffic is a result of the generation of events. Figure 2-3 shows an example of a client logon event.

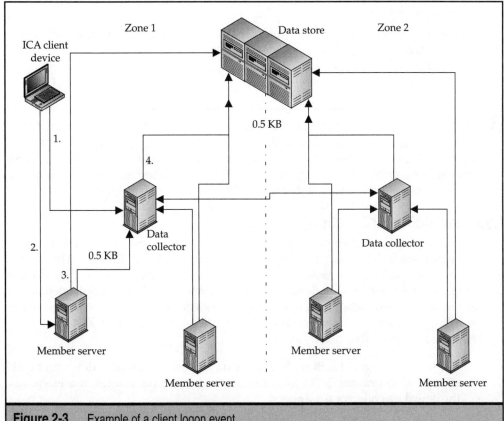

Figure 2-3.   Example of a client logon event

> **Misconception** "If a data collector goes down, the farm will go down, thus the data collector is a single point of failure."
>
> **Actual** The data collector election process is triggered automatically without administrative intervention. Existing, as well as incoming users, are not affected by the election process, as a new data collector is elected almost instantaneously. Data collector elections are not dependent on the data store.

When a client connects, disconnects, logs off, etc. the member server must update its load, license count, and such to the ZDC. The data collector in turn must replicate this information to all the other data collectors in the farm. There are four steps to a logon event:

1. The client sends a request to the data collector to resolve the published application to the IP address of the least loaded servers in the farm.

2. The client will then connect to the least loaded member server, per the response from the data collector.

3. This member server will update its load, licensing, and connected session information to the data collector for its zone.

4. The data collector will forward this information to all the other data collectors in the farm.

NOTE: Notice in the client logon event example shown in Figure 2-3 that there is no communication to the data store. Connections are independent of the data store and can occur when the data store is not available. Connection performance is not affected by a busy data store. Note also that license communication is not included in the diagram shown in Figure 2-3. The bandwidth utilized for contacting the license server is covered later in the "Network Bandwidth" section of this chapter.

New Data Collector Election

When a communication failure occurs between a member server and the data collector for its zone or between data collectors, the election process will be initiated. This is true whether network problems prevent communications to the network, whether the existing data collector for the zone is shut down gracefully, or whether it has an unplanned failure for some reason, (for example a RAID controller fails causing the server to blue screen). Figure 2-4 shows an example of farm communication after election of a new ZDC.

There are four steps that illustrate the process.

1. The servers in Zone 1 will recognize the data collector has gone down and will start the election process. In this example the backup data collector is elected as the new data collector for Zone 1.

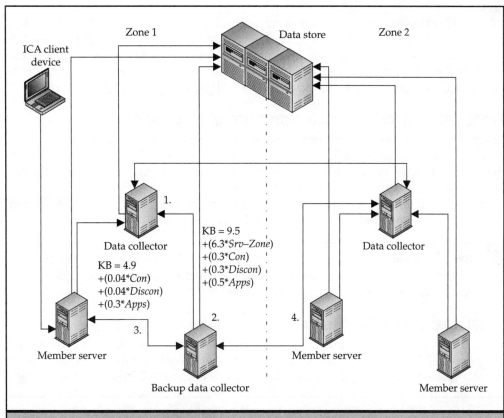

Figure 2-4.   Example of communication of a farm after election of a new ZDC

2. The servers in the zone will recognize that the data collector has gone down and will start the election process. The member servers in Zone 1 will then send all of their information to the new data collector (the Backup Data Collector) for the zone. This information includes the number of live sessions, disconnected sessions, and published applications.

3. The member servers in Zone 1 will next send all of their information to the new data collector (the Backup Data Collector) for the zone. This information includes the number of live sessions, disconnected sessions, and published applications.

4. The new data collector for Zone 1 will, in turn, replicate this information (a full zone transfer) to all other data collectors in the farm. In Figure 2-4, this includes just the data collector in Zone 2.

Presentation Server Console Communication Bandwidth

When the Presentation Server Console is launched, it gathers information from several different sources. It pulls static information, such as the server list, from the data store, dynamic data session information from the data collector, and Resource Manager-specific information from the farm metric server.

Table 2-3 illustrates bandwidth consumption to the data store when the following actions are performed using the Presentation Server Console.

TIP: When using the Presentation Server Console to monitor a farm at a remote site, bandwidth across the WAN can be conserved by publishing the Presentation Server Console application on a remote server and connecting to it using an ICA Client locally.

Local Host Cache Change Events

When configuration changes are modified in the Presentation Server Console, the changes are propagated across the farm using directory change notification broadcasts. These broadcasts take place when a change is made that is under 10KB in size. The broadcasts

MetaFrame Presentation Server 3.0	
Action	**Data Transmitted (in KB)**
Server enumeration (one server)	0
Server details (one server)	169.88
Server query	26.10
Application enumeration (one application)	11.97
Application query	145.06
Add Resource Manager metric to application	11.33
Add Resource Manager metric to application and configure	21.95
Change farm metric server	15.88
Any Resource Manager report on the local server	6.58

Table 2-3. Data Store Bandwidth Consumption Resulting from Presentation Server Console Actions

MetaFrame XPe / SP3

Action	Data Transmitted (in KB)
Server enumeration (one server)	.66
Server details (one server)	14.31
Server query	7.13
Application enumeration (one application)	.71
Application query	15.57
Add Resource Manager metric to application	3.69
Add Resource Manager metric to application and configure	6.76
Change farm metric server	5.29
Any Resource Manager report on the local server	1.56

MetaFrame XPe / SP2

Action	Data Transmitted (in KB)
Server enumeration (one server)	13
Server details (one server)	20
Server query	193
Application enumeration (one application)	6
Application query	4
Add Resource Manager metric to application	11
Add Resource Manager metric to application and configure	21
Change farm metric server	45
Any Resource Manager report on the local server	5.13

Table 2-3.   Data Store Bandwidth Consumption Resulting from Presentation Server Console Actions *(continued)*

help to minimize WAN traffic and alleviate contention on the data store. The propagation of the change notification is not guaranteed. If a server misses a change notification, it will pick up the change the next time it does an LHC coherency check.

Figure 2-5 shows an example of LHC change events communication.

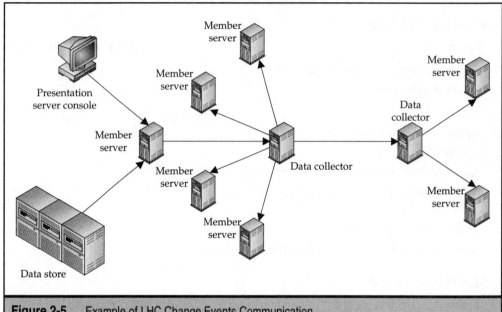

Figure 2-5. Example of LHC Change Events Communication

The following steps illustrate how this process occurs:

1. The administrator makes a change in the Presentation Server Console affecting all the servers in the farm.

2. The member server that the Presentation Server Console is connected to will update its LHC and write the change to the data store.

3. The member server will then forward the change to the data collector for the zone in which it resides. The data collector will update its LHC.

4. The data collector in turn will forward the change to all the member servers in its zone and all other data collectors in the farm. All servers will update their LHCs with the change.

5. The data collectors in the other zones will, in turn, forward the update to all the member servers in their zones, and they will subsequently update their LHCs.

NOTE: Almost all IMA changes are under 10KB in size.

LICENSE SERVER SIZING AND SCALABILITY

The overall sizing of a license server can be broken down into two pieces: the rate at which licenses are acquired and the number of licenses in use. The rate at which licenses are acquired is dependent on the speed of the CPU and network. The number of licenses in use impacts both memory and disk resources. In order to configure the optimal solution, it is important to understand requirements for processor speed, hard disk space, network bandwidth and memory.

Processor Speed

One of the most important considerations in determining license server requirements is the processor speed of the machine running the license server. Although CPU usage is not usually high, CPU time increases when license check-out requests and License Management Console activity increase. The time it takes to execute these transactions is dependent on the speed of the CPU. In general, the size of the farm and the number of simultaneous client connections will dictate the power of the server needed for licensing.

The license server is a single threaded application; the number of processors the license server can utilize depends on whether the license server is a dedicated or shared machine. For dedicated license servers, one fast processor is a better choice than multiple slower processors because the license server cannot exploit multiple processors. When the license server is installed in conjunction with MetaFrame Presentation Server, installing the license server on a computer with multiple processors will improve overall server performance.

Analysis of license server performance conducted in the Citrix eLabs shows that a Dell PowerEdge 2650 with a 2.2 GHz processor can handle 170 license check-outs per second, license check-ins are not measured since they consume virtually no CPU resources.

When sizing a license server it is important to determine the number of client logins per second in the MetaFrame deployment. To accomplish this, use the PerfMon counters available with MetaFrame Presentation Server 3.0 and the load evaluator logging feature in the Presentation Server Console. This number will determine the speed of processor needed for optimal license server performance.

To use the performance monitor counters, open the performance monitor on the farm's Data Collector(s) and begin monitoring the Application Resolutions/sec counter under the object "Citrix MetaFrame Presentation Server" during peak login times. The number of Application Resolutions/sec will directly correspond to the number of license check-outs occurring on the License Server. The performance of license check-outs can be further monitored on a farm member server by using the Last Recorded License Check-out time (ms) counter, also under the object "Citrix MetaFrame Presentation Server."

Hard Drive Space

Installing MetaFrame Access Suite licensing requires approximately 30MB of hard drive space. The most significant factor, however, in determining hard drive space is the amount of space the usage log files require. The license server logs license activity in *usage logs* for historical reporting.

Hard drive space requirements are determined by two factors:

▼   The length of time desired for keeping usage log files

▲   The amount of license activity

The more license activity on the license server, the larger the usage log grows. It is important to determine both the desired length of time for keeping usage logs as well as the frequency for archiving and/or rotating these files.

Usage Log Size

For best performance when generating historical usage reports in the License Management Console, keep the size of the usage logs under 150MB. This can be accomplished by writing a script that monitors the size of the usage log and backs it up when a certain size is reached. For more details on backing up usage log files and the *lmswitchr* and *lmreread* commands, consult the "MetaFrame Access Suite Licensing Guide."

The amount of disk space the usage logs consume is dependent on the number of client logons generated in the MetaFrame environment. 1.2KB of disk space is used for every 50 license transactions (license check-out and check-in).

Network Bandwidth

When deploying a license server into a MetaFrame environment it is important to understand the communication paths and bandwidth costs associated with licensing. This is especially important when communication is over a WAN. This section will describe the communication characteristics of the license server and the amount of bandwidth consumed with each transaction. Figure 2-6 shows the communication characteristics of the license server.

There are four transactions consuming bandwidth:

1. When a MetaFrame Presentation Server is brought online, it will read the location of the license server from the data store. The server will then establish a static connection to the license server and check-out a Citrix startup license through this connection. This action will consume 1.67KB of bandwidth. All servers in the farm will take one startup license. Once a startup license is checked-out, the license server will hold this license until it is either taken offline or until its location is changed in the Presentation Server Console.

2. All communication to and from the license server is over the connection established in Step 1. During the client logon process, the MPS server will request a license from the license server on behalf of the client. The amount of bandwidth consumed for a license check-out or check-in request is 1.67KB.

3. Every 2 minutes the MPS server will exchange a heartbeat with the license server to determine if the license server is still available. The amount of bandwidth in this transaction is 456 bytes for each server.

4. Every 60 minutes the MPS server will request a refresh of the license server data, this is to check if license allocation has been increased or decreased. The amount of bandwidth in this transaction is 2.4KB for each server.

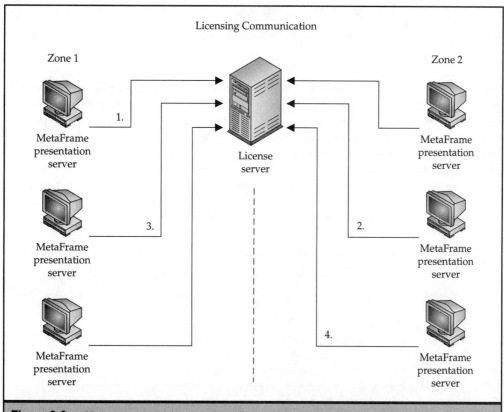

Figure 2-6. License server actions in a MetaFrame presentation server environment

MetaFrame Presentation Servers	# of Licenses in Use	Citrix Vendor Daemon Physical Memory in KB	Citrix Vendor Daemon Virtual Memory in KB
0	0	4072	1552
8	512	5476	2988
16	1024	7196	4696
40	2560	12336	9840
80	5060	20912	18424
160	10012	38036	35536
327	20143	73640	71140
500	30335	110020	107472

Table 2-4.   Citrix Vendor Daemon Memory Utilization

Memory

The size of the MetaFrame Presentation Server environment will determine the memory requirements for the license server. Memory utilization of the licensing processes is dependent on the number of licenses checked-out. The Citrix Vendor Daemon is a process that runs on the licensing server and tracks the number of licenses that are checked out and which product has them. The term "Daemon" is a UNIX term for a process that does a specific operation in response to a predefined event or at a preset time. The Windows equivalent is a service or a System Agent. Table 2-4 shows the constant memory utilization of the Citrix vendor daemon (*Citrix.exe*) at various levels of license consumption.

Figure 2-7 shows a graphical representation of the license server memory usage versus licenses in use.

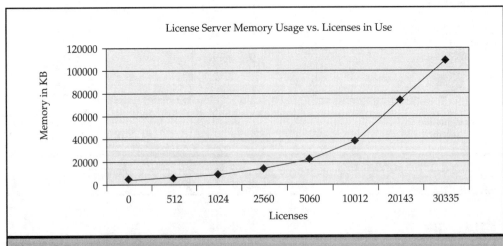

Figure 2-7.   License server memory usage

CHAPTER 3

Server Configuration Design and Recommendations

This chapter is intended to assist in the MetaFrame Presentation Server design and configuration architecture that must be addressed in the planning and pilot phases prior to deploying MetaFrame Presentation Server in a large enterprise. The concepts discussed in this chapter include hardware configurations and server sizing, operating system configurations, data store sizing, CPU utilization, and performance analysis planning.

RECOMMENDATIONS FOR METAFRAME PRESENTATION SERVER CONFIGURATION

Server sizing has long been considered more of an art than a science, since the most significant performance variables in any Citrix environment—the applications and the number of users, plus how they will interact and behave in the environment—simply cannot be predicted without empirical data and simulation testing. This section covers general recommendations for server hardware and operating system configurations that should be considered prior to deploying Citrix MetaFrame Presentation Server 3.0 for Windows. Although these guidelines will provide an excellent starting point, the final hardware plan should be tested in a simulated environment to fully understand the scaling and bottleneck parameters specific to your applications and users. Please see Chapters 10 and 11 of *Citrix MetaFrame Access Suite for Windows Server 2003: The Official Guide* for a more in depth discussion of pilot testing, regression testing, and non-production test lab configurations.

Hardware Configurations

Over the last several years, much progress has been made within Citrix *e*labs to truly understand the server hardware bottlenecks in a Citrix environment. One of the more significant findings has been the discovery of the impact of input/output (I/O) bottlenecks. Server hard drives remain one of the slowest components in a server, by an order of magnitude. Addtionally, they also remain a large source of failure, due to the moving parts and heat associated with those parts. Thus, Citrix recommends a RAID (Redundant Array of Independent Disks) setup. The recommended configuration is RAID 5 (Striping with Parity), which offers both a redundancy and a read speed increase. If cost is a huge concern, RAID 1 (mirroring) can be utilized to alleviate the impact of a hard disk failure. See the *MetaFrame Presentation Server Administrator's Guide* for more information regarding available RAID configurations. For speed purposes, Ultra 320, with 15,000 RPM drives will curtail disk bottlenecks. In larger environments with I/O intense applications, solid state disk drives (TiGi Corporation, http://www.tigicorp.com, is one manufacturer of solid state drives) have shown to dramatically increase (50–100%) the number of users a given server platform can support.

For quad and eight-way servers, use a solid state disk or install at least two controllers: one for OS disk usage and the other to store applications and temporary files, and to isolate the operating system as much as possible, with no applications installed on its controller. If solid state drives will not be used, it is also critical to distribute the hard drive access load as evenly as possible across the controllers.

Improve Logon Performance

Misconception   "Heavy usage of the data store causes logons to be slow."

Actual   The logon process is not dependent on the data store. Logons are dependent on dynamic information and, thus, are handled by a data collector in the farm. Logon times are impacted by the size of user profiles and the speed in which they are copied from their storage space to the local machine. Other items that can also have a significant impact include printer mappings, drive mappings, domain controller location and performance, data collector location and performance, and logon scripts.

The sizes of the partitions and hard drives are dependent on both the number of users connecting to the MetaFrame server and the applications deployed from the server. Microsoft Internet Explorer, Microsoft Office, and other applications can cause user profile directory sizes to increase to hundreds of megabytes, and thus large numbers of user profiles can consume gigabytes of disk space on the server. The server must be designed with sufficient disk space for these profiles to be copied locally to the server when a user logs in.

NOTE: Roaming profiles and permanent user data should be stored on a centralized file server [Storage Area Network (SAN) or Network Attached Storage (NAS) for larger environments] that can adequately support the environment. In addition, this storage medium should be logically located near the MetaFrame Presentation Servers, preferably with Layer 3 Gigabit network connections, so that login times are not unnecessarily increased.

Citrix *e*Labs tests show that there will be an improvement in simultaneous logon performance if you enable disk write caching on the server's RAID controller.

HP DL360 G3 Battery Backed Write Cache Login Test

The following tests were performed in the Citrix *e*Labs in collaboration with Hewlett Packard (HP) to compile performance measurements of user logon time on HP DL360 G3 servers running Citrix MetaFrame Presentation Server XP with Feature Release 3, with and without a Smart Array 5i Controller Battery Backed Write Cache (BBWC) Enabler Option Kit.

Test Setup
Hardware
   The HP DL360 G3 consisted of the following configuration:

▼   Dual Intel Xeon 2.8 GHz processors

■   533 MHz FSB

- ■ 4GB RAM
- ▲ Single 36GB SCSI drive

Session logon performance was compared using results obtained with and without the BBWC unit installed in the server under test.

Software

Test Server Configuration:

- ▼ Citrix MetaFrame Presentation Server XPe with Feature Release 3
- ▲ Windows 2003

An automation utility was utilized to launch simultaneous multiple user logons.

Test Methodology   User Logon Time-Progressive Load (no BBWC).
Automation utility configured on 25 client servers.

1. Configure the automation utility to launch three user sessions on each server.

2. Tests run on progressive groups of 5, 10, 15, 20, 25 servers:
   - ■ Logon time measured.
   - ■ Disk, Processor, and Memory utilization measured.

User Logon Time-Progressive Load (BBWC installed)

1. Install BBWC (wait three hours for full battery charge).

2. Configure the automation utility to launch three user sessions per client server.

3. Tests run on progressive groups of 5, 10, 15, 20, 25 servers.

   - ■ Logon time measured.
   - ■ Disk, Processor, and Memory utilization measured.

Performance Results   The following table shows the results that were measured utilizing user logon times and PerfMon counters. Three test runs were measured for each indicator and an average of the three runs is reported.

Client Servers	Sessions/Server	Total Client Logons	No BBWC	BBWC
5	3	15	16 s	13 s
10	3	30	25 s	16 s
15	3	45	43 s	38 s
20	3	60	57 s	51 s
25	3	75	80 s	60 s

System Performance Without BBWC–20 Servers

The Performance Monitor graph shown in Figure 3-1 is illustrative of typical system performance for two iterations of user logon tests without a BBWC unit. Note the "PhysicalDisk" object/"%Disk Time" counter averages 20.740%.

System Performance–BBWC Installed–20 Servers

The Performance Monitor graph in Figure 3-2 is illustrative of typical system performance for two iterations of user logon tests with a BBWC unit installed. Note that the PhysicalDisk object/"%Disk Time" counter average decreased from 20.740% to 3.047%. All other counters remain essentially unchanged.

NOTE: Further information regarding HP BBWC performance improvements in a Server Based Computing environment can be found on the HP website:
http://h71019.www7.hp.com/ActiveAnswers/Render/1,1027,6461-6-100-225-1,00.htm

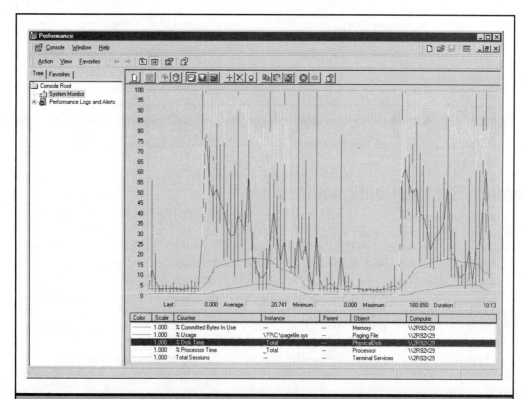

Figure 3-1. Performance Monitor graph of user logon tests without Battery Back Write Cache (BBWC) enabled

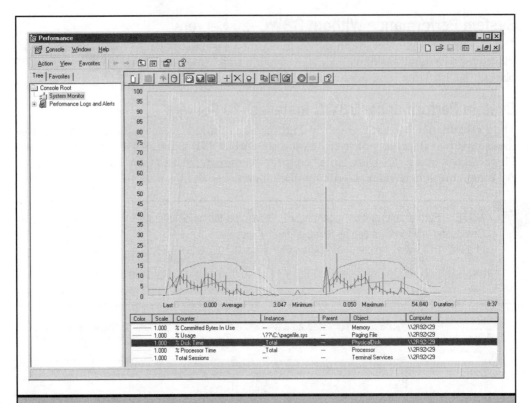

Figure 3-2. Performance Monitor graph of user logon tests with Battery Back Write Cache (BBWC) enabled

Operating System Configurations

All partitions, especially the system partition, must be in NT File System (NTFS) format to allow security configuration, optimal performance, and fault tolerance. NTFS also saves disk space usage because NTFS partitions have much smaller and constant cluster sizes (the minimum NTFS cluster size is 4KB). FAT partitions require much larger cluster sizes as the size of the partition increases, with the minimum size being 32KB. More space is wasted on FAT partitions because the file system requires an amount of physical disk space equal to the cluster size of the partition used to store a file, even if the file is smaller than the cluster size. For more information about cluster sizes of FAT and NTFS partitions, see Microsoft Knowledge Base article 140365.

If possible, install only one network protocol on the server. This practice frees up system resources and reduces network traffic. If multiple protocols are needed, set the bind order so the most commonly used protocol is first.

Increase the registry size to accommodate the additional user profile and applications settings that are stored in the registry with Terminal Services. On a single-processor server, reserve at least 40MB for the registry, and at least 100MB on quad and eight-way servers.

Performance can also be increased by properly tuning the pagefile. For more information about the pagefile, see Microsoft Knowledge Base article 197379.

Service Packs and Updates

Microsoft, Citrix, and most hardware manufacturers provide patches, service packs, hotfixes, or other updates intended to insure optimum performance, security, and stability of the systems. It is critical to not only keep up to date, but also to regression test all updates prior to installing them in a production environment.

NOTE: Before installing MetaFrame Presentation Server, please review the online Pre-installation Update Bulletin. The Pre-installation Update Bulletin offers late-breaking information and links to critical updates to server operating systems and to Citrix installation files. A link to the bulletin is available on the Installation Checklist accessed through the autorun feature of the installation CDs.

Windows Service Packs   Service packs and hotfixes should be applied uniformly across all servers in the server farm. By ensuring this level of uniformity, consistency is assured and troubleshooting time will be reduced. MetaFrame Installation Manager (included with the Enterprise Edition) is an effective tool for the deployment (and uninstallation, if needed) of patches and hotfixes across a large farm.

MetaFrame Presentation Servers use Microsoft Jet drivers extensively. The Microsoft Jet Database Engine is used by the local host cache on every MetaFrame Presentation Server. It is also used when Resource Management is installed. Citrix recommends installing Microsoft service packs for the Microsoft Jet Database Engine. Older versions contain memory leaks that appear as IMA service memory leaks. Apply these service packs and patches before installing MetaFrame Presentation Server on the servers. See Microsoft Knowledge Base article 239114 for more information.

NOTE: A memory leak in the Microsoft Jet Database Engine is fixed in Windows 2000 Service Pack 2. To use MetaFrame Presentation Server XP with Feature Release 3 or earlier versions on a Windows 2000 system on which Windows 2000 Service Pack 2 is not installed, you must install the hotfix described in the Microsoft TechNet article 273772. MetaFrame Presentation Server 3.0 requires Windows 2000 Service Pack 4.

The amount of memory consumed by the IMA service can be reduced by changing MaxBufferSize in a registry entry for Microsoft Jet 4.0 Database Engine.

CAUTION: Using Registry Editor incorrectly can cause serious problems that can require you to reinstall the operating system. Citrix cannot guarantee that problems resulting from incorrect use of Registry Editor can be solved. Use Registry Editor at your own risk. Make sure you back up the registry before you edit it.

To change MaxBufferSize, perform the following steps:

1. Run regedt32.
2. Locate the registry entry: HKLM\SOFTWARE\Microsoft\Jet\4.0\Engines\Jet 4.0
3. Double-click MaxBufferSize in the right pane.
4. In the DWORD Editor dialog box, enter **0x200** in the Data box. Accept the default radix, Hex, in the Radix box. This will set the MaxBufferSize to 512KB. (The IMA service will consume less memory if the value is changed from 0 to 512KB.)
5. Click OK.

NOTE: Installing a new MDAC or Microsoft Jet Database Engine service pack may reset MaxBufferSize to its default setting. Be sure to check this setting after applying any MDAC or Jet updates.

Data Store Hardware Guidelines

When selecting the hardware to host the data store, consider the following variables:

▼ Number of objects in the farm, including servers, applications, printers, etc.

■ Frequency of events, such as adding/removing servers.

▲ Maximum number of servers starting the IMA service simultaneously.

Since each of these variables has a bearing on the type of hardware used to host the data store, the individual issues will be discussed in the following section.

Objects in the Data Store

To properly select the hardware to host a data store, a general understanding about the objects stored in the data store is beneficial. Nearly every item displayed in the Presentation Server Console represents one or more entries in the data store. These objects are

▼ Applications

■ Administrators

■ Folders

■ IM Groups

■ IM Package properties

■ Servers

■ Load Evaluators

■ Printers

- Printer Drivers
- Policies
- ▲ RM Metrics

Some objects, such as applications and servers, create multiple entries in the data store. As the number of entries in the data store grows, the time required for IMA to search and retrieve the entries also grows.

As servers are added to the farm, the data store will need to service more requests. Plan the data store hardware platform based on the total number of servers that will eventually be in the farm.

The Size of Data Store Objects

When an object is created in the Presentation Server Console, such as a publishing application or new MetaFrame Administrator, a record is created for that object in the data store database. In Table 3-1, Citrix eLabs has calculated the estimated size of objects' records as created in a data store utilizing an SQL 2000, Service Pack 3 database. Please note that the following measurements should only be considered as guidelines because the size of an object's entries in the data store depends on many factors, such as the name of an object and its configurations.

Hardware Guidelines   As with any client-server database application, the CPU power and speed of the database server can improve the response time of an application. In the MetaFrame Presentation Server environment, the following events are improved by increasing the processing power of the data store:

- ▼ Starting the IMA service on multiple servers simultaneously
- Installing a server into the farm
- ▲ Removing a server from the farm

The response time of other farm events [such as starting the IMA service on a single server, recreating the Local Host Cache (LHC), or replication of printer drivers to all farm servers] is more related to the farm size, rather than the response time of the data store. The IMA response time and network requirements are discussed in depth in Chapter 2.

Citrix eLabs testing shows that adding processors to the data store can dramatically improve response time when multiple simultaneous queries are being executed. If the environment has large groups of servers coming online frequently, the additional processors will service the requests faster.

However, with serial events, such as installing or removing a farm server, the additional processors show lower performance gains. To improve the processing time for these types of events, increase the processor speed of the data store hardware platform.

Database Object	Size (Bytes)
Publish an application (Wordpad.exe, application name "Wordpad").	11338
Create a blank policy named "policy one."	7122
Configure all rules and assign policy to domain users group.	986
Create a Resource Manager application named "notepad" configured for one server.	7467
Import a Network Printer Server/Printer Driver.	2183
Add printer driver "QuadLaser I."	2485
Add Resource Manager Metric for one server (Citrix MetaFrame Presentation Server/Data Store bytes written/sec).	1808
Add One Domain Administrator as a MetaFrame Administrator.	3164
Configure Installation Manager Properties (account, path).	1635
Add a package.	24275
Create a package group named "Group1."	4225
Add a Server Folder named "Server Folder" w/permission copied.	1188
Add an Application folder "App folder."	1191
Create a load evaluator with one evaluation rule (server user load).	1786
Create an Installation Manager server group named "group 1" containing one server named "ell1600Sc."	1113
Join a server to the farm.	81891

Table 3-1. Data Store Objects' Estimated Size

Effects of Varying the Number of CPUs and Hyper-Threading on MetaFrame Presentation Servers

The number of users that a server can support depends on several factors including the following:

▼ The MetaFrame server's hardware specifications

■ The applications that are being run (because of the applications' CPU and memory requirements)

■ The amount of user input being processed by the applications

▲ What is considered to be maximum desired resource usage on the server, for example, 90% CPU usage or 80% memory usage

This section discusses the increase in user capacity when more CPUs are added, as well as the effect of Hyper-Threading in the processor. First, the Citrix benchmarking test for user capacity, known as ICAMark, is described.

Citrix ICAMark

Citrix ICAMark is a tool based on the Citrix Server Test Kit (CSTK) and used by Citrix Engineering for benchmarking purposes to quantify the optimal number of simulated client sessions that can be connected to a MetaFrame Presentation Server with acceptable performance. Extending the number of concurrent simulated users beyond the optimal results will cause a decrease in performance and may impact end-user experience. Please see Chapter 11 of the *Citrix MetaFrame Access Suite for Windows Server 2003: The Official Guide* (McGraw-Hill/Osborne, 2003) for detailed information on user-load simulation.

The ICAMark test simulates users constantly typing and performing actions in Microsoft Excel, Microsoft Access, and Microsoft PowerPoint. Other applications can utilize more or less memory and CPU than Microsoft Office and therefore could produce different results. Note also that because the simulated users in this test are constantly typing into these applications, they may be considered more "rigorous" than normal users. The use of the applications and the actual activities are intended simply to tax the system in a similar way that a user might use the system.

In this test, a step size "number of users" is defined as five. During the course of the test, after the first five users are logged in, ICAMark launches simulated user scripts on all five sessions. Each script opens Microsoft Excel and simulates the creation of a spreadsheet, including calculations and charts. Once the Excel phase is complete, Excel is closed and Microsoft Access is opened. The script then simulates the creation of an Access database, including a table, query, and form, with data manipulation. Once the Access phase is complete, a Microsoft PowerPoint presentation is created of six slides, including spell checking, font changes, and slide copies and deletions.

Based on how long the scripts take to complete, an ICAMark score is calculated. After significant empirical testing and usability studies, a score of **80** was mapped to be the optimal load for a server. This means that the server has sufficient additional CPU and memory resources to handle spikes in performance. When the test iteration score drops below 80, additional users added to the server consume more resources, producing lower test scores and slower performance.

Server	Client
Dell PowerEdge 6650 Quad Processor - 1.6 GHz Xeon with 256KB L2 and 1MB L3 Cache Hyper-Threading is enabled 35GB HDD with Dell PERC 3/DC Raid Controller and 1GB RAM 4GB Page File Citrix MetaFrame XP Microsoft Windows 2000 Advanced Server with Service Pack 2 Microsoft Office 97	Dual Pentium P3 667 with 256KB Cache 256MB RAM 9GB HDD with Adaptec SCSI Controller Citrix ICA Program Neighborhood Client version 6.30.1050 Microsoft Windows 2000 Service Pack 2

Table 3-1. Server and Client Configurations for Benchmark Test

Number of CPUs Effect on User Capacity

A benchmark test was performed with the server and client configurations listed in Table 3-2.

Tests were performed by keeping the hardware static and by disabling processors on the server. Results were collected on the following configurations:

▼ Dell PowerEdge 6650 with one processor enabled

■ Dell PowerEdge 6650 with two processors enabled

▲ Dell PowerEdge 6650 with four processors enabled

Table 3-3 and Figure 3-3 display the results collected from this test.

The results of this test conclude that the performance of the Dell PowerEdge 6650 with four processors enabled and 160 concurrent simulated users is equivalent to the performance of two processors enabled with 140 concurrent simulated users, which is equivalent to the performance of one processor enabled with 80 concurrent simulated users.

# of CPUs	# of Simulated Users	% Performance Increase
1	80 ± 1	N/A
2	140 ± 1	75%
4	160 ± 1	14%

Table 3-2. Effect of the Number of CPUs on Server User Capacity

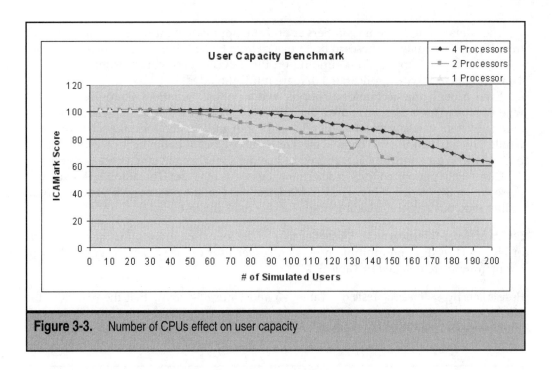

Figure 3-3.   Number of CPUs effect on user capacity

Adding more CPUs, however, results in diminishing returns. Moving from a single to a dual processor system equates to a 75% increase in performance while moving from a dual to a quad processor system equates to only a 14% increase in performance. Server scalability is not linear with the number of processors and drops off sharply between two and four CPUs. Some of this nonlinear behavior results from factors other than processing, such as I/O, becoming the critical bottleneck as user count increases. Recent preliminary tests with solid state hard drives from TiGi Corporation show 100–200% improvements in user capacity on four processor servers.

NOTE: When sizing MetaFrame Presentation Servers, the number of actual users per server varies based on the applications deployed and their use of resources including network, memory, and hard drive read/write processes.

The Affect of Hyper-Threading on User Capacity

Hyper-Threading technology enables a single physical processor to appear as two logical processors. Intel introduced this technology in the Pentium 4 line of processors. Hyper-Threading allows multi-threaded programs to take advantage of extra execution units on the processor resulting in as much as a 30% performance increase to some applications.

The MetaFrame Presentation Server and the applications it hosts can also benefit from Hyper-Threading. Increases in performance from Hyper-Threading are highly dependent on the type of applications running on the server. The greatest benefit of Hyper-Threading is seen with applications that are multi-threaded.

Even though this technology sounds like a no-lose situation, there are scenarios where Hyper-Threading can cause a decrease in performance. For example, since the operating system is unaware of Hyper-Threading, it utilizes the logical processors as it would physical processors. Thus two current active threads could be sent to two logical processors on the same physical processor leaving the other physical processors idle.

Citrix *e*Labs performed tests to determine the affects of Hyper-Threading on MetaFrame Presentation Server scalability. The ICAMark test used on the previous MPS test was used again to run this Hyper-Threading single-server scalability test.

Effects of Hyper-Threading on MPS User Capacity   The following graphs illustrate the effects of Hyper-Threading on multiple processor server user capacity. The server and client configuration are detailed in Table 3-4.

Results from Hyper-Threading Testing   Table 3-5 and Figure 3-4 show that the results of the Single Server Scalability test conclude that the Dell PowerEdge 2650 with Hyper-Threading enabled performed 30% better than the same server with Hyper-Threading disabled.

Server	Client
Dell PowerEdge 2650	CPQ ML350 600 MHz Pentium III with
Dual Intel Pentium 4 Xeon Processor:	256KB Cache
3.06 GHz with 512KB L2 Cache and	256MB RAM
1MB L3 Cache	Windows 2000 Service Pack 4
533 MHz front side bus speed	Citrix ICA Windows 33-bit Program
Hyper-Threading enabled and	Neighborhood
disabled	
36GB HDD with Dell PERC 3/Di Raid	
Controller	
4GB RAM	
4GB Pagefile	
Windows Server 2003	
MetaFrame Presentation Server 3.0	
Enterprise Edition	
Microsoft Office XP – Excel XP,	
PowerPoint XP, and Access XP	

Table 3-3.   Server and Client Configurations for Hyper-Threading Testing

Configuration	# of Simulated Users	% Difference
Hyper-Threading Disabled	123 ± 1.5	N/A
Hyper-Threading Enabled	177 ± 1.5	+ 30%

Table 3-4. Impact of Hyper-Threading on MetaFrame Presentation Server User Capacity

Extending the number of concurrent users beyond the recommendation in this test environment will result in decreased server performance, and consequently, will negatively impact the end-user experience. Again, when sizing MetaFrame Presentation Servers, the number of actual users per server varies based on the applications deployed and amount of user interaction.

In Figure 3-4, each iteration on the Y-axis represents five users, and the score on the X-axis is the ICAMark score described in the previous CPU MPS tests.

Summary of Hyper-Threading Test Results   The increase in performance from Hyper-Threading is highly dependent on the type of applications running on the server. The true benefit of Hyper-Threading is seen on the single and dual processor scenarios where the processor is the bottleneck, thus allowing an additional 40% and 24% respective increase in capacity when enabled. With Hyper-Threading enabled on a quad processor

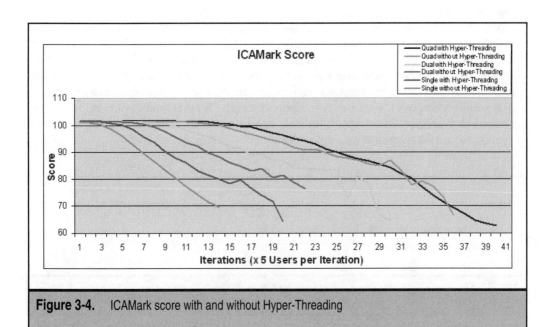

Figure 3-4. ICAMark score with and without Hyper-Threading

system, there are eight logical CPUs. In this instance, the benefit of Hyper-Threading is no longer evident. As the processing capacity of the server increases, less of a bottleneck is placed on the processor's execution resources and more on the system bus, disk, and memory resources. Additionally, operating system limitations that prevent the utilization of the eight logical processors results in only a 1% increase in performance with Hyper-Threading enabled.

NOTE: When sizing MetaFrame Presentation Servers, the number of actual users per server varies based on the type of applications deployed and the amount of user interaction within those applications.

Performance Analysis of Blades versus Standalone Servers

As datacenters grow larger to support thousands of users, datacenter space becomes increasingly expensive. Space, power, and HVAC all come at a price, prompting many organizations to look for ways to reduce the number of servers and the amount of rack space associated with housing the servers. To this end, Dell, HP, IBM, and others have developed blade servers that support higher density than previous form factors. This density provides a tremendous savings in rack space and datacenter space, but there is a decrease in the number of users supported on a blade since the current genre of blade servers generally support slower processors, less memory, and slower hard disks. Using the Single Server Scalability test, designed to quantify the maximum number of client sessions that can be connected to a MetaFrame Presentation Server with acceptable performance, Table 3-6 shows the number of users supported by a blade server versus a standalone server.

With the variables defined in this test scenario, the results of the Single Server Scalability test conclude that the performance of the Dell PowerEdge 1655MC servicing 99 concurrent users is equivalent to the performance of the Dell PowerEdge 1650 servicing 108 concurrent users. Extending the number of concurrent users beyond the recommendation in this test environment will result in decreased performance and, thus, will negatively impact the end-user experience on the MetaFrame Presentation Server. As stated throughout this chapter, though, server performance and user capacity will vary significantly depending on applications.

Server	Results (Simulated Users)
Dell PowerEdge 1655MC Blade Server	99 ± 1
Dell PowerEdge 1650	108 ± 1

Table 3-5. Number of Users Supported by a Blade Server Versus a Standalone Server

CHAPTER 4

Farm Design

This chapter covers MetaFrame Presentation Server 3.0 farm design and implementation. The farms, within the context of MetaFrame Presentation Server, represent the logical and physical location(s)/layout of the servers. The farm design is critical to server login/logout performance, as well as LAN/WAN network utilization. Farm design concepts include a discussion on when to use multiple farms as opposed to a single farm, and the corresponding zone and data store implications including redundancy options to enable continuous on-demand access. This chapter also includes an in depth discussion on the implementation of the data store database on all the supported platforms.

METAFRAME PRESENTATION SERVER FARM DESIGN

In this section we will discuss design techniques to be considered prior to deploying a MetaFrame Presentation Server farm, including enterprise farm design, zone design, multihoming, and data store guidelines. At the end of the section, a variety of farm configuration scenarios are outlined with corresponding zone and data store recommendations.

Enterprise Farm Design

A single farm can be used for the enterprise. However, there are several factors concerning hardware, database performance, and network congestion that can decrease performance of the farm. Although multiple farms can be deployed, there are different benefits associated with a single farm design and multiple farm designs.

Benefits of Deploying a Single Farm

The following are benefits of implementing a single farm:

▼ Simple maintenance and administration

▲ Easier to design fault tolerance and business continuity solutions

Simple Maintenance and Administration   A Citrix administrator needs only to log into one farm for all maintenance and administrative tasks. An administrator need not open multiple Management Console windows to view all servers in the enterprise. Not only does this simplify the environment, but it also reduces resource utilization, as opening multiple Management Console windows on a server requires more resources than a single Management Console window.

Another way a single MetaFrame Presentation Server farm can simplify administration is by ensuring settings such as policies and printers are consistent. This is easier to do in a single farm. By creating policies in only one farm you avoid the possibility of misconfigurations or omissions in the desired policy settings.

Easier to Design Fault Tolerance and Business Continuity Solutions   With a single MetaFrame Presentation Server farm you reduce the amount of complexity and redundancy that might be required when planning for a multiple farm design.

Benefits of Deploying Multiple Farms

The following are benefits of implementing multiple farms:

- ▼ Reduced IMA network traffic
- ■ No data store replication
- ■ No unsecured IMA Internet traffic
- ▲ No required firewall changes

Reduced IMA Network Traffic   A single farm with remote zone data collectors must communicate frequently to keep published application and user connection information synchronized across the farm. Previous versions of MetaFrame queued up these communications and sent them across an ICA gateway at configurable intervals. MetaFrame Presentation Server sends these communications as they are generated, requiring a dedicated WAN connection between the zone data collectors. MetaFrame Presentation Server 3.0 introduced enhancements to coalesce updates together when they are sent in rapid succession, further reducing bandwidth utilization. If the WAN cannot support the network traffic outlined in Chapter 2, then performance may be optimized by setting up a separate farm at each remote site.

No Data Store Replication Required   As discussed later in this chapter, Citrix recommends that the data store be replicated to remote sites when using a single farm in a WAN environment. The use of multiple farms eliminates the need for data store replication, because each remote site maintains its own data store.

No Unsecured IMA Internet Traffic   When multiple farms are used, they do not span an Internet WAN connection. IMA traffic and ODBC connection information cannot be intercepted. However, it should be noted that if farms share a license server, there will be WAN traffic caused by farms checking out licenses across the WAN.

No Required Firewall Changes   By default, IMA uses TCP ports 2512 and 2513 to communicate. The *imaport* utility may be used to alter the IMA communication ports. Regardless of the ports being used, when the farm spans the firewall, these ports must be opened for IMA communication. The implementation of a separate farm per site eliminates the need to open Ports 2512 and 2513 on the firewall and any ODBC ports used for data store communication. Likewise, if a single license server is deployed for the farm, Port 27000 needs to be opened on the firewall to allow licenses to be checked out by the MetaFrame Presentation Servers.

Benefits of Deploying Multiple Farms at a Single Site

Application Service Providers can implement a separate farm for each customer, further easing security concerns and allowing Citrix administrators to have access to some farms and not others.

NOTE: MetaFrame Presentation Server 3.0 allows enhanced object-based delegated administration, which allows for granular administration of application and server folders.

IMA architecture eases the maintenance of multiple farms by providing remote administration through the Presentation Server Console. All farms can be managed from a single server or workstation where the Presentation Server Console is installed. The MetaFrame administrator can specify the farm to which the Presentation Server Console connects by specifying the server name of a server within that farm. In addition, multiple instances of the Presentation Server Console can be loaded simultaneously—one for each farm, for example—although this scenario uses more resources on the server running the multiple Presentation Server Console instances.

Zone Design

Layout and distribution of zones in a MetaFrame Presentation Server farm is crucial to the end-user's perception of performance. The distribution of zones will impact user login and logoff times, as well as overall LAN/WAN performance.

Zone Data Collector Hardware Recommendations

The hardware recommendations discussed in this section come from extensive testing in the Citrix *e*Labs.

A 500 MHz Pentium III data collector can support approximately 190 resolutions per second. The number of resolutions per second that a data collector can handle is directly related to the number of servers on which an application is published.

The following criteria should be examined when designing zones:

▼ Number of users connecting to the farm

■ Length of time the average user stays logged onto a session (a single daily session or repeated short sessions)

■ Number of simultaneous user logons

▲ Number of published applications with load evaluators attached

The last two items produce a much higher load on the data collector. Monitor the CPU and memory usage on the data collector to ensure that the data collector is not being overloaded with requests.

Zone Deployment

Each zone keeps information on all servers in the farm. Member servers in each zone frequently update their session and load information to their Zone's Data Collector. For MetaFrame Presentation Server 3.0, if load sharing is enabled between data collectors, or with Feature Release 3 or older, when a user logs on or off, connects or disconnects, the data collector is responsible for relaying new information to all other data collectors in the farm.

The amount of bandwidth used by each operation increases proportionally to the number of zones. To optimize performance, keep the number of zones in the MetaFrame farm as low as possible, while still being able to fulfill all enumeration and resolution requests in a timely manner.

MetaFrame Presentation Server 3.0 by default has load sharing between disabled zones. If a farm has multiple zones, load information for the servers in a zone will be kept local to that server's data collector instead of being forwarded to all other data collectors in the farm. During a logon, logoff, or such, event information regarding the session details is still forwarded to all other data collectors in the farm, minus the updated load information. If the data collector has not received a load update from the servers in its zone, it will query for the server's updated load by default every five minutes. With load sharing disabled, this updated data is no longer forwarded to the other data collectors in the farm.

NOTE: Disabling load sharing should decrease the amount of network traffic sent between zones in most cases. However, it does not affect the overall architecture of the farm, nor does it increase the performance of zones or increase the number of zones a farm should have.

Special considerations need to be made when determining if it is better to disable or enable load sharing between zones. Disabled load sharing works best when used in conjunction with zone preference and failover. Zone preference and failover dictates which zone the user should connect to first. If the user only has one primary zone defined, only the data collector for this primary zone will perform the resolution for the published application. If a user has multiple zones defined as their primary zone, multiple data collectors will perform the resolution and the user will be sent to the least loaded zone. This causes an increased load on the other data collectors involved as each must perform a resolution instead of a single data collector.

Likewise, if zone preference and failover is not set on the farm, and applications are published across multiple zones, all data collectors for the zones in which the application is published will always perform resolutions. This can increase the time to perform a resolution, especially if the zones are linked by high latency WAN links.

TIP: In situations where zone preference and failover is not used, the application spans multiple zones, and bandwidth is not a concern, it is best to enable load sharing across zones.

A large number of zones can impact the performance of the network and server farm, producing high network bandwidth consumption and decreased performance of the data collectors. If the network experiences congestion or performance degradation in the server farm, the following recommendations may help minimize network traffic:

▼   Reduce the number of zones.

▲   Configure data collectors to reside on the same subnet as the majority of the member servers in its zone.

Misconception "Increasing the number of zones in the farm increases scalability."

Actual Increasing the number of zones in the farm places a higher load on the existing data collectors, as they must replicate all of the events they receive to all other data collectors in the farm. They must also keep up with all of the updates they receive from the data collectors in the other zones in the farm. All of this consumes more bandwidth and places a higher load on the data collector's CPU. In the event that the CPU for a zone is overloaded, it is recommended to increase the processing power of the data collector rather than splitting the zone up into multiple zones. If a Zone Data Collector is also used to supply applications to users, consider making the data collector dedicated to only application enumeration/resolution requests to alleviate the server's load prior to increasing the processing power. See the section "Use a Dedicated Data Collector" later in this chapter.

TIP: Keep the total number of zones in the farm at a level supported by the network infrastructure. For more information, see the zone bandwidth discussion in Chapter 2.

When sizing a zone, start with 300 servers per zone. Depending on the server hardware and farm activity, a data collector can support more than 300 servers. Monitor the CPU usage on the data collector during normal farm activity to determine what the data collector hardware can support. If the data collector begins to get overwhelmed with enumeration/resolution requests and/or regular reporting, consider the following to reduce the load on the current data collector:

▼ Increase the processor speed of the server hosting the data collector or add an additional processor.

▲ Dedicate the data collector to handle ICA Client requests only and to not accept ICA Client connections.

IMPORTANT: When installing servers on multiple subnets in the same zone, do not use the default zone name. The default zone name is based on the subnet of the server joining the farm. When installing servers on multiple subnets into the same zone, specify the zone name during install. If the zone name was not changed during install, it can be changed after installation using the Presentation Server Console under Farm Properties.

Zone Considerations

For most installations, a zone should be limited to a group of well connected (high bandwidth, low latency connections) MetaFrame Presentation Servers that reside in a single data center. This helps keep client resolutions local to where the servers are and also minimizes the amount of traffic sent across the WAN during data collector updates.

Conversely, in some instances it is beneficial to have a single zone span multiple sites. If the number of servers in the main site far outnumbers the servers in a remote site, consider placing these servers in the same zone. In this case, thousands of events can be generated by the MetaFrame Presentation Servers in the main data center. If there are multiple zones, these events would then need to be forwarded to all the other data collectors in the farm, consuming significant traffic across the WAN. A better solution is to place the servers in the data center and the remote site into the same zone. This eliminates the need to forward events that occur in the data center to data collectors in the zones at the remote sites. The only drawback to this configuration is that client resolutions will have to occur over the WAN and zone preference, and failover will have to occur at the regional level instead of the site level.

NOTE: In this scenario, the data collector should be placed in the site with the most servers.

If the network link goes down between servers that reside in the same zone, multiple data collectors can be elected for the same zone, one for each site. This will allow client connections to continue to work, allowing new client connections to be sent to the subset of MetaFrame Presentation Servers that still have network connectivity. When the communication is restored, the MetaFrame Presentation Servers will automatically converge back to one data collector.

NOTE: The data collector election process is not dependent on connectivity to the data store.

Use a Dedicated Data Collector   The decision to dedicate a MetaFrame Presentation Server for use solely as a Zone Data Collector depends upon several factors, as follows:

▼   The number of member servers within the zone

■   The number of zones within the farm (interzone communication)

■   The frequency of user logons/application enumerations

▲   The frequency of restarts of member servers in the zone

Misconception   "If a data collector goes down, there is a single point of failure."

Actual   The data collector election process is triggered automatically without administrative intervention. Existing, as well as incoming users, are not affected by the election process, as a new data collector is elected almost instantaneously. Data collector elections are not dependent on the data store.

In general, if users experience slow connection times due to high CPU utilization on the data collector, consider dedicating a MetaFrame Presentation Server for the Zone Data Collector.

To determine if the existing data collector is overloaded, track the WorkItem Queue Ready metric listed under the MetaFrame Presentation Server Performance Monitor object. The WorkItem Queue Ready metric shows the number of items that IMA has waiting to be processed. This counter is analogous to the Processor Queue Length (PQL) and Disk Queue Length (DQL) counters provided in Windows 2000. This counter should not stay above 0 for extended periods of time. A steady state value greater than 0 indicates that the data collector may be overloaded. This PerfMon counter is not a default metric in Resource Manager, however it should be added as a metric to all of the farm's data collectors.

DATA STORE NETWORK OPTIMIZATIONS

The MetaFrame data store can be designed in several different ways to increase the performance and throughput of the database server. In large farms with powerful database servers, the network can become the performance bottleneck when reading information from the data store during startup. This is particularly true when the database server hosts various resource-intensive databases. As with the MetaFrame Presentation Servers, Citrix recommends that a teaming Network Interface Card (NIC) solution be used, such as switch-assisted load balancing, to improve the available bandwidth of the data store. To find out if the network is the bottleneck, monitor the CPU usage on the data store. If the CPU utilization is not at 100% while the IMA service is starting, and it is still in the process of starting, the network may be the bottleneck. If the CPU utilization is at or near 100%, it is likely that additional processor(s) may be needed.

Data store connectivity testing was performed in the Citrix eLabs on a 100 Mbps switched LAN. This testing was also repeated in a Gigabit Ethernet environment. It was found that two NICs that were teamed via switch-assisted load balancing (that is, 400 Mbps throughput) provided ample throughput without the additional cost associated with gigabit NICs, cables, and switch ports. However, in very large environments, gigabit connectivity may be beneficial.

Teaming Network Interface Card Configurations

In all cases, the NICs and switch ports should each be manually configured to support full duplex and the highest speed available on both devices since autosensing does not always result in an optimal or compatible configuration. If the speed or duplex settings are configured incorrectly, frames will likely be dropped.

Many new servers can be procured with two factory-installed NIC ports. These NICs may be configured as follows, as listed in the order of Citrix' recommendation:

▼   Utilize both NICs and team via switch-assisted load balancing within the same subnet if connecting to different blades within a large Layer 3 switch.

■   Utilize both NICs and team via adaptive load balancing within the same subnet if connecting to different blades within a large Layer 3 switch.

■   Utilize both NICs and configure for failover onto two separate switches.

■   Utilize one NIC and disable the second.

▲   Utilize both NICs and multihome to two different subnets.

Historically, most organizations have only used one NIC in each server. However, if two NIC and switch ports are available, these can be teamed, configured for failover, or multihomed. Of these two options, NIC teaming is considered a Citrix Best Practice when the switch ports are located on different blades within a large Layer 3 switch (such as Cisco 6500 series) because this enables both failover and redundancy, in addition to higher throughput. Although the Layer 3 switch does represent a single point of failure in this case, the availability of most large Layer 3 switches is in the 99.999% range and represents a minimal failure rate. More commonly, though, an individual blade may fail. If a large Layer 3 switch that supports teaming across blades is not available, then a failover configuration is the best option. While multihoming is a supported practice, NIC teaming is considered to be the better option in nearly all situations. Multihoming is often configured incorrectly, and security holes can be opened since access control lists configured on the router are bypassed.

If insufficient switch ports or other business decisions make it impossible to team the NICs and switch ports of all MetaFrame and related servers, it is best to apply this recommendation to the following servers:

▼   Data store

■   Web Interface server(s)

■   Secure Gateway server(s)

■   Secure Ticket Authority server(s)

■   Secure Access Manager server(s)

▲   Zone Data Collector(s)

The following teaming NIC configurations have been tested on MetaFrame Presentation Servers and on an SQL Server housing the data store. In all cases, Citrix recommends teaming NICs using the MAC address, not the IP address. Because the MAC address is at a more basic and at a lower OSI layer, as well as not subject to modification unless the burned-in address (BIA) is modified, this is a more basic and stable configuration. The switch vendor's recommended practice for manually configuring teaming or aggregating of the switch ports should be followed.

Network Fault Tolerance (Failover)

This failover option provides the safety of an additional backup link between the server and the switch. If the primary adapter fails, the secondary adapter takes over with very minor interruption in server operations. When tested in the Citrix eLabs, failover caused an interruption of less than 0.5 seconds and did not provide any noticeable impact on existing ICA sessions. There is no performance gain with this setting, but fault tolerance is improved.

Transmit Load Balancing (Formerly Adaptive Load Balancing)

This option creates a team of adapters to increase transmission throughput and ensure that all network users experience similar response times. All adapters must be linked to the same network switch. As adapters are added to the server, they are grouped in teams to provide a single virtual adapter with increased transmission bandwidth. For example, a transmit load balancing team containing two Fast Ethernet adapters configured for full-duplex operation provides an aggregate maximum transmit rate of 200 Mbps and a 100 Mbps receive rate resulting in a total bandwidth of 300 Mbps. One adapter is configured for transmit and receive; while the others are configured for transmit only. Adapter teams configured for transmit load balancing provide the benefit of network fault tolerance because if the primary adapter that supports both transmit and receive fails, another adapter will then support this functionality.

Switch-Assisted Load Balancing (Formerly Fast EtherChannel)

Unlike transmit load balancing, Fast Ether Channel (FEC) can be configured to increase both transmitting and receiving channels between the server and switch. For example, an FEC team containing two Fast Ethernet adapters configured for full-duplex operation provides an aggregate maximum transmit rate of 200 Mbps and an aggregate maximum receive rate of 200 Mbps, resulting in a total bandwidth of 400 Mbps. All adapters are configured for transmit and receive, with the load spread roughly equal.

FEC works only with FEC-enabled switches. The FEC software continuously analyzes load on each adapter and balances network traffic across the adapters as needed. Adapter teams configured for FEC not only provide additional throughput and redundancy but also provide the benefits of Network Fault Tolerance (NFT). The switch ports should also be manually configured to support this configuration so that that autosensed aggregation does not occur. For more information, please see Citrix Knowledge Base article CTX434260 and/or contact your hardware vendor.

Multihoming MetaFrame Presentation Servers

MetaFrame Presentation Server 3.0 provides support for multihomed servers. The following section provides the details necessary for implementing MetaFrame Presentation Server on a server operating with two or more Network Interface Cards (NICs).

Multihoming is commonly used to connect MetaFrame Presentation Server directly to a database server that is located in another subnet. This may be advantageous where access to the remote subnet requires crossing several routers that have high latency or other bottlenecks. However, this practice can create security holes since the normal access medium, the router, is bypassed, as well as its security configuration. Multihoming should be carefully considered, and security implications should be reviewed.

For example, in the diagram shown in Figure 4-1, if multihoming is not configured properly on the MetaFrame Presentation Servers, it is possible that external users may gain access to the SQL and Oracle database servers by means of the MetaFrame Presentation Servers, bypassing the router security.

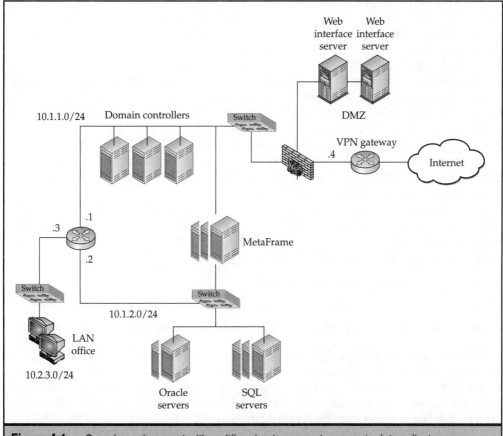

Figure 4-1. Sample environment with multihoming to connect servers to data collectors on different subnets

CAUTION: Multihoming is frequently configured improperly. The steps described in this section must be followed exactly as specified in order for multihoming to function correctly and be supported.

In all cases, all NICs should be manually configured to support full duplex and the maximum speed of the associated switch port, which is generally 100 Mbps. The switch port should be hard coded for this same configuration.

MetaFrame Presentation Server multihoming can be used to provide access to two network segments with no direct route to each. However, each network will utilize the same MetaFrame Presentation Server resources making the addition of another MetaFrame Presentation Server farm redundant. Another application of multihoming a MetaFrame Presentation Server would be to separate a network configured as the main corporate backbone dedicated to server-to-server traffic from a second subnet dedicated to ICA Client-to-MetaFrame Presentation Server traffic. The latter configuration is illustrated in Figure 4-2 and is the subject of the remaining example provided in this section.

Citrix recommends that multihomed MetaFrame Presentation Servers not be configured to operate as a router (TCP/IP Forwarding). In addition, MetaFrame Presentation Server relies upon a properly configured local routing table for accurate operation. Since Windows servers automatically build their routing tables, some care must be taken when configuring the network card binding order and default gateway. This aspect is covered in more detail in the subsection titled "Configure a Default Gateway."

Figure 4-2 illustrates two multihomed MetaFrame Presentation Servers, each with a connection to the 10.8.1.0/24 and 172.16.1.0/24 networks. Neither server is configured to route between their two network interfaces.

ICA Clients requesting a server name or published application get a TCP/IP address to a MetaFrame Presentation Server that contains them. This address is resolved and returned by the MetaFrame Presentation Server that receives the request. Some types of address resolution requests by ICA Clients are the following:

▼ Find the address of the data collector.

■ Find the TCP/IP address of a given MetaFrame Presentation Server name.

▲ Find the TCP/IP address of the least loaded server for a published application.

A MetaFrame Presentation Server receives an address resolution request from an ICA Client and compares the TCP/IP address of the ICA Client to its local routing table to determine which network interface to send the appropriate reply to the requesting ICA Client. It is for this reason that the proper functioning of a multihomed MetaFrame Presentation Server relies heavily upon the correct configuration of the routing table.

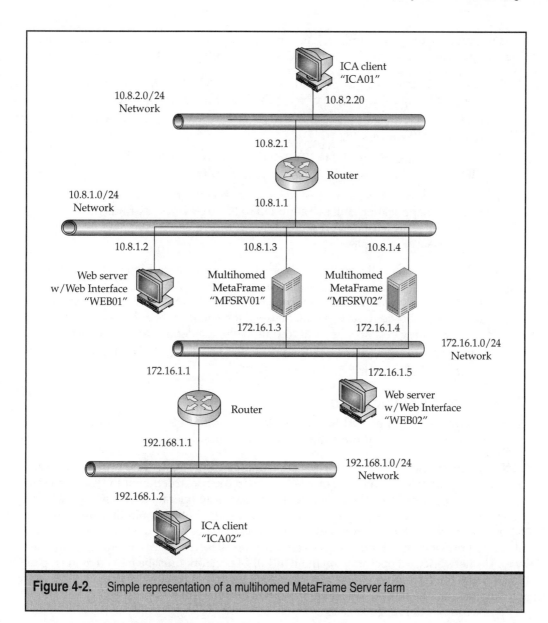

Figure 4-2. Simple representation of a multihomed MetaFrame Server farm

Continuing with our example, the following steps describe the process from an ICA Client request to MetaFrame Presentation Server resolution and response.

1. The ICA Client with TCP/IP address 10.8.2.20, ICA01, sends an address resolution request to the MetaFrame Presentation Server, MFSRV01.

2. MFSRV01 has the TCP/IP address 10.8.1.3. This server also has a second NIC with TCP/IP address 172.16.1.3.

3. ICA01 is configured with MFSRV01 as its service location. ICA01 contacts MFSRV01 and requests a load-balanced application.

4. The TCP/IP address of the least loaded server containing the requested published application must be supplied to ICA01. MFSRV01 finds that MFSRV02 is the least loaded server.

5. MFSRV02 has two TCP/IP addresses, 10.8.1.4 and 172.16.1.4.

6. MFSRV02 looks at the source address of ICA01. The MetaFrame Presentation Server uses its local routing table to determine what network interface will be used to respond to the client. In this case, the NIC configured on the 10.8.2.0/24 network is chosen to send the response to the client. If there is no corresponding entry in the local routing table, the default route will be used.

7. MFSRV01 uses the local routing table to correctly respond with the 10.8.1.4 address when referring the client to MFSRV02.

Configure the Routing Table

A routing table on a multihomed MetaFrame Presentation Server is set up by configuring a single default gateway and the addition of static routes.

Configure a Default Gateway   Windows servers automatically build their routing tables by default. For this reason, some care must be taken in the construction of the routing table to allow a multihomed MetaFrame Presentation Server to operate properly. While Windows servers will build multiple default gateways, the network binding order of the NICs in the server determine which default gateway will be utilized. Using our example, illustrated previously in Figure 4-2, we selected the 10.8.1.1 address as our default gateway. The network card operating on the 10.8.1.0/24 network must be moved to the top of the network binding order.

To configure the network binding order, perform the following:
For Windows Server 2000/2003

1. Open Start | Settings | Control Panel | Network and Dial-up Connections.

2. Select Advanced | Advanced Settings.

3. Under the section titled "Connections," place the NIC to operate as the default gateway first in the list.

There may be certain environments where the configuration of the network binding order will not be sufficient for proper MetaFrame Presentation Server functionality.

An example would be a MetaFrame Presentation Server with two connections to the Internet, where each provides ICA connectivity for a diverse range of IP subnets. The MetaFrame Presentation Server will only use the default gateway of the first NIC in its network binding order, referenced as Network 1. If the MetaFrame Presentation Server were to receive a request from a Client on Network 2 of its second NIC, which is not the default gateway, and there was no routing table entry for Network 2 in the local routing table of the MetaFrame Presentation Server, then the response to the client request will be sent through Network 1. This will likely cause the request to fail.

Alternatively, the additional default gateway configurations can be removed from each additional NIC on the server. This is done through the server's TCP/IP configuration. Using servers MFSRV01 and MFSRV02 from Figure 4-2, we select 10.8.1.1 as our default gateway for both servers and thus remove the default gateway setting from the NICs operating on the 172.16.1.0/24 network.

Running the command line utility **IPCONFIG** on MFSRV01 shows the following:

Windows IP Configuration
Ethernet adapter Local Area Connection #1:
        Connection-specific DNS Suffix . :
        IP Address. . . . . : 10.8.1.3
        Subnet Mask . . . . : 255.255.255.0
        Default Gateway . . . . : 10.8.1.1
Ethernet adapter Local Area Connection #2:
        Connection-specific DNS Suffix . :
        IP Address. . . . . : 172.16.1.3
        Subnet Mask . . . . : 255.255.255.0
        Default Gateway . . . . :

        Running **IPCONFIG** on MFSRV02 shows:

Windows IP Configuration
Ethernet adapter Local Area Connection #1:
        Connection-specific DNS Suffix . :
        IP Address. . . . . : 10.8.1.4
        Subnet Mask . . . . : 255.255.255.0
        Default Gateway . . . . : 10.8.1.1
Ethernet adapter Local Area Connection #2:
        Connection-specific DNS Suffix . :
        IP Address. . . . . : 172.16.1.4
        Subnet Mask . . . . : 255.255.255.0
        Default Gateway . . . . :

Adding Static Routes   Defining static, persistent routes is the best way to avoid potential routing conflicts and, depending on the network configuration, may be the only way to provide ICA connectivity to a multihomed MetaFrame Presentation Server. Refer again to the diagram in Figure 4-2.

Executing the **ROUTE PRINT** command from the command prompt on the routing table on MFSRV01 shows the following:

```
=================================================================
Interface List
0x1 .......................... MS TCP Loopback interface
0x2 ...00 a0 c9 2b f8 dc ...... Intel 8255x-based Integrated Fast Ethernet
0x3 ...00 c0 0d 01 12 f5 ...... Intel(R) PRO Adapter
=================================================================
=================================================================
Active Routes:
```

Network Destination	Netmask	Gateway	Interface	Metric
0.0.0.0	0.0.0.0	10.8.1.1	10.8.1.3	1
10.8.1.0	255.255.255.0	10.8.1.3	10.8.1.3	1
10.8.1.3	255.255.255.255	127.0.0.1	127.0.0.1	1
10.255.255.255	255.255.255.255	10.8.1.3	10.8.1.3	1
127.0.0.0	255.0.0.0	127.0.0.1	127.0.0.1	1
172.16.1.0	255.255.255.0	172.16.1.3	172.16.1.3	1
172.16.1.3	255.255.255.255	127.0.0.1	127.0.0.1	1
172.16.1.255	255.255.255.255	172.16.1.3	172.16.1.3	1
224.0.0.0	224.0.0.0	10.8.1.3	10.8.1.3	1
224.0.0.0	224.0.0.0	172.16.1.3	172.16.1.3	1
255.255.255.255	255.255.255.255	10.8.1.3	10.8.1.3	1
Default Gateway:	10.8.1.1			

```
=================================================================
Persistent Routes:
None
```

Currently MFSRV01 is configured with a default gateway using the router at 10.8.1.1. Note that the second client, ICA02, is located on the 192.168.1.0/24 network, which is accessed via the router at 172.16.1.1. For MFSRV01 to have network connectivity and to avoid using the default gateway when responding to requests from ICA02, a static route must be defined for the 192.168.1.0/24 network.

ROUTE -p ADD 192.168.1.0 MASK 255.255.255.0 172.16.1.1

Executing **ROUTE PRINT** from a command prompt on MFSRV01 from Figure 4-2 now shows the following:

```
==================================================================
Interface List
0x1 ......................... MS TCP Loopback interface
0x2 ...00 a0 c9 2b f8 dc ...... Intel 8255x-based Integrated Fast Ethernet
0x3 ...00 c0 0d 01 12 f5 ...... Intel(R) PRO Adapter
==================================================================
==================================================================
```

Active Routes:

Network Destination	Netmask	Gateway	Interface	Metric
0.0.0.0	0.0.0.0	10.8.1.1	10.8.1.3	1
10.8.1.0	255.255.255.0	10.8.1.3	10.8.1.3	1
10.8.1.3	255.255.255.255	127.0.0.1	127.0.0.1	1
10.255.255.255	255.255.255.255	10.8.1.3	10.8.1.3	1
127.0.0.0	255.0.0.0	127.0.0.1	127.0.0.1	1
172.16.1.0	255.255.255.0	172.16.1.3	172.16.1.3	1
172.16.1.3	255.255.255.255	127.0.0.1	127.0.0.1	1
172.16.1.255	255.255.255.255	172.16.1.3	172.16.1.3	1
192.168.1.0	255.255.255.0	172.16.1.1	172.16.1.3	1
224.0.0.0	224.0.0.0	10.8.1.3	10.8.1.3	1
224.0.0.0	224.0.0.0	172.16.1.3	172.16.1.3	1
255.255.255.255	255.255.255.255	10.8.1.3	10.8.1.3	1

Default Gateway: 10.8.1.1

```
==================================================================
```

Persistent Routes:

Network Address	Netmask	Gateway	Address	Metric
192.168.1.0	255.255.255.0		172.16.1.1	1

MFSRV02 is handled the same way. When the static routes are set up, both ICA Clients can ping both MetaFrame Presentation Servers' TCP/IP addresses and the servers can ping the clients.

Each MetaFrame Presentation Server can now correctly resolve the network interface to which either ICA Client is connecting. The TCP/IP addresses that the ICA01 client can receive are 10.8.1.3 and 10.8.1.4. The TCP/IP addresses that the ICA02 client can receive are 172.16.1.3 and 172.16.1.4.

Data Store Guidelines

The general guidelines for categorizing a data store are listed in Table 4-1 and are also found in the *MetaFrame Presentation Server Administrator's Guide*.

The following are general recommendations for the server farm's data store:

▼ Microsoft Access and Microsoft SQL Desktop Engine (MSDE) are suitable for all small and many medium-sized environments.

▲ Microsoft SQL Server, Oracle, and IBM DB2 are suitable for any size environment and are especially recommended for all large and enterprise environments.

	Small	Medium	Large	Enterprise
Servers	1–50	25–100	50–100	100 or more
Named Users	< 150	< 3000	< 5000	> 3000
Applications	< 100	< 100	< 500	< 2000

Table 4-1.   General Data Store Size Guidelines

The following is a list of things to consider when choosing a data store for a farm:

▼ Microsoft Access and MSDE are best used for centralized farms.

■ Microsoft Access and MSDE support only indirect mode for all servers other than the host server and, therefore, have slower performance than a direct mode data store in large farm implementations.

■ Database replication is not supported with Microsoft Access.

■ For MSDE replication information, please visit http://www.microsoft.com/sql/techinfo/development/2000/msde2000.asp

■ Use databases that support replication when deploying large farms across a WAN. You can obtain considerable performance advantage by distributing the load over multiple database servers.

▲ In the Citrix *e*Labs, Microsoft SQL Server, Oracle, and IBM DB2 perform similarly with large farms. Oracle Real Application Clusters (RAC) includes the added advantage of load balancing incoming requests between the servers.

Use Replicated Data Store Databases

Having a single data store is recommended where appropriate, but in some situations, a replicated data store can improve farm performance. This section covers the concerns and situations that arise from using replicated database technology.

High Latency WAN Concerns   High latency links without the use of replicated databases can create situations where the data store is locked for extended periods of time when performing maintenance from remote sites. This means that the IMA service may start after extended periods of time and some normal operations may fail when performed from the remote site.

TIP: Performing farm maintenance using the Presentation Server Console from a remote site that has high latency is not recommended.

In networks with high-latency,

▼   Data store writes take longer to complete and, for a period of time, block all additional writes from local or remote sites.

▲   Data store reads will probably not adversely affect local connections, but the remote site will experience slower performance.

Replicated Data Store Database Issues   Using replicated databases to speed performance may be justified. The farm servers perform many more reads from the data store than writes to the data store. Most reads occur during startup, when each server populates its local host cache.

In a LAN environment, using replicated databases can speed the startup time of the IMA service and improve the responsiveness of the servers in large farms.

In a WAN environment, the configuration of the data store is important. Because MetaFrame Presentation Server is read-intensive, place replicas of the data store at sites where a considerable number of servers reside. This practice minimizes reads across the WAN link. Limit the use of replicated databases to situations where the remote site has sufficient MetaFrame Presentation Servers to justify the cost of placing a replicated copy of the database at the site.

TIP: Database replication consumes bandwidth. The database server software configuration, not MetaFrame Presentation Server, controls the frequency of database updates.

Data Store Requirements

Table 4-2 shows the versions and releases of tested and supported third-party databases.

Databases	Versions	Platform
Microsoft Access Jet Engine 4.*x*	4.*x* up to SP8	Windows
Microsoft SQL Server Desktop Engine (MSDE)	8.00.760 up to MSDE 2000 RelA	Windows
Microsoft SQL Server	7.0 SP2 or later, 2000 up to SP3A	Windows
Oracle	7 (7.3.4) 8 (8.0.6)	Windows

Table 4-2.   Supported and Tested Third-Party Databases

Databases	Versions	Platform
Oracle	8*i* (8.1.5, 8.1.6, 8.1.7)	Windows /UNIX
	9*i* (9.0.1)	Windows
	9*i* R2	Windows /Solaris
IBM DB2 UDB	7.2 (FixPac 5 or later), 8.1 (FixPac 4)	Windows

Table 4-2. Supported and Tested Third-Party Databases *(continued)*

NOTE: For information regarding Oracle Database 10*g* support, see Citrix Knowledge Base article CTX103686.

Table 4-3 denotes the supported and tested ODBC Client Database versions. Updates to the third-party ODBC clients occur frequently; please use the table as a guideline. Citrix recommends updating to the latest available ODBC client version for the particular database being used prior to the installation of MetaFrame.

CAUTION: Oracle client 8.1.5 is not supported. It must be upgraded to 8.1.55 prior to the installation of MetaFrame XP 1.0 or higher.

The minimum requirements for the five supported database platforms (Microsoft Access, MSDE, Microsoft SQL Server, Oracle, and IBM DB2) as data stores for a MetaFrame Presentation Server farm are listed below. Although MetaFrame Presentation Server uses ODBC for connectivity, other ODBC compliant databases are not supported with MetaFrame Presentation Server.

IMPORTANT: The 8.1.7 and 8.1.7.2 native Oracle clients require a registry modification prior to the installation of MetaFrame XP 1.0. This does not apply to later versions. The Citrix Knowledge Base article CTX949726 refers to this issue. Please see the Citrix Support Knowledge Base on the Web at http://support.citrix.com/ for more information.

Use Microsoft Access

Choosing "Use a local database as the data store" and selecting MS Access during installation configures Microsoft Access as the data store. The ODBC connection to Access uses the Microsoft Jet Engine 4.*x*.

Client Databases	Driver Versions
SQL 7.0 Enterprise for NT MDAC 2.5	3.70.0820
SQL 7.0 Enterprise for NT MDAC 2.5 SP1	3.70.0821
SQL 2000 Enterprise for NT MDAC 2.5 SP2	3.70.0961
SQL 2000 Enterprise for NT MDAC 2.6 SP1	2000.80.380.0
SQL 2000 Enterprise for NT MDAC 2.7	2000.81.7713.00
SQL 2000 Enterprise for NT MDAC 2.7 SP1	2000.81.9030.04
SQL 2000 Enterprise for NT MDAC 2.8	2000.85.1022.00
Oracle 7.3.4 for NT	2.50.0301
Oracle 8.0.6 for NT	8.0.6.00
Oracle 8.1.55 for NT	8.01.55.00
Oracle 8.1.6 for NT	8.1.6.00
Oracle 8.1.6 for NT and UNIX/Solaris	8.1.6.00
Oracle 8.1.7.2 for NT	8.1.7.2.00
Oracle 9.0.1 for NT	9.00.11.00
Oracle 9i R2 for NT and UNIX/Solaris	9.2.0.1.0
Oracle 9i R2 for NT	9.2.0.1.0
IBM DB2 UDB 7.2, FixPak 5 for NT	7.01.00.55
IBM DB2 UDB 7.2, FixPak 7 for NT	7.01.00.65
IBM DB2 UDB 8.1, FixPak 4 for NT	8.01.04.341

Table 4-3.   Supported and Tested Third-Party ODBC Client Database Versions

Misconception   "Access data stores cannot have more than ten servers in a farm."

Actual   Access data stores can support well over 100 servers in a single farm. The decision of which data store to use should be based on how risk adverse you are (avoiding a single point of failure) and the feature sets of the various databases such as backup, restore, maintenance, and so on.

Minimum Requirements

▼ Allow for approximately 50MB of disk space for every 100 servers in the farm. The disk space used can increase if a large number of published applications are in the farm.

▲ Allow for an additional 32MB of RAM if the MetaFrame Presentation Server hosting the data store will also host user connections.

Microsoft Authentication to the Data Store Database

The default user name/password on the *Mf20.mdb* file is **citrix/citrix**. To change the password on the database, use the

```
dsmaint config /pwd:newpassword
```

command with the IMA service running. Keep the new password in a secure place because it might be needed for migration to another database.

TIP: Perform a backup using **dsmaint backup** before changing the password on the *Mf20.mdb* file. For more information on the dsmaint command see the *MetaFrame Presentation Server Administrator's Guide*.

Automatic Backup of the Access Data Store

Each time the IMA service is stopped or a server is restarted, the existing *Mf20.mdb* file is backed up, compacted, and copied as *Mf20.unk*. Each time the IMA service starts, it deletes *Mf20.bak*, if it exists, and renames the *Mf20.unk* file to *Mf20.bak*. This process helps ensure that the *Mf20.bak* file is a valid farm database. This file is used when the **dsmaint recover** command is executed. The *Mf20.mdb* file and all automatic backup files are located by default in the %ProgramFiles%\Citrix\Independent Management Architecture folder.

CAUTION: Run **dsmaint backup** prior to executing **dsmaint recover**. Do not execute **dsmaint recover** if no *Mf20.bak* file exists. This command will remove the existing *Mf20.mdb* from the server.

Additional Notes on Using Access for the Data Store   All indirect servers connect and maintain connections to the host server.

1. By default, the server that hosts the database is also its Zone's Data Collector.

2. Tuning the Jet Database Engine with registry settings can improve performance for large farms. Consult the Microsoft documentation about performance tuning for the Jet Database Engine. Back up both the registry and the *Mf20.mdb* file before changing the tuning parameters.

3. Use **dsmaint backup** to perform an online backup of the data store. This can be scripted easily in a batch file.

4. Backup the MetaFrame Presentation Server data store before using the Presentation Server Console to make changes in the data store. Scheduling a daily backup is sufficient in most cases.

CAUTION: If the server runs out of disk space on the drive where the *Mf20.mdb* file is stored, automatic backups cease. Always ensure that free disk space is at least three times the size of the *Mf20.mdb* file.

Microsoft SQL Server Desktop Engine (MSDE)

MSDE (essentially a free, run-time version of MS SQL) is a more scaleable and stable option for a Citrix data store than Microsoft Access, but not as feature rich or capable as the enterprise databases covered later. The big draw to MSDE, though, is that it is free and as such is the best supported option for the data store if cost is the number one concern, and the environment is small. The practices outlined in this section suggest the best practices for using MSDE as the data store. This is not intended to be a substitute for the Microsoft MSDE documentation. Please read all of the Microsoft MSDE documentation prior to installing and using MSDE.

IMPORTANT: To use MSDE to host a data store with remapped server drives, remap the server drives prior to installing MDSE.

In order to use MSDE for the data store, install MSDE prior to installation of MetaFrame Presentation Server. MSDE with Service Pack 3 is included on the MetaFrame Presentation Server CD within the Support\MSDE directory. Run the **SetupMsdeForMetaFrame.cmd** batch file, which will install MSDE, Service Pack 3 and create a named instance called "CITRIX_METAFRAME" needed for the default installation of the MetaFrame Presentation Server. Then choose the "Use a local database on this server" option during installation and select the MSDE Database entry from the list of possible databases when installing MetaFrame Presentation Server.

IMPORTANT: If MSDE will be used to host a server farm's data store, double-byte characters in the name of the server on which the MSDE database will be stored will not be supported.

Minimum Requirements for the MSDE Server

The MetaFrame Presentation Server that hosts the MSDE database should meet the following minimum requirements:

▼ Approximately 50MB of disk space is required for every 100 servers and 25 applications in the farm.

■ Plan for an additional 32MB of RAM if the MetaFrame Presentation Server hosting the data store will also host connections.

▲ 70MB of disk space is required, in addition to the size of the MSDE database.

Security and Authentication of the MSDE Database

Windows NT authentication is supported for the MSDE database. For security reasons, Microsoft SQL Server authentication is not supported. Please consult Microsoft documentation for further details on MSDE security.

Connect to the Data Store

Although it is possible to configure multiple MetaFrame Presentation Servers to connect directly to a single MSDE database, Citrix does not recommend this configuration because it is not supported by MSDE. MSDE allows only five connections per installed instance of MSDE. A MetaFrame Presentation Server may use multiple connections to the MSDE instance. Therefore, if more than one MetaFrame Presentation Server attempts to connect to the MSDE database at the same time, the connections may be denied resulting in intermittent failures. Citrix therefore recommends that the first server connection to the MSDE database be configured using direct access and all other server connections configured for indirect access.

To create the named instance of "CITRIX_METAFRAME" for MSDE, follow these steps:

1. Run the SetupMsdeForMetaFrame.cmd to install MSDE support and create a named instance used by the MetaFrame Presentation Server Feature installation.

2. This file is located in the Support\MSDE directory within the MetaFrame Presentation Server CD.

3. This will also create the files and directories for MSDE support under \Program Files\Microsoft SQL Server.

4. There will also be a named instance directory of MSSQL$CITRIX_METAFRAME which is created by running the above-mentioned command.

This batch file installs MSDE with the recommended defaults for use with MetaFrame Presentation Server.

To create and install a Named Instance of MSDE other than the default CITRIX_ METAFRAME, follow these steps:

1. Insert the MetaFrame Presentation Server CD in the computer's CD-ROM drive. Do not use the autorun feature.

2. Open up a command prompt and change directories to the CD-ROM drive.

3. Navigate to Support\MSDE\MSDE.

4. Type the following at the command prompt: **msiexec -i "MSDE For MetaFrame .msi" INSTANCENAME=<*name*>** where <name> is the name to be given to the MSDE installation.

After performing these steps, proceed with the installation of MetaFrame Presentation Server, and select MSDE for the data store.

For further details please consult the *MetaFrame Presentation Server Administrator's Guide*.

NOTE: If MSDE is selected for the database, the correct named instance of MSDE installed on the server must be known. By default, Setup looks for the MSDE named instance of CITRIX_METAFRAME as noted in the previous steps.

Use Microsoft SQL Server

Microsoft SQL Server provides administrative tools, backup tools, and additional scalability over what is found in MSDE and Microsoft Access databases. As such, Microsoft SQL tends to be a popular choice for the data store database. The practices outlined in this section suggest the best practices for using Microsoft SQL Server as the data store. This is not intended to be a substitute for the Microsoft SQL Server documentation. Please read all of the Microsoft SQL Server documentation prior to installing Microsoft SQL Server. These recommendations will apply to both Microsoft SQL Server 7 and Microsoft SQL Server 2000. These instructions do not refer to MSDE; see the previous section for information about using MSDE as the data store.

Minimum Requirements

The minimum requirements are the following:

▼ Approximately 100MB of disk space for every 250 servers in the farm. The disk space used can increase if a large number of published applications are in the farm.

■ Set the "temp" database to Auto Grow on a partition with at least 1GB of free space.

▲ Verify that enough disk space exists on the server to support growth of both the temp database and the farm database.

For the server configuration:

▼ When using Microsoft SQL Server in a replicated environment, be sure to use the same user account on each Microsoft SQL Server for the data store.

■ Each MetaFrame Presentation Server farm requires a dedicated database. However, multiple databases can be running on a single Microsoft SQL Server. Do not install the MetaFrame Presentation Server farm in a database that is shared with any other client/server applications.

■ Set the "Truncate log on Checkpoint" option in the database to control the log space. Please note this recommendation only applies to SQL 7; SQL 2000 does not contain this option. To truncate the transaction log on SQL 2000, create a maintenance plan or follow the next recommendation.

■ On both SQL 7 and SQL 2000, follow Microsoft's recommendations for configuring database and transaction logs for recovery.

- ■ Whenever a change is made using the Presentation Server Console, back up the database. Scheduling a daily backup is sufficient in most cases.

- ▲ If installing more than 256 servers into a farm with a Microsoft SQL Server data store, the number of worker threads available for the database must be equal to or greater than the number of servers in the server farm.

To increase SQL Server worker threads, follow these steps:

1. Launch the Microsoft SQL Server Enterprise Manager.
2. Select Server Configuration Properties.
3. Click the Processor tab.
4. Change the maximum worker thread count from 256 to a number greater than the number of servers in the server farm.

Compare SQL Fibers and Threads

Using fibers may provide better performance in some configurations of the SQL Server used to house the data store. The operating system code that manages threads is in the kernel. Switching threads requires mode switches between the user mode of the application code and the kernel mode of the thread manager, a moderately expensive operation. Fibers, a subcomponent of threads, are managed by code running in user mode. Switching fibers does not require the user-mode to kernel-mode transition needed to switch threads. The application manages the scheduling of fibers. The Windows operating system manages the scheduling of threads. Each thread can have multiple fibers.

Using fibers reduces context switches by allowing SQL Server to handle scheduling rather than using the Windows NT or Windows 2000 Scheduler. Utilize the lightweight pooling option to configure SQL Server to use fibers. If applications are running on a multiple-processor system and there are a large number of context switches, try setting the lightweight pooling parameter to 1, which enables lightweight pooling. After setting this parameter, monitor the number of context switches again to verify that they are reduced. The default value is 0, which disables the use of fibers causing SQL Server to schedule one thread per concurrent user command, up to the value of maximum worker threads. In fiber mode, an instance of SQL Server allocates one thread per CPU, and then allocates a fiber per concurrent user command, up to the maximum worker threads value. An instance of SQL Server uses the same algorithms to schedule and synchronize tasks when using either threads or fibers.

Fibers work best when the server has multiple CPUs and a relatively low user-to-CPU ratio. For example, on an Enterprise installation with 32 CPUs and 250 users, a noticeable performance boost is seen with fibers. When there are 8 CPUs and 5000 users, a performance decrease may be seen with fibers.

NOTE: Threads will be most beneficial for the majority of MetaFrame Presentaion Server data store implementations.

At the time of this writing, additional information and instructions about configuring fibers can be found at the following addresses:

http://msdn.microsoft.com/library Search using keywords: SQL Server Task Scheduling.

http://www.microsoft.com/technet Search using keywords: Configuring, Threading, Priority, and Fiber.

http://www.microsoft.com/learning_tools Search using keywords: Microsoft SQL Server 7.0 Performance Tuning, then select sample chapter.

Security and Authentication of the SQL Server

Microsoft SQL Server supports Windows NT, Active Directory, and Microsoft SQL Server authentication. Consult the Microsoft SQL Server documentation for configuring Windows NT authentication support.

▼ For high-security environments, Citrix recommends using Windows NT authentication only.

■ During MetaFrame Presentation Server installation, the account used for the data store connection must have db_owner (database owner) rights on the database that is being used for the data store.

▲ For better security, after the initial installation of the database as database owner, set the user permissions to read/write only.

CAUTION: Changing user rights from database owner can prevent future service packs or feature releases from being installed correctly. Always change permissions back to database owner during the installation of a service pack or feature release.

Use Sockets Rather than Named Pipes

It is preferable to use TCP/IP sockets when choosing a method to connect MetaFrame Presentation Servers to a Microsoft SQL Server. Data transmissions are more streamlined for TCP/IP sockets and have less overhead. Performance enhancement mechanisms, such as windowing and delayed acknowledgements, can provide significant performance improvement in a slow network.

Named Pipes is an authenticated protocol. Any time a user attempts to open a connection to the SQL Server using Named Pipes, the Windows NT authentication process occurs. TCP/IP sockets do not rely on the Windows NT authentication to establish a connection, but provides user/password authentication to the SQL Server after the connection is established. This eliminates the possibility of an error if the SQL Server and the MetaFrame Presentation Server do not have the correct domain/ADS trust relationship. To use TCP/IP sockets for MetaFrame Presentation Server to Microsoft SQL Server connections, follow the next two procedures.

Here's how to create a SQL Server data source connection while installing MetaFrame Presentation Server.

When Microsoft SQL is selected as the data store, a prompt appears for creating a new data source connection to the SQL Server.

1. Type the Data Source description and SQL Server to which to connect. Click Next.

2. Select NT Authentication or SQL Server Authentication.

3. Click Client Configuration.

4. Select TCP/IP from the available network libraries. Click OK.

To modify a Data Source Name (DSN) after the MetaFrame Presentation Server installation, follow these steps:

1. Open the ODBC Data Source Administrator from the Control Panel or from the Administrative Tools.

2. Select the File DSN tab.

3. Browse to %Program Files%\Citrix\Independent Management Architecture.

4. Select the MetaFrame DSN created in the prior installation. Select Configure.

5. In the Microsoft SQL Server DSN Configuration dialog box, select Next | Client Configuration.

6. Select TCP/IP from the available network libraries. Select OK. Select Next. Select Finish.

7. Restart the MetaFrame Presentation Server.

Replicate a SQL Server 2000 Database

This section outlines the steps necessary to configure replication of a data store environment on Microsoft SQL Server 2000.

The purpose of replication is to insure that if the main database server has hardware failure or corruption problems, the data store will not be lost. Note that replication does not guarantee uptime of the data store—please see the "Failover and Clustering of SQL Server 2000" section immediately following this section for details on ensuring uptime of the data store.

To replicate a SQL Server 2000 database, use SQL Enterprise Manager. Begin by creating a new database on the SQL Server that will be used as the source for all replicas you create. Be sure that the account you use to create the database has db_owner permissions and is the same one used on the replicated database.

Before setting up replication, ensure the following:

▼ Ideally, the Windows installations should be clean, fresh (from CD) installations instead of images. If images of Windows are used, make sure that they do not come from the same image but from different ones for each server. If your Windows installations come from the same image, then replication will not work.

- Do not mix Windows 2000 with Windows Server 2003. The Distributed Transaction Coordinator service operates differently in Windows Server 2003 than it does in Windows 2000. If you mix the operating systems, replication will fail.

- For Windows Server 2003, verify that both Publisher and Subscriber SQL Servers are in the same domain. If they are not, please review Microsoft Knowledge Base article 817064.

- Install SQL Server on the servers designated for the data stores.

▲ Verify that the Microsoft Distributed Transaction Coordinator is installed on the servers designated for the data stores.

Set Up the SQL Server Data Store Replication for Distribution   In order to ensure that the data store replication is available for use, perform these steps for both servers:

1. From the Start menu, start the Services Manager.

2. From Services Manager, set up the same domain logon account for the following services (the local system account does not work):

   - SQLServerAgent
   - MSSQLServer
   - MSDTC (Distributed Transaction Coordinator on Windows 2000)

> **NOTE:**   If you are configuring SQL replication on a Windows Server 2003, verify the MSDTC service is using the Network Services security account. (Note: This account uses a blank password.)

The general tasks to successfully replicate an SQL Server database are the following:

1. Establish the distributor server.
2. Set the distributor properties.
3. Publish the source database.
4. Push the published database out to subscribers.

Each of these four tasks is explained in more detail in the following sections.

Step 1: Establish the Distributor Server   Complete the following steps to define the server that will act as the distributor.

MS SQL 2000 servers acting as Publisher, Distributor, and Subscriber need to be in the same NT/AD domain and the SQL services should be started under the same account.

1. Open Enterprise Manager on the server on which the source database is located.

2. Right-click the Replication folder and select Configure Publishing | Subscribers | Distribution Wizard.

3. On the Select Distributor page, select the current server to act as the distributor.

4. Keep the default Snapshot folder.

5. On the Customize the Configuration page, choose the option "No, use the following default settings."

6. Click Finish.

Step 2: Set the Distributor Properties   Complete the following steps to set the distributor properties:

1. Right-click the Replication Monitor folder and choose Distributor Properties.

2. On the Publication Databases tab, check the Trans box next to the database you want to replicate, as shown in Figure 4-3.

Step 3: Publish the source database   Complete the following steps to publish the database that you want to replicate.

1. Right-click the database name and go to New | Publication to start the Create Publication wizard.

2. Click "Show advanced options in this wizard" and then click Next.

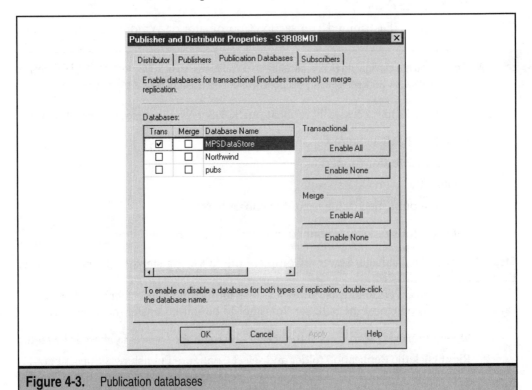

Figure 4-3.   Publication databases

3. On the Choose Publication Database screen, select the database you want to replicate and then click Next.

4. On the Select Publication Type page, choose Transactional Publication.

5. On the Updatable Subscriptions page, select the Immediate Updating option, as shown in Figure 4-4.

6. On the Specify Subscriber Types page, select the Servers running SQL Server 2000 option.

7. On the Specify Articles page, shown in the Figure 4-5, select both Show and Publish for the Tables object type on the left side of the page. Do not publish stored procedures to the replicated databases.

8. Click Next on the Article Issues page.

9. Name the publication.

10. On the Customize the Properties of the Publication page, choose "No, create the publication as specified."

11. Click Finish to complete the wizard. The publication is displayed in the Publications folder, as shown in Figure 4-6.

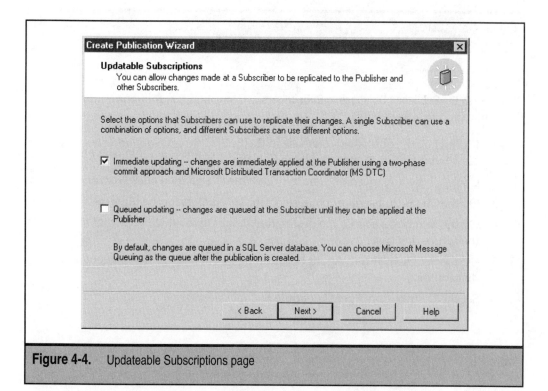

Figure 4-4.   Updateable Subscriptions page

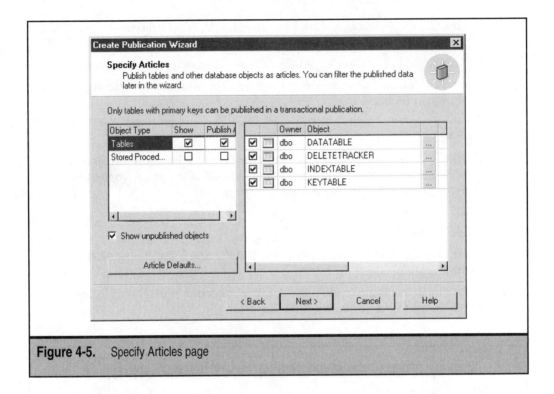

Figure 4-5. Specify Articles page

Step 4: Push the Published Database to Subscribers   Complete the following steps to push the publication to subscribers:

1. Right-click the published database in the Publications folder and choose Push New Subscription to start the Push Subscription wizard.

2. Click "Show advanced options in this wizard" and then click Next.

3. On the Choose Subscribers page, select the subscribers for the published database.

4. On the next page, choose the destination database to which you want to replicate the source database.

5. On the Set Distribution Agent Location page, choose to run the agent at the distributor.

6. Set the Distribution Agent Schedule to "continuously."

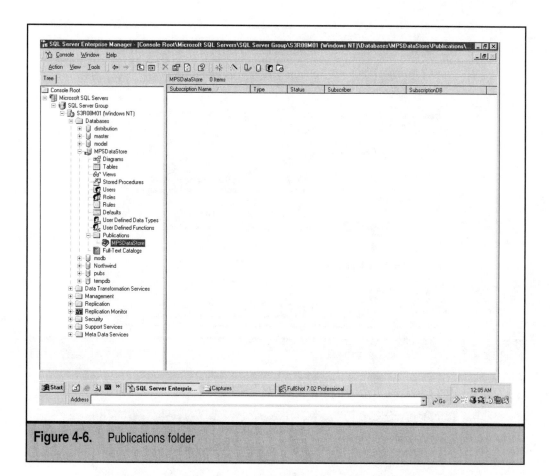

Figure 4-6.   Publications folder

7. On the Initialize Subscription page, shown in Figure 4-7, choose "Yes, initialize the schema and data" and select the option "Start the Snapshot Agent to begin the initialization process immediately."

8. On the Updateable Subscriptions page, select the Immediate Updating option.

9. On the Start Required Services page shown in Figure 4-8, the services that must be running are listed. Verify that the applicable required services are running on the distributor server.

10. Click Finish on the next screen to complete the wizard.

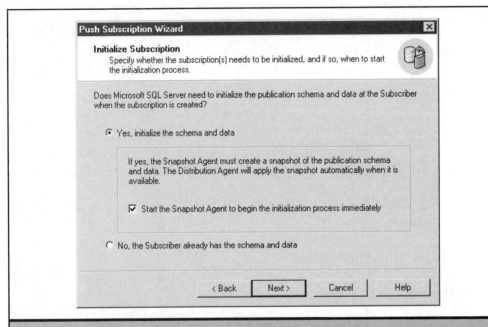

Figure 4-7. Initialize Subscription page

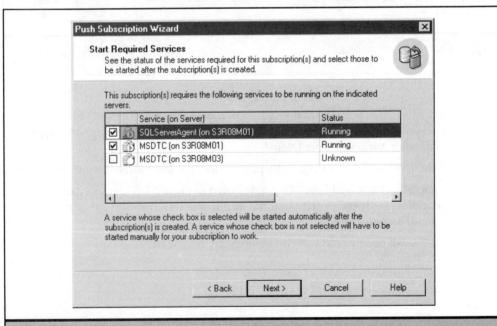

Figure 4-8. Start Required Services page

Setting the Password on the Replica Database on the Subscriber   When the subscription (replica) database is created on the subscriber, the password for the **sa** account is not passed for security reasons. The password for the **sa** account needs to be manually set on the subscriber for the replica database. The following steps represent one way to change the password for the sa account:

1. Select the subscription database on the subscriber.
2. Select Tools | SQL Query Analyzer.
3. In the SQL Query Analyzer window, type and run the following stored procedure:

    ```
    sp_link_publication '<Distributor>', '<Database>',
    '<Publication>', 0, 'SA', '<Pwd>'
    ```

where:

▼ *Distributor* = The name of the distributor server

■ *Database* = The name of the published database on the distributor

■ *Publication* = The name of the publication that is to be linked

▲ *Pwd* = The password for the sa account on the distributor

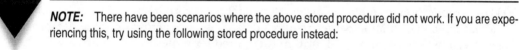

NOTE: There have been scenarios where the above stored procedure did not work. If you are experiencing this, try using the following stored procedure instead:

```
sp_link_publication 'publisher', 'database',
'publication', 0, 'sa', 'password', 'distributor'
```

For more information about linking a publication and other SQL replication troubleshooting, please see Chapter 17.

Additional Concerns for Windows 2003 Servers   As a final step on both Subscriber and Publisher, run the following procedure using Query Analyzer:

```
exec sp_serveroption 'myServer', 'data access', 'true'
```

where *myServer* is the name of the remote server. Example runs on Publisher and Subscriber would be the following:

Example run on: Subscriber

```
exec sp_serveroption 'SubscriberServer', 'data access', 'true'
```

Example run on Publisher:

```
exec sp_serveroption 'PublisherServer', 'data access', 'true'
```

Failover and Clustering of SQL Server 2000

For fault tolerance with Microsoft SQL Server, use Microsoft Cluster Services (MSCS). This provides failover and failback for clustered systems.

An MSCS cluster group is a collection of clustered resources, such as disk drives, that are owned by one of the failover cluster nodes. You can transfer the ownership of the group from one node to another, but each group can be owned by only one node at a time.

The database files for an instance of Microsoft SQL Server 2000 are placed in a single MSCS cluster group owned by the node on which the instance is installed. If a node running an instance of Microsoft SQL Server 2000 fails, MSCS switches the cluster group containing the data files for that instance to another node. Because the new node already has the executable files and registry information for that instance of Microsoft SQL Server 2000 on its local disk drive, it can start up an instance of Microsoft SQL Server 2000 and start accepting connection requests for that instance.

NOTE: MSCS clustering does not support load balancing between clustered servers because it functions in active-passive mode only.

Distributed SQL Databases

MetaFrame Presentation Server supports distributed databases. These are useful when the data store becomes a bottleneck due to too many read requests. Microsoft SQL Server 2000 uses replication to create the distributed database environment.

MetaFrame Presentation Server requires data coherency across multiple databases. Therefore, a two-phase commit algorithm is required for writes to the database.

When configuring Microsoft SQL Server 2000 for a two-phase commit, you must use the Immediate Updating Subscriber model. See your Microsoft SQL Server 2000 documentation for information about setting up replication with the Immediate Updating Subscriber model.

CAUTION: Using merged replication will corrupt the data store.

Misconception   "Merge replication can be used for replicating the data store."

Actual   Immediate-Updating Transactional Replication must be used or the data store will get corrupted. A highly coherent database is required by IMA. Due to the usage of identity fields in the database, merge replication does not work.

To set up a distributed environment for an existing MetaFrame Presentation Server farm, follow these steps:

1. Configure a Publisher (the Microsoft SQL Server 2000 currently hosting the data store), and Subscribers (remote sites) using Microsoft SQL Server Enterprise Manager.

2. Execute the **dsmaint publishsqlds** command from an existing farm server. This step executes the necessary SQL statements to create the published articles on the current Microsoft SQL Server 2000 (Publisher). For more information about the dsmaint command, see the MetaFrame Presentation Server Administrator's Guide.

3. Configure the remote sites (Subscribers) to subscribe to the published articles created in Step 2.

For more detailed information on installing the Citrix data store on Microsoft SQL Server 2000, please see *Citrix MetaFrame Access Suite for Windows Server 2003: The Official Guide* (Kaplan et al., McGraw-Hill/Osborne, 2003).

Using Oracle for the Data Store

The practices outlined in this section are suggested implementations for the Oracle data store. They are not intended to be a substitute for the Oracle documentation. Read all of the Oracle documentation prior to installing Oracle. Guidelines given here can be used on Oracle7, Oracle8, Oracle8i, and Oracle9i, except as noted otherwise.

Minimum Requirements

The minimum requirements are the following:

▼ Use approximately 100MB of disk space for every 250 servers in the farm. The space used can increase if a large number of published applications are in the farm.

▲ The Oracle Client (version 8.1.55 or later) must be installed on the terminal server prior to the installation of MetaFrame Presentation Server. The 8.1.5 client is not supported with any version of MetaFrame Presentation Server.

NOTE: If you do not restart the server after installing the Oracle Client, the MetaFrame Presentation Server installation will fail to connect to the data store.

For the server configuration:

▼ Creating a separate tablespace for the data store simplifies backup and restoration operations.

■ Using Shared/Multi-Threaded Server (MTS) mode can reduce the number of processes in farms with more than 100 servers. However, performance may be affected under high data store load. Consult your Oracle documentation for information about configuring the database to run in MTS mode.

■ Add one additional process for each farm server connected directly to the Oracle database when using an Oracle server in dedicated mode. If the Oracle server uses 100 processes before installing MetaFrame Presentation Server and the server farm has 50 servers, set the processes value to at least 150 in the *init.ora* file on the Oracle server. Consult the Oracle documentation for more information.

■ If you are running Oracle in MTS mode, verify the following parameters in the *init.ora* file are greater than or equal to the following values. (If running multiple farms on the same Oracle database, include all MetaFrame Presentation Servers for the calculations listed here. Round up for fractional values.)

MTS_SERVERS = {#MFXP Servers} / 10
MTS_MAX_SERVERS = {#MFXP Servers} / 5
SERIALIZABLE = False
ROW_LOCKING = Always

■ Whenever a change is made using the Presentation Server Console for MetaFrame Presentation Server, back up the database. Scheduling a daily backup is sufficient in most cases.

▲ Online backups using *archivelog* mode are recommended. Archivelog mode reduces the recovery time of a crashed database and allows you to perform backup and recovery of individual tablespaces.

NOTE: For security reasons, Citrix recommends setting up a unique tablespace for each farm with its own user/password. Do not use the default system account within Oracle.

Oracle Client Configuration

In order to use the Oracle 8.1.7 client to access the data store, several steps should be taken to ensure proper operation with MetaFrame Presentation Server. The Oracle 8.1.7.0 driver installs a security feature, called NT Security (NTS) that uses Windows NT credentials to authenticate to the Oracle server. Because the IMA Service is configured to use the System account to access the data store, IMA fails to connect to the Oracle server when the NTS feature is enabled. If this happens, IMA reports error code 2147483649.

NOTE: The following steps are not required with the Oracle 8.1.6 client because it does not use NTS.

For the MetaFrame Presentation Server installation to recognize that the Oracle 8.1.7.*x* client is installed, do the following:

1. Install the Oracle 8.1.6.x client and upgrade to 8.1.7.*x*.

2. Run the Net8 Assistant.

3. Navigate to Configuration | Local | Profile.

4. Select Oracle Advanced Security.

5. Select the Authentication tab.

6. Remove NTS from the Selected Methods list if it is present.

7. Install MetaFrame Presentation Server.

If `dsmaint` will be used to migrate from an Access data store to an Oracle 8.1.7 data store, the IMA Service fails to start because the Oracle 8.1.7.0 driver alters the logon authentication method. To avoid this problem, when migrating from Microsoft Access to Oracle 8.1.7, disable the Oracle NTS feature.

To disable the Oracle NTS feature, follow these steps:

1. Run the Net8 Assistant.

2. Navigate to Configuration | Local | Profile.

3. Select Oracle Advanced Security.

4. Select the Authentication tab.

5. Remove NTS from the Selected Methods list if it is present.

Security and Authentication of the Oracle Server

▼ Oracle for Solaris supports Oracle authentication only. It does not support Windows NT authentication.

■ Oracle for Windows NT supports both Windows NT and Oracle authentication. Consult the Oracle documentation for information about configuring Windows NT authentication.

■ The Oracle user account must be the same for every server in the farm because all servers share a common schema.

■ Each farm in the database must have a different user account because the data store information is stored in the Oracle user account's schema.

■ The account used for the data store connection needs to have the following Oracle permissions:

   ■ Connect

   ■ Resource

   ■ Optionally, assign the following permission:

   ■ Unlimited Tablespace

Failover of the Oracle Data Store

Oracle allows administrators to maintain a standby database for quick disaster recovery. A standby database maintains a copy of the production database in a permanent state of recovery. If there is a disaster in the production database, the standby database can be opened with a minimum amount of recovery.

Some important items concerning Oracle failover include the following:

▼ With Oracle8*i*, the management of standby databases is fully automatic.

■ The standby database must run on the same version of the kernel that is on the production system.

■ Standby databases only fail one way. They cannot fail back.

■ If a database fails, use **dsmaint config** to reconfigure the MetaFrame Presentation Servers to point to the standby database.

▲ Citrix recommends the use of a standby database for MetaFrame Presentation Server farms.

Please see the Oracle documentation for detailed instructions on setting up a standby database.

Distributed Oracle Data Store Databases

MetaFrame Presentation Server supports distributed databases. These are useful when the data store bottlenecks because of too many read requests. Oracle uses replication to create the distributed database environment. Important items concerning distributed databases are listed below.

To reduce the load on a single database server, install read-write replicas and distribute the farm servers evenly across the master and replicas.

MetaFrame Presentation Server requires data coherency across multiple databases. Therefore, a two-phase commit algorithm is required for writes to the database.

Using Oracle as a distributed database solution requires the following:

▼ All participating databases must be running Oracle.

■ All participating databases must be running in MTS/Shared mode (rather than Dedicated mode).

■ All clients (MetaFrame Presentation Server direct servers) must be SQL*Net Version 2 or Net8.

■ Install the farm database first on the master site, and then configure replication at the snapshot sites.

▲ Replicate all the objects contained in the data store user's schema (tables, indexes, and stored procedures).

TIP: If the performance at the replicated database site is significantly slower, verify that all the indexes for the MetaFrame Presentation Server user's schema are successfully replicated.

When configuring Oracle for a two-phase commit, Citrix recommends the following:

▼ Use updateable, synchronous snapshots with a single master site. MetaFrame Presentation Server does not work with read-only snapshots. Some functions need write access to the data store.

■ Use Fast Refresh where possible (this requires snapshot logs).

■ Do not configure conflict resolution when setting up the replication environment.

▲ Set the replication link interval to be as frequent as the network environment allows (one minute is recommended). With Oracle Replication, if no changes are made, no data is sent over the link.

If Oracle is configured in MTS mode and remote reads or writes are initiated from the remote site, these can block reads or writes locally because, in MTS mode, all connections share a set of worker threads called MTS servers. To remedy this, increase the value of the `Max_Mts_Servers` parameter in the *init.ora* file.

Citrix recommends consulting the Oracle documentation when setting up replication. The documentation for Oracle8*i* is at the following web address:

http://technet.oracle.com/docs/products/oracle8i/doc_index.htm.

Use IBM DB2 for the Data Store

MetaFrame XP Feature Release 2 and higher supports using IBM DB2 Universal Database Enterprise Edition Version 7.2 for Windows 2000 with FixPak 5 or higher for the server farm's data store.

MetaFrame Presentation Server 3.0 supports this database as well as Version 8.1 for Windows 2000 with FixPak 4 or greater.

To get started using DB2 for the data store, install the IBM DB2 runtime client and apply FixPak 5 on each MetaFrame Presentation Server that will directly access the database server.

To configure the DB2 data store for multiple MetaFrame Presentation Server farms, create a separate database/tablespace for each farm's data store. Plan to restart the system after the installation of the IBM DB2 runtime client and FixPak 5 and before the installation of MetaFrame Presentation Server. See the IBM DB2 documentation for more information.

IMPORTANT: MetaFrame Presentation Server uses the data type of binary large object (BLOB) to store information in an IBM DB2 database. IBM DB2 does not support the use of BLOB data types in an updateable replication scenario. Therefore, if a server farm needs to have updateable replicas, use Microsoft SQL Server or Oracle for the farm's data store instead of IBM DB2.

Depending on the size of the server farm, the following options may need to be modified in the IBM DB2 Control Center:

▼ **appheapsz, app_ctl_heap_sz, maxlocks**   You may need to modify these options if you have a large server farm (50 or more servers) that is relatively active.

■ **Maxappls**   This setting must be greater than the number of servers in the farm, or the servers will fail to connect (the default is 40).

■ **avg_appls**   This setting should be equal to the number of servers in the farm.

▲ **logfilsiz, logprimary, logsecond**   You may need to adjust these settings upward if you are migrating the farm from another database.

Minimum Requirements for the DB2 Data Store

The practices outlined in this section are suggested practices for using an IBM DB2 database for the server farm's data store. Be sure to read the DB2 documentation before installing and configuring the DB2 databases.

▼ There should be approximately 100MB of disk space for every 250 servers and 50 published applications in the farm. The required disk space increases if a large number of published applications are in the farm.

■ If a data source name (DSN) is created for use with an unattended installation of IBM DB2, Citrix recommends that the DSN be created using the Microsoft ODBC Data Source Administration screen. Doing so ensures that the DSN is populated according to MetaFrame requirements for proper connectivity to the DB2 database or tablespace.

■ The Citrix *e*Labs tested the IBM DB2 environment with the following permissions assigned to the user:

  ■ Connect database

  ■ Create tables

  ■ Register functions to execute to database manager's process

  ■ Create schemas implicitly

IMPLEMENT THE DATA STORE IN A STORAGE AREA NETWORK

A Storage Area Network (SAN) is a logically separated high-speed network dedicated to hosting a disk storage array. The SAN is a back end network that carries only I/O traffic between servers and a disk storage pool while the front-end network, the LAN, carries e-mail, file, print, and web traffic. For their backbones, SANs utilize Fibre Channel Technology, Gigabit Ethernet, or soon to be common, 10GB Ethernet (Ethernet SANs are often referred to as IP SANs).

SAN Backup Support

SANs provide easy, on-the-fly backup strategies. Not only can the SAN be utilized for snapshots and incremental disk-to-disk backups, but it also allows for faster tape back-ups that consume fewer resources. This is because all of the disk access occurs on the SAN's network, and not on the LAN. The data store can consequently be backed up easily even while it is in use.

SAN Cluster Failover Support of the Data Store

The data store is an integral part of the MetaFrame Presentation Server farm architecture. An inherent part of building access infrastructure for an on-demand enterprise is to have the database available all the time. For maximum availability, the data store should be in a clustered database environment with a SAN backbone.

Hardware redundancy allows the SAN to recover from most component failures. Additional software such as Oracle9*i* Real Application Cluster or SQL Server 2000 utilizing MSCS allows for the failover in a catastrophic software failure and in Oracle's case, performance improvements.

NOTE: Software such as Compaq's SANWorks is required to manage database clusters in certain hardware configurations.

MSCS, available on Windows 2000 and Windows Server 2003Advanced Server and DataCenter products, provides the ability to failover the MetaFrame Presentation Server farm data store to a functioning server in the event of a catastrophic server failure.

MSCS monitors the health of standard applications and services, and automatically recovers mission-critical data and applications from many common types of failures. A graphical management console allows the monitoring of the status of all resources in the cluster and to manage workloads accordingly. In addition, Windows 2000 and 2003 Advanced Server and Datacenter Server integrate middleware and load balancing services that distribute IP network traffic evenly across the clustered servers.

Redundancy and recovery can be built into each major component of the data store. Deploying the following technologies can eliminate single points-of-failure from the data store:

▼   Microsoft Cluster Service

■   Redundant hardware

▲   Software monitoring and management tools

The basic SAN configuration in Figure 4-9 shows each clustered server with dual Host Bus Adapters (HBAs) cabled to separate FC-AL switches. A system with this redundancy can continue running when any component in this configuration fails. Inherently, SAN architecture is intended to be very reliable. It provides redundant systems in all aspects of the configuration with multiple paths to the network. The number of supported nodes that can be clustered for your chosen operating system can be found in the Microsoft Knowledge Base article 288778.

If there is a software or hardware failure on the owner of the cluster node, the MetaFrame Presentation Servers lose their IMA connection to the database. When the servers sense that the connection has been dropped, the farm goes into a two-minute wait period. The servers then attempt to reconnect to the database. If the IMA cannot immediately reconnect to the data store, it retries, indefinitely, every two minutes. The MetaFrame Presentation Servers automatically reconnect to the database, which has the same IP address, once it fails over to the other node of the cluster.

Microsoft SQL Clustering of the Data Store   SQL clustering does not mean that both databases are active and load balanced. With SQL clustering, the only supported clustering method allows one server to handle all the requests while the other server simply stands by waiting for the other machine to fail.

NOTE: For increased security, when installing a MetaFrame Presentation Server data store to a clustered SQL Server, Windows NT authentication should be used for connecting IMA to the database.

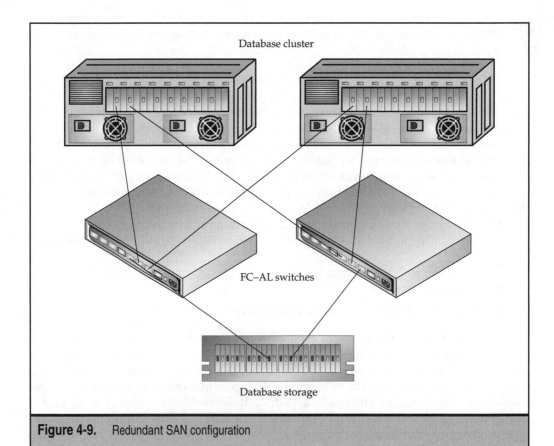

Figure 4-9.   Redundant SAN configuration

Oracle Clustering of the Data Store Oracle Real Application Cluster (RAC) does allow true active-active clustering. As database requests are sent via ODBC, they will be load balanced between the nodes of the cluster. This configuration provides both fault tolerance and increased performance.

SAN Tuning for the Data Store

In addition to increased reliability, a SAN can provide better database performance. In testing at the Citrix *e*Labs, the data store is mainly used as a repository for reading configuration information. In this configuration, the number of reads far exceeds the number of writes. The Array Controller on the SAN can be tuned for 100% reads and 0% writes. This allows optimal performance for data access to the data store through the SAN.

NOTE: Having the SAN tuned to 100% reads and 0% writes still allows servers to write to the data store.

Special Data Store Scenarios

This section covers situations where deviating from the default installation and configuration may be desired or can be beneficial to an environment.

Use Indirect Mode to Access the Data Store

Microsoft SQL Server, Oracle, or IBM DB2 can be used in indirect mode to reduce the number of database connections. This practice is not recommended for use in large farms because it creates a single point of failure at the server hosting the indirect connections.

CAUTION: Although this configuration is possible, it is not a recommended architecture for a MetaFrame farm. Using Microsoft SQL Server, Oracle, or IBM DB2 in indirect mode creates a bottleneck and can cause performance issues.

To prevent a single point of failure for the entire farm, install a core set of direct servers and then point groups of member servers to each of the core direct servers. This process provides better performance than sharing a single server for all queries.

Using a MetaFrame Presentation Server in indirect mode does not reduce the number of queries made to the third-party database. Instead, it channels them through a single ODBC connection.

To use indirect mode with a third-party database, follow these steps:

1. Install the first server into the server farm in direct mode and configure it to properly point to the third-party database.

2. You can install subsequent servers in indirect mode by specifying the direct server from Step 1.

3. When prompted for the account permissions, specify the username and password of the MetaFrame Administrator created in Step 1.

Dedicate a Host Server in an Indirect Mode Server Farm

When a Microsoft Access or MSDE data store resides on a MetaFrame Presentation Server, there is only one direct server connection to the data store. The other servers in this indirect mode server farm access the data store through this host server. The host server acting as a single point of access can potentially be a performance bottleneck. The host server can have further demands on its resources if it is also handling ICA connections.

When the host server has a full user load, the following problems can occur:

▼ Delays when using the Presentation Server Console to configure applications

■ Longer Presentation Server Console refresh times

▲ Longer IMA start times for member servers because the data store server is splitting processor time between users and the IMA service

For these reasons, set up the host server to have a lighter user load than the other member servers of the server farm. The exact tuning of this is dependent on the applications being used and the usual load on the servers.

Make user load on the host server one-half to two-thirds of the load on member servers. If using load balancing, tune the parameters so that the host server is sent less user traffic than the other servers. If servers are restarted often, you must factor in longer start times. In large MetaFrame environments running in indirect mode, it can be necessary to dedicate the host server to handle data store requests exclusively.

NOTE: If the same server is used as the Zone Data Collector, the recommendations for dedicating a server as a Zone Data Collector take precedence over the recommendations in this section. However, better performance can be achieved by utilizing separate machines for the data collector and direct server in a large farm.

CHAPTER 5

MetaFrame Presentation Server 3.0 Deployment

Following the design principals introduced in the previous four chapters, this chapter introduces best practice deployment principals. The deployment aspects covered in this chapter include finding and installing any pre- and post-installation critical updates, remapping server drives, manual installation, automated installation, and rapid deployment of large numbers of MetaFrame Presentation Servers. This chapter also includes discussion on deploying the MetaFrame Presentation Server 3.0 Client and Domain Name System implementation.

METAFRAME PRESENTATION SERVER 3.0 DEPLOYMENT

Part of the planning and design process of any IT project is architecting an efficient process to deploy the infrastructure. Although some of the deployment planning may seem trivial, and the temptation to just get going can be immense, some small tweaks and tricks can reduce deployment time by weeks or even months in larger environments. More significant deployment architecture decisions can have even larger impacts. Additionally, this planning will reduce the risk of major failures and end-user frustration upon turn-up of the environment. It is critically important to test all deployment scenarios in a small test environment prior to rolling out the deployment on a larger scale.

Critical Updates for Citrix MetaFrame
Presentation Server 3.0 for Windows

Before beginning deployment, it is important to investigate and test all new critical updates, hotfixes, and patches.

After inserting the MetaFrame Presentation Server 3.0 for Windows CD and before installing the product, Citrix recommends reading the Installation Checklist. The Installation Checklist can be viewed by selecting View Installation Checklist on the Citrix MetaFrame Presentation Server Setup window that appears after inserting your CD. It outlines, among other items, the following:

1. Downloading and installing critical updates before you install the product
2. Meeting system requirements
3. Installing and configuring the MetaFrame Access Suite licensing
4. Remapping server drive letters
5. Installing MetaFrame Presentation Server
6. Downloading and installing critical updates after you install the product.

The focus of this section will be on installing the required Pre-installation Updates, Critical Installation, and Post-Installation Updates—Steps 1 and 6 respectively—which may be required to properly install or run the product.

Pre-Installation Update Bulletin

The Pre-Installation Update Bulletin offers late-breaking information and links to critical updates to server operating systems and to Citrix installation files. These updates may be required to install or run the product and should be applied prior to installation. Information regarding the required updates can be found on the Pre-Installation Update Bulletin. A link to the bulletin is available on the Installation Checklist. The bulletin is divided into three sections, described in the following sections.

Pre-Installation Updates   Follow the instructions in Step 1 of the bulletin to download and install the updates to Microsoft operating system components required to install or run the product. Links to both the Microsoft Knowledge Base articles and patch for download are provided. Read the Knowledge Base articles for detailed descriptions of the updates.

Installation Updates   Follow the instructions in Step 2 of the bulletin to download and apply critical updates to Citrix installation packages. After downloading and executing the update package, the Critical Update Wizard will be a guide through the process of applying the update to the Citrix components. The Critical Update Wizard creates a modified administrative image of the original CD-ROM of MetaFrame Presentation Server 3.0 for Windows on your hard drive. Use the modified administrative image containing the critical installation updates instead of the original CD-ROM to install MetaFrame Presentation Server.

Post-Installation Updates and the Critical Updates Web Page   Follow the instructions in Step 3 of the bulletin to download and install critical post-installation hotfixes. The instructions in Step 3 of the bulletin will direct you to the Critical Updates web page where the hotfixes can be downloaded. The Critical Updates web page should be visited frequently, on an on-going basis, to determine if any critical hotfixes have been released by Citrix.

Remap Server Drives

If you intend to change the server's drive letters to allow users to retain their original drive letters on client devices, do so before installing MetaFrame Presentation Server or prior to upgrading to MetaFrame Presentation Server. If the server drive letters are going to be changed after installing or upgrading, do so before installing any applications. To change the server's drive letters, use the MetaFrame Presentation Server CD's Autorun feature. Select the Remap Drives option from the Product Installations Screen.

IMPORTANT: If you are upgrading from an earlier release, the Remap Drives option is not available from Autorun. The existing drive mapping is preserved for the upgrade. To modify the existing drive mapping, run the DriveRemap utility (*driveremap.exe*) located in the root folder of the MetaFrame Presentation Server CD.

When running *driveremap.exe* with no parameters, the drive letter choices in the drop-down list may be grayed out. This happens because some aspect of being able to remap the existing drive letters cannot be done.

Some reasons for this are the following:

▼ Noncontiguous drive letters, for example, C, D, X. The mapped drive letters are spread over the interval [a…z] and no reasonable interval shifting can be performed. Shifting C to M is a shift of ten. Drive letter X would not be able to shift ten letters and wrap around the alphabet. Even network drives are taken into account. To work around this, change the drive letters to C:, D:, E: and re-run the utility.

■ At the command prompt, if you silently remap to a letter that is IN USE, such as a mapped network drive, nothing will happen. The process just returns to the prompt. To see if mappings take place, launch Windows Explorer.

▲ MetaFrame Presentation Server drive remapping is not supported on Windows 2000 or Windows 2003 Dynamic Disks.

For more detailed information, please refer to Citrix Knowledge Base article CTX950520 on http://www.citrix.com.

Manual Installation/Upgrade to MetaFrame Presentation Server

This section will detail the steps to manually install or upgrade MetaFrame Presentation Server. In most, larger environments, we strongly recommend the use of automated procedures as outlined in later sections of this chapter.

NOTE: MetaFrame Presentation Server can be installed or upgraded in silent mode using **msiexec / i MPS.msi /qn**.

To install or upgrade to MetaFrame Presentation Server 3.0, follow the procedure outlined in these five steps:

1. Start Autorun from the MetaFrame Presentation Server CD, a network sharepoint, or a mapped network drive containing all the files from the CD image.

NOTE: If you install MetaFrame Presentation Server 3.0 directly by *mps.msi* from MetaFrame Presentation Server, such as a silent or unattended install, make sure that all the prerequisite components are installed. Run Autorun from the installation CD and select the option View Installation Checklist. A copy of the checklist can be printed for easy reference.

2. Click Product Installations and then select Install MetaFrame Presentation Server and its Components.

3. Accept the License Agreement and click Next.

4. Select the components to be installed and click Next.

5. Choose the option to install a Citrix License Server or choose to install Citrix License Server at another time and click Next.

NOTE: In order to be functional, MetaFrame Presentation Server 3.0 requires connectivity to a Citrix License Server. The license server can be installed in the environment before or after MetaFrame Presentation Server is installed and the name of the Citrix License Server can be provided either during an installation or after installation in the Presentation Server Console.

Upgrade to MetaFrame Presentation Server

When upgrading to MetaFrame Presentation Server, consider the following:

1. If MetaFrame 1.8 for Windows 2000 was installed with remapped drives, the COM+ Catalog may have been damaged. To determine if the server is in this state, go to Start | Programs | Administrative Tools | Component Services. In the Console Root, go to Component Services | Computers | My Computer | COM+ Applications. If it is damaged, use the *drvremap* utility located on the MetaFrame 1.8 for Windows 2000, Feature Release 1 or MetaFrame 1.8 for Windows 2000 Service Pack 3 CDs. Use these steps:

   a. **subst C: M:/**

   b. **drvremap /drive:M /remap /com**

   c. **subst C: /d**

   d. Restart the server.

   Refer to Citrix Knowledge Base article CTX240747 for more information.

NOTE: Installation automatically detects which version of MetaFrame is installed, if any. If a previous version is found, setup will then ask you if you want to upgrade to MetaFrame Presentation Server 3.0.

2. SSL settings are intentionally not migrated for security reasons. When upgrading to MetaFrame Presentation Server 3.0, reconfigure SSL manually. For more information about configuring SSL, see the SSL Relay utility's online help.

3. If upgrading a server that does not have Installation Manager and Resource Manager installed, these components will not be installed during the upgrade. To install these components, verify that an Enterprise Edition license is loaded in the Citrix License Server, and install these components using the Add/Remove Programs applet in the Control Panel.

Downgrade from MetaFrame Presentation Server 3.0

MetaFrame Presentation Server 3.0 is a platform upgrade. Once it has been installed, it cannot be downgraded to previously installed versions of MetaFrame.

Rapid Deployment of MetaFrame Presentation Servers

Having a means to quickly build or rebuild a MetaFrame Presentation Server ensures not only a fast deployment of multiple servers, but also that users are impacted for the minimum period of time if an unplanned failure occurs. Optimally, an automated process provides the fastest and most efficient means of building or rebuilding a server. This section covers practices regarding rapid deployment of MetaFrame Presentation Server in the Enterprise environment, including server cloning, unattended installations, and simultaneous installations.

Rapid Deployment of Servers Using Imaging (Cloning)

One efficient approach to rapid deployment of five or more Citrix Servers is cloning. Chapter 11 of *Citrix MetaFrame Access Suite for Windows Server 2003: The Official Guide* (McGraw-Hill/Osborne, 2003) goes into detail on using cloning software such as Norton Ghost and Symantec PowerQuest DeployCenter to rapidly clone nonblade server hardware.

A few manual steps are required for cloning MetaFrame Presentation Servers. These steps vary depending on the type of data store used for the farm, and are described in the following sections. MetaFrame Presentation Server is compatible with server cloning, but cloning software can contain issues that cause the operating system or its add-ons to function incorrectly after being cloned. When using server cloning, it is important to clone one server and test its operation before deploying the rest of the farm.

CAUTION: Do not attempt to image a server with an SSL certificate installed because SSL certificates are unique to the hardware.

Pre-Cloning Considerations   Zone settings are not retained when cloning a server. When the IMA Service on the cloned server starts for the first time, the MetaFrame Presentation Server joins the default zone. The name of the default zone is the ID of the subnet on which the cloned server resides. When deploying images to servers on multiple subnets, assign zone information for each server after the imaging process completes.

CAUTION: Do not attempt to use drive image software to restore an image of a MetaFrame Server with remapped drives. Remapped drives will partially revert to the original configuration on the deployed server rendering the server unusable. Servers with remapped drives may be duplicated using a hardware solution such as Compaq Smart Array controllers with RAID1 drive mirroring.

Prior to changing the Security ID (SID) on the machine used to access the Presentation Server Console, add one of the following as a Citrix Administrator with read/write privileges:

1. A domain administrator
2. The Local Administrators group
3. A local administrator from a machine where the SID is not being changed

NOTE: If cloning is not an option, such as when configuring a server with remapped drives, a custom unattended installation script can be created for both the operating system and applications, including MetaFrame Presentation Server.

The following steps must be performed prior to reimaging a server that is already a member of a MetaFrame Presentation Server farm:

1. From the Presentation Server Console, remove the list of servers configured to host any applications.

2. Remove the server from the server farm by uninstalling MetaFrame Presentation Server.

3. If the server entry still exists in the Presentation Server Console server list, right-click and manually remove the server name from the server list.

4. Apply the system image and add the server to the server farm.

IMPORTANT: If a server is not removed from a MetaFrame Presentation Server farm before a new system image is applied to it, performance problems may result. The Presentation Server Console can display invalid data if the server is added back to the same server farm. This is because the old server's host record in the data store is applied to the newly imaged server.

Rapid Deployment in Environments Using Microsoft Access or MSDE for the Data Store

In environments using Microsoft Access or MSDE, manually install the first server in the new MetaFrame Presentation Server farm that will host the data store. The second server in the farm can then be imaged for the deployment of additional servers.

To image a server for rapid deployment using Access or MSDE for the data store, perform the following procedures:

1. Follow all the necessary steps from the MetaFrame Presentation Server Administrator's Guide to install the first MetaFrame Presentation Server into the farm.

2. Install a second MetaFrame Presentation Server into the farm with an indirect connection to the data store created on the first server.

3. With the second server successfully installed and restarted, log onto the console of the second server as a local or domain administrator.

4. On the second server, delete the *wfcname.ini* file, if it exists, from the root drive of the server.

5. Stop the IMA service using the Services Control Panel. Set the startup type to Manual.

6. If Enterprise Edition components are installed, see Cloning on MetaFrame Presentation Server, Enterprise Edition Systems.

7. Take the image of the second server and then restart the second server.

8. Deploy the image obtained in Step 7.

> **IMPORTANT:** It is important that some type of SID generation utility be executed when deploying images.

To set up the server and verify that it is added, perform the following steps:

1. Set the SID of the server with the SID generator of choice.

2. Rename the new server with a unique name.

3. Manually start the IMA service and set the service to start automatically.

4. Verify that the server was successfully added to the farm by executing **qfarm** at the command prompt. The newly imaged server will appear in the list of servers.

Rapid Deployment with Microsoft SQL Server, Oracle, or IBM DB2 Data Stores

When using Microsoft SQL Server, Oracle, or IBM DB2 for the server farm data store, the first server in the farm can be imaged and used to deploy all other servers.

> **NOTE:** Removal of the WSID line from the DSN file is no longer necessary when imaging and deploying MetaFrame XP with Feature Release 3 or later.

To image a server for rapid deployment with SQL Server, Oracle, or IBM DB2, perform the following steps:

1. Follow the steps from the MetaFrame Presentation Server Administrator's Guide for installing the first MetaFrame Presentation Server into the farm.

2. When the server is successfully restarted, log onto the console as a local or domain administrator.

3. Delete the *wfcname.ini* file, if it exists, from the root drive of the server.

4. Save the changes to the DSN file.

5. Stop the IMA Service and set the startup option to Manual.

6. If Enterprise Edition components are installed, see Cloning on MetaFrame Presentation Server, Enterprise Edition Systems.

7. Take the image of the server and then restart the server.

8. Deploy the image obtained.

IMPORTANT: It is important that some type of SID generation utility be executed when deploying images.

To set up the server and verify that it is added, perform the following steps:

1. Set the Security ID of the server with the SID generator of choice.

2. Rename the new server with a unique name.

3. Manually start the IMA Service and set the service to start automatically.

4. Verify that the server was successfully added to the farm by executing **qfarm** at a command prompt on any server in the farm. The newly imaged server will appear in the list of servers.

Special Considerations for Cloning MetaFrame Presentation Server, Enterprise Edition Systems

If Resource Management is installed, recreate the RMLocalDatabase prior to making an image of the server. To recreate the RMLocalDatabase, follow these steps:

1. Delete *%Program Files%\Citrix\Citrix Resource Manager\LocalDB\ RMLocalDatabase.**.

2. The next time the IMA service is started, it will recreate the database.

Rapid Deployment of Blade Servers Using Imaging

Blade servers are an ideal fit for Citrix MetaFrame Presentation Server environments. With server sprawl and increasing data center costs, the most asked question has been shifting from "How many users can I get on a box?" to "How many users can I get per square foot?" Blade servers in the market are traditionally twice as dense as 1U dual processor servers (sometimes referred to as "pizza boxes"). This means 84 servers currently can be placed into a single 42U Rack.

Blade servers offer a wide range of options, depending on the manufacturer, from SAN connectivity to storage blades to unique imaging solutions.

Most blade servers ship with some form of imaging software. Dell provides Dell Net Start, HP provides Rapid Deployment Pack, and IBM provides IBM Director. Each of these imaging solutions offers image capture and deployment to servers. A base image can be installed on a single machine, stored on the image server, and then be deployed to all other like servers in the data center.

The base OS can be imaged and the imaging software can perform an unattended install of MetaFrame Presentation Server using an answer file, or an image can be taken of a system with MetaFrame Presentation Server already installed.

NOTE: If a MetaFrame Server is to have remapped drives, it is best to run drive remap after the imaging process is complete due to incompatibilities with some imaging solutions.

Script Configuration After Imaging

If a cloned version of MetaFrame Presentation Server is deployed, a few steps must first be performed to allow the MetaFrame Presentation Server to function properly.

Most imaging software suites allow the administrator to define scripts to be run on the server after imaging completes. MetaFrame Feature Release 3 and later includes a utility called *Apputil*. *Apputil* is a command line utility that adds a server to the Configured Servers list of a published application. If the application does not exist on the server then *Apputil* can also be used to deploy the application using a MetaFrame Installation Manager package.

With this utility, the administrator can script various different configurations of a MetaFrame Presentation Server installation depending on the application silo in which it resides. Once the machine has finished imaging, the script will execute and the Installation Manager package will be deployed to the server.

For more information regarding this utility, please refer to the *MetaFrame Presentation Server Administrator's Guide*.

Rip and Replace   In the event of a hardware failure, blades present the opportunity to simply pull out the failed blade and replace it with a new server blade. MetaFrame Presentation Server can then be imaged back down to the new blade. If the blade server assumes the same name, it will continue to function in the capacity as the previous MetaFrame Presentation Server that had the same name.

NOTE: For servers that were previously hosting an indirect data store, the data store will need to be migrated using the **dsmaint** command. Refer to Chapters 2 and 4 for instructions.

Simultaneous Installation Limitations

When using a high-powered server for the data store (current generation dual CPU database server or above), Citrix recommends that no more than 30 servers be simultaneously installed. For older database server hardware, no more than 10 servers should be installed at the same time. During installation, servers must write configurations to the same indexes in the data store. The more servers installed at once, the greater the probability of creating deadlocks on the database server.

IMPORTANT: Deadlocks occur when one server times out while waiting to write to a piece of data that is locked by another server. In this event, the IMA Service simply retries after a short interval.

When installing servers to a new zone, Citrix recommends that a single server initially be installed into the new zone. MetaFrame Presentation Server will set the first server in a zone as the Most Preferred data collector. This avoids problems with new servers in the zone becoming the Zone Data Collector during installation. After installation is completed, the data collector election preference can be changed using the Presentation Server Console.

If a MetaFrame XP farm is on Feature Release 2 or later, Installation Manager can be used to deploy the MSI package to upgrade the servers to MetaFrame Presentation Server 3.0.

NOTE: MSI 2.0 must be installed on all the servers in the farm you plan to upgrade. If you already have MSI 2.0 installed, skip the instructions to install MSI 2.0. The MSI 2.0 install program—*instmsiw.exe*—is located in the folder support\MSI20 on the CD-ROM. To install MSI 2.0, do one of the following:

▼   Install MSI 2.0 manually on each target server. Copy the *intmsiw.exe* file from the support\msi20 folder of the MetaFrame Presentation Server CD to the target servers and then execute the file.

▲   Create an unattended installation package for the MSI 2.0 install using Installation Manager's Packager and deploy it to the target servers. The **/q** option may be used for unattended installation.

NOTE: Citrix recommends that the *Force Reboot After Install* option in Installation Manager is set when scheduling the installation. This ensures the server will restart after installation.

Before beginning this upgrade, check the following:

1. Ensure that there are no users logged into the MetaFrame Presentation Servers, since the upgrade installation will require a server restart.

2. Ensure that the network account being used for Installation Manager package deployment is a member of the Local Administrators group on each target server.

Follow the steps in the next sections to install MetaFrame Presentation Server.

Create a Transform File for Upgrading to MetaFrame Presentation Server

To create the transform file used to upgrade to MetaFrame Presentation Server, follow these steps:

1. Use a transform editor to create a transform file using *mps.msi*. Use the transform editor of your choice to the instruction that is included with the editor. If you use Microsoft Orca as your editor, use version 2.0.26 or higher.

2. From within the editor, choose the Property table in *mps.msi*.

3. Generate a transform file with all desired changes in property values and give it a unique name such as *mpstransform.mst*. Do not alter the original *mps.msi* file.

NOTE: Transform templates are provided in the Support\install directory on the MetaFrame Presentation Server CD. The first server installed should use the *Point for LicenseServerChoice* setting with a valid license server name provided in *LicenseServerName*. The remaining servers joining the same farm should use *UseFarmSettings* with no license server name required. Follow the directions presented in the next section to create two transform files; one for the first server you upgrade and a second transform file for all remaining servers in the farm.

Perform the Upgrade to MetaFrame Presentation Server Using the Transform File

The next step in the MetaFrame upgrade using Citrix MetaFrame Installation Manager is to perform the actual upgrade using the transform file created in the previous section.

NOTE: Follow the directions steps presented here to add two Installation Manager packages to the management console; one for the first server to be upgraded, using the transform file which specifies the License Server name, and a second package using the second transform file created for the remaining servers in the farm.

1. Copy the contents of the MetaFrame Presentation Server CD to a file share on a network sharepoint.

2. Copy the MST file to the folder that contains the MSI package (*mps.msi*).

3. Ensure there are no users logged in on the target servers.

4. Use the Management Console to connect to the MetaFrame farm and in the left pane click Installation Manager.

5. The Installation Manager's network account must have administrator's privileges on each target server and must have permission to access the files on the network file share. This cannot be a Netware Account.

6. Add the *mps.msi* package to the Installation Manager database. You will be asked if you wish to add transforms, select OK.

7. Add the MST to the MSI package.

NOTE: This MST file must be located in the same directory as the MSI package. Otherwise, the deployment will fail.

8. Deploy the MSI package to the target servers.

9. When the deployment is complete and the servers restart, log onto the server farm from the Presentation Server Console.

10. If any server is not included in the package deployment (for example, if you are using the Management Console from a server in the server farm), upgrade that server to MetaFrame Presentation Server 3.0, either from the files on the network share, or by logging onto a different server and deploying the package to the server.

Deploy MetaFrame with Active Directory

Follow these guidelines when deploying MetaFrame Presentation Server using Active Directory Services.

1. Place target and source servers in the same domain. The source server hosting the MetaFrame Presentation Server Windows Installer package and any transforms to be applied must be a member of the same domain as the servers to which MetaFrame Presentation Server is being deployed.

2. Because Active Directory does not notify the user if a deployment fails, enable the Windows Installer Logging. Event viewer can also be used to track the install status. To enable Windows Installer Logging, do the following:

   a. Run **regedt32**.

   b. Locate the registry entry:

      `HKLM\SOFTWARE\Policies\Microsoft\Windows\Installer`

   c. Right-click in any blank space on the right window and select String Value.

   d. Name the string value **Logging**, and then click OK.

   e. Double-click the new Logging value and enter the string **voicewarmup** under Value Data.

   f. Be sure to restart the system so the new registry value can take effect.

CAUTION: Ensure Windows Installer Logging is turned off at the end of the procedure. Otherwise it will log all Windows Installer deployments.

When logging is enabled using the procedure just specified, log files are stored in the directory *%SystemRoot%\Temp*. Open the log file and search for the line above "Return Value 3" to determine why a deployment failed.

Deploy MetaFrame Presentation Server with Computer Associates Unicenter

This section describes the basic steps for deploying MetaFrame Presentation Server using Computer Associates (CA) Unicenter Software Delivery product. For more detailed information, see the Unicenter documentation, available from the CA Web site at http://www.ca.com. Follow the next nine steps to deploy MetaFrame with CA Unicenter.

1. Edit any Windows Installer transforms to be applied to the MetaFrame Presentation Server Windows Installer installation package. Sample transforms that can be edited to fit most installation scenarios are included on the MetaFrame Presentation Server CD in the support\install folder. For more information about the MetaFrame Presentation Server Windows Installer package and the sample transforms, see the *MetaFrame Presentation Server Administrator's Guide*,

located in the Documentation\Docs directory on the MetaFrame Presentation Server CD.

2. Copy the MetaFrame Presentation Server Windows Installer installation package and your customized transforms to a shared directory on a source server to which the Unicenter server has read permission.

IMPORTANT: Install the Unicenter Software Delivery Agent on each server on which you want to install MetaFrame Presentation Server. Consult the CA documentation for information about unattended installation of the Agent.

3. Create a new volume using the Software Library node. On the Register Software dialog box, enter the name **MetaFrame Presentation Server** and the version **1.0**. A node is created with this name.

4. On the General tab of the Register Procedure dialog box, choose the Install task and select Windows 32-bit from the list of operating systems.

5. On the Embedded File tab, enter **mps.msi** in the File field. In the Subpath field, enter the path to the location of the MetaFrame Presentation Server installation package and transforms. If you copied these files to the server's root directory, enter \.

6. Select Install for the MSI method. In the Transforms field, enter the name of any customized transforms you created using the sample transforms from the MetaFrame Presentation Server CD.

7. On the Options tab of the Register Procedure dialog box, select all logging options. Click OK to close the Register Procedure dialog box.

8. Right-click the MetaFrame Presentation Server node and select Seal.

9. Deploy the MetaFrame Presentation Server package. The package can be dragged and dropped to the target servers listed under the All Computers and Users node.

Deploy MetaFrame Presentation Server from an Administrative Sharepoint

MetaFrame Presentation Server supports the installation of the MSI package from an administrative sharepoint.

Use the following command to create the administrative sharepoint:

```
Msiexec.exe /a [path] mps.msi.
```

MetaFrame Presentation Server setup properties parameters can be used to create a customized administrative sharepoint that can be used to deploy MetaFrame Presentation Server.

An administrative sharepoint can be created to install the first server to create the server farm. Another can be created and used to install the servers that join the server farm. In that scenario, all the setup properties do not need to be filled in during the actual installation time. All that needs to be done is a silent installation from the administrative sharepoint.

Following is a sample command line to create a customized administrative sharepoint. This command line example will create an administrative installation sharepoint that can be used to install MetaFrame Presentation Server that creates a farm using a third-party database (SQL) as the data store:

```
msiexec /a mfxp001.msi /l*v c:\msi.log TARGETDIR="Y:\wh32\sqlnt2k_1"
INSTALLDIR="c:\Citrix\" CTX_MF_FARM_SELECTION="Create"
CTX_MF_CREATE_FARM_DB_CHOICE="Thirdparty" CTX_MF_ZONE_NAME="SQLZONE"
CTX_MF_SILENT_DSNFILE="c:\sql.dsn" CTX_MF_ODBC_USER_NAME="username"
CTX_MF_ODBC_PASSWORD="password" CTX_MF_NEW_FARM_NAME="FarmSQL"
CTX_MF_USER_NAME="Uname"
CTX_MF_DOMAIN_NAME="dname" CTX_MF_SHADOWING_CHOICE="Yes"
CTX_MF_SHADOW_PROHIBIT_REMOTE_ICA="No" CTX_MF_SHADOW_PROHIBIT_NO_NOTIFICATION="No"
CTX_MF_SHADOW_PROHIBIT_NO_LOGGING="No" CTX_MF_XML_CHOICE="separate"
CTX_MF_XML_PORT_NUMBER="2000" CTX_MF_NFUSE_DEF_WEB_PAGE="No"
CTX_MF_LAUNCH_CLIENT_CD_WIZARD="No"
CTX_MF_TURN_FEATURE_RELEASE_ON="Yes" CTX_MF_SERVER_TYPE="E"
CTX_MF_REBOOT="Yes" CTX_MF_PRODUCT_CODE="0D00-06A7"
CTX_MF_ADD_LOCAL_ADMIN="Yes"
CTX_MF_LIC_CHOICE_FOR_CREATE="Point"
CTX_MF_LICENSE_SERVER_NAME="[LicenseServerInUse]"
CTX_RDP_DISABLE_PROMPT_FOR_PASSWORD="Yes"
CTX_MF_ENABLE_VIRTUAL_SCRIPTS="Yes"
```

NOTE: Customized administrative sharepoints can also be created using transform files. Please refer to the *MetaFrame Presentation Server Administrator's Guide* for further information.

Deploy a MetaFrame Presentation Server Farm Using Oracle Real Application Clusters

For a MetaFrame XP for Windows with Feature Release 3 deployment, the Citrix *e*Labs configured an Oracle Real Application Cluster (RAC) environment using an EMC^2 Celerra Network Enterprise Server for the shared disk subsystem. The configuration tested used the Oracle Cluster File System (CFS) on Oracle servers running Microsoft Windows 2000 SP3.

When using an Oracle RAC configuration, all Oracle server nodes actively process requests against the same backend database. Running with a RAC configuration provides the following benefits:

▼   All nodes can run using the same Oracle Home executable files. Using shared executables guarantees that all nodes are using the same version, which decreases upgrade time.

■ All nodes can simultaneously access the same data, providing multiple front-end servers to access the data. This provides exceptional performance gains with read-intensive database operations.

■ Requests are automatically load-balanced across active nodes.

▲ New requests to a failed server are automatically routed to a surviving node.

In addition to the fault tolerance benefits, using a RAC cluster for the MetaFrame Presentation Server data store will provide improved response time for the IMA Service on startup and during read-intensive operations such as LHC updates.

Tested Environment

For the testing environment, the Citrix *e*Labs set up the following environment:
Two Cluster Servers with the following configuration:

▼ Compaq ProLiant 1850R Dual P3 600 MHz

■ 1GB RAM

■ 16GB SCSI Local Disk

■ Emulex LightPulse 9000 Host Bus Adapter (HBA) connected via Fiber Optic cable directly to the EMC^2 Celerra

▲ 1 100MB Compaq NIC used for both normal and cluster communication

One EMC^2 Celerra Enterprise Network Server with the following configuration:

▼ 51GB partition available to the cluster servers

■ Arbitrated Loop SAN configuration

▲ Dedicated Fiber Adapter (FA) ports for access by the Emulex HBA cards

Process Overview

The process for building the MetaFrame Presentation Server environment using Oracle Clustering is as follows:

1. Configure physical connection to the shared disk subsystem.

2. Configure the shared disks on Windows 2000.

3. Install Oracle Cluster File System (CFS).

4. Install Oracle9*i*R2.

5. Patch the Oracle RAC files.

6. Reconfigure the Oracle listeners.

7. Create the database using the Database Configuration Assistant (DBCA).

8. Create a *TNSNAMES.ORA* file for the cluster configuration.

9. Install MetaFrame Presentation Server.

Each of these steps will be discussed in detail next.

Configure the Physical Connection to the Shared Disk Subsystem   To configure the physical connection to the shared disk subsystem, perform the following steps:

1. Create a metavolume of the appropriate size to host both the Oracle Home files (8GB) and the Oracle data files. The MetaFrame database will reside in the Oracle data files partition, so verify that the space created is appropriate. For MetaFrame sizing guidelines, refer to the *MetaFrame Presentation Server Administrator's Guide.*

2. Using dedicated FA ports on the EMC^2 Celerra server, map the newly created metavolume to each FA port to be used by the Oracle servers.

3. Install the HBA cards into the Oracle servers and connect them to the EMC^2 Celerra server.

4. Verify the Oracle servers can see the EMC^2 Celerra shared disk using the HBA.

Configure the Shared Disks on Windows 2000   When configuring Windows 2000 to view the shared disks, adhere to the following guidelines:

▼   Do not allow Windows 2000 to write a disk signature on the drive.

■   Do not assign drive letters to the Windows 2000 partitions.

▲   Do not format the Windows 2000 partitions.

Perform the following steps to configure the shared disks in Windows 2000:

1. Log into the Oracle Server as an administrator.

2. Launch Computer Management and create a new partition to hold the Oracle server files.

    a. From within Computer Management, select the Disk Management Folder.

    b. Right-click on the EMC^2 disk and choose Create Partition from the Context menu. This launches the Create Partition wizard.

    c. Select Next.

    d. Select Extended Partition.

    e. Set "Amount of disk space to use" and click Next.

    f. Click Finish.

3. Create a logical drive inside the partition to hold the Oracle Home files.

    a. Right-click on the new partition and choose Create Logical Drive.

    b. Click Next.

    c. Set "Amount of disk space to use" to 8GB for the Oracle Home files and click Next.

    d. Choose "Do not assign a drive letter or drive path" radio button, click Next.

    e. Choose "Do not format this partition."

    f. Click Finish.

4. Create a logical drive inside the partition to hold the Oracle data files.

    a. Right-click on the new partition and choose Create Logical Drive.

    b. Click Next.

    c. Set "Amount of disk space to use" to 8GB for the Oracle Home files and click Next.

    d. Choose "Do not assign a drive letter or drive path" radio button, click Next.

    e. Choose "Do not format this partition."

    f. Click Finish.

5. Repeat Steps 3 and 4 for all Oracle servers in the cluster.

6. Verify TCP/IP and shared disk connectivity between all Oracle servers.

Install the Oracle Cluster File System   When installing the Oracle CFS, adhere to the following guidelines:

▼   Do not run the executables from the Oracle9*i* CD media, instead use the executables provided with download.

▲   The Oracle cluster name should be a derivative of the Oracle server machine names. For instance, if the Oracle server machine names are OCLUSTER1 and OCLUSTER2, then the cluster name should be OCLUSTER.

To install the Oracle CFS, follow these steps:

1. Start the *preinstall_rac**clustersetup**clustersetup.exe* program to create the cluster nodes. This starts the Oracle Cluster Setup Wizard. Complete this *before* installing the Oracle9*i* server.

2. Choose Create Cluster.

3. Select the appropriate network interconnect type and configure for the environment.

4. Enter the cluster name.

5. Choose "CFS for Oracle Home and Datafiles."

6. Configure CFS for Oracle Home and set it to the 8GB logical drive created earlier.

7. Configure CFS for Datafiles and set it to the data logical drive created earlier.

8. Complete the wizard.

9. Start the \install\win32\setup.exe program to install the OraCFS file system on the cluster nodes.

10. Select the 8GB logical drive for Oracle Home files.

At this point the drive letters assigned to the shared disk should be visible from all cluster nodes. In addition, several new services should now be visible in the Services Control Panel applet.

Install Oracle9i R2   When installing Oracle9i R2, do not select a pre-installed database. Before installing a database, certain files must be patched for RAC to work properly. Selecting a pre-installed database causes the DBCA wizard to start and automatically create a database before the RAC components are successfully patched.

To install Oracle9i, perform the following steps:

1. From the Oracle9i CD, start the *setup.exe* program to install database server software.

2. On the node selection page, select all the Oracle servers to be included in this cluster.

3. Navigate to the \stage\products.jar directory on the CD to select the appropriate products file.

4. Set the Oracle Home name.

5. In the path field, select the 8GB logical drive path you created earlier for the Oracle Home files.

6. On the next page, select Enterprise Edition.

7. On the Database Type page, select Custom so the DBCA wizard does not autocreate a database at the end of install.

8. Complete the remainder of the installation wizard.

9. Complete the Network Configuration Assistant, Click Yes to ignore the warning message. This is a known issue with cluster servers.

10. The Database Configuration Assistant starts. Click Cancel to quit out of this wizard. CFS patches must be applied before running this wizard.

11. End the installation.

12. If Enterprise Manager starts, click Cancel to close it.

Patch the Oracle RAC Files   To patch the Oracle RAC files, perform the following three steps:

1. Navigate to the \patch folder from the downloaded file.

2. On each node, perform the patch procedures indicated in the *srvm.txt* file.

3. On each node, perform the patch procedures indicated in the *dbca.txt* file.

Reconfigure Listeners   To reconfigure the listeners, perform these steps:

1. Stop the Oracle<OracleHome>TNSListener service from the Windows Services Control Panel applet.

2. Change the startup type to Disabled.

3. Open a command prompt window and run the command: **lsnrctl start listener_** *<nodename>*. For example: **lsnrctl start listener_ocluster1.**

4. Repeat Steps 1–3 on each node in the cluster.

Configure the Database   To configure the database, follow these steps:

1. Create an *oradata* directory on root of the data files logical drive.

2. Open a command prompt window and run the DBCA from the command prompt specifying the file location created in Step 1 above. For example, **dbca –datafileDestination P:\oradata.**

3. Choose Create Database and click Next.

4. Select the nodes to create the database on.

5. When complete, restart all Oracle servers.

6. Refer to the *"MetaFrame Presentation Server Administrator's Guide"* for steps to correctly configure an Oracle database for a MetaFrame Presentation Server farm.

Create a *TNSNAMES.ORA* File for the Cluster Configuration   To create the *TNSNAMES.ORA* file for the cluster configuration, follow these steps:

1. Add an entry to the *TNSNAMES.ORA* file for the cluster configuration.

2. Include each Oracle server in the cluster in the address list:

```
OCLUSTER.TEST.COM =
 (DESCRIPTION =
 (ADDRESS_LIST =
  (ADDRESS = (PROTOCOL = TCP)(HOST =
 ocluster1.test.com)(PORT = 1521))
  (ADDRESS = (PROTOCOL = TCP)(HOST =
 ocluster2.test.com)(PORT = 1521))
  )
 (CONNECT_DATA =
  (SERVICE_NAME = ocluster.test.com)
  )
  )
```

3. Use TNSPING to verify that all nodes of the cluster are reachable.

Install MetaFrame Presentation Server   To install MetaFrame Presentation Server on the cluster, follow these steps:

1. Copy the *TNSNAMES.ORA* file to the \network\admin folder of the Oracle client.

2. Start the MetaFrame Presentation Server install.

3. Specify "Use a 3rd Party Database" and select Oracle.

4. Specify the cluster service name for the Service Name field.

5. Specify the username/password configured above.

6. Complete the rest of the wizard using the guidelines for MetaFrame Presentation Server databases as outlined in the *"MetaFrame Presentation Server Administrator's Guide."*

Installation of Administrative Tools

This section covers the Presentation Server Console and the Web Console Administration Tools installation scenarios.

Skip the Installation of the Management Console

Use the following command to skip the installation of the Presentation Server Console during the MetaFrame Presentation Server installation:

```
msiexec /i mps.msi CTX_ADDLOCAL=all REINSTALL=CTX_MF_CMC
```

NOTE: CTX_MF_CMC must be in upper case.

Install or Upgrade the Presentation Server Console on Standalone Servers

To install or upgrade the MetaFrame Presentation Server Console on standalone servers, perform the following tasks:

1. Run Autorun from the MetaFrame Presentation Server CD.

2. Select Product Installations.

3. Select Install Management Consoles.

4. Accept the license agreement and click Next | Next to select Presentation Server Console.

5. Follow the dialog boxes to finish the installation of the Presentation Server Console.

Install the Management Console for the MetaFrame Access Suite on Standalone Servers

To install the Access Suite Console on a standalone server, perform the following tasks:

1. Run Autorun from the MetaFrame Presentation Server CD.
2. Select Product Installations.
3. Select Install Management Consoles.
4. Accept the license agreement and click Next | Next to select Access Suite Console.
5. Follow the dialog boxes to finish the installation of the console.

Install the Citrix Web Console on Standalone Servers

To install the Citrix Web Console on standalone servers, perform the following tasks:

1. The following software must be installed and requirements met prior to installing the Citrix Web Console as a standalone application on a non-MetaFrame Presentation Server:

   a. Internet Information Server 5.0

   b. The MetaFrame Presentation Server 3.0 MFCOM SDK

2. Download *mpssdk.exe* from the Citrix Web site to install MFCOM SDK following the instructions distributed with the SDK.

3. When prompted, enter the name of the MetaFrame Presentation Server on which you want to run MFCOM.

4. Download *cwc.msi* from the Citrix Web site and run **msiexec /i cwc.msi CWC_ MFCHECK="N"**

5. Follow the wizard and complete the installation.

To change the MetaFrame Presentation Server to which the Citrix Web Console is pointed, run the command **MFREG <*servername*>** from a command prompt or from the **run** command.

NOTE: On Windows Server 2003, the Active Server Pages web service extension is prohibited by default. After installation of the Citrix Web Console, enable the Active Server Pages in order to use the console. Please refer to Windows Server 2003 documentation about how to enable the Active Server Pages web service extensions.

Deployment of the MetaFrame Presentation Server Client for Win32

This section outlines best practices, recommendations, and advanced scenarios when dealing with the various MetaFrame Presentation Server Clients for Win32 and MetaFrame

Presentation Server. Please refer to the respective client administrative guides for additional information.

Install Program Neighborhood Agent as a Pass-Through Client

Program Neighborhood Agent may be installed on the MetaFrame Presentation Server during the MetaFrame Presentation Server setup to be used as a pass-through client. This allows users to connect to the server desktop and use the functionality of the Program Neighborhood Agent.

To install the Program Neighborhood Agent, click the Program Neighborhood Agent component during the component selection of the MetaFrame Presentation Server install, and select "Will be installed on local hard drive."

NOTE: By default, Program Neighborhood Agent is not selected to be installed during a MetaFrame Presentation Server install.

▼   When installing the Program Neighborhood Agent, the installer will be prompted later during setup to enter the URL of the server running the Web Interface for MetaFrame Presentation Server. This server hosts the Program Neighborhood Agent configuration file. By default, MetaFrame Presentation Server attempts to resolve the "localhost" as a server running the Web Interface for MetaFrame Presentation Server.

■   When upgrading from a previous release of MetaFrame Presentation Server, the administrator will not be given an opportunity to setup the Program Neighborhood Agent as a pass-through client.

▲   If you performed a fresh install and did not choose to install the Program Neighborhood Agent, or if you performed an upgrade, you can install the client after the MetaFrame Presentation Server setup process.

Add the Program Neighborhood Agent as a Pass-Through Client Post Installation   This section describes how to install the Program Neighborhood Agent and use it as a pass-through client on the MetaFrame Presentation Server if the Program Neighborhood Agent was not a selected component during the initial MetaFrame Presentation Server installation.

1.   Launch Add/Remove Programs in the Control Panel.

2.   Select Change on Citrix MetaFrame Presentation Server for Windows entry name.

3.   Select to "Modify" the Windows Installer packages installed on the system and click Next.

4.   Select the Program Neighborhood Agent component, select "Will be installed on local hard drive," and click Next.

5.   Enter the server URL for the Web Interface Server or leave as "localhost" if Web Interface is installed on the same computer as MetaFrame Presentation Server.

6. Select whether or not to enable Pass-Through Authentication and click Next.

7. Verify the component changes and click Finish.

Dynamic Client Name vs. Machine Name

Dynamic Client Name is a feature that is included in version 7.00 and later of the MetaFrame Presentation Server Client for Win32. Prior versions of the client only reported the client name that was statically configured during install of the client and stored in the *wfcname.ini*. If the Dynamic Client Name feature is not enabled, the client name that is reported to the MetaFrame Presentation Server when connecting to a session is stored in the registry key, as follows:

```
HKLM\Software\Citrix\ICA Client\ClientName
```

When the Dynamic Client Name feature is enabled, the MetaFrame Presentation Server Client calls the Windows function GetComputerName which gets the computer's NetBIOS name which is then reported to the MetaFrame Presentation Server.

The `ClientName` registry value should not be present when the Dynamic Client Name feature is enabled. Dynamic Client Name is initially enabled or disabled during the install process. In the Program Neighborhood client, this can be changed after install by opening Program Neighborhood and setting the Dynamic Client Name checkbox under Tools | ICA Settings | General. In all other MetaFrame Presentation Server Clients including Program Neighborhood Agent, this feature can be enabled or disabled by creating or deleting the `ClientName` registry value in the following:

```
HKLM\Software\Citrix\ICA Client
```

These changes should take effect on all new connections.

NOTE: Earlier releases of the client (prior to version 6.30) stored the client name in the file *C:\wfcname.ini*.

CAB-Based Client Packages

The client cab-based packages were reintroduced with MetaFrame XP for Windows with Feature Release 3. There are three different CAB packages that are being shipped with MetaFrame Presentation Server 3.0:

1. *wfica.cab*: The full Program Neighborhood client packaged in CAB format (3,967,216 bytes).

2. *wficat.cab*: The "thick" web client packaged in CAB format (2,208,665 bytes).

3. *wficac.cab*: The "Zero Footprint" web client packaged in CAB format (1,304,454 bytes). This is the new "zero install" client that customers requested.

There are several benefits to the thin (Active-X) web clients (*wficat.cab* and *wficac.cab*), such as

▼ The user doesn't initiate the install. The internet browser (IE) initiates the install on a need-to-download-and-install basis.

■ The CAB file package install is fast as it is limited in size.

▲ The CAB file is exploded in a scratch directory, leaving no or little footprint on the target desktop. Changes made to the locked down desktop are none or minimal (registration of ActiveX ICA control).

Along with the benefits, there are trade-offs to be made to keep the thin web package small and efficient. Since a smaller footprint means a reduction in size of the client package, certain features from the full-fledged MetaFrame Presentation Server Client represented by Program Neighborhood or Program Neighborhood Agent are not available for the two smaller sized Cab-based client packages *wficat.cab* and *wficac.cab*.

Supported Features of *wficat.cab*   The following features are supported by the *wficat.cab* install:

▼ Client engine

■ Thinwire

■ Client drive mapping

■ Licensing

■ Connection Center

■ Autoclient reconnection

■ Zero Latency

■ Font Manager

■ Client Audio Mapping

■ Client Printer Mapping

■ Universal Printer Driver

■ Client COM port mapping

■ Netscape plug-in

■ Protocol Driver (128bit)

■ Protocol driver (old compression)

■ Smartcard support

■ Active X control

■ ICA Client Object

- SSL support
- Auto-client update
- Name Resolver (TCP/IP)
- Name Resolver (HTTP)
- INI files
- Support DLLs
▲ TCP/IP protocol support

In addition to the features above the following new features for MetaFrame Presentation Server 3.0 are also supported: Bi-directional Audio, Session Reliability, Dynamic Session Resizing and the new login look and feel.

Unsupported Features of *wficat.cab*   SpeedScreen Multimedia Acceleration is not supported.

Supported Features of *wficac.cab*   The following features are supported by the *wficac.cab* install:

Client engine, Thinwire, Client drive mapping, Licensing, Connection Center, Auto-client reconnection, Client Printer Mapping, Smartcard support, Active X control, ICA Client Object, SSL support, Name Resolver (TCP/IP), Name Resolver (HTTP), INI files, Support DLLs, and TCP/IP protocol support.

In addition to these features, the following new features for MetaFrame Presentation Server 3.0 are also supported: Session Reliability, Dynamic Session Resizing, new login look-and-feel.

Unsupported Features of *wficac.cab*   The following features are not supported: Zero Latency, Font Manager, Client Audio Mapping, Universal Printer Driver, Client COM port mapping, Netscape Plug-in, Protocol Driver (128bit), Protocol Driver (old compression), and Auto Client update.

In addition to these features, the following new MetaFrame Presentation Server 3.0 features are also not supported: SpeedScreen Multimedia Acceleration and Bi-directional audio.

Limitations/Constraints of *wficaC.cab*   The following are limitations and constraints of the *wficaC.cab*:

▼ Any user wishing to use the CAB based ActiveX Win32 web client needs permissions to download an ActiveX control via Internet Explorer. Appropriate level of permissions to be able to create subkeys under HKR registry hive is necessary for the user in order to correctly register the ActiveX control and to register the *.ICA* file type extension to support launching of ICA connections outside the browser.

- The only supported browser for these versions of the CAB-based client is Internet Explorer 4.0 and above.

▲ Only a limited number of client features, as noted previously, will be available in the thin version (*wficac.cab*) of the CAB based Win32 ActiveX based client.

Considerations for Use of *wficac.cab*   Listed here are some of the known issues and considerations regarding the *wficac.cab* file coupled with any known workarounds.

▼ Upgrade considerations: If one version of the MetaFrame Presentation Server Client for 32-bit Windows is already installed on the target machine by any of the following methods, the same version CAB-based web client package will not be downloaded and installed by the Internet Explorer browser.

  - Full Program Neighborhood client using Installshield (*ICA32.exe*)
  - Full Program Neighborhood MSI (*ica32pkg.msi*) install
  - Program Neighborhood Agent using Installshield (*ICA32a.exe*)
  - Program Neighborhood Agent MSI (*ica32pkg.msi*) install
  - Thin web client (*wficac.cab*) install package

- For the same version of a web client installed on a target machine that was installed via the thin (*wficac.cab*) CAB file, users will not be able to install the web client using the thick (*wficat.cab*) CAB file if a need arises to use more features. The reason for this is the version numbers on the CAB files will remain the same and Internet Explorer will not download and explode the thick (*wficat.cab*) CAB-based client.

  Workaround: The users will have to first uninstall the thin (*wficac.cab*) CAB-based web client via the Add/Remove applet in the Control Panel and then visit a web page that points them to the location to download the thick version (*wficat.cab*) of the web client.

▲ If a previous version of the full web ICA Client is installed on the target machine and the client users visit a web page that points them to a later version of the CAB-based web client, Internet Explorer will always prompt the users to download and install the latest web client. This leads to multiple ICA Client installations on the target machine.

  Workaround: Uninstall the previous web client and then visit the web page that points to a higher version CAB-based client.

NOTE: By installing a smaller-sized CAB client, even if it is a higher version, some features will be lost due to the streamlining of the client.

Deploy and Publish the Program Neighborhood Agent or Program Neighborhood Client Windows Installer Packages Using Active Directory

Active Directory can be used to publish or assign MetaFrame Presentation Server Client for 32-bit Windows. This section describes how to publish or assign an application for a group of users or computers using Active Directory. The Microsoft definition of "publish" is to make an application available to a user for installation through Add/Remove Programs or by launching a file associated with the application. If the MSI package is "assigned" to a user, whenever the user logs into a workstation the Windows Installer service will "advertise" the set of applications that are listed in the Active Directory Organizational Unit for that particular user. Advertising means that the class IDs, extensions, and shortcuts will be installed for the user so that when the user double-clicks on a file with an associated extension, or double-clicks on the advertised shortcut, the application will then be fully installed for that user. For more information regarding assigning and publishing applications to users and computers using Active Directory group policies, please refer to the Windows online documentation.

The requirements for Active Directory Publishing are the following:

1. Program Neighborhood Agent (Version 7.00.13547 or greater).
2. Program Neighborhood Client (Version 7.00.13547 or greater).
3. Web Client (Version 8.*x* or greater).
4. Windows Installer Service. The Windows Installer service (*Instmsi.exe*) is present by default on computers running the Windows 2000 operating system. If the client device is running Windows NT 4.0 or Windows 9*x*, you must install Windows Installer Version 2.0 or higher.

To deploy the client MSI package on a computer or set of computers, follow these steps:

1. Start with a clean client machine with no clients installed.
2. Join an ADS Domain. Joining the ADS Domain will enable you to assign or publish a Windows Installer application for computers and users in that domain or an organizational unit within the ADS domain.
3. On a machine that belongs to the ADS Domain, launch the Microsoft Management Console (MMC) and load the Active Directory Users and Computers snap-in or go to Start | Programs | Administrative Tools | Active Directory Users and Computers.
4. For this example, create a new Organizational Unit (OU) called "MSI test," and a new user called "MSIuser." Go to the Computers group and find the machine you added to the ADS Domain. Right-click on the machine and select Move. Select the "MSI Test" folder and click OK. Follow the same steps to add the new user from the Users group to the new OU folder.

NOTE: The previous step is necessary to test a contained number of users and computers. In the next step, we edit the Group Policy of that container. This way any changes made to the Group Policy will not affect the rest of the ADS Domain.

5. Right-click on the "MSI test" OU and go to Properties. Select the Group Policy tab and create a new Group Policy Objects Link called "MetaFrame Presentation Server Client Install."

6. Highlight the "MetaFrame Presentation Server Client Install" policy and click Edit. Under Computer Configuration | Software Settings | Software Installation, right-click Software Installation, and select New | Package.

7. Browse to a network share containing the *ica32pkg.msi*, select the MSI package, and set the deployment method to Assigned. This step is to ensure that all environment settings are present for the Automated Install for the MetaFrame Presentation Server Client. Once you have clicked OK, Software Installation should display a software package assignment for deployment.

8. Restart the client machine. As the client restarts, ADS Group Policy will automatically install the MetaFrame Presentation Server client on the computer. On the Windows Startup dialog status box, there should be a message displayed that the Citrix MetaFrame Presentation Server Client is being installed by Remote Managed Apps. This message appears before the login dialog box appears.

9. Log onto the client machine and verify that the client is installed.

NOTE: For Windows XP Professional operating systems, the machine has to be rebooted twice before the ADS Group Policy will automatically install the MetaFrame Presentation Server Client on the computer. However, if the Active Directory is a Windows Server 2003 Active Directory, you can avoid the second reboot after creating the policy by going to a command line on the client machine and typing **gpupdate /force**. This command will prompt you to reboot, but it will only be necessary to reboot the Windows XP Professional operating system once.

Uninstall the MetaFrame Presentation Server Client MSI Package from a Computer or Set of Computers via Active Directory   The process to uninstall the MetaFrame Presentation Server Client MSI package from a computer or set of computers via Active Directory is as follows:

1. On a machine which belongs to the ADS Domain, launch the MMC and load the Active Directory Users and Computers snap-in or go to Start | Programs | Administrative Tools | Active Directory Users and Computers.

2. Right-click the MSI Test OU folder and select Properties. Select the Group Policy tab and Edit the ICA Client Install policy. Under Computer Configuration | Software Settings | Software Installation, right-click on the client package and select All Tasks | Remove. Make sure that "Immediately Un-install…" is checked, and then click OK.

3. Restart the client machine. As the system restarts, ADS Group Policy will automatically uninstall the client from the computer. On the Windows Startup dialog status box, there should be a message displayed that the client is being removed by Remote Managed Apps. This message appears before the login dialog box appears.

4. Log onto the client machine and verify that the client was completely removed.

Publish the MetaFrame Presentation Server Client MSI Package to a User or Group of Users in an Active Directory Domain   To publish the client MSI package to a user or group of users in an Active Directory domain, follow these steps:

1. On a machine which belongs to the ADS Domain, launch the MMC and load the Active Directory Users and Computers snap-in or go to Start | Programs | Administrative Tools | Active Directory Users and Computers.

2. If you have not already created a new test OU from the previous example, create a new OU called "MSI Test," and a new user called "MSIuser."

3. Under the Users folder, right-click MSIuser and select Move. Select the MSI Test OU folder and click OK.

4. Right-click the "MSI Test" OU and select Properties. Go to the Group Policy Tab and highlight the MetaFrame Presentation Server Client Install policy and click Edit. If you do not already have a MetaFrame Presentation Server Client Install policy from a previous example, create a new Group Policy Objects Link named MetaFrame Presentation Server Client Install.

5. Under User Configuration | Software Settings | Software Installation right-click Software Installation, and select New | Package. Browse to a network share containing the *ica32pkg.msi*, select the MSI package, and set the deployment method to Published. Once you have clicked OK, Software Installation should display a software package assignment for deployment.

6. Close all management windows and restart the client machine.

7. Log onto client machine as MSIuser.

8. Go to Add/Remove Programs and click on Add New Programs. Verify that Citrix MetaFrame Presentation Server Client is included in the list and is ready to be added. Click Add and verify that the Citrix MetaFrame Presentation Server Client is successfully installed.

NOTE: When using the Published method to make the client MSI package available to users for installation, the user can also initiate installation of the MetaFrame Presentation Server Client by opening a file with the *.ica* extension.

The client MSI package can also be made available to users using the Assigned deployment method. If a package is assigned to users, the client will not be installed automatically for the user upon login, but only the class IDs, extensions, and shortcuts will be installed so that when the user double-clicks on a file with an *.ica* extension or double-clicks on the shortcut, the client will be fully installed for that user.

If you answer Yes to the option "Would you like to enable and automatically use your local user name and password for MetaFrame sessions from this client?", at least one reboot will be required following the installation of the client.

Unpublishing MetaFrame Presentation Server Client MSI Package from a User or Group of Users in an Active Directory Domain   To unpublish (uninstall) the client MSI package from a user or group of users in a Active Directory Domain, follow these steps:

1. Log onto the client machine as MSIuser. Go to Add/Remove Programs and Remove MetaFrame Presentation Server Client.

2. Go to Add/Remove Programs and click on Add New Programs. Verify that Citrix MetaFrame Presentation Server Client is still listed and is ready to be added. Even though the client has been un-installed, the MSI package is still available for install due to the group policy. The client can also be uninstalled from the client machine automatically with the continuing steps.

3. On a machine which belongs to the ADS Domain, launch the MMC and load the Active Directory Users and Computers snap-in or go to Start | Programs | Administrative Tools | Active Directory Users and Computers.

4. Right-click the MSI Test OU and select Properties. Go to the Group Policy tab and highlight the MetaFrame Presentation Server Client Install policy and click Edit.

5. Under User Configuration | Software Settings | Software Installation, right-click on the client package and select All Tasks | Remove. Make sure that "Immediately Un-install…" is checked and click OK.

6. Reboot client machine and log in as MSIuser. ADS Group Policy automatically removes the client from the Add New Programs list as the MSIuser logs in. Go to Add/Remove Programs and verify that client is not published in the available list under Add New Programs.

NOTE: These same steps can be used to deploy, uninstall, publish, and unpublish the Program Neighborhood Agent Client and the Web Client (*ica32pkg.msi*) using Active Directory.

Troubleshoot Active Directory Publication of the ICA Client

Publishing the Program Neighborhood Agent, Program Neighborhood Client, and the Web Client MSI Packages to users on a Windows 2000 Server or Windows Server 2003 is not supported. The only available method of using Active Directory to deploy Citrix ICA Clients to Windows 2000 Servers or to Windows Servers 2003 is to assign the package to a computer or to a group of computers.

To enable logging for a client MSI package install, you can add an entry to the group policy for Windows Installer logging, as follows:

1. On a machine which belongs to the ADS Domain, launch the MMC and load the Active Directory Users and Computers snap-in or go to Start | Programs | Administrative Tools | Active Directory Users and Computers.

NOTE: This is a per-machine setting. When deploying clients to users, an OU that contains target computers is required.

2. Right-click the OU containing the target computers and select Properties.

3. Go to the Group Policy tab and highlight the MetaFrame Presentation Server Client Install policy and click Edit. If you have created a separate OU for your target servers, create a new policy for the OU. Within the properties of the policy, go to Computer Configuration | Administrative Templates | Windows Components | Windows Installer | Logging.

4. Choose Enabled and select the type of logging desired from the list of available options.

5. Enter **voicewarmup** to enable all possible logging. The log file will be created in *%systemroot%\Temp\msi*.log*. Use the creation dates to differentiate log files.

Silent Installation of Program Neighborhood, Program Neighborhood Agent, or Web Client Using MSI

This section describes how to create Program Neighborhood Agent, Program Neighborhood, or Web Client MSI Packages for use in a silent installation with SMS or the Windows Installer service. A "silent installation" is an installation without user interaction. With version 8.*x* of the Client Packager, adminstrators can create custom client MSI packages to install any or all of the available clients (Program Neighborhood Agent, Program Neighborhood, or Web Client) and be able to pre-select information that is usually prompted for, such as Web Interface Server. With past client versions, to make the deployment of the MSI package truly silent, some modifications had to be made to the MSI file, or a transform had to be created. Now, with client version 8.*x*, after creating a custom client package, SMS, Active Directory, or Installation Manager can be used to deliver the new ICA Clients without any user interaction.

The requirements are the following:

▼ MetaFrame Presentation Server Client Packager (Version 8.*x*)

▲ Microsoft Windows Installer (Version 2.0 or above)

Create a Custom Client Package To create a custom client package, perform one of the two following tasks:

1. Insert the MetaFrame Presentation Server Client CD in the CD-ROM drive, select MetaFrame Presentation Server Clients, and then select Create a Custom Windows Client Installation Package.

   OR

1. Locate the *ica32pkg.msi* file on the client CD in the *ICAINST\en\ica32* directory and from the command line type the following:

```
msiexec /a <path to msi file>\ica32pkg.msi
```

2. Select Next on the Welcome screen.

3. Select a network installation point, what kind of Windows installer package you want to create, and click Next.

4. Accept the Licensing Agreement and select Next.

5. Select which client or clients you want to include in the package, select the install location, and click Next.

6. If installing the Program Neighborhood Client, select the Server URL for Web Interface and click Next.

7. Select the Program Folder name and click Next.

8. Select whether to use the machine name or let the user specify and click Next.

9. Select whether or not you want to use the local name and password and select Next.

> **NOTE:** If the Yes radio button is selected, a checkbox will be unhidden to allow the option to use Kerberos only as the single sign-on method.

10. Select whether to upgrade or overwrite existing clients and click Next.

11. The Select User Dialog Boxes screen allows you to select the dialog boxes and options you want the user to see when installing the custom package. To make the installation silent, select Remove All and click Next.

12. Click Next for the Installation Summary screen.

13. The custom client package is now created and located in the directory specified in Step 3, and is ready to be deployed.

Deploy the Client Package   Because all dialogs were hidden, there is no need to add any additional command line switches to install the MSI file in silent mode. When the user double clicks the custom *ica32pgk.msi* or when it's deployed via SMS, Active Directory, or Installation Manager, the client or clients will be installed silently and the client or clients will contain all preconfigured information.

General Notes on Custom Client Packaging   The following are some general notes on using custom client packaging:

▼   The new client package will still be named *ica32pgk.msi* unless it was changed. This may cause some confusion as the original file on the Component CD is also *ica32pkg.msi*.

▲   If Compressed or Uncompressed is selected when deciding what kind of MSI package to create, the network installation point selected must be accessible by all users installing the MSI package.

MetaFrame Presentation Server Client Deployment on the Compaq iPaq

The MetaFrame Presentation Server Client is supported on Compaq iPaq devices. This device can be used as a client as well as a server farm management tool for high-density MetaFrame Servers.

The client version should be MetaFrame Presentation Server Client for WinCE ARM version 7.*x* or later.

TIP: The MetaFrame Presentation Server Client supports input from both the iPaq keyboard and character recognizer and transcriber within a session.

iPaq Configuration   Configure the following settings in the MetaFrame Presentation Server Client for better performance with cellular digital packet data (CDPD) or code division multiple access (CDMA) connections:

1. Disable sound.
2. Select Enable Palette Device.
3. Limit session color depth to 256 colors.
4. Set the encryption level to Basic.
5. Avoid accessing the client drives in the session, if possible.

To run the Presentation Server Console in an ICA session, set the ICA settings as follows:

1. Window Size: Absolute (in pixels), 640 x 480. The ICA Client can dynamically zoom the session window.
2. Window Color: 256.
3. Data Compression: On.

The version of Internet Explorer that comes installed on the iPaq supports the Citrix Web Console if it is installed on the MetaFrame Server. Some manual adjustment of the screen is necessary; however, the console will be fully functional. To access the console, enter the URL of the server where the console is installed; for example http://webserver/citrix/webconsole/default.asp.

Wireless LAN (802.11b) and Traditional Network Connections   Expect any network settings selected for the iPaq to have minimal impact on session performance because of the high speeds and available bandwidth on most networks and wireless LANs. To alleviate poor CDPD connections, or to better support roaming on a wireless LAN, adjust the Keep Alive settings on the MetaFrame Presentation Servers. This improves performance in the environment and helps keep connections from dropping on networks that contain dead spots. See the Citrix Knowledge Base article CTX708444 for configuration settings posted on http://support.citrix.com.

DOMAIN NAME SYSTEM (DNS) IMPLEMENTATION IN METAFRAME PRESENTATION SERVER CLIENT TO SERVER CONNECTIONS

When a MetaFrame Presentation Server Client connects to a server or application, the client can use several methods and protocols to enumerate the server name and address where the connection is destined. This section describes how the client interacts with DNS servers and what protocols take full advantage of this implementation.

In this section, the example domains used are corp.company.com and remote.company .com. Figure 5-1 will be referenced throughout this section to provide examples of usage.

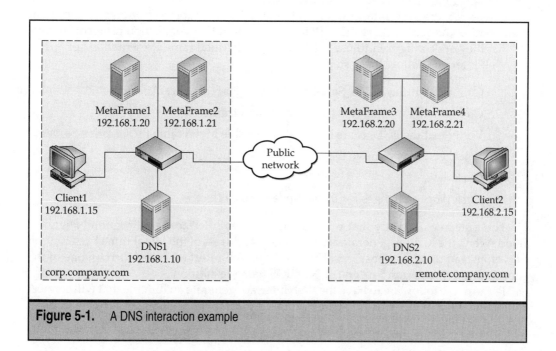

Figure 5-1.   A DNS interaction example

TCP/IP+HTTP and TCP/IP+SSL Connections

When using Program Neighborhood with TCP/IP sessions, the client enumerates the MetaFrame Presentation Server through DNS first. If the server location has the NetBIOS name of the server, that is MetaFrame1, then the client will query DNS and WINS for resolution. If the server location is set to the Fully Qualified Domain Name (FQDN), i.e. MetaFrame1.corp.company.com, then the client will only query DNS. Using FQDN for resolution is very useful for Internet-ready connections through public networks. Also a significant performance gain and network traffic reduction in enumeration/connection exists when only DNS is used. WINS was not used in the Citrix *e*Labs tests for this section.

NOTE: WINS Lookups are only performed if the client machine has WINS addresses set in the network device's TCP/IP properties.

The server location settings (Custom Connection Settings/ICA Settings) can hold up to 15 server addresses; 5 addresses in the *Primary* group, 5 addresses in *Backup1* group, and 5 addresses in the *Backup2* group. The client will resolve all addresses in the groups, even if the first address responds to the request. This resolution is done automatically by the OS rather than by the MetaFrame Presentation Server Client. If DNS Round Robin is not being used, it is recommended that all of the MetaFrame Servers FQDN addresses be entered into the server location settings. This will ensure proper communication to the farm if one of the servers becomes unavailable.

By default, the Web Interface for MetaFrame Presentation Server and the Program Neighborhood Agent will use TCP/IP for their default ICA connection protocol. To verify that they are configured to use the FQDN of the MetaFrame Presentation Servers in the Web Interface, follow these steps:

1. Connect to http://<WI_Server>/Citrix/MetaFrame/WIAdmin.
2. Go to MetaFrame Servers from the content frame.
3. Verify that the FQDNs are set for all applicable MetaFrame Presentation Servers.
4. If not, you may remove the names and add the FQDNs.
5. Click Save.
6. Click Apply Changes for the settings to take effect

These steps will ensure that when using the Web Interface and Program Neighborhood Agent, the ICA file generated has the FQDN address of the MetaFrame Presentation Server instead of a "localhost" resolution (if the Web Interface is installed on one of the MetaFrame Presentation Servers) or NetBIOS name resolution.

Perform the following to have the Web Interface generate an ICA file that will connect to the MetaFrame Presentation Server using the FQDN:

1. Log into the Presentation Server Console.
2. Right-click on the Farm object and go to Properties.

3. Go to MetaFrame Settings and select the option Enable XML Service DNS Address Resolution.

4. Click OK to save the settings.

This will enable the Web Interface and Program Neighborhood Agent to generate the FQDN in the address field of the ICA file, thus ensuring proper resolution of the MetaFrame Presentation Server even in dynamic environments. If the MetaFrame Presentation Server's IP address changes and the DNS system support dynamic updates, there will be no need to change ICA and Web Interface configurations on the clients to support the change.

Program Neighborhood Agent and DNS

On a default installation of the Web Interface, Program Neighborhood Agent's *config.xml* file is populated with the NetBIOS name of the Web Interface server. It is recommended that this file is edited to change the NetBIOS name to FQDN. This will facilitate communications throughout DNS and HTTP(S) connections.

To ensure the Web Interface server name is listed as FQDN:

1. Open a web browser and go to http://<WI_Server>/Citrix/PNAgentAdmin

2. Go to Server Settings.

3. Verify that the Server URL contains the FQDN of the Web Interface server. If it does not, replace the NetBIOS name with the FQDN.

4. Click on the Save button to save the changes. This action will replace all values listed in the previous step.

For additional information on the Web Interface and Program Neighborhood Agent configurations, see Chapter 16 of *Citrix MetaFrame Access Suite for Windows Server 2003: The Official Guide* (McGraw-Hill/Osborne, 2003) and the *Web Interface Administrator's Guide*.

DNS Round Robin and ICA

DNS Round Robin is used in cases where the MetaFrame Administrator would like to distribute TCP/IP connections across several servers. This does not mean that sessions are load-balanced, but that enumeration requests are distributed equally across a group of MetaFrame Presentation Servers. Windows Server 2003 Standard, Enterprise, and Data Center editions, as well as Windows 2000 Server Enterprise Edition all include support for Network Load Balancing (NLB), which is one implementation of DNS Round Robin.

DNS Round Robin is beneficial for MetaFrame Administrators that have more than 15 servers and would like to use all of the servers at enumeration time. In most cases, the client has to perform an enumeration of the servers in the farm in order for IMA to load-balance the server loads.

To use DNS Round Robin, following the network diagram in Figure 5-1, the MetaFrame Administrator will create the following DNS host (A) records in DNS1:

```
enum.corp.company.com IN A 192.168.1.20
enum.corp.company.com IN A 192.168.1.21
```

and will create the following DNS A host records in DNS2:

```
enum.remote.company.com IN A 192.168.2.20
enum.remote.company.com IN A 192.168.2.21
```

When the records are created, the MetaFrame Administrator can add enum.corp.company.com and enum.remote.company.com as the Server Location for Client1. For Client2, the MetaFrame Administrator will reverse the order of the enumerator addresses: first enum.remote.company.com and second, enum.corp.company.com, to ensure that the client enumerates the *corp* domain only when necessary. The same applies for Client1 enumerating the remote domain only when necessary.

When the client attempts to connect to a session, the DNS will return all addresses of the MetaFrame Presentation Servers. Each response from the DNS server will include the IP addresses of the MetaFrame Presentation Servers. If Client1 connects to a load-balanced application, the DNS server will return the IP address for MetaFrame1 and MetaFrame2 in the first response for enum.corp.company.com. It will also return the IP address for MetaFrame3 and MetaFrame4 for the second response for enum.remote.company.com.

When Round Robin is enabled on the DNS server, it restructures the list for each client resolution that it receives by moving the first host to the end of the list. For client versions 6.31.1051 and later, the client attempts to contact each of the servers listed in the order received from the DNS server.

NOTE: For client version 6.30.1050 and earlier, the first server on the list is contacted. If that server fails to respond, the client will then re-query DNS and attempt to contact the first server on the new list. For example, if Client1 connects to the published application, the DNS server will return a list with MetaFrame1 as the first server in the list (192.168.1.20). If the first server fails to respond, Client1 will requery the DNS server and receive a list that has MetaFrame2 as the first server in the list (192.168.1.21), provided the DNS server did not respond to any intermediate queries for enum .corp.company.com in the meantime.

This process ensures all the MetaFrame Servers in the Round Robin loop alternate taking client enumeration requests. In some cases, clients will have a client-side DNS cache enabled and they will not requery the DNS server. By default, Windows 2000 Professional and Windows XP Professional have this feature enabled and Round Robin will appear to fail. To ensure that these clients always try to query the DNS server, see the Microsoft Support Knowledge Base Article 245437: *How to Disable Client-Side DNS Caching in Windows*.

If a MetaFrame Presentation Server farm environment is using Dynamic DNS (DDNS) and DHCP, then the best practice would be to use FQDN locators in the MetaFrame Presentation Server Clients. Using DNS is one of the fastest and easiest methods for ICA traffic addressing.

CHAPTER 6

Novell Directory Services Integration

NOVELL DIRECTORY SERVICES INTEGRATION

MetaFrame Presentation Server 3.0 supports NDS (Novell Directory Services) authentication. This chapter explains how to use NDS with MetaFrame Presentation Server, Web Interface 3.0, and the MetaFrame Presentation Server Win32 Client (version 6.20 and later). In addition to discussing setup, the chapter also discusses the best practices for management of the MetaFrame Presentation Server farm within a Novell environment.

This chapter assumes familiarity with NDS and related Novell products. See the Novell Web site at http://www.novell.com for more information about the Novell products referred to in this chapter.

Prior to Feature Release 1 for MetaFrame Presentation Server XP 1.0, a MetaFrame Presentation Server farm offered limited support for NDS users through the BUILTIN group. The BUILTIN group is selected to specify dynamic local users, managed by Novell's ZENworks for Desktops, when an application is published and users are assigned to network printers.

While use of the BUILTIN group is supported in MetaFrame Presentation Server 3.0 for backward compatibility, Citrix recommends enabling NDS support. Enabling NDS support provides tighter integration between the MetaFrame Presentation Server farm and NDS trees and allows NDS users to take advantage of more features. MetaFrame Presentation Server 3.0 does not require any additional licenses beyond the basic licensing to enable NDS support.

Implement NDS Support in MetaFrame Presentation Server

MetaFrame Presentation Server can now publish applications, desktops, and content for users managed by NDS or Directory Services in Windows 2000 and Windows NT. However, using MetaFrame Presentation Server in a network environment that employs multiple directory services requires careful planning.

Read the following sections carefully before installing MetaFrame Presentation Server in an NDS environment.

Plan the Deployment of MetaFrame Presentation Server for NDS Support

Using MetaFrame Presentation Server in an NDS environment requires the following tasks in the order they are listed:

1. Decide which servers will host applications and content published for NDS users when MetaFrame Presentation Server is installed.

2. Install the Novell Client for Windows onto the servers. For Windows 2000, you can use Novell client version 4.81 or later. For Windows Server 2003, Novell supports only Novell client version 4.9 or later.

3. Install MetaFrame Presentation Server:

▼ Activate the required MetaFrame Presentation Server licenses.

▲ Enable the Dynamic Local User (DLU) policy in ZENworks for Desktops or make sure the same user accounts and passwords exist in both NDS and NT4 or Windows 2000/2003 Active Directory Services (ADS) domains. You may also enable the SyncedDomainName key in each MetaFrame Presentation Server with NDS Integration. This will not require the ZENworks DLU Component requirement.

NOTE: To enable the SyncedDomainName, open the Registry Editor on the MetaFrame Presentation Server, go to HKLM\SOFTWARE\Citrix, and add a new key called **NDS**. On the new key, add a new SZ Sub Key called **SyncedDomainName**. Set the value to the NetBIOS name of the domain you want to synchronize the usernames with. It is not required to restart the server or IMA Service; users will now synchronize the NetWare users with those of the NT/ADS domain. Both users will still need to exist on the NetWare tree and the NT/ADS domain. Both user accounts should also use the same password.

4. Enable NDS support in the MetaFrame Presentation Server farm.

5. Assign Citrix administrator privileges to NDS objects.

6. Log onto the Presentation Server Console with NDS credentials.

7. Publish applications, desktops, or content for NDS users on MetaFrame Presentation Servers to which only NDS users will connect.

8. If Web Interface 2.0 (or later) or NFuse Classic 1.7 will be used, enable NDS support in the Web Interface Admin or the NFuse Classic Admin Page. NDS authentication is supported on IIS only, because this requires native Win32 Novell NetWare Client DLLs to perform the lookup for the context search. Additionally, to use this feature, the NDS client must be installed on the server running the Web Interface.

9. If Program Neighborhood Agent will be deployed, enable NDS support in the Program Neighborhood Agent.

10. Instruct end-users how to connect to published applications and content using their NDS credentials.

The rest of the chapter outlines the procedures required to use MetaFrame Presentation Server in an NDS environment.

Farm Layout and System Requirements

Using MetaFrame Presentation Server in a network environment that employs multiple directory services requires careful planning. While the MetaFrame Presentation Server farm can contain servers that are in Windows NT, Windows 2000, or Windows Server 2003 domains as well as servers enabled for NDS, MetaFrame Presentation Servers that run the

Novell Client and that use DLU functionality should be members of a workgroup and not members of a domain. The DLU feature of Novell ZENworks for Desktops must be used in this configuration.

To implement MetaFrame Presentation Server in an NDS environment, designate application servers to host applications and content published only for NDS users. These servers must run version 4.81 or later of the Novell Client for Windows 2000 or Novell client version 4.9 or later for Windows Server 2003 and MetaFrame Presentation Server XP 1.0 with Feature Release 3 or later. Figure 6-1 illustrates the recommended layout of a MetaFrame Presentation Server farm supporting NDS.

The following software must be installed for MetaFrame Presentation Server to successfully access NDS:

▼ On the NDS server (a server supporting NDS authentication and responding to NDS queries from clients):

■ NDS eDirectory 8.5 for Windows, for Novell NetWare 5 with Support Pack 6 or later, for Novell NetWare 5.1 with Support Pack 2 or later, or for Novell Netware 6 and later.

■ On MetaFrame Presentation Servers:

■ Novell Client for Windows NT/2000 version 4.81 or later, or for Windows Server 2003 (Novell client 4.9 or later is supported by Novell).

▲ MetaFrame XP for Windows, Feature Release 3 or later.

If you are using ZENworks DLU function to gain access to Windows, you must install Novell ZENworks for Desktops 3 or later.

If you are not using ZENworks DLU function to gain access to Windows, you must have accounts with the same username and password that exist in both NDS and NT4 or ADS Domains.

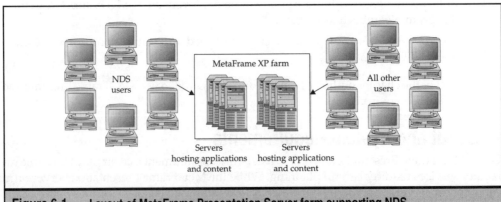

Figure 6-1.   **Layout of MetaFrame Presentation Server farm supporting NDS**

To synchronize domains, perform either of the following:

▼   Manually synchronize accounts.

▲   Use third-party software, such as Novell's Account Manager 2.1 for NT or DirXML, that can automatically synchronize accounts between NDS and NT domains.

NOTE: IP (Internet Protocol) is the only supported protocol for interaction between MetaFrame Presentation Server, NDS, and ZENworks for Desktops.

Install Required Software

Citrix recommends installing the Novell Client and related service packs on a server before installing MetaFrame Presentation Server. If the server is already running MetaFrame Presentation Server, see the section titled "Install the Novell Client on a Server with MetaFrame Presentation Server" later in this chapter.

Install the Novell Client on a Server Without MetaFrame Presentation Server   Complete the following tasks prior to installing MetaFrame Presentation Server:

1.   Install and configure the Novell Client for Windows NT/2000, version 4.81 or later.

NOTE: If you choose to use ZENworks DLU, it may be necessary to perform a custom installation of the Novell Client and add the Workstation Manager component; some clients do not install this component when performing a typical install.

2.   Restart the server.

3.   Verify that you can log onto NDS.

If you cannot log onto NDS, you may need to add a Directory Agent (DA) location to the Novell Client. A DA is needed when the NDS server is located on a different subnet. If a DA does not exist, make sure the NDS server and the MetaFrame Presentation Server are part of the same subnet.

1.   To optimize logon and browsing response times, change the order of the network providers using the following steps:

   For Windows 2000 Servers:

   a.   Right-click My Network Places on the server's desktop.

   b.   Choose Properties from the short-cut menu. The Network and Dial-up Connections window appears.

   c.   Choose Advanced Settings on the Advanced menu. The Advanced Settings dialog box appears.

    d. On the Provider Order tab, adjust the order of the network providers so that Microsoft Windows Network is above NetWare Services.

    e. Click OK to close the Advanced Settings dialog box.

For Windows Server 2003:

    a. Open Network Connections.

    b. Click the connection to be modified, and on the Advanced menu, click Advanced Settings.

    c. On the Provider Order tab, in Network Providers, click the Microsoft Windows Network provider and then click the Up or Down button so that Microsoft Windows Network is above NetWare Services.

2. To optimize logon time, add the Windows fonts directory located in %systemroot% to the system path environment variable.

3. To suppress a MetaFrame Presentation Server setup program error message informing you that the FileSysChange parameter is invalid, complete the following steps:

    a. Open the *System.ini* file located in %systemroot%.

    b. In the **[386Enh]** section of *System.ini*, set the following value:

       FileSysChange=off

    c. Save and close *System.ini*.

NOTE: The appearance of this error message causes unattended setup of MetaFrame Presentation Server to fail. Make sure the FileSysChange parameter is set to Off before running an unattended installation.

4. Install MetaFrame Presentation Server.

If MetaFrame Presentation Server fails to install, complete the following steps:

1. Uninstall the Novell Client from the server.

2. Install MetaFrame Presentation Server and then install the Novell Client by following the instructions in the section "Install the Novell Client on a Server with MetaFrame Presentation Server" in the next section.

3. If the system is working properly, skip to "Configure ZENworks for Desktops Settings for MetaFrame Presentation Server Support" later in this chapter.

Install the Novell Client on a Server with MetaFrame Presentation Server   If MetaFrame Presentation Server is already installed on the server before the installation of the Novell Client, the Windows registry must be changed on the server before *and* after the installation of the Novell Client. If the Novell Client being installed is version 4.9 or later, the following steps will not be needed since the 4.9 client detects Graphical Identification and Authentication (GINA) chaining and respects such chaining with Citrix.

NOTE: If the MetaFrame server has the IPX protocol installed along with the Novell Client, the MetaFrame Presentation Server installation may fail with a wowexec error message. To work around this issue, disable the NWLink protocol on all adapters in the server. After MetaFrame Presentation Server is installed, reenable NWLink.

If MetaFrame Presentation Server is already installed on the server, complete the following tasks:

1. Run regedt32.
2. Edit the following registry key:

   `HKLM\SOFTWARE\Microsoft\WindowsNT\CurrentVersion\Winlogon`

3. Double-click the GinaDLL entry located in the right-hand pane. In the String Editor window that pops up, replace the value **Ctxgina.dll** with the value **Msgina.dll**.
4. Install and configure the Novell Client for Windows NT/2000, Version 4.81 or later.
5. **Do not restart** when prompted by the Novell Client setup program.
6. Edit the registry entry for GinaDLL as in Step 2. In the String Editor window that appears, replace the value **nwgina.dll** with the value **Ctxgina.dll**.
7. With the key path for Winlogon still selected, choose Edit | Add Value.
8. Type **CTXGINADLL** in the Add Value dialog box. The data type is REG_SZ.
9. Enter **Nwgina.dll** in the String Editor window to assign this value to the new CTXGINADLL entry.
10. Restart the server.

On MetaFrame Presentation Servers, *Ctxgina.dll* is loaded by *Winlogon.exe* to process the auto-logon information transmitted by ICA clients. *Ctxgina.dll* can process auto-logon credentials in excess of 20 characters. For example, if *Ctxgina.dll* is not loaded, then auto-logon usernames greater than 20 characters are truncated to 20 characters by *Termsrv.exe*. When *Ctxgina.dll* acquires the user's auto-logon credentials, they are passed in their entirety to the installed *Gina.dll* file to complete the authentication process. In most cases, the installed GINA is *Msgina.dll*. When the Novell Client is installed, the GINA is *Nwgina.dll*. The above steps are required to ensure that the Citrix GINA is installed on the MetaFrame Presentation Server. *Ctxgina.dll* is required for logging on automatically with usernames that exceed 20 characters. If the Novell Client being installed is 4.9 or later, the above steps will not be needed since the 4.9 client detects GINA chaining and respects such chaining with Citrix.

NOTE: If the Novell Client is upgraded after the installation of MetaFrame Presentation Server, the GINA values are overwritten and it is necessary to reconfigure the registry with the above steps.

1. To optimize logon and browsing response times, change the order of the network providers using the following steps:

   For Windows 2000 Servers:

   a. Right-click My Network Places on the server's desktop.

   b. Choose Properties from the short-cut menu. The Network and Dial-up Connections window appears.

   c. Choose Advanced Settings on the Advanced menu. The Advanced Settings dialog box appears.

   d. On the Provider Order tab, adjust the order of the network providers so that Microsoft Windows Network is above NetWare Services.

   e. Click OK to close the Advanced Settings dialog box.

   f. For Windows Server 2003:

   g. Open Network Connections.

   h. Click the connection you want to modify, and on the Advanced menu, click Advanced Settings.

   i. On the Provider Order tab, in Network Providers, click the Microsoft Windows Network provider and then click Up or Down so that Microsoft Windows Network is above NetWare Services.

2. To optimize logon time, add the Windows fonts directory located in %systemroot% to the system path environment variable.

The system is now ready to set up the Windows account authentication to be used to access the servers.

Windows Account Authentication

When a NetWare Client is running on a Windows Server, users are required to have two accounts: one for authentication to NDS and one to gain access to Windows.

There are two different approaches to give Windows access to users. The first option uses Novell's DLU functionality, available in Novell's ZENworks for Desktop Product (this is the only supported method in MetaFrame Presentation Server XP with Feature Release 1).

The second option is by having the same username and password in both NDS and NT or Active Directory Services (ADS) domains for each user (this support is available for MetaFrame Presentation Server XP with Feature Release 2 and higher). This allows integration of MetaFrame and NDS without the use of Novell's ZENworks.

If you are using MetaFrame with NDS integration with ZENworks, continue with the section "Configure ZENworks for Desktops Settings for MetaFrame Presentation Server Support".

If you are using MetaFrame with NDS integration without ZENworks, skip to "Configure NDS Support in MetaFrame Without ZENworks" later in this chapter.

Configure ZENworks for Desktops Settings for MetaFrame Presentation Server Support

When a Novell Client is running on a Windows NT, Windows 2000, or Windows 2003 Server, users are normally required to enter separate credentials to log onto Windows and NDS. Enabling the DLU policy in ZENworks for Desktops eliminates this requirement.

The following section explains how to configure the Container Package and User Package in ZENworks for Desktops to eliminate the need to specify two sets of credentials when connecting to a MetaFrame Presentation Server. Configure the Container Package to specify which users (by container) will have the DLU policy applied to them. Configure the User Package to specify how the DLU policy is applied to those users.

NOTE: These settings are configured on the NDS server through ConsoleOne.

Configure the ZENworks for Desktops Container Package   The Container Package searches for policies located within the tree and then applies them to users who are associated with a particular container. Follow the next example to create a Container Package that searches only the local container for policies applied to users within that container.

NOTE: This sample configuration is useful for small companies.

Perform the following steps for containers that hold user objects that require the DLU policy:

1. Select a container that holds user objects.

2. On the New Object menu, choose Policy Package | Container Package.

3. Choose Define Additional Properties and click Finish.

4. On the Policies tab, enable the search policy.

5. In the Search Policies Up To field, choose Object Container to search only the container in which the search policy resides. The other choices are

   ■ **Root (default)** Searches the local container and any container in the direct path to the root of the tree. This is not recommended for medium to large trees.

   ■ **Partition** Searches the local container and any container up to the root of the partition. This method works well for large environments, but you need to locate the partition boundaries.

   ■ **Selected Container** Searches the container between the current container and the root of the tree that you select.

6. Leave the search level at the default setting of 0.

7. Click Apply, then Close.

8. Click the Associations tab.

9. Choose Add and browse to the container that holds the Container Package you just created.

10. Click OK, then Close.

Configure the ZENworks for Desktops User Package

The User Package in ZENworks for Desktops enables DLU functionality for users who are associated with that particular package. Follow these steps to create a User Package that enables the DLU functionality.

IMPORTANT:　If the Container Package, the User Policy Package, and the user are not located in the same container, the User Policy Package, which contains the DLU settings, will not be applied to the user.

1. Choose the Organizational Unit that holds the Container Package from the previous section.

2. Choose New Object | Policy Package | User Package.

3. Near the end of the wizard, choose Define Additional Properties and then click Finish.

4. Choose WinNT-2000 on the Policies tab.

5. Choose Enable Dynamic Local User and then choose Properties.

6. Choose Dynamic Local User at the top of the page.

7. Choose Manage Existing NT Account (if any). This changes the password and other items to match for a seamless integration.

NOTE:　Novell recommends that a separate DLU policy be created for users who have the username Administrator, if the local administrator account has not been renamed.

8. Choose Use NetWare Credential. This creates a local Microsoft user who has the same name and password as the NDS user. If this is not enabled, the DLU feature creates a random user name and password, resulting in a loss of MetaFrame functionality.

9. Do not enable Volatile User unless you have very large profiles and want to conserve disk space. Enabling the Volatile User setting will increase logon times.

10. On the Not Member Of tab, choose User | Add. Select the users or groups to which the policy will apply. This gives them rights to log on and run MetaFrame applications.

11. Click Apply and then click OK two times to finish the policy.

12. If the MetaFrame Presentation Server is a Windows Server 2003, make sure that you add a Custom Group to the Policy. The Custom Group name should be Remote Desktop Users; this is the group that is granted Log On Locally in order to log in remotely through Terminal Services.

Configure NDS Support in MetaFrame Without ZENworks

In an environment with a Novell Client running on Windows Server 2003 or Windows 2000 Server, users are required to enter separate credentials to log onto Windows and NDS. Using synchronized accounts between NDS and NT4 or ADS domains eliminates this need. MetaFrame Presentation Server XP Feature Release 2 and later adds support for this type of configuration.

To enable NDS support in MetaFrame without ZENworks, set the following registry key on all servers that have the Novell Client installed but are not using the ZENworks for Desktops DLU functionality. Set the Value to the NT or ADS downlevel domain name that contains the user accounts that match the accounts in NDS.

1. Run regedt32.

2. Edit the registry key: `HKLM\SOFTWARE\Citrix`

3. With the key path for Citrix still selected, choose Edit | New Key.

4. Rename the newly created key to NDS.

5. Highlight the new NDS key.

6. With the NDS still selected, choose Edit | New String Value.

7. Type **SyncedDomainName** in the String Value dialog box.

8. Enter the name of the domain that has the same user accounts as NDS in the String Editor window to assign this value to the new SyncedDomainName entry.

NOTE: When this registry key is set, *ctxgina.dll* will replace the NDS tree name that is passed from the client to the server with the string that is placed in SyncedDomainName. *Ctxgina.dll* will then pass the credentials on to *nwgina.dll*. This will allow the passed on username and password to authenticate to NDS, then authenticate to the domain specified in the SyncedDomainName.

Enable NDS Support in the MetaFrame Presentation Server Farm

By default, a MetaFrame Presentation Server farm supports only Microsoft Windows users. Follow these steps to specify the preferred NDS tree for the farm. MetaFrame Presentation Server supports only one NDS tree in each farm.

1. Log onto the Presentation Server Console and connect to a MetaFrame Presentation Server configured for NDS support.
2. Right-click the farm node in the left pane of the console and choose Properties.
3. Click the MetaFrame Settings tab in the Properties dialog box.
4. Specify the tree name in the NDS Preferred Tree field and then click OK. To disable NDS support for the farm, erase the value in the NDS Preferred Tree field and then click OK.

Assign Citrix Administrator Privileges to NDS Objects

Follow these steps to assign Citrix administrator privileges to objects in an NDS tree (such as country, organization, organization unit, group, user, or alias):

1. Log onto the Presentation Server Console.
2. Right-click the MetaFrame Administrators node in the left-hand pane and choose Add Citrix Administrator from the menu that appears.
3. In the Add Citrix Administrator dialog box, open the NDS tree. Objects in the NDS tree represent container and leaf objects.
4. When prompted to log onto the tree, enter the distinguished name and password of an NDS user.
5. Select the Show Users option to display user and alias objects in this hierarchy.
6. Double-click to open container objects. Select the objects to be granted MetaFrame administrator privileges. Add at least one NDS user account that has read and write privileges.

NOTE: While it is possible to grant MetaFrame administrator access rights to a context, users within the context or in contexts that are children of the granted context will also be MetaFrame administrators. This is not recommended due to the difficulty in managing permissions granted to contexts.

7. Click Add. Choose View Only, Full Administration, or Custom privileges.
8. Click Finish to close the Add Citrix Administrator dialog box.

Novell Integration with MetaFrame Presentation Servers

Although the setup and configuration of NDS on the MetaFrame servers is critical, the integration of the users and Citrix Clients is also necessary to complete a seamless Citrix-Novell user experience.

Log Onto the Presentation Server Console Using NDS Credentials

Follow these steps to log onto the Presentation Server Console using NDS credentials to administer a MetaFrame Presentation Server farm.

1. Launch the Presentation Server Console.
2. Enter a distinguished name in the User Name field. A fully distinguished name starts with a period and has a period between each object name up to the root of the tree. For example, user JoeX, within two container objects (the Admin organization unit within the ABC organization) would enter **.JoeX.Admin.ABC** in the User Name field.
3. Enter a password in the Password field.
4. Enter the NDS tree name in the Domain field.
5. Click OK.

NOTE: Citrix MetaFrame Conferencing Manager does not support NDS authentication. Only Windows authentication is supported.

Configure NDS Permissions to MetaFrame Presentation Server Resources

NDS objects like Users, Groups, Aliases, Organizational Units, Organization, Country, and Locality can be specified when configuring permissions for MetaFrame Presentation Server resources like Published Applications and Content, Printer Autocreation, MetaFrame Administrators, and User Policies. More detailed information and instructions are contained in this section.

NOTE: The Assign Shadowing Permissions policy does not allow NDS objects to be configured as Shadowers.

Publish Applications for NDS Users

Follow these steps to publish applications on MetaFrame Presentation Servers configured for NDS support. Only NDS users can connect to the applications you publish on these servers.

1. Log onto the Presentation Server Console using NDS credentials.
2. From the Actions menu, choose New | Published Application.
3. Follow the instructions in the Published Application wizard. Click Help to obtain detailed help for each step.
4. In the Specify What to Publish dialog box, type the UNC (universal naming convention) path to the application you want to publish in the Command Line

field. For example, the NDS tree named MYNDSTREE contains the organization object MYORG, which contains NetWare volume NW50_SYS. The executable path on NW50_SYS is \APPS\OFFICE\WINWORD.EXE. The full UNC path to Winword.exe is \\MYNDSTREE\MYORG\NW50_SYS\APPS\OFFICE\WINWORD.EXE.

5. Leave the Working Directory field blank.

6. Because the application publishing wizard cannot access the application's icon, default MetaFrame icons appear in the Program Neighborhood Settings dialog box. To use the application's icon, copy the icon file (ending with an .ico extension) or the entire executable to a MetaFrame Presentation Server that is not configured to only support NDS. Click Change Icon to browse for the icon or executable on this other MetaFrame Presentation Server.

7. In the Specify Servers dialog box, be sure to select *only* those servers running the Novell Client version 4.81 or later.

8. In the Specify Users dialog box, select the NDS tree from the list. This enumerates the objects in the tree. Double-click container objects to open them. Choose the Show Users option to view users and alias objects in the current container. Select the desired object and click Add.

NDS usernames can also be manually entered. Choose Add List of Names and enter one or more NDS account names separated by a semicolon (;). Each account name must be entered in the fully distinguished name format prefixed by an NDS tree name and a slash (\ ). For example, enter **CitrixNDSTree\.joeX.admin.pnq;CitrixNDSTree\.mary.test.pnq**. Click Check Names to validate the account names or click OK if you are done adding accounts. Double-click to open container or leaf objects until the object to be granted access is displayed. Select the object and click Add.

Configure Printer Autocreation in NDS

Use the Presentation Server Console to choose Windows NT or Windows Active Directory print queues and assign them to NDS objects for autocreation. Permissions to the print queue must be granted to the DLU created when the NDS user logs onto a server. This may require enabling the guest account on the print server. See the Microsoft Knowledge Base article 271901 for information about enabling the guest account.

MetaFrame Presentation Server does not support autocreating NDS printers. See Novell's documentation for autocreating NDS printers (NDPS and non-NDPS) in ZENworks for Desktops.

Enable NDS Support in Web Interface/NFuse Classic 1.7

Complete the following tasks to configure Web Interface/NFuse Classic 1.7 for NDS support.

NOTE: For the following set of instructions, the Web Interface Console can be used rather than the manual process outlined, if Web Interface 3.0 is used. See the *Web Interface Administrator's Guide* for more details.

1. Open the *WebInterface.conf* or *NFuse.conf* file located in the %SystemRoot%\ Inetpub\wwwroot\Citrix\MetaFrame\conf or %ProgramFiles%\Citrix\NFuse\ conf\ directory on the Web Interface/NFuse Web server.

2. Edit the following parameters:

   ■ Set the *LoginType* to **NDS**.

   ■ Set the *NDSTreeName* to the name of the preferred NDS tree for the MetaFrame Presentation Server farm.

3. Restart the IIS Admin Service for the changes to take effect.

If the optional parameter **SearchContextList** is not set, the Web Interface/NFuse "Contextless" authentication feature searches the entire tree to locate a user. This may take a long time in a tree that has a lot of objects. Use **SearchContextList** to reduce the time required for Contextless authentication. Set this parameter to a comma-delimited list of contexts from the NDS tree. The Web Interface/NFuse Contextless authentication feature searches only these contexts to locate the user instead of the entire tree.

NOTE: The Novell Client must be running on the Web Interface or NFuse Classic 1.7 Web server to allow Contextless authentication.

Specify NDS User Credentials in Web Interface/NFuse   On the Web Interface/NFuse logon page, NDS user credentials can be entered as follows:

▼ **User Name**   The following options may be specified:

   ■ The full NDS distinguished name of the user (.joe.department.company or .CN=joe.OU=department.O=company) or

   ■ The full NDS distinguished name of the alias for a user (.joeAlias.department .company or .CN=joeAlias.OU=department.O=company) or

   ■ A partial name ("joe") and select **[Find Context]** from the Context field to find all contexts where a user/alias with this name exists.

■ **Password**   Password is the NDS user's password.

■ **TreeName**   TreeName shows the name of the NDS tree supported by the farm. MetaFrame XP supports only one NDS tree per farm. This field cannot be edited.

▲ **Context**   Select from this list by either of the following:

   ■ A context used in a previous Web Interface/NFuse login

   ■ Find Context tab

By selecting the Find Context tab and clicking Log In, the Web Interface/NFuse searches the NDS tree for all contexts that contain the partial user/alias name. This search feature requires the Novell Client be installed on the Web Interface/NFuse Web server and have access to the NDS tree. Since searching the entire NDS tree may be slow, you can specify the NDS contexts that Web Interface/NFuse should search. To do this, specify them in the SearchContextList setting in the *nfuse.conf* file. For example:

SearchContextList=subdepartment.department.company

Context names should not be prefixed with a dot (.) and multiple contexts should be separated by a comma (,).

NOTE: Web Interface/NFuse does not support Pass-Thru Authentication for NDS users.

NDS Support in the ICA Win32 Client

When users launch the ICA Win32 Client, they can log on and be authenticated using their NDS credentials. Supported NDS credentials are username (or distinguished name), password, directory tree, and context.

NDS support is integrated into the following:

▼ **Program Neighborhood and Program Neighborhood Agent** If NDS is enabled in the MetaFrame Presentation Server farm, NDS users enter their credentials on an NDS tab on the ICA Client logon screen. If users have the Novell Client (version 4.81 or later) installed, they can browse the NDS tree to choose their context. See the section titled "Enable NDS Support in the ICA Program Neighborhood Agent" later in this chapter to configure the Program Neighborhood Agent for NDS support.

▲ **Pass-Thru Authentication** If users have the Novell Client (version 4.81 or later) installed, their credentials are passed to the MetaFrame Presentation Server, eliminating the need for multiple system and application authentications.

NOTE: To enable Pass-Thru Authentication when using Novell's ZENworks for Desktops DLU functionality, set the Use NetWare Credentials value in ZENworks for Desktops DLU policy package to On.

▼ **Session Sharing** The session sharing feature is not currently supported for custom ICA connections that are configured with NDS user credentials (under Properties | Login Information). To use the session sharing feature for Custom ICA Connections, do not specify user credentials in the Login Information tab for a connection.

■ **Custom ICA Connections** When users run the Add New ICA Connection wizard, they must enter a distinguished name in the User Name field, a password in the Password field, and place the NDS tree name in the Domain field. This will also work with earlier versions of ICA Win32 Clients.

- **Single Sign On**   When the Novell Client is installed on the client machine and Single Sign On is enabled, Single Sign On, by default, will send the user's NDS credential to the server. If Windows credentials are desired, add the following to the *Appsrv.ini* or *.ica* file:

    - **Appsrv.ini**   Under the [WFCLIENT] section, add or modify the SSOnCredentialType entry to SSOnCredentialType=NT

    - **.ICA**   Under the application name section, add or modify the SSOnCredentialType entry to SSOnCredentialType=NT

Configure Default Contexts for Users   Configuring default contexts for users eliminates the need for users to know their context when they log on. Listed below are ways to configure default contexts on ICA Client devices:

To enable Single Sign On in the ICA Client:

1. If the ICA Client device is running the Novell Client, enable Single Sign On in the ICA Client. If Single Sign On is enabled in the ICA Client, the username context and password are passed from the Novell Client to the MetaFrame server.

2. Edit the Windows registry on the client device.

3. Create a script using regini or regedit that modifies the registry entry **HKCU\ Software\Citrix\CtxLogon** with the correct context of the user. Edit the value *RecentContexts* to specify context(s). Each context must appear on a new line.

To add a Default Context to the MSI install of Program Neighborhood: At a command prompt, type **msiexec /I <*MSI_Package*> /qn+ Default_NDSCONTEXT= <*Context* >** Where <*MSI_Package*> is the name of the installer package and <*Context*> is the Default NDS context you want to display in the client. If you are including more than one context, separate the contexts by a comma.

Tp add a Default Context to the Self Extracting Executable of Program Neighborhood:

1. Extract the ICA Client files from *Ica32.exe* by typing at a command line: **ica32.exe -a -unpack:<*Directory Location*>** where <*Directory Location*> is the directory to which you want to extract the client files.

2. Locate and open the *appsrv.src* file in a text editor.

3. Locate the section named [WFClient].

4. Add the following line to the list of parameters and values in the [WFClient] section: DEFAULT_NDSCONTEXT=<*Context1* [,]>. Include this parameter if you want to set a default context for NDS. If you are including more than one context, place the entire value in quotation marks, and separate the contexts by a comma.

5. Examples of correct parameters:

```
DEFAULT_NDSCONTEXT=Context1
DEFAULT_NDSCONTEXT="Context1,Context2"
```

NOTE: The executable install of Program Neighborhood Agent does not support this method.

Enable NDS Support in the ICA Program Neighborhood Agent

Complete the following tasks to allow NDS users to log onto the ICA Win32 Program Neighborhood Agent:

1. Open the *Config.xml* file located in the **InetPub\Citrix\PNAgent** directory on the Web Interface/NFuse Classic 1.7 Web server.

2. Set Logon/SupportNDS to True.

3. Set Logon/NDS_Settings/DefaultTree to the name of the preferred NDS tree for the MetaFrame Presentation Server farm.

4. Restart the IIS Admin Service on the Web Interface/NFuse Classic 1.7 Web server for the changes to take effect.

5. Restart the Program Neighborhood Agent.

Organize Published Applications for NDS Users

It may be helpful to set up groups in NDS and associate published applications with them. For example, an NDS group called Default_User_Apps can be created for business and office applications. This group should be added when specifying which users have access to those published applications. When new users are added to this group, they are granted rights to the applications.

Another good practice is to create a separate group for specialty applications that are not distributed to a wide audience. For example, a group can be created in NDS called Accounting_Program, where an application called Microsoft Great Plains is published in MetaFrame Presentation Server. In the Presentation Server Console, specify the NDS group Accounting_Program to the published application called Microsoft Great Plains. When assigning new users to the accounting application, simply add them to the group called Accounting_Program in NDS.

Tips and Techniques

This section contains a variety of special tips to complete a smooth integration of the Citrix environment with Novell NDS.

Create Aliases

To create aliases in NDS, make sure of the following:

▼   Ensure the distinguished name of the object does not exceed 48 characters.

▲   Alias object names are unique within the tree. The Alias object can be the same name as the actual object.

NOTE: Third-party tools, such as the Lyncx tool from Centralis, can automate the process of creating aliases for large trees. See the Centralis Web site at http:// www.centralis.co.uk for more information.

NOTE: When users log on, they are given the rights of the object to which the alias object points.

Debug NDS Issues

To capture tracing for debugging problems related to NDS support in MetaFrame Presentation Server, tracing must be enabled for IMA_AAMS, WinDrvSS, and NDSDrvSS components.

CHAPTER 7

MetaFrame Secure Access Manager Design and Configuration

This chapter covers advanced concepts of the design and configuration of MetaFrame Secure Access Manager, including key component services, deployment requirements, and server scalability. Other topics also covered are modifying the Java Client for use with MetaFrame Secure Access Manager, changing page title names generated by the Access Center, and customizing the logon agent page. Basic concepts and in-depth examples and integration topics for MetaFrame Secure Access Manager can be found in *Citrix MetaFrame Access Suite for Windows Server 2003: The Official Guide* by Steve Kaplan, Tim Reeser, and Alan Woods (McGraw-Hill/Osborne, 2003).

METAFRAME SECURE ACCESS MANAGER

MetaFrame Secure Access Manager is a full-blown Access Solution designed to be a common interface for the aggregation of many different types of corporate data and applications rather than just Windows and UNIX applications. MetaFrame Secure Access Manager provides a wizard-based tool with content delivery agents (CDAs) that automate such tasks as placing MetaFrame ICA icons within the Web Access page, or grabbing Microsoft Exchange content and placing it within the web page.

MetaFrame Secure Access Manager can quickly, and through a wizard-based tool, create a single secured web interface that has a portion of the window showing a message from the president of the company, another portion of the window showing the number of customers in a call queue for support, another portion of the window that is a customer information lookup for pertinent data, a portion of the window showing applications available (both ICA and web-based), and a final tag across the top that shows the corporate stock price. All of these sections are dynamically controlled based on the role of the user. Figure 7-1 shows a simple MetaFrame Secure Access Manager page.

Key MetaFrame Secure Access Manager Component Services

MetaFrame Secure Access Manager, in its most basic Internet-based deployment, has the following components: a State Server, a Microsoft SQL Server or Microsoft Data Engine (MSDE) Database, one or more Agent Servers, one or more Web Servers (or web service extensions, if installed on Windows Server 2003), Secure Gateway for MetaFrame, Secure Ticket Authority (STA) server, and Login Agent. There are also the additional ancillary components: the user-side MetaFrame Secure Access Manager Gateway Client and the Index Server for MetaFrame.

State Server

When you create a new access server farm, the first server on which you install MetaFrame Secure Access Manager becomes the State Server. The State Server maintains configuration information for the Access Centers in the Access Server farm including CDA information, custom user information, session information, and much more.

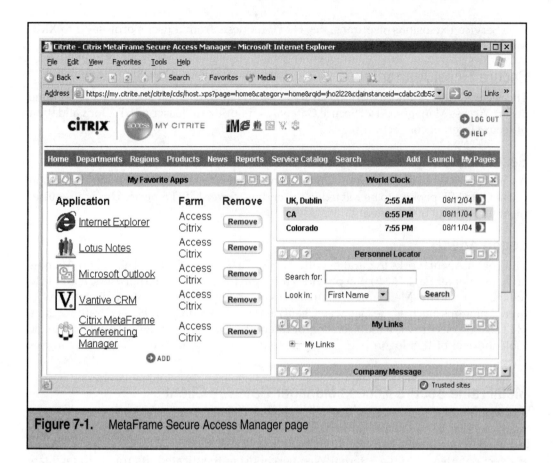

Figure 7-1.   MetaFrame Secure Access Manager page

Microsoft SQL Server or Microsoft Data Engine (MSDE) Database

The database stores the configuration information for an Access Server farm. Citrix recommends the use of Microsoft SQL Server for improved performance and scalability.

Agent Server

Agent Server(s) handle CDA execution for the Access Server farm. Agent Servers can be very loosely compared to MetaFrame Presentation Server farm servers because they generate the bulk of the content/information for end users. The information processed, though, is data for CDAs instead of feature-rich GUI applications.

Web Server or Web Service Extensions

The Web Server or Web Service Extensions format the output from processing CDAs to create and provide the pages that are sent to the user's web browser. The Web Server or

Web Service Extensions also translates HTTP requests from a user's browser into XML for the Agent Server.

Secure Ticket Authority

The Secure Ticket Authority (STA) is installed automatically when you install MetaFrame Secure Access Manager. Also, Secure Gateway will utilize at least one STA for validation of secure Internet connection states.

Secure Gateway for MetaFrame

As in a secure Web Interface deployment, Secure Gateway services enable the encryption of data into SSL packets to be related to the end user over HTTPS ports. This is a requirement for Internet deployments.

Logon Agent

The Logon Agent works in parallel with the Secure Gateway install. The Logon Agent is an Active Server Page (ASP) that provides the login interface to external users. It is able to log the user into the MetaFrame Secure Access Manager environment and install any required plug-ins (such as the Gateway Client) and can be secured for HTTPS traffic. Again, HTTPS (SSL) security is a requirement for Internet-based deployments. To customize the look-and-feel of this logon page, see "Customize the Logon Agent Page" later in this chapter.

MetaFrame Secure Access Manager Gateway Client

The MetaFrame Secure Access Manager Gateway Client is key to proper Internet deployments and can be somewhat compared to having a MetaFrame Presentation Server Client installed in that it is an ActiveX component downloaded to the users' computers when a connection attempt to the internal Web Servers is authenticated. Its role is to facilitate communications with the MetaFrame Secure Access Manager internal environments and act as a tunneling client, which will allow a remote client into LAN-based resources at the data center. For example, if there is a Web site CDA that links to an internal data center URL, the Gateway Client enables the remote user to view the contents of that URL by tunneling the web browser requests to the Secure Gateway Server, which then links to the internal resource.

Index Server for MetaFrame

By installing Index Server for MetaFrame, users are able to search Intranet or Internet Web sites as well as search documents located within the Intranet. The Index Server uses existing security settings so users can only access the documents they have rights to see.

DEPLOYMENT REQUIREMENTS FOR METAFRAME SECURE ACCESS MANAGER

In order to optimally deploy MetaFrame Secure Access Manager, consideration must be given to the requirements for the STA installation path, address translation, and using UNC paths with Secure Gateway.

Secure Ticket Authority Installation Path

Installing MetaFrame Secure Access Manager also installs STA by default. During this install, the STA installer locates the directory containing the files for the server's default Web site. The STA files are then installed into the *scripts* directory under this location. If the location of the default Web site files has been changed, then the location must also be changed in the following registry key in order for the STA files to be installed in the correct location:

```
HKLM\System\CurrentControlSet\Control\ContentIndex\Catalogs\Web
```

This location must be changed to the match the location of the files for the Web site under which the STA installation is desired.

Address Translation and MetaFrame Secure Access Manager

Special consideration should be taken when using Secure Gateway, a Proxy Server, or a Network Address Translation (NAT)-enabled firewall to reach your access center. These devices all mask the actual client address. When configuring addressing modes, use the visible IP address for the client IP address. This will be the IP address of the Secure Gateway Server, the external IP address of the Proxy Server, or the external address of the firewall.

Use UNC Paths with Secure Gateway

Secure Gateway provides native access to URLs, but does not provide access to UNC paths. If data, however, resides on UNC shares, it can be accessed through Secure Gateway by using MetaFrame Secure Access Manager's content redirection feature.

When you use MetaFrame Secure Access Manager's content redirection feature, provided the MetaFrame Presentation Server can reach the UNC path via its local network, the application associated with the data will be opened on a MetaFrame Presentation Server rather than on the user's local machine. The user will then be able to view the data presented via a secure ICA session accessed through Secure Gateway.

For example, using the Shared Documents CDA, give users access to a share point referenced by its UNC path containing Microsoft Word documents. Configure a MetaFrame Presentation Server farm that has Word published. In the MetaFrame Secure Access Manager farm configuration select "Apply MetaFrame XP content redirection". Additionally, configure the farm to launch applications through Secure Gateway when users connect externally. When a user logs into MetaFrame Secure Access Manager, they will see their documents in the Shared Documents CDA. Normally the user would not be able to open the documents because the UNC path is not valid externally. Now, however, when the user opens one of these documents it will launch a MetaFrame Presentation Server session through Secure Gateway and open the requested document within the session.

MODIFY THE CLIENT FOR JAVA FOR USE WITH METAFRAME SECURE ACCESS MANAGER

MetaFrame Secure Access Manager integrates with the MetaFrame Presentation Server Client for Java to connect to published applications on MetaFrame Presentation Servers. Secure Access Manager does not provide an integrated GUI utility for managing the Client for Java. Modifications to the Client for Java configuration are done by modifying the JavaLaunch CDA. This can be done in two ways: by using the CDASDK (CDAPad) or by directly modifying the *configuration.xml* file for the CDA . The configuration file is located in *$(INSTALLDIR\Config\State Server*(access center name)*\ConfigStore\{\A\ {A5DBC0E4-0F42-11D4-8FF1-0050DA2FEE7E}|JAVA ICA CLIENT.txt*. Changes made directly to the *configuration.xml* file will not be applied until the MetaFrame Secure Access Manager State Server services are restarted.

Archive File Description

The MetaFrame Presentation Server Client for Java is divided into several feature-related packages in order to avoid having to download features that are unused or not desired. Table 7-1 shows the descriptions of each package.

MetaFrame Presentation Server Client for Java Version 7.0.*x* vs. Version 8.0 Notes

The JavaLaunch CDA (version 1.*x* and 2.*x*) by default is not compatible with the MetaFrame Presentation Server Client for Java version 8.0 because the CDA code is looking for the legacy *JICA*J.jar* files which have been replaced by *JICA*N.jar* files. To enable Client for Java version 8.0 compatibility, *configuration.xml* file for the JavaLaunch CDA must be modified to reference the *JICAN*.jar* files. This can be accomplished using CDAPad (recommended) or by directly editing the configuration file.

Java Client Packages	Descriptions
JICAEngM.cab	Complete archive. This archive contains the contents of all of the other archives apart from *cryptojM.cab* and *sslM.cab*, which must be included if required.
cryptojM.cab	Encryption component. Required for all encryption.
sslM.cab	SSL component. Adds SSL and TLS encryption support.
JICA-configM.cab	User configuration component. Adds the Status bar, buttons, and ICA Settings dialog box.
JICA-coreM.cab Core archive	This archive provides only a basic connection. You add functionality by using it in conjunction with the other component archives described in this table.
JICA-audioM.cab	Audio component. Adds client audio mapping.
JICA-cdmM.cab CDM component	Adds client drive mapping.
JICA-clipboardM.cab	Clipboard component. Adds client clipboard support.
JICA-commM.cab	Communications component. Adds serial port mapping support. Also requires the javax.comm standard extension package.
JICA-printerM.cab	Printer component. Adds client printer mapping.
JICA-sicaM.cab ICA	Encryption component. Adds ICA Encryption Support.
JICA-tw1M.cab Thinwire 1 component	Required for connections to MetaFrame 1.8, MetaFrame component 1.8 SP1, MetaFrame for Unix servers, or any server set to use Thinwire version 1.
JICA-zlcM.cab ZLC component	Adds SpeedScreen Latency Reduction support.

Table 7-1.   Java Client Packages Descriptions

CDAPad Method

Load CDAPad and select the Access Center that you want to modify. On the View menu, ensure the Framework CDAs item is checked. In the tree control on the left side, locate the "Java ICA Client" CDA and select the "default" action. Use the Replace function (CTRL-R) to modify the file (Find: *J.jar* and Replace: *N.jar*) and Commit the changes.

Edit the *configuration.xml* File

Open the file *$(INSTALLDIR\Config\State Server\(access center name)\ConfigStore\{\A\ {A5DBC0E4-0F42-11D4-8FF1-0050DA2FEE7E}|JAVA ICA CLIENT.txt* with Wordpad.

Use the Replace function (CTRL-H) to modify the file (Find: *J.jar* and Replace: *N.jar*) and save the changes. Restart the MetaFrame Secure Access Manager State Server services. The changes will not be applied until the services are restarted.

Changing the Java Client Package Inclusion Default

By default, the core, encryption, configuration, printer, client drive mapping, and secure socket layer packages are included. To change the default inclusion of packages for the client for Java, load CDAPad and select the Access Center that you want to modify. On the View menu, ensure the Framework CDAs item is checked. In the tree control on the left side, locate the "Java ICA Client" CDA and select the "default" action. Scroll down in the code until you find the section here:

```
JARS = """"JICA-coreJ.jar,JICA-sicaJ.jar,cryptojJ.jar,JICA-configJ.jar,
    JICA-dmJ.jar,JICA-printerJ.jar""""
CABS = """"JICA-coreM.cab,JICA-sicaM.cab,cryptojM.cab,
JICA-configM.cab,JICA-cdmM.cab,JICA-printerM.cab""""
''''''' if you want clipboard, comment the next two lines out
JARS = JARS & """",JICA-clipboardJ.jar""""
CABS = CABS & """",JICA-clipboardM.cab""""
''''''' if you want audio, comment the next two lines out
''''JARS = JARS & """",JICA-audioj.jar""""
''''CABS = CABS & """",JICA-audioM.cab""""
''''''' if you need thinwire, comment the next two lines out
''''JARS = JARS & """",JICA-tw1J.jar""""
''''CABS = CABS & """",JICA-tw1M.cab""""
''''''' if you need speedscreen latency reduction,
comment the next two lines out
''''JARS = JARS & """",JICA-zlcJ.jar""""
''''CABS = CABS & """",JICA-zlcM.cab""""
```

In order to add audio support, for example, uncomment the two lines below the comment describing the audio package. Comments in CDAs are specified with a leading apostrophe. The code would then look like the following:

```
''''''' if you want audio, comment the next two lines out
JARS = JARS & """",JICA-audioj.jar""""
CABS = CABS & """",JICA-audioM.cab""""
```

Basic Configuration

The quickest way to launch applications with the least amount of features is to only include the "core" package. This can be done by modifying the code to look like the following:

```
JARS = """"JICA-coreJ.jar"""",JICA-sicaJ.jar,cryptojJ.jar,JICA-configJ.jar,
JICA-cdmJ.jar,JICA-printerJ.jar""""
CABS = """"JICA-coreM.cab"""",JICA-sicaM.cab,cryptojM.cab,
JICA-configM.cab,JICA-cdmM.cab,JICA-printerM.cab""""
'''''''' if you want clipboard, comment the next two lines out
''''JARS = JARS & """",JICA-clipboardJ.jar""""
''''CABS = CABS & """",JICA-clipboardM.cab""""
'''''''' if you want audio, comment the next two lines out
''''JARS = JARS & """",JICA-audioj.jar""""
''''CABS = CABS & """",JICA-audioM.cab""""
'''''''' if you need thinwire, comment the next two lines out
''''JARS = JARS & """",JICA-tw1J.jar""""
''''CABS = CABS & """",JICA-tw1M.cab""""
'''''''' if you need speedscreen latency reduction,
comment the next two lines out
''''JARS = JARS & """",JICA-zlcJ.jar""""
''''CABS = CABS & """",JICA-zlcM.cab""""
```

This is achieved by only including the JICA-core*.* packages and commenting out the rest.

Add Thinwire Support

To communicate with MetaFrame for Unix, it is necessary to include the thinwire components. This can be enabled by uncommenting to following lines. The code would then look like this:

```
'''''''' if you need speedscreen latency reduction,
comment the next two lines out
JARS = JARS & """",JICA-zlcJ.jar""""
CABS = CABS & """",JICA-zlcM.cab""""
```

Add Certificates

If you want to add a certificate to use secure connections, first find the following code:

```
'''''''' if you need SSL, comment the next two lines out
JARS = JARS & """",sslJ.jar""""
CABS = CABS & """",sslM.cab""""
'''''''' if you need certificates comment out the next lines
''''set the jar and cab files to the names of the files that contain your
    certificates
''''set the certificates variable to all the certificates (separate each
```

```
  certificate by a comma)
''''JARS = JARS & """",MyCertificate.jar""""'''' change
this to your certificate file
  name
''''CABS = CABS & """",MyCertificate.cab""""
''''certificates = """"file1.cer,file2.cer,file3.cer,file4.cer""""
```

You will need to create a *cab* and a *jar* file (if using Sun's JVM) that contains all of your certificate files. This can be done by using the cabarc and jar tools. *Cabarc.exe* can be downloaded from Microsoft at http://support.microsoft.com/default.aspx?scid=KB;en-us;310618.

```
cabarc N MyCertificate.cab file1.cer file2.cer file3.cer
jar cvf MyCertificate.jar file1.cer file2.cer file3.cer
```

Place the *cab* and *jar* files in the same location as the other *jar* and *cab* files (by default C:\Inetpub\wwwroot\<*access center name*>\cds\icaweb\en\icajava\), then change the following lines in the Java ICA Client CDA to look like this:

```
JARS = JARS & """",MyCertificate.jar""""''''
change this to your certificate file name
CABS = CABS & """",MyCertificate.cab""""
certificates = """"file1.cer,file2.cer,file3.cer""""
```

Add Certificates Using XSLT

An alternate way to add/modify security certificates after creating *jar/cab* files and putting them in their correct folder is to change the *ICAFile.xslt* file, which is located at \Program Files\Citrix\MetaFrame Secure Access Manager\bin\binders. Find the line that looks like the following:

```
SSLNoCACerts=0
```

Change the 0 to the number of certificates that are going to be added. Then add a line for each certificate you want included in the following format:

```
SSLCACert0=file1cer
SSLCACert1=file2.cer
SSLCACert2=file3.cer
Etc.
```

Notice that the certificate numbers start at zero and increment from there.

SERVER SCALABILITY FOR METAFRAME SECURE ACCESS MANAGER

This section describes server scalability for MetaFrame Secure Access Manager when being used to deploy content, whether from applications published on a MetaFrame Presentation Sever farm or from other sources. The discussion covers the number of user accesses per agent server and the number of Agent Servers per Web Server.

When many users are accessing the MetaFrame Secure Access Manager Access Center, the Agent Servers perform the majority of the processing in the system. The two operations that tax the Agent Servers are the servicing of concurrent accesses to the portal and servicing the general pages per minute. Since these operations are CPU intensive, CPU considerations are also discussed in this section.

The measurements in this section were collected using a "complex portal," which is defined as having the following three components:

▼   One page containing the following CDAs:

  ■   Alert Broadcaster

  ■   Message Center

  ■   Web Site Viewer

  ■   Web Site Favorites

■   Authentication is turned on.

▲   A menu containing 10 folders, each with 10 pages. It is also integrated with a MetaFrame XP, Feature Release 3 farm hosting 40 published applications in the menu.

Using this MetaFrame Secure Access Manager configuration, the number of Agent and Web Servers varies, as described in each following section, to understand and define the scaling parameters. The State, Agent and Web Servers were Dell 1400 Dual Pentium III 800 MHz with 512MB of RAM and a single 100 Mbps network card.

Several of the tests described in this chapter are broken into three parts: *Logon*, *Initialization*, and *Cache*. *Logon* refers to the process of a client logging onto an authenticated portal. *Initialization* (Init) is the user's first access to the Access Center, and is the point at which the cache is created. *Cache* is when the user refreshes a page, or hits the portal for a second time during one contiguous Access Center session. These three separate tasks give a better understanding of where bottlenecks occur in the Access Center farm.

Concurrent Accesses

Concurrent accesses are the number of simultaneous accesses that the Agent Server can process within a given time. Table 7-2 and the associated graph in Figure 7-2 show the number of concurrent accesses that MetaFrame Secure Access Manager can service within three seconds based on the number of concurrent sessions requested at once. For the purposes of this measurement, the acceptable time to service a request (given in Figure 7-2 as Time to Last Byte [TTLB]) is considered to be less than three seconds.

Throughput vs. Agent Servers

Given the maximum throughput of an Access farm, the total number of users that can be serviced can be derived through the following formula:

Total Users = ((Pages per Minute * 60 Minutes) / 20 Pages per Hour) / 0.9 Active Users

These variables change depending on the hardware and user environment.

Throughput is typically measured in Pages per Minute (PPM). Essentially, this measurement denotes the number of pages the portal can service within one minute. This number is arrived at by allowing multiple accesses to the portal during a period of five minutes, and then calculating the average. Figure 7-3 shows the maximum throughput as the number of Agent Servers increases.

CPU Effect on Agent Server Performance

The operations performed by the Agent Server are CPU intensive; the Agent Server will only use approximately 150MB of RAM above the requirements for Microsoft Windows 2000 Server. However, performance gains will occur when the number or speed of the CPUs is increased.

Concurrent Sessions	TTLB (Hit)	TTLB (Cache)
1	1.552	0.798
2	1.621	0.798
5	3.279	1.01
10	7.06	1.783
20	11.153	2.743

Table 7-2.   Agent Server Concurrent Accesses

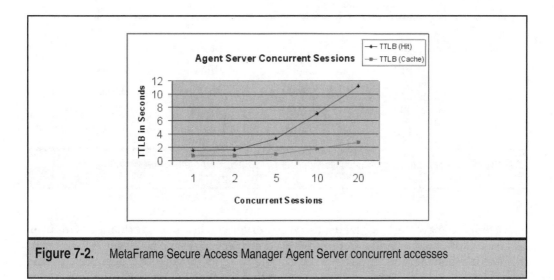

Figure 7-2.   MetaFrame Secure Access Manager Agent Server concurrent accesses

Table 7-3 and associated graph in Figure 7-4 show a comparison of a single, dual, and quad Intel Pentium III Xeon 700 MHz processor Agent Server.

Number of Agent Servers per Web Server

The load on the Web Server is also CPU intensive. The Agent Servers, however, run out of CPU cycles long before the Web Servers do. As the number of Agent Servers increases in

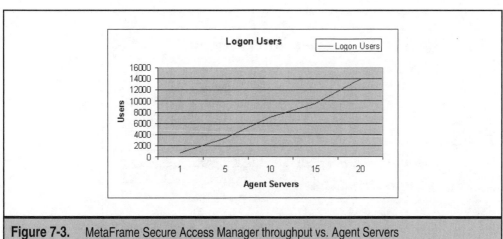

Figure 7-3.   MetaFrame Secure Access Manager throughput vs. Agent Servers

# of Processors	Init		Cache	
	PPM	Users	PPM	Users
1	49.8	166.00	96.00	320.00
2	90.6	302.00	219.00	730.00
4	150	500.00	408.60	1362.00

Table 7-3.   MetaFrame Secure Access Manager CPU Effect on Agent Server Performance

order to handle greater user loads, the Web Server can become overloaded with user accesses. Citrix recommends that in a MetaFrame Secure Access Manager Access farm, the ratio of Agent Servers to Web Servers should be 6:1. For every six Agent Servers, one Web Server should be installed. This assumes that the Web Server hardware and Agent Server hardware are similar in configuration. If the Web Server contains more CPUs, the number of Agent Servers it can support increases. The CPU usage on the Web Server should be monitored in order to determine when another should be installed.

CAUTION: When adding Web Servers, a third-party hardware load-balancer (such as Cisco's Content Services Switches or Content Switching Modules) or software load-balancing solution (such as Microsoft's Network Load Balancing) should be used to load balance the Web Servers. Web servers are not dedicated to specific Agent Servers. All Web Servers can redirect communication to any Agent Server in the Access farm.

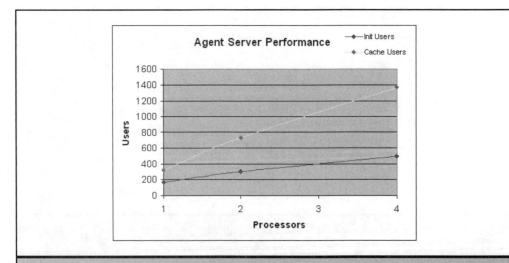

Figure 7-4.   MetaFrame Secure Access Manager CPU effect on Agent Server performance

Overhead Incurred When Using Secure Gateway

Communication with the Access farm through a double hop secure environment using Secure Gateway will generally decrease MetaFrame Secure Access Manager performance. *Logon time* will increase 20–30 percent due to the web-based logon, while *Initialization* and *Cache time* will normally increase 10–15 percent due to the overhead associated with encrypting and proxying web traffic through multiple Secure Gateway Servers.

For our test environment, the double hop secure environment was set up with SSL encryption between the following components:

▼   Client →Secure Gateway Sever

■   Secure Gateway Server → Secure Gateway Proxy

▲   Secure Gateway Proxy Server → MetaFrame Secure Access Manager web server

NOTE: Actual performance of the Access Center using Secure Gateway depends on the network environment and hardware in which Secure Gateway Servers are deployed. If routers, firewalls, or Secure Gateway Servers (due to hardware constraints) introduce a bottleneck or add a large amount of latency to packets traversing the network, then performance of the Access Center over the Secure Gateway connection will be reduced.

CHANGE PAGE TITLE DISPLAY NAMES

To further customize a user's experience of the MetaFrame Secure Access Manager Access Center, you may find it desirable to change the page title display names seen when viewing your Access Center pages. It is possible to change the page names that are automatically generated by MetaFrame Secure Access Manager.

MetaFrame Secure Access Manager sets the page name to the value that is specified between the header title open and close tags in the CDS configuration file. To change the page name, simply alter the text between these tags. The CDS configuration file, an XML file, allows you to change the setting of this autogenerated name. To change the page title display name, follow these steps:

1. Open the file *C:\[MSAM Install Path]\Config\State Server\{Access Center Name}\ConfigStore\{\2{235F25C0-F04D-11D3-8113 00C04F607D9F}|cdsconfig.txt*

2. Locate this line in the file: <header.title>(Access Center Name) - Citrix Secure Access Manager</header.title>

3. Modify the text between the tags to reflect the desired browser title display name and save the changes, for example, <header.title>*Company Name - Custom Description*</header.title>

The MetaFrame Secure Access Manager State Server service must be restarted before the changes are applied. Restarting the MetaFrame Secure Access Manager State Server

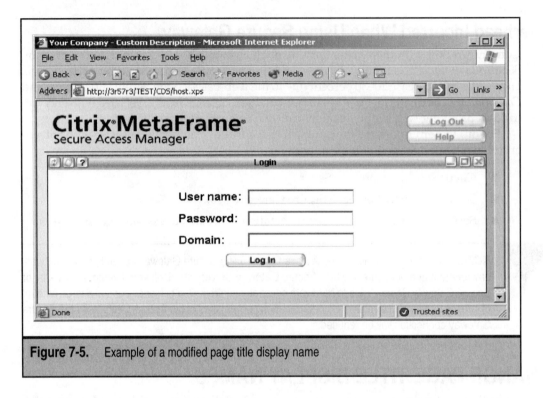

Figure 7-5.   Example of a modified page title display name

service also restarts the MetaFrame Secure Access Manager Admin Server, MetaFrame Secure Access Manager Repository, and MetaFrame Secure Access Manager Agent Server services. You can see an example of the resultant modification in Figure 7-5.

CUSTOMIZE THE LOGON AGENT PAGE

When a user accesses an Access Center through Secure Gateway, the logon process is controlled by the Logon Agent rather than by the default MetaFrame Secure Access Manager logon mechanism. The Logon Agent implementation is web template-based and allows MetaFrame Administrators to easily customize the logon web pages to incorporate graphical elements and color schemes in keeping with the corporate style of the enterprise. The Logon Agent web template consists of a web-based Logon form, an Authentication Service VBScript, and configuration data files.

The Web-Based Logon Form

The web-based logon form is implemented as a server-side ASP script—*Login.asp*. *Login.asp* includes the script file *CCSGLogonProxy.vbs* which contains VBScript APIs that communicate with the Authentication Service. The *CSGLogonProxy.vbs* script file includes configuration data files which contain configuration information used by the VBScript

API. The *Login.asp* script also contains the logon form used to collect user credentials and buttons to submit the user credentials for authentication. User credentials are forwarded to the Authentication Service when the user submits the data.

The web-based logon form provides the fields required to collect user credentials during the logon process. The presentation details of the web-based logon form are the aspects you may want to customize. The look and feel can be modified as required, provided you maintain the logic of the authentication process.

When installed in the default mode, the Logon Agent template contains a single web page comprising a logon form. The Logon Agent web templates are installed to the following locations:

▼ /inetpub/wwwroot/logonagent/basictemplate/*.*

▲ /inetpub/wwwroot/logonagent/securidtemplate/*.*

When the authentication method is specified during install, the relevant template files are copied to /inetpub/wwwroot/logonagent/*.*. If changes are made within the template directories, you will need to either manually copy them to the Logon Agent Directory, or directly edit the template files in the Logon Agent Directory. This logon form is used to collect the following information:

Username

Password

Domain

To simplify the application logic within the *Login.asp* script, form data must conform to a fixed set of named fields and buttons, as shown in Table 7-4.

The Logon Agent template consists of three configuration data files shown in the next three sections.

Form Element Name	Input Type	Description
CSG_UserName	TEXT	Input field for user name
CSG_UserPassword	PASSWORD	Input field for user password
CSG_UserDomain	TEXT	Input field for user domain
CSG_CmdDoLogon	SUBMIT	Button to submit logon request

Table 7-4. Form Data Conventions

AuthService_conf.asp   This is the main configuration file that contains customizable parameters.

AuthService.wsdl   This is a SOAP/WSDL definition file that specifies the methods and URL of the Authentication Service. This file must be present and must not be modified in any way.

Authenticate.xml   This is a template file that contains the SOAP XML message used for sending user credentials to the Authentication Service. This file must be present and must not be modified in any way.

The configuration parameters in *AuthService_conf.asp* that can be modified to customize the Logon Agent are listed in Table 7-5.

NOTE: The Logon Agent ASP script page is prefixed by a scripting block that performs user authentication processing. DO NOT modify the scripting block in any way. The scripting block is followed by the HTML content that constitutes the logon form displayed on the client web browser. Apart from the required form data elements as just described, the HTML content can be fully customized.

Parameter Name	Description	Possible Values
LP_PageTitleStr	A text string used as the title of the logon pages. This text string is shown in the client web browser title bar.	Any text.
LP_LogLevel	This is a numeric value defining the desired log level.	0 = Fatal 1 = Error + Fatal 2 = Warning + Error + Fatal 3 = All (Default)
LP_CookieSecure	If set to TRUE, all cookie values are marked as secure.	TRUE (Default) FALSE
LP_DomainMode	This is a numeric value that specifies the user domain mode.	0 = Default 1 = Forced domain 2 = Drop-down mode
LP_ForceLogonDomain	This is a text string defining the user domain to be used for all logon interactions.	A valid domain name.
LP_Domains	This is an array of strings defining the available domains.	List of valid domain names.
LP_DomainCount	This is a numeric value specifying the number of domain names to be included in the drop-down box.	This value must be one less than the actual number of strings in the LP_Domains array.

Table 7-5.   Configuration Parameters in *AuthService_conf.asp* to Customize the Logon Agent

CHAPTER 8

MetaFrame Password Manager: Planning and Deployment

The inability of users to remember passwords can be an impediment to an on-demand enterprise, especially as IT increasingly demands that the passwords be complex in format and that they change regularly. In order to deal with the problem, users frequently take one of three actions: they call the help desk when they forget a password (Gartner Research says 25% of Help Desk calls are password related), they write down their passwords on a sheet of paper in their drawer or on a sticky note, or they give up accessing certain applications from certain environments.

MetaFrame Password Manager helps to enable access infrastructure by providing password security and Single Sign On access to Windows, Web, proprietary, and host-based applications running in the MetaFrame Access Suite environment. Users authenticate once with a single password, and MetaFrame Password Manager does the rest, automatically logging into password-protected information systems, enforcing password policies, monitoring password-related events, and even automating end-user tasks, including password changes. MetaFrame Password Manager also works on standalone workstations or servers running Windows 2000 Professional, Windows XP, Windows 2000 Server, or Windows Server 2003.

This chapter covers various aspects of MetaFrame Password Manager including deployment models and scenarios, upgrading, working with MetaFrame Secure Access Manager MSAM), supporting Host Emulator Software, working with Novell authentication and with ZENWorks, and performance and scalability.

DEPLOYMENT MODELS AND SCENARIOS

This section details the most common deployment methods for MetaFrame Password Manager in various scenarios. The methods detailed will be MetaFrame Presentation Server's Installation Manager feature, Active Directory Group Policy Objects, and standard file sharing. We also look at integrating MetaFrame Password Manager with Distributed File System (DFS), file synchronization, user questions, and Entrust integration.

Install MetaFrame Password Manager

MetaFrame Password Manager consists of three primary components; the MetaFrame Password Manager Agent, the MetaFrame Password Manager Console, and the central credential store (the synchronization point). The agent runs in the background of the MetaFrame Presentation Server or desktop PC and links to a local credential store (database file) which stores the user password information. Credentials are also saved in the central store. The central store can be in a Microsoft NTFS File Share, Novell NetWare publicly accessible folder, or Microsoft Active Directory. The agent synchronizes the local store with the central store, allowing users to maintain their credentials from any workstation. The console is the administrator's management tool used to control all aspects of application password management. It is possible to deploy the MetaFrame Password Manager Agent by installing the agent from the installation CD and applying a *.reg* file with the synchronization point location; however, this is not the recommended approach.

Citrix recommends installing the MetaFrame Password Manager Agent from a custom Microsoft Installer (MSI) package. Instructions to generate a customized MSI package can be found in the *MetaFrame Password Manager Administrator's Guide*.

Agent Settings

When creating the MSI package, include agent settings that describe the synchronization point and any custom defined user questions.

Other Settings

The MetaFrame Password Manager Agent will obtain all other settings from the synchronization point, including application definitions, agent settings, and policies. These other settings should be deployed at the synchronization point. Creating a custom MSI with application definitions, agent settings, and custom passphrases configured will still result in the agent ignoring the custom MSI settings if they are not deployed at the synchronization point.

MetaFrame Presentation Server and Installation Manager

The MetaFrame Password Manager Agent must be installed on all MetaFrame Presentation Server systems that are hosting applications requiring authentication. The Enterprise Edition of MetaFrame Presentation Server 3.0 has a feature called Installation Manager that allows for efficient deployment of MSI-based installs across a MetaFrame Presentation Server farm. Installation Manager deploys the agent MSI in silent mode so no user interaction is needed for deployment on remote servers.

The following steps show how to quickly deploy MetaFrame Password Manager to your MetaFrame Presentation Server farm:

1. Create the custom agent MSI as detailed in the *MetaFrame Password Manager Administrator's Guide*.

2. Save or copy this MSI to a network share that will be accessible to all the servers in your farm.

3. Open the Presentation Server Console.

4. If Installation Manager was not previously configured with a network account, right-click on the Installation Manager node. Select Properties, and enter a valid administrator account, which has read access to the share above, and write access to all the servers to which you wish to deploy the package.

5. Right-click on the Packages node and select Add Package.

6. Browse to where you saved your custom MSI created previously.

7. Follow the Installation Manager prompts to deploy the package to all desired servers in the server farm (see the *MetaFrame Presentation Server Administrator's Guide* for details).

Use Installation Manager to Deploy an MSI Based on MetaFrame Password Manager 2.0

If using Installation Manager to deploy an MSI based on MetaFrame Password Manager 2.0, the following changes must be made to the registry in order to allow sessions to log off properly once applications are closed:

HKLM\SYSTEM\CurrentControlSet\Control\Citrix\wfshell\TWI
Value Name: LogoffCheckSysModules
Type: REG_SZ
String: ssoshell.exe,ssobho.exe,ssomho.exe

NOTE: MetaFrame Password Manager 2.5 does not experience this issue when deploying via Installation Manager.

Active Directory Group Policy Objects

Group Policy is a feature available in an Active Directory Domain and can be used to install software on systems within the domain. Detailed information on how to use Group Policy Objects can be found on the Microsoft Web site. If your server farm is in a pure Active Directory (AD) environment, you can use a Group Policy to deploy the MetaFrame Password Manager Agent by taking the following steps:

1. Create the desired custom MSI install as detailed in the *MetaFrame Password Manager Administrator's Guide.*

2. Save or copy this MSI to a network share that will be accessible to all the servers to which you wish to deploy.

3. Create a Group Policy Object for the groups of computers or users to which you wish to deploy the agent. (Search the Microsoft Knowledge Base (http://www .support.microsoft.com) for articles on how to use Group Policy Objects—there are many to choose from, depending on your particular environment.)

File Share Deployment

In smaller environments or in certain situations, deployment by file share may be desirable. The following steps show how to deploy MetaFrame Password Manager by file share:

1. Copy the agent MSI file from the MetaFrame Password Manager Installation CD (or your own custom MSI file) to a file share location, which is accessible to the machines on which you will deploy.

2. Make sure MSI 2.0, which is the Microsoft Installer Service, is already present on your machine.

3. Run the following command:

```
Msiexec /i <path_to_MSI_file_and_its_filename>
```

If you wish to suppress rebooting after the install, use the following:

```
Msiexec reboot=suppress /i <path_to_MSI_file_and_its_filename>
```

Integrate MetaFrame Password Manager with Distributed File System

The MetaFrame Password Manager File Synchronization Point is the file-based database that stores the user password information. The File Synchronization Point can be implemented using Windows 2000 or Windows Server 2003 Distributed File System (DFS). The ability to both distribute the workload across multiple servers and to provide fault tolerance are two of the reasons to consider using DFS as an alternative to a single synchronization point. The following steps enable configuration of DFS for use with MetaFrame Password Manager.

Step 1: Create a Domain DFS Root

The first step to integrating MetaFrame Password Manager with DFS is to create a Domain DFS Root.

NOTE: Creating a Domain DFS Root is not needed if your Windows Deployment already has one Domain DFS Root in place. If this is the case, then skip to "Step 2: Prepare the Shares for MetaFrame Password Manager."

1. Open the MMC Snap-in for the DFS, typically located in Start | Programs | Administrative Tools | Distributed File System.
2. Right-click on the Distributed File System Icon and select the option New DFS Root.
3. Click Next.
4. Select Create a Domain DFS Root.
5. Click Next.
6. Select the host domain of the DFS Root.
7. Click Next.
8. Select the name of the host server for this DFS Root.
9. Click Next.
10. Either use an existing share on the server or create a new share to host the DFS tree.
11. Click Next.
12. Type a name for the DFS Root.
13. Click Finish.

Step 2: Prepare the Shares for MetaFrame Password Manager

After creating a Domain DFS Root, the shares hosting the File Synchronization Point should be created in the designated servers. The *ctxfilesyncprep* utility will be used; it will create the directory c:\citrixsync on the C:\ Drive and shares it as \\%servername%\ citrixsync$ assigning the proper permissions.

1. On two or more Windows 2000/2003 Servers open a command prompt.
2. Insert the MetaFrame Password Manager Distribution CD.
3. Type **CD x:** where *x* is the letter of your CD-ROM, and then click ENTER.
4. Type **CD x:\Tools** and press ENTER.
5. Type **ctxfilesyncprep.exe** and then press ENTER.

Step 3: Create the DFS Link

The third step of the process is creating a DFS link to host the first of the shares created in Step 2. The share name used for the DFS link is **citrixsync$**.

1. Open the MMC Snap-in for the Distributed File System, typically located in Start I Programs I Administrative Tools I Distributed File System.
2. Right-click on the New DFS Root and select New DFS Link.
3. In the Link Name field enter **citrixsync$**.
4. In the Shared Folder, insert the UNC Location (**%server1name%\citrixsync$**) of the first server hosting the Synchronization Point.
5. Press OK.

Step 4: Add the Replicas

In order to have a redundant, fault-tolerant solution, replicas should be added to the synchronization point. The replicas will be the additional server shares that we created on the other servers.

1. Open the MMC Snap-in for the Distributed File System, typically located in Start I Programs I Administrative Tools I Distributed File System.
2. Right-click on the DFS Link created in Step 3 and select New Replica.
3. In the Send User to this Shared Folder field, insert the UNC Location (**%server2name%\citrixsync$**) of the server hosting the other synchronization point prepared in the section titled "Step 2: Prepare the Shares for MetaFrame Password Manager."
4. Change Replication Policy from Manual Replication to Automatic Replication.
5. Click OK.

6. On the following screen, highlight the first server and Enable Replication.

7. Highlight the second server and Enable Replication.

8. Click OK.

9. Repeat Steps 2 through 8 for each of the servers.

Step 5: Connect to the Share from the Console

Connecting to the DFS Share Folder and configuring MetaFrame Password Manager to export the configuration to the synchronization point is the final task of the procedure.

In order to successfully connect, the agents and the console must be part of the domain where the DFS was created.

1. Deploy the MetaFrame Password Manager on a workstation that is part of the same Active Directory Domain.

2. Log on with a user that has administrative rights to the active directory domain and select Directory | Connect To | Shared Folder.

3. The Shared folder name will be **activedirectorydomainname****DFS****citrixsync$**.

Step 6: Distributed File System Replication

The final step to configuring DFS for use with MetaFrame Password Manager is to implement file system replication.

Replica Synchronization   Replica Synchronization is managed by the File Replication Service (FRS). FRS operates on Windows Active Directory Domain Controllers and Member Servers. It is a multithreaded, multimaster replication engine that replicates system policies, login scripts, fault tolerant DFS Root and Child nodes Replicas.

FRS replicates whole files in sequential order according to when files are closed, meaning the entire file will be replicated even if only a single byte in the file is changed.

Changes for intersite replication are set using a three second aging cache so only the last iteration of a file that is constantly modified is sent to the replica members.

Five minutes is the maximum replication value for servers hosting replicas, but it can be only seconds if the server is not overwhelmed.

Knowledge Consistency Checker   In Active Directory deployments, the Knowledge Consistency Checker (KCC) is responsible for building NT Domain Services (NTDS) connection objects to form a well-connected topology between domain controllers in the domain and the forest.

RepAdmin.exe   *RepAdmin.exe* is a utility available in the *support.cab* archive of the Windows 2000 Servers' Installation CD, which can be used to check if replication is taking place using the default intervals for intersite replication. The default intervals are once every 3 hours between domain controllers in different sites (the minimum is 15 minutes).

FRS Tuning References The following two Microsoft Knowledge Base articles will be useful for administrators to set up and tune the FRS:

▼ Microsoft Knowledge Base article 220938: Description of the FRS Replication Protocol, Notification and Schedule for DFS Content

▲ Microsoft Knowledge Base article 224512: FRS Builds Full-Mesh Replication Topology for Replicated DFS ROOT and Child Replicas

File Synchronization and MetaFrame Password Manager

In MetaFrame Password Manager, the agent acts as an intermediary between users and applications that require authentication. MetaFrame Password Manager can be configured to synchronize with a Microsoft NTFS File Share, Novell NetWare publicly accessible folder, or Microsoft Active Directory. When configuring MetaFrame Password Manager to synchronize with a shared folder, the administrator may do any of the following:

▼ Create multiple sets of user credentials for an agent and store them centrally

■ Define a shared folder to synchronize information between the MetaFrame Password Manager Console and Agent

▲ Define individual file synchronizations for individual users

Configure Synchronization Points

Synchronization points can be configured with the MetaFrame Password Manager tools. From a command prompt, access the /Tools directory on the MetaFrame Password Manager CD and type the following:

CtxFileSyncPrep /Path:<*pathname*> /Share:<*sharename*>

Run the following tool for each individual synchronization point to be deployed:

Tools>ctxfilesyncprep /Path:c:\%username% /Share: %username%

Once the above command has been run, the shared folder and people folder are created with appropriate sharing and security permissions, and the shared folders are now ready to be used for synchronization.

NOTE: Citrix recommends that you do not use the system volume to host the synchronization folder.

To use the Novell NetWare File Synchronization setup tool, at a command prompt, access the /Tools directory on the MetaFrame Password Manager CD-ROM, and type

CtxNWFileSyncPrep /path:<*UNCpath*>

You must include the path parameter, and it must be specified using the following format:

*<NetWare server>**<volume>*\\folder

NOTE: The use of Novell NetWare File Synchronization requires that users' Novell password be identical to their Windows NT password.

Prepare for Per User File Synchronization

Confirm the following before configuring Per User File Synchronization:

▼   Each synchronization point has been created using the *CtxFileSyncPrep* or *CtxNWFileSyncPrep* tools.

■   Each client workstation has MetaFrame Password Manager Agent installed.

▲   Each MetaFrame Password Manager Agent has been configured to use File Synchronization [In the console, configure a synchronizer of type Microsoft NTFS File Share (or Novell NetWare File Share) but do not configure a synchronization point and push this registry file to the agent.]

The main purpose for configuring the client workstation with a synchronizer of type Microsoft NTFS File Share or Novell NetWare File Share with no synchronization point is to preserve the hierarchy of precedence, meaning that the agent should use the HKCU synch point first, unless the registry file is pushed out, in which case it will read the location from HKLM first and ignore the location specified in the HKCU. If there is a synchronization point defined in the registry file pushed out to agent workstations, the following will populate the field:

HKLM\Software\Citrix\MetaFrame Password Manager\Extensions\ SyncManager\Syncs\%SyncName%\Server1\Server1

If a value exists under HKLM under Server1, then the agents will automatically be directed to this synchronization point without checking HKCU for a server entry.

User File Synchronization

User File Synchronization can be used to ensure that users who work on a laptop or other computer that is often disconnected from the network can have their password information synchronized to their network environment. To configure User File Synchronization, perform the following steps:

1.   Log into the user workstation as the user that is being configured to use a specific synchronization point.

2.   As each user, enter the user's corresponding share as a Registry String Value in the Windows registry hive:

HKCU\Software\Citrix\MetaFrame Password Manager\Extensions

3. Create a new key called **SyncManager**.

4. Under the SyncManager key, create a new string value called **Server1**.

5. For the Server1 string, set the Value Data to the full UNC path for the user's corresponding file share.

6. Restart the agent.

7. Configure the agent and confirm that agent settings correspond to the synchronization point.

8. Repeat these steps for each user that requires an individually configured file synchronization point.

If users only work on one machine, then the user's local MMF file will be stored only on that machine. In theory, the Days Before Delete setting could be set to 0 without any issues in a single machine scenario. If the scenario is different, however, and the user roams to different machines, has a laptop and a desktop, or uses multiple servers in a MetaFrame Presentation Server farm, then you should set this value to something higher than 0 (the default is 30 days). See the section titled "Set the Days Before Delete Variable" for more detailed information on this setting.

CAUTION: Under any scenario other than a single machine, with Days Before Delete set to zero, the MetaFrame Password Manager Agents would conflict with each other by deleting and re-adding credentials.

Configure Per User File Synchronization

The eight steps to configure file synchronization are as follows:

1. Log into the user workstation as the user that is being configured to use a specific synchronization point.

2. As each user, enter the user's corresponding share as a Registry String Value in the Windows registry hive

    HKCU\Software\Citrix\MetaFrame Password Manager\Extensions

3. Create a new key called **SyncManager**

4. Under the SyncManager key, create a new string value called **Server1**

5. For the Server1 string, set the Value Data to the full UNC path for the user's corresponding file share.

6. Restart the agent.

7. Configure the agent and confirm that agent settings correspond to the synchronization point.

8. Repeat these steps for each user that requires an individually configured file synchronization point.

NOTE: MetaFrame Presentation Server 3.0 now contains a policy for specifying the synchronization point for a user. Open the Presentation Server Console, and view the properties of a policy. The MetaFrame Password Manager policies are located under User Workspace | MetaFrame Password Manager. The synchronization point policy is titled Central Credential Store.

User Questions with MetaFrame Password Manager

A user who begins using MetaFrame Password Manager for the first time is required to define secondary credentials by selecting an identity verification question (also referred to as a *user question*) and providing an answer to this question. The combination of question and answer is known as the identity verification phrase. The process of creating the identity verification phrase must be completed before MetaFrame Password Manager will begin working for a user.

First Time User Profile Setup

The first part of the profile setup procedure is where the users are prompted to enter their Windows domain credentials. After successfully authenticating their user credentials, they will be prompted to answer the user question. Whichever user question the user answers (custom created, or default) will be the one that is permanently linked with their data.

Whenever the user's window domain passwords are changed, the MetaFrame Password Manager Agent will ask the user question (in order to identify the user), and the user will need to provide the answer they originally entered during the initial profile setup. In this situation, the user's password storage databases will be opened and the new windows domain password will be updated.

Since the user question is stored in the First Time User (FTU) list where it is encrypted. The user question also serves to protect the user's password database from the administrator, who could easily change a user's windows domain password, but would not know the user's answer to the user question.

User Question GUID

Each question has its own Globally Unique ID (GUID), meaning that if the administrator modifies the user question, the GUID does not change and the users can open their databases by answering the modified questions with their old answers. In some cases, the questions can be misleading and the text of the question should not be modified if users have already answered the question. Please refer to the example in the *MetaFrame Password Manager Administrator's Guide*.

The answer is stored in the user's database with the Question GUID. Once the user question has been answered, the answer cannot be modified nor can the user switch to a different user question and provide a different answer.

Custom User Questions

Currently, if the administrator creates a custom user question and then later deletes the *FTUlist.ini* file from the synchronization point, any users that answered any user question from that file will not be able to unlock their password storage database when their password is changed.

On the console, when an administrator creates a custom user question it cannot be deleted, only disabled. It can be overwritten from another console, or deleted manually from the file system or AD tree.

Administrators can use extended characters when creating custom user questions. Users also can use extended characters when answering their user question.

Overwrite the FTU File

If multiple administrators are working on different consoles and a second administrator overwrites the FTU file that was created by the first administrator on the synchronization point, then all user questions that the first administrator created will be overwritten.

In order to avoid this situation, a centralized XML file should be used for the console. Whenever the second administrator opens the console, the administrator needs to import all of the objects from the synchronization point by using Bring to Console. The administrator can modify or make changes to the current settings once they have been successfully loaded.

Delete a User Profile

An administrator can delete a user profile by deleting all the data from the following points:

▼ HKCU\Software\Citrix\MetaFrame Password Manager.

■ The folder from C:\Documents and Settings\<*username*>\ApplicationData\ Citrix\MetaFrame Password Manager.

■ For file synchronization: The data from the user's folder under the People folder on the File Synchronization.

▲ For Active Directory synchronization: Delete the SSOConfig objects from under the user's object in the Active Directory.

Disable the Default Identity Verification Question

When creating the identity verification phrase during the FTU setup, in MetaFrame Password Manager 2.0, and by default in MetaFrame Password Manager 2.5, end users can choose from console defined questions or the default question. Since the default question does not provide the user with any clue as to what the answer might have been, some administrators see this as a source of confusion. Disabling this question will allow administrators to further customize the user experience by controlling the set of questions from which the users can choose.

Administrators must be careful with this option as it may prevent existing users from authenticating to the agent. When users are challenged to answer their identity verification question and their chosen question is no longer defined or no longer available, they will be unable to authenticate themselves to MetaFrame Password Manager. It is therefore important to disable this default question before users begin using the agent. This will ensure that an existing user's identity verification question is not disabled.

If the administrator disables the default question without creating or enabling any custom questions, new users will be unable to configure the agent for First Time Use. Users will receive an error message that states, "No identity Verification questions have been configured. Please contact your administrator."

To disable the default identity verification question, complete the following:

Under Agent Settings | Authenticator in the MetaFrame Password Manager Console, set

```
"IdentityVerification" = "Disable Default Question"
```

Set the Days Before Delete Variable

This setting is important because it allows the agent to remember what credentials have been deleted. It remembers them for the specified amount of time so that the user will have the opportunity to synchronize all the MetaFrame Password Manager Agents on the other machines. The Delete on Shutdown setting will not affect this since the data is stored in the MMF file and then synchronized to the synchronization point as the agent is shutting down. The following steps are an example of what could happen if the agent deleted the credentials without remembering:

1. The user runs the MetaFrame Password Manager Agent on ComputerA (for example, the user's desktop PC).

2. The user adds credentials for AppA.

3. AppA's credential is stored in the local MMF and synchronized to the central credential store.

4. The user then runs the agent on ComputerB (for example, the user's laptop PC).

5. The MetaFrame Password Manager Agent gets synchronized and AppA gets stored in the local MMF on ComputerB.

6. The user decides to delete AppA's credential and it is removed from the local MMF and the central credential store.

7. Later that day the user logs back onto ComputerA.

8. The agent on ComputerA synchronizes with the central credential store. It still has AppA's credential stored in its local MMF, but it does not see this credential in the central credential store; therefore it adds the AppA credential back.

In summary, with Days Before Delete set to zero, the MetaFrame Password Manager Agents would be conflicting with each other by deleting and re-adding credentials.

MetaFrame Password Manager and Entrust Integration

MetaFrame Password Manager and Entrust/PKI (public-key infrastructure) Authority can be successfully integrated deploying Entrust Authority in a Windows 2000 Active Directory Domain and leveraging Microsoft Lightweight Directory Access Protocol (LDAP) implementation with Entrust Certificates. Once the Entrust Authority has been deployed and the Entrust client packaged and configured on a per-user base, MetaFrame Password Manager can be integrated in the environment. This can be done by following certain steps for the AD Schema for Entrust, Certification Authority deployment, Certification Authority initialization, client configuration, and for MetaFrame Password Manager Agent deployment.

The following versions were used during the Citrix *e*Labs testing: Entrust Software Versions 6.01 for the Authority Server and 6.1 SP1 for the Entrust Client Entelligence–Desktop Solutions.

Modify the AD Schema for Entrust

To modify the Active Directory Schema to support Entrust, perform the following steps:

1. On the Domain Controller that is the Schema Master, logon with a user who is part of the Domain Admins and Schema Admins Groups and extend the schema.
2. Insert the Entrust/PKI Authority CD in the CD-ROM drive, navigate to the \Utilities folder and run *entadconfig.exe* to start the Entrust Active Directory Configuration Wizard.
3. Select the Entrust/Authority checkbox.
4. Select Configure the Active Directory Schema.
5. Create a CA Entry for Entrust/Authority and give it a name.
6. Publish the CA Certificate in the Certification Authorities Container.
7. Create a New Domain Account or Use an Existing one.
8. Grant Access for Entrust Authority to Existing Users.
9. Execute the changes and save the log.

Certification Authority Deployment

To deploy the Certification Authority, perform the following steps:

1. The first step will be the deployment of the Informix Database, needed to create the Entrust/Authority Database.
2. The server used for Entrust should be different from the Active Directory Domain Controller for security reasons.
3. The Certification Authority will be installed after the Informix Database.
4. The Authority will require licensing information such as Serial Number, Enterprise User Limit, and Enterprise Licensing Code.

5. The following screen will ask for Directory Node and Port. Enable the Using Microsoft Active Directory checkbox.

6. The following screen will require the fully qualified name of the Domain Controller.

7. Next, the Authority will require a distinguished name, which may be customized if required by the deployment scenario.

8. Confirm the CA Name.

9. The Directory Attributes dialog box should be left as LDAP Version 3 with the default transfer mode dimmed.

10. Enter the CA Name. Use the same name and password specified when configuring AD.

11. On the Advanced Directory Attributes, type the First Officer Domain Name.

12. Verify directory information.

13. After a short wait, the ENTDVT Log File dialog box appears and will show Directory Verification completed successfully.

14. The current User's Windows Login Password is needed to start Entrust Services and is the login and the password for the Entrust/Authority Service to start when logging to Entrust/Authority Master Control.

15. Select Yes for the Microsoft Crypto-API enabled application Interoperability Setup window.

16. On the Entrust Authority Port Configuration, review the default data and make sure that the node name is the one of the server that is running the Entrust Authority.

17. In the Cryptographic Information dialog box, choose the required parameters for the deployment.

18. Select a lifetime for the CA and complete the CA configuration.

Certification Authority Initialization

The Entrust/PKI Authority must be initialized before it can be used. During the Initialization Process, the three Master Users and the First Officer should be present.

1. In the Entrust/Authority Master Control window, choose Log In.

2. A dialog box will appear stating that the initialization will take a few minutes.

3. After an Initial Password Entry dialog box appears, each of the three Master Users and the First Officer must privately choose, type, and verify their passwords.

4. The next screen will communicate that the installation was successful.

5. Logon with one of the Master Users or First Officer accounts and start the Entrust/Authority Service.

Client Configuration

To configure the client, perform the following steps:

1. On the Authority Server, start the Authority/RA Console Administration Program and enumerate the users in the Active Directory Domain.

2. Open the Properties Page of the user you would like to add to Entrust, and add it.

3. Note the reference number and the authorization code.

4. On a workstation, deploy the Entelligence Desktop Designer and create a deployment package. Deploy the package to the client workstation and change the *entrust.ini* initialization file to point to the correct Authority and Directory Server.

5. Log onto the client with the user you added to Entrust Authority.

6. Create a new Entrust User Profile. Specify the Reference Number and the authorization code.

7. Assign the user a password and log onto Entrust.

MetaFrame Password Manager Agent Deployment

To deploy the agent and create a new application definition with the console for the Entrust Logon, complete the following steps:

1. Open the Console.

2. Select Applications Node.

3. Select New Windows App.

4. Enter **Entrust Login** as name.

5. Select Detect Field Wizard.

6. Select Logon.

7. Right-click the Entrust Icon and select Log Into Entrust.

8. Refresh the Form Wizard and select Entrust Login Form.

9. Define UserID as Combo Box, Password, and OK Button.

10. Save the definition and send to the synchronization point.

11. Because Entrust doesn't use standard calls to the OS, the logon screen provided by Entrust is not detected automatically by MetaFrame Password Manager. When new users need to log onto Entrust they should right-click the MetaFrame Password Manager Icon and select Log On Using MetaFrame Password Manager.

UPGRADE METAFRAME PASSWORD MANAGER

If you are not using custom user questions in your MetaFrame Password Manager deployment and are not adding new software that changes the GINA chain, follow the normal installation instructions found in the *MetaFrame Password Manager Administrator's Guide*. Only the MetaFrame Password Manager Agent installation affects the GINA chain. If you are installing new software or want to save custom user questions, there are several upgrade considerations with respect to both GINA altering software and user questions.

Upgrade Considerations with GINA Altering Software

The recommended upgrade installation path from MetaFrame Presentation Server XP, Feature Release 3 with MetaFrame Password Manager 2.0 is to first upgrade to the latest version of MetaFrame Presentation Server 3.0, and then to upgrade the MetaFrame Password Manager installation to version 2.5.

CAUTION: If you are installing another software package that uses a custom GINA in addition to upgrading to MetaFrame Password Manager 2.5, install the MetaFrame Password Manager Agent *last*. This installation order is required to ensure that the GINA chain is never broken. GINA software cannot identify its location within the chain. The GINA knows what was there when it was installed, but after that it can never be sure because other applications may alter the GINA chain without notifying the other GINAs involved. Since MetaFrame Password Manager has no current mechanism to track the state of the GINA chain, administrators should verify that MetaFrame Password Manager is always the last GINA-related software installed.

Third Party Custom GINAs

If software that uses a custom GINA is installed after you install the MetaFrame Password Manager Agent, it may prevent your users from logging onto the agent. See "Preserving the GINA Chain" in the *MetaFrame Password Manager Administrator's Guide* for more information.

NOTE: You do not need to upgrade all of your MetaFrame Password Manager 2.0 agents to MetaFrame Password Manager 2.5 at the same time. Agents running MetaFrame Password Manager 2.0 are able to communicate with a central credential store that has been updated by MetaFrame Password Manager 2.5. It must be noted that agents running MetaFrame Password Manager 2.0 will not reflect the new features until they are upgraded.

Upgrade Considerations with User Questions (Formerly Known as Passphrase)

If MetaFrame Password Manager 2.0 was initially deployed with custom user questions, the MetaFrame Password Manager Administrator will need to make special considerations when upgrading to the latest version. Custom user questions are assigned a unique

GUID when they are originally created. That GUID is how the questions are referenced in the code. Recreating the same question on a new installation will not result in the same GUID and will be treated as a different question.

Users cannot re-authenticate if the user question they originally answered is not displayed by the agent. To preserve the original questions and their associated GUIDs, the questions must be imported from the existing synchronization point and used for any Custom MSI packages or FTU related activities. To preserve the existing user questions, follow the steps in the section titled "Retrieve Previous MetaFrame Password Manager Data."

Retrieve Previous MetaFrame Password Manager Data

When upgrading Password Manager, there are five steps to follow in order to retrieve previous data:

1. Upgrade or install the MetaFrame Password Manager 2.5 Console.

2. In the console, highlight the Directory node, right-click and select the Connect To option.

3. Specify your synchronization point type and path (if applicable).

4. Once connected, locate the MetaFrame Password Manager objects from the right pane of the console.

5. Highlight each one, right-click, and select Bring to Console.

Save Data to the Synchronization Point

There are two steps to follow in order to save existing and new data to the synchronization point prior to performing an upgrade. Following these steps will ensure that no user data gets overwritten with new questions and will prevent the configured users from losing access to their credentials.

1. Add any new applications, settings, and user questions to the settings previously retrieved.

2. Highlight the synchronization point or Organizational Unit (OU), right-click, and select Configure SSO Support to push this new data back out to the synchronization point.

USE METAFRAME PASSWORD MANAGER WITH METAFRAME SECURE ACCESS MANAGER

MetaFrame Password Manager and MetaFrame Secure Access Manager (MSAM) combine to solve a set of enterprise access needs around security, aggregation, and personalization services. While Password Manager is designed to integrate well with MSAM, there are some considerations of which administrators should be aware in regard to working with MSAM CDAs.

Access Center CDAs and the MSAM Login Page

MetaFrame Password Manager does not autorecognize most MSAM access center CDAs or the MSAM login page. The administrator must create web application definitions in order for these to work with MetaFrame Password Manager.

Certain CDAs use Windows authentication and are exceptions to this rule (such as, Lotus Notes, Exchange, and Share Point) and no further configuration at the administrator console is required.

MSAM 2.0 Issues

With MSAM 2.0, if an administrator defines a web application definition for the login page and then pushes this out to the agents, whenever an agent machine logs out from an MSAM site, the user will automatically get logged back into MSAM. The end user should either close their browser or the administrator should not define the login page. To correct this problem, the administrator can install MSAM 2.0 SP1 or later on their MSAM servers.

Password Manager Control of CDAs

Every CDA on each MSAM page, which the end user wishes to have under MetaFrame Password Manager's control, must be individually defined as individual web application definitions within the MetaFrame Password Manager Administrator Console.

CDAs modified through CDA pad and then redeployed to MSAM will require the creation of a new web application definition.

 NOTE: It is advisable to define the Submit button when generating MSAM web application definitions.

Add and Copy CDAs

MSAM administrators can move CDAs around in a page and MetaFrame Password Manager will recognize them with no adverse effects. However, CDAs that are added to a page, copied, or that are moved from one page to another (or one folder to another) require the creation of a new web application definition. Exporting and importing a portal does not require new web application definitions.

Multiple CDA Password Requirements

MetaFrame Password Manager will log into MSAM CDAs on a given page serially. In the event that the end user has many CDAs requiring passwords, several page redraws will ensue.

MetaFrame Password Manager Handling CDA Logins

If you want MetaFrame Password Manager to handle the login of a CDA, you must disable the autologin feature in the given CDA's Advanced Configuration Wizard.

SUPPORT HOST EMULATOR SOFTWARE WITH METAFRAME PASSWORD MANAGER

MetaFrame Password Manager has the ability to provide Single Sign On for mainframe applications as well as Windows and web applications.

MetaFrame Password Manager Requirements for Host Emulator Software Support

The following requirements must be met before MetaFrame Password Manager can detect and interact with a mainframe application:

1. Host/Mainframe emulator program must support HLLAPI. (For more information on HLLAPI, see section "What is HLLAPI?".)

2. The HLLAPI short session name must be defined and unique to the current user's desktop session.

3. Host/Mainframe emulator program must be defined in the *mfrmlist.ini* file located on the agent at %Program Files%\Citrix\MetaFrame Password Manager\Helper\Emulator

4. Enable Host/Mainframe support on the agent by choosing one of the following methods:

   - **From the agent** Click the Password Manager Systray icon and choose Configuration | Settings. Select the Host/Mainframe tab and click the Enable Host/Mainframe support checkbox.

   - **From the central console** Select AgentSettings | AccessManager | HostMainFrameSupport | Host/Mainframe Support Enabled. Push settings to the synchronization point and have the agent synchronize.

5. Create a host application definition. For more information on this process, refer to the *MetaFrame Password Manager Administrator's Guide*.

What is HLLAPI?

HLLAPI is short for High Level Language Application Program Interface, an IBM API standard that allows a PC application to communicate with a host computer, such as an IBM iSeries or zSeries host. HLLAPI requires PC emulation software and then defines a set of APIs that allow other PC applications to interface with the emulation software.

Telnet and MetaFrame Password Manager

MetaFrame Password Manager requires that the host/mainframe emulator support the use of HLLAPI. Most emulators do not support the use of HLLAPI for telnet applications. During testing, Citrix found that the only HLLAPI implementation that worked reliably with telnet was NetManage Rumba. The symptoms indicate that the problem revolves around the interpretation of the @T and @E symbols sent by HLLAPI for the TAB and ENTER keys. Apparently, most emulators interpret these symbols incorrectly when working with a VT100 application, yet they work fine when tested with 3270/5250 mainframe displays. For now, the only supported telnet application is NetManage Rumba.

Display the Password Field with Telnet Another issue with using telnet is that the password field is not displayed until a username is entered. Therefore, host definitions need to have two separate forms configured, one for the username and another for the password.

Configure HLLAPI Support for Supported Emulators

The following is an example of how to setup HLLAPI support for some of the emulator programs that ship with MetaFrame Password Manager.

NOTE: After installing a Host/Mainframe emulator program, you must reboot the server.

Attachmate Extra! 6.4 Attachmate Extra! version 6.4 terminal emulation software can be configured for use with MetaFrame Password Manager by following these steps:

1. Install Attachmate. Reboot the machine.
2. Select File | Create New Session.
3. Choose type of session, such as 3270 Display. Click Next.
4. Choose type of connection, such as TN3270. Click Next.
5. Click Add and enter the IP address of your host machine. Click Next.
6. Choose type of transfer. Click Finish.
7. Verify your information and Click OK.
8. In the new window, select File | Save Session As....Choose a filename (e.g., *IBM-Mainframe.EDP*) and click Save.
9. Back in the new "IBM-Mainframe - myEXTRA! For Windows 95/NT" window, select Options | GlobalPreference.
10. Click the Advanced tab. Choose a Short Session letter (A–Z) that is unique for this emulator.
11. Click Browse, select your session (e.g., *IBM-Mainframe.EDP*), and click Open. Click OK.

12. Exit Attachmate.

13. Run Attachmate. Choose the existing session and open *IBM-Mainframe.EDP*. If the agent is configured with the host application definition, it should recognize the connection screen and pop up the form to enter the credentials for storage.

Attachmate myEXTRA! Enterprise 7.11   Attachmate myEXTRA! Enterprise version 7.11 terminal emulation software can be configured for use with MetaFrame Password Manager by following these steps:

1. Select File | Create New Session.

2. Select session type, such as IBM AS/400, click Next.

3. Select display type, such as 5250 Display, click Next.

4. Select connection protocol, such as TN5250, click Next.

5. Type the host address into the HostName field, click Next.

6. Select None, click Next.

7. Click Finish.

8. In the new window, select File | Save Session As....

9. Choose a filename (like *Session1.EDP*) and click Save.

10. Back in the new "Session1 - myEXTRA! Enterprise" window, select Options | GlobalPreferences.

11. Click the Advanced tab.

12. Choose a Short Session letter [A–Z] that is unique for this emulator.

13. Click Browse.

14. Select your session (like *Session1.EDP*) and click Open. Click OK.

15. Exit Attachmate.

16. Run Attachmate.

17. Select File | Session1.EDP to load the session you just saved. It should now use the Short Session name assigned.

WRQ Reflection for IBM 10.0.4   WRQ Reflection for IBM version 10.0.4 terminal emulation software can be configured for use with MetaFrame Password Manager by following these steps:

1. Connection, choose Session Setup, and enter the IP address of the Host.

2. Select Setup | View Settings. At the Reflection settings, find "HLLAPI Short Name"; at the Settings details, enter Short Name for [A–Z]. Click OK.

3. Go to File | Save As and save the session with a name. For example, *Test.rsf*.

4. When opening WRQ, choose to open the saved session; the MetaFrame Password Manager should recognize it if the host application definition is created properly.

NetManage Rumba Office 7.2   NetManage Rumba Office version 7.2 terminal emulation software can be configured for use with MetaFrame Password Manager by following these steps:

1. Go to Rumba and open the AS/400 Display or Mainframe Display.

2. Choose Options | API... | Session Short Name, and assign a session name that is unique [A–Z]. Save the session with a unique name.

3. When opening Rumba, choose to open the saved session; the MetaFrame Password Manager should recognize it if the host application definition is created properly.

IBM Personal Communications 5.6   IBM Personal Communications version 5.6 terminal emulation software can be configured for use with MetaFrame Password Manager by following these steps:

1. Go to IBM Personal Communications and run Start and Configure Sessions.

2. Choose New Session. Note that this version is HLLAPI enabled by default and it also creates the short name for sessions by default; this emulator does not need any additional configuration except the IP/Host Name.

3. In the Link Parameters, enter the Host Name or IP Address. Save it and run it.

Zephyr 2002-621 PASSPORT PC-to-Host   Zephyr 2003-621 PASSPORT PC-to-HOST terminal emulation software can be configured for use with MetaFrame Password Manager by following these steps:

1. Go to PASSPORT and launch PASSPORT PC-to-Host.

2. In the setup, enter the IP or Host address. Check that HLAPPI is set to Automatically Select.

> **NOTE:**   If desired, you can switch to Manually Select, but you will need to choose the Short Name [A–Z].

Scanpak Aviva for Terminal Servers   Scanpak Aviva for Terminal Servers terminal emulation software can be configured for use with MetaFrame Password Manager by following these steps:

1. Run Destination Wizard. Enter names for *new destination, connection,* and *emulator type.* For example: IBMTest, TN3270, and 3270 Display.

2. On the next page, enter destination IP or Host address. Enter display properties. On the third page, click Finish.

204
Citrix MetaFrame Access Suite Advanced Concepts: The Official Guide

3. Run Session Wizard. Enter name, choose Display type, and choose the session you want to base on. On the third screen, choose the destination you created in Step 2. On the last screen, click Finish.

4. Run the created session. Go to Session | Properties | Automation, and check in HLLAPI support: Choose the first available Short Name, or you can choose it manually.

BosaNova   BosaNova terminal emulation software can be configured for use with MetaFrame Password Manager by following these steps:

1. Install the emulator.

2. Go to the Administrator icon. It should open Connectivity (connection type); choose Configure. Click Add and enter Host address. Click Run to make a connection.

NEXUS   NEXUS terminal emulation software can be configured for use with MetaFrame Password Manager by following these steps:

1. Install the emulator.

2. Go to Session | API Setup and choose Short Name. Enable HLLAPI for current session and as a default.

3. Go to Session | Session Setup and enter the Host address.

PowerTerm   PowerTerm terminal emulation software can be configured for use with MetaFrame Password Manager by following these steps:

1. Install Power Term Pro.

2. Open the emulator. It will launch Connect setup.

3. Choose IBM at the left panel. Choose protocol 5250 Display or 3270 Display.

4. Apply the settings. Click Setup at the bottom. Go to General tab and enter **Short "A"** name for HLLAPI Names.

Create MFRMLIST.INI Entries

As mentioned earlier in the chapter, for MetaFrame Password Manager to recognize applications for a specific host emulator program, HLLAPI support is required. The method that MetaFrame Password Manager uses to locate installed emulators is simple. At startup, if Mainframe/Host Emulator support is enabled, SSOShell spawns the *SSOMHO.EXE* process. When this process is started, it first reads the *MFRMLIST.INI* file located at %Program Files%\Citrix\MetaFrame Password Manager\Helper\Emulator. The process then looks for all the configured emulators and attempts to load the HLLAPI DLL assigned in the file. A sample section of this file is included here:

```
[Emulators]
Ver=20040510
EMU1=Rumba6
EMU2=Attachmate myExtra!
EMU3=Attachmate Extra! 6.3
EMU4=Attachmate Extra! 6.4
EMU5=Attachmate Extra! 6.5
EMU6=Attachmate Extra! 2000
EMU7=Attachmate Extra! 7.1
EMU8=Reflection7
EMU9=Reflection8
EMU10=Reflection9
EMU11=Reflection10
EMU12=PCOM
EMU13=HostOnDemand 4.0
EMU14=Aviva
EMU15=ViewNow
EMU16=ZephyrPC
EMU17=BOSaNOVA
EMU18=Nexus
EMU19=PowerTermPro
EMU20=Rumba Web2Host Client
EMU21=PowerTermEnterprise
[Rumba6]
DisplayName=Rumba
RegistryLoc=WALLDATA\Install
ValueName=
DLLFile=SYSTEM\EHLAPI32.DLL
UpdateNotificationHandling=0.FirstLogin
Process=shared
ConvertPosType=long
QuerySessionsType=long
QuerySessionStatusType=long
QueryHostUpdateType=long
StartNotificationType=long
IntSize=16
WindowClass=WdPageFrame
WindowTitle=RUMBA
```

Emulator Entries

The emulator entries in the [Emulators] section of the *MFRMLIST.INI* file must be in sequence (EMU1–EMU21). Any break in sequence will cause the SSOMHO process to terminate before reading all the entries. The values EMU1–EMU99 are acceptable. To comment out an entry, complete the following steps:

1. Move the entry to the bottom of the list.
2. Place a semicolon (;) in front of the entry.
3. Renumber the EMU entries so no numeric value is skipped.

Removing or commenting out any emulators that will not be used in the deployment can improve the SSOMHO startup process. By removing the additional entries, SSOMHO will not waste resources or time scanning for the location of the HLLAPI DLLs.

MFRMLIST.INI File

Since there is no method within MetaFrame Password Manager to globally update this *MFRMLIST.INI* file, administrators will need to manually overwrite the file after installing the agent using other means. For large deployments, Citrix recommends using batch files or scripts run through Microsoft System Management Server (SMS), CA-Unicenter, or Active Directory Software installation.

Create a New MFRMLIST.INI Entry

Not all emulators will function by creating new *MFRMLIST.INI* entries. The success depends on whether they follow the HLLAPI standard used by an existing emulator that is currently supported. The only way to determine if the vendor's implementation will work with MetaFrame Password Manager is to test it.

Table 8-1 defines the *MFRMLIST.INI* entries.

Entry	Value
[*EmulatorName*]	The value for EmulatorName must match the value used for the EMU*nn*=*EmulatorName* line in the [Emulators] section.
GroupName	Used for displaying information in a debug dialog. Can be any value in the retail build.
DisplayName	The display name of the emulator, which will be one of the two parameters used when spawning a new process to handle the session. Should be unique to the *MFRMLIST.INI* file.
RegistryLoc	The registry key in HKLM\Software that points to the path where the HLLAPI DLL is stored. If the program does not store this information in HKLM\Software, the administrator will need to manually add these entries to the HKLM\Software registry key.

Table 8-1.   *MFRMLIST.INI* Entries

Entry	Value
ValueName	The name of the value in the RegistryLoc key that contains the actual path value.
DllFile	The name of the HLLAPI DLL file.
StripFileName	Indicates the value stored in ValueName contains a "\" that must be stripped when assembling the HLLAPI DLL path from ValueName and DLLFile entries.
IntSize	Defines the "int" size supported by the emulator, 16-bit or 32-bit.
WindowClass	The Window Class name for the emulator. Obtained by using MetaFrame Password Manager Console or a window spy program such as SPY++.
WindowTitle	A portion of the Window Title that can be used by MetaFrame Password Manager to identify this window is associated with the emulator. Should contain at least one word that will always be in the window title.
UseSendKeys	Instructs MetaFrame Password Manager to use SendKeys for communicating with the emulator.

Table 8-1.   *MFRMLIST.INI* Entries *(continued)*

Add a New Host Emulator to the MFRMLIST.INI File

In this example, the Nexus Host emulator will be added to the *MFRMLIST.INI* file. This example assumes the default *MFRMLIST.INI* file that ships with the MetaFrame Password Manager Agent. In order to add the emulator, follow these steps:

NOTE: Nexus was officially added to *mfrmlist.ini* in MetaFrame Password Manager 2.5, and is only being used here as an example.

1. Verify that the chosen emulator has HLLAPI support.
2. Install the emulator and view the registry settings in HKLM\Software\Nexus Integration.
3. Launch the emulator and use the console to detect the WindowClass name of the emulator by following these steps:

    a. Open Console and choose new Windows application definition.

    b. Enter a name and use Detect Field Wizard.

    c. Choose Logon Wizard.

    d. When the Application Window form is opened, find the opened emulator window. The third column indicates the WindowClass.

4. Use the emulator to connect to the mainframe host and note the window title.

5. You now have all the necessary information to create an *MFRMLIST.INI* file entry.

6. Open *MFRMLIST.INI* file under \%Program Files%\Citrix\MetaFrame Password Manager\Helper\Emulator folder.

7. Under [Emulators], add **EMU22=Nexus** after the EMU21=PowerTermEnterprise entry.

8. Create an INI section titled [Nexus].

9. Under this entry add the following INI values:

```
GroupName=Nexus
DisplayName=Nexus
RegistryLoc=Nexus Integration\Nexus Mainframe Terminal
ValueName=InstallDir
DLLFile=NIAPI.DLL
Process=shared
IntSize=32
WindowClass=Afx:.*:b:.*
WindowTitle=Nexus
```

10. Save the *MFRMLIST.INI* file.

11. Synchronize the host definition to the agent by closing and restarting the agent.

METAFRAME PASSWORD MANAGER, NOVELL AUTHENTICATION, AND ZENWORKS

When using Novell authentication as a primary authenticator for MetaFrame Password Manager, it is important that the Windows logon account has the same password as the Novell logon account. If a Windows domain controller will not be used for authentication, another option is to use Novell ZENworks. ZENworks can configure a local Windows account with the same password as the Novell logon account on a given machine. Using ZENworks, a user policy package can be created that specifies DLU settings. This policy can then be assigned to all the Password Manager users that will use Novell as their primary authenticator to ensure Windows/Novell password synchronization upon each successful logon.

When configuring DLU settings within ConsoleOne, enable Manage Existing NT Account and Use Netware Credentials. This will ensure that Novell users with this policy will create Windows accounts upon logon, and that the Windows password will be set from the Netware credentials. Other third party utilities can be used to provide this password synchronization, but the important part is that the Windows logon account must have the same password as the Novell account. When troubleshooting, note that Password Manager detects changes in primary credentials based on interaction with the Windows GINA chain.

Since a Windows user's application data folder holds a local copy of the user's encrypted data, Citrix recommends enabling Password Manager's DeleteOnShutdown setting when using ZENworks. This will ensure that encrypted files are not left in the DLU account. This setting can be found under Shell | Agent Settings in the console. ZENworks provides similar functionality with the Volatile Users option, which will remove the Windows DLU upon logout from the Novell tree.

For more information on using ZENworks and DLUs, please refer to Chapter 6 of this book and Novell's Web site: http://www.novell.com/documentation/zdpr/index.html.

Best Practices with MetaFrame Password Manager and the Novell Client

Citrix recommends installing the latest service packs for both ZENworks and the Novell Client, using Novell settings to enhance performance, to create synchronization points, and to create Novell share types.

Install the Latest Service Packs

Install the latest service packs for the NetWare operating system and apply the latest service packs for ZENworks. Re-apply the manufacturer's latest Network Interface Card (NIC) drivers (Novell recommends this always be done as Support Packs are prone to overwrite NIC drivers).

Novell Client Settings to Enhance Overall Performance

If slow responsiveness to MetaFrame Presentation Servers with the Novell Client is experienced, there are Novell Client settings that can be applied to enhance overall performance. Citrix has tested with the following client32 settings with improved results:

▼ LIP=Start size set to 512 or try turning off LIP

■ Net Status Busy Timeout=1

▲ Burst Mode=On

It is recommended that the Novell Client not be configured with more than two Directory Agents, as this lengthens the network query time.

Novell Server Settings

The following Novell server settings can also enhance overall MetaFrame Presentation Server performance:

▼ Set Maximum Concurrent Disk Cache Writes=300

▲ Set Maximum Concurrent Directory Cache Writes=100

Create the Synchronization Point

For security purposes, Citrix does not recommend creating the MetaFrame Password Manager synchronization point on the *sys* volume. The sys volume is used for operating system files and the best practice is to use nonsystem volumes for programs and other files.

Always Use Novell Share Types

When configuring the synchronization point for Novell synchronization, always use Novell share types throughout the configuration. In other words, do not use the Microsoft NTFS File Share type when configuring your Universal Naming Convention (UNC) path to the Netware synchronization point.

Novell Modular Authentication Server NMASS.dll Error

Occasionally a Windows 2000 or Windows Server 2003 with the Novell 4.9 SP1 client may display a Novell Modular Authentication Server (NMAS)error after locking the desktop's console. The following error may be displayed when unlocking the console: "Error: "NMAS.DLL could not initialize cryptographic services or cryptographic services are not available. (-1497)". A work-around for this error is to disable the NMAS Authentication after the installation or remove the NMAS Client using Add/Remove Programs.

METAFRAME PASSWORD MANAGER 2.5 PERFORMANCE AND SCALABILITY

There are several factors affecting the performance and scalability characteristics of MetaFrame Password Manager running with MetaFrame Presentation Server including number of users per MetaFrame server, Credential Synchronization using NTFS File Share, Network Bandwidth Utilization between MetaFrame Password Manager agents and the File Share Server, Credential Synchronization using Microsoft Active Directory, and Credential Synchronization using Novell File Share.

NOTE: All testing was done with MetaFrame Presentation Server 3.0 using Windows 2000 Server or Windows Server 2003.

Number of Users per MetaFrame Server

Installing MetaFrame Password Manager on a MetaFrame Presentation Server can affect the capacity of the server. Capacity is normally discussed in terms of the effective number of users the server can support.

When installed on a Presentation server, an instance of MetaFrame Password Manager will run for each client session. For each MetaFrame Password Manager instance, the following processes may be running:

- ▼ **ssoshell.exe**   Primary agent process which also handles windows applications
- ■ **ssobho.exe**   Process which handles web applications
- ▲ **ssomho.exe**   Process which handles mainframe host emulators

In addition, when synchronizing data with the synchronization point, an additional temporary *ssoshell.exe* process is spawned. This process disappears when the synchronization is complete. All of these processes consume server resources, which can impact the effective number of users per server.

Single Server Scalability Test

The Single Server Scalability Test is designed to quantify, for benchmarking purposes, the optimal number of simulated client sessions that can be connected to a MetaFrame server with acceptable performance. Extending the number of concurrent simulated users beyond the acceptable performance recommendation will result in decreased performance and will impact end-user experience. The test simulates users constantly typing and performing actions in Microsoft Excel, Microsoft Access, and Microsoft PowerPoint. In addition, the simulation includes a custom password-protected Win32 application that is periodically started. Note that other applications can utilize more or less memory and CPU than these and therefore could produce different results. Also note that the simulated users in this test are constantly typing into these applications and may be considered more "rigorous" than normal users.

A baseline test was first run using MetaFrame Presentation Server without MetaFrame Password Manager. The simulation script simulated user credentials being typed for the password-protected application. The test was then rerun with MetaFrame Password Manager installed on the MetaFrame server. The simulation script was modified to allow MetaFrame Password Manager to provide credentials when needed. During the test, mainframe host support was not enabled; therefore, the *ssomho.exe* process was not running on the MetaFrame server. Figures 8-1 and 8-2, respectively, show a graphical plotting of the ICAMark scores by number of users for Windows 2000 and for Windows Server 2003 respectively (both with and without MetaFrame Password Manager), while the corresponding four tables (Table 8-2, Table 8-3, Table 8-4, and Table 8-5, respectively) show the data underlying the graphs.

The easiest way to determine the server's degradation point is to look at the ICAMark Score column in the test results. For the Single Server Scalability Test, a score of 80 has been determined as the optimal load for a server. This means that the server has sufficient additional CPU and memory resources to handle spikes in performance. When the test

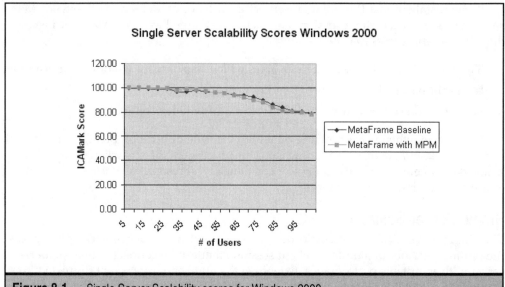

Figure 8-1.   Single Server Scalability scores for Windows 2000

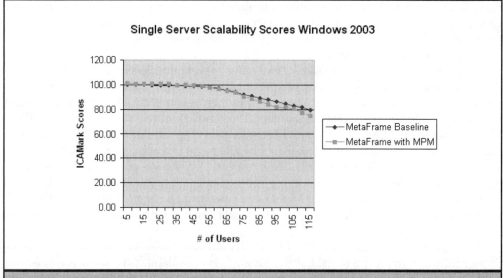

Figure 8-2.   Single Server Scalability scores for Windows Server 2003

# of Users	Time	Bytes Sent	KBps	ICAMark Score
5	18:13	108,123.07	0.30	99.49
10	18:19	85,097.23	0.24	99.46
15	18:27	76,729.69	0.21	99.19
20	18:27	72,804.59	0.20	98.76
25	18:25	69,682.91	0.19	98.90
30	18:19	68,455.27	0.19	96.97
35	18:32	67,101.47	0.18	96.99
40	18:42	65,769.30	0.18	97.77
45	18:47	64,940.36	0.17	96.95
50	18:56	64,684.49	0.17	96.06
55	18:57	63,999.84	0.17	95.68
60	19:30	65,629.84	0.17	94.39
65	19:54	63,867.90	0.17	93.66
70	19:58	64,237.43	0.16	92.63
75	19:58	63,668.27	0.16	89.58
80	21:04	63,471.35	0.15	86.32
85	21:19	64,952.42	0.16	83.98
90	22:21	65,084.86	0.15	81.19
95	22:07	64,120.79	0.15	80.42

Table 8-2. MetaFrame Presentation Server 3.0 Single Server Scalability Baseline Score (Windows 2000)

iteration score drops below 80, additional users added to the server consume more resources. This produces lower test scores and slower performance.

On this specific hardware with this specific test (Windows Server 2003), extrapolating the results allows for 105 simulated users to be concurrently and constantly running Microsoft Office applications and MetaFrame Password Manager without significant performance degradation. This is compared to 113 users without MetaFrame Password Manager installed on the server, a 7.1% decrease in the total number of users. This decrease is attributed to additional memory resources required by the MetaFrame Password Manager Agent.

# of Users	Time	Bytes Sent	KBps	ICAMark Score
5	18:09	106,201.93	0.30	100.15
10	18:05	85,254.17	0.24	100.29
15	18:14	79,655.38	0.22	100.17
20	18:17	76,458.88	0.21	100.05
25	18:11	75,108.34	0.21	99.63
30	13:12	74,163.08	0.20	98.12
35	18:27	73,357.71	0.20	98.94
40	18:32	72,388.23	0.20	98.50
45	13:30	72,384.02	0.19	97.09
50	13:39	72,483.73	0.19	95.90
55	19:09	73,933.44	0.20	95.48
60	19:54	70,981.03	0.18	93.62
65	19:24	69,665.47	0.18	91.96
70	20:18	72,738.51	0.18	90.00
75	20:44	71,748.21	0.18	88.11
80	20:57	72,218.58	0.17	83.72
85	21:39	71,481.08	0.17	81.02
90	21:46	70,401.69	0.16	80.32
95	23:20	70,072.51	0.16	79.56

Table 8-3. MetaFrame Password Manager Single Server Scalability Score on MetaFrame Presentation Server 3.0 (Windows 2000 and Active Directory Synchronization)

Server Hardware Configuration The server hardware configuration utilized for this test was as follows:

▼ IBM x-Series 335
  ■ Dual Xeon 2.4 GHz Processors with 512KB L2 Cache
  ■ 34GB Ultra 320 SCSI HD

- 3GB RAM
- 4GB pagefile

# of Users	Time	Bytes Sent	KBps	ICAMark Score
5	18:12	104,302.67	0.29	99.67
10	18:15	81,701.27	0.23	99.62
15	18:11	72,930.80	0.20	99.70
20	18:15	68,158.98	0.19	99.58
25	18:14	65,859.41	0.18	99.56
30	18:18	64,240.06	0.18	99.49
35	18:17	62,858.50	0.17	99.36
40	18:26	61,950.02	0.17	98.94
45	18:24	61,107.67	0.17	98.59
50	18:26	61,848.07	0.17	97.97
55	19:08	61,899.61	0.17	97.47
60	18:32	61,327.67	0.17	96.93
65	18:51	60,459.90	0.16	95.32
70	19:54	60,072.68	0.16	94.10
75	20:26	61,390.74	0.16	91.71
80	20:52	59,855.00	0.15	90.88
85	21:25	59,684.77	0.15	89.23
90	22:06	59,417.45	0.14	87.69
95	22:21	58,185.51	0.14	86.18
100	23:19	58,142.51	0.14	84.62
105	23:27	58,242.44	0.13	82.88
110	23:13	57,599.87	0.13	81.80
115	25:07:00	58,406.61	0.13	79.18

Table 8-4.   MetaFrame Presentation Server 3.0 Single Server Scalability Baseline Score (Windows Server 2003)

# of Users	Time	Bytes Sent	KBps	ICAMark Score
5	18:02	104,122.93	0.29	100.88
10	18:06	80,692.93	0.23	100.58
15	18:05	73,347.33	0.21	100.52
20	18:08	68,601.60	0.19	100.52
25	18:09	65,603.69	0.18	100.33
30	18:06	63,623.37	0.18	100.34
35	18:08	62,457.20	0.17	99.55
40	18:12	61,502.56	0.17	99.75
45	18:18	60,904.09	0.17	99.19
50	18:22	62,785.23	0.17	98.61
55	18:25	61,689.86	0.17	97.37
60	19:37	62,491.12	0.17	96.23
65	20:10	61,536.09	0.16	94.47
70	20:17	61,293.97	0.16	93.36
75	20:40	60,257.54	0.15	90.13
80	20:23	60,111.80	0.15	88.39
85	23:09	60,256.07	0.14	86.33
90	21:43	58,718.98	0.14	84.04
95	22:17	60,180.96	0.14	81.63
100	22:24	58,381.59	0.13	81.32
105	23:06	59,645.90	0.13	80.21

Table 8-5. MetaFrame Password Manager Single Server Scalability Score on MetaFrame Presentation Server 3.0 (Windows Server 2003 and File Share Synchronization)

Client Hardware Configuration   The Client hardware configuration utilized for this test was as follows:

▼ Compaq Proliant 800
- ■ Dual 500 MHz PIII Processors with 256KB L2 Cache
- ■ 8GB SCSI HD
- ■ 512MB RAM
- ■ 1GB pagefile

MetaFrame Server Software Configuration   The MetaFrame Presentation Server configuration utilized for this test was as follows:

▼ Windows 2000 Server w/ Service Pack 4 or Windows Server 2003 w/ Service Pack 1

    ■ MetaFrame Presentation Server 3.0

    ■ MetaFrame Password Manager 2.5

    ■ Microsoft Office XP: Excel, Access, and PowerPoint

Client Software Configuration   The client software configuration utilized for this test was as follows:

▼ Windows 2000 Server w/ Service Pack 4

    ■ Citrix ICA Program Neighborhood Version 8.00.24737

    ■ 10 ICA sessions exist on each machine

Test Configuration   The test configuration utilized for this test was as follows:

▼ Step Size: 5 users

■ Iterations: 13

■ Total simulated users in test: Windows 2000=115, Windows Server 2003=120

▲ Script Version: 1.0

MetaFrame Password Manager Memory Usage   Table 8-6 shows the average memory usage observed for each MetaFrame Password Manager process running in a MetaFrame client session. These measurements were taken while the processes were idle, but had previously responded to credential requests. These numbers can be used to estimate the amount of additional memory that will be needed for MetaFrame Password Manager.

Process	Private Bytes Windows 2000	Private Bytes Windows 2003
ssoshell.exe	3.63MB	3.26MB
ssobho.exe	2.85MB	1.71MB
ssomho.exe	1.34MB	1.40MB

Table 8-6.   Average Memory Usage for Each MetaFrame Password Manager Process

Credential Synchronization Using NTFS File Share

There are several scalability and performance characteristics related to using an NTFS file share for password synchronization including

- ▼ Disk space utilization of the File Share Server
- ■ Network bandwidth utilization between MetaFrame Password Manager Agents and the File Share Server
- ■ CPU utilization of File Share Server
- ▲ MetaFrame Password Manager Agent response times

NOTE: MetaFrame Presentation session login time was not significantly impacted by the MetaFrame Password Manager Agent.

The following test bed was used for this phase of testing:

File Server Hardware Configuration

The File server hardware configuration utilized for this test was as follows:

- ▼ Dell PowerEdge 2650
  - ■ Dual 2.4 GHz Xeon Processors with 512KB L2 Cache
  - ■ 16GB SCSI HD
  - ■ 1024MB RAM
  - ■ 2GB pagefile

MetaFrame Server Hardware Configuration

The Terminal Server/MetaFrame Server hardware configuration utilized for this test was as follows:

- ▼ Dell PowerEdge 2650
  - ■ Dual 2.4 GHz Xeon Processors with 512KB L2 Cache
  - ■ 16GB SCSI HD
  - ■ 1024MB RAM
  - ■ 2GB pagefile

Client Hardware Configuration

The client hardware configuration utilized for this test was as follows:

- ▼ Dell PowerEdge 2650

File Server Software Configuration

The file server software configuration utilized for this test was as follows:

▼   Windows 2000 w/ Service Pack 4 or Windows Server 2003 w/ Service Pack 1

MetaFrame Server Software Configuration

The Terminal Server/MetaFrame Server software configuration utilized for this test was as follows:

▼   Windows 2000 Server w/ Service Pack 4 or Windows Server 2003 w/ Service Pack 1

■   MetaFrame Presentation Server 3.0

■   MetaFrame Password Manager v 2.5

■   Microsoft Office XP: Excel, Access, and PowerPoint

Client Software Configuration

The client software configuration utilized for this test was as follows:

▼   Windows 2000 Server w/ Service Pack 4

■   Citrix ICA Program Neighborhood Version 8.00.24737

■   10 ICA sessions exist on each machine

Disk Space Utilization of the File Share Server

With file share synchronization, the file share includes a separate directory for each user. Within each user's directory, credential information is stored for each application de-fined for use with MetaFrame Password Manager. Table 8-7 shows the disk space utilized for a single user.

With the measurements shown in Table 8-7, the amount of disk space required on a File Share Server can be calculated with the following formula:

Disk Space required = (# of users) * (3.04 Kbytes + (# of defined apps * 0.7 Kbytes))

For example (using Windows Server 2003 as a MetaFrame Server), 1000 users with 20 applications defined for each user would require 17,040KB, or 17MB of disk space.

Disk Utilization Measurement	Windows 2000	Windows 2003
Disk usage with no applications defined	3.04Kb	3.04Kb
Disk usage per application	0.69Kb	0.70Kb

Table 8-7.   Disk Space Utilized for a Single User

Network Bandwidth Utilization Between MetaFrame Password Manager Agents and the File Share Server

Different events, such as logging on or changing a password, can trigger synchronization between the Password Manager Agent and the file share. These synchronizations will put traffic on the network. The amount of network traffic between an agent and the file share will depend on the following factors:

▼ Number of application definitions per user

■ Whether or not aggressive synchronization is enabled

▲ Frequency of synchronization events

Network Monitor was used to measure the amount of data passed between the File Share Server and the MetaFrame Password Manager Agent for various synchronization events. Each measurement was taken multiple times to obtain the average value for each event. The users were configured with 20 defined applications divided among Win32 applications, web applications, and mainframe host applications. It is important to note that more or less application definitions could produce different results. Table 8-8 shows

Synchronization Event	Windows 2000 (Agent)	Windows 2003 (Agent)
User runs MetaFrame Password Manager for the first time with 20 applications defined in an FTU list.	224KB	239KB
User runs MetaFrame Password Manager for the first time without any applications defined.	77KB	89KB
User runs MetaFrame Password Manager (not first time) with no new application definitions or password changes to synchronize.	41KB	34KB
User changes Windows logon password.	48KB	49KB
User configures a Windows application for use with MetaFrame Password Manager using the Agent.	39KB	45KB
User configures a web application for use with MetaFrame Password Manager using the Agent.	51KB	58KB

Table 8-8. Synchronization Events

Synchronization Event	Windows 2000 (Agent)	Windows 2003 (Agent)
User launches a MetaFrame Password Manager-defined Windows application with aggressive synchronization enabled.	11KB	16KB
User launches a web application with aggressive synchronization enabled.	11KB	16KB
User opens the Agent's Logon Manager and hits the Refresh button.	88KB	99KB
Synchronization after MetaFrame Password Manager files in user's profile have been deleted.	239KB	241KB

Table 8-8.   Synchronization Events *(continued)*

the synchronization events for the MetaFrame Password Manager Agent under both Windows 2000 and Windows Server 2003.

With the data listed, the amount of network bandwidth required for synchronization over a given period of time can be estimated with the following formula:

$$N = \frac{((S_1 * B_1) + (S_2 * B_2) + \ldots + (S_n * B_n)) * 8 * U}{T}$$

N   Network bandwidth utilization measured in bits per second.

S_n   For synchronizat time (in ion event type n, the expected frequency of the event, per user, during time T.

B_n   The expected number of bytes transferred between an agent and the file share for event n. This value may be dependent on the number of applications defined for use with MetaFrame Password Manager. If this number is expressed in bytes, then it must be multiplied by 8 as above.

U   Number of concurrent MetaFrame Password Manager users during time T.

T   Amount of elapsed (in seconds) being analyzed.

Network Bandwidth Utilization Example   A company has 5,000 employees using MetaFrame Password Manager to access 20 different password protected applications. Aggressive synchronization is enabled. The most active period of synchronization will be in the morning, when most employees begin logging into applications. Between 9:00 A.M. and 9:30 A.M. (30 minutes), it is estimated that all employees will log into a MetaFrame Presentation

Server (Windows 2000 Server) with MetaFrame Password Manager and run two password-protected Win32 applications. Using the previous formula, we have the following:

$$N = \frac{((1 * 41K) + (2 * 11K)) * 8 * 5000}{1800}$$

$$N = 1.4 \text{ Mbps}$$

Synchronization Event₁ Windows logon (not first time use)
Synchronization Event₂ Launch Win32 application
S₁ 1
S₂ 2
B₁ 11K (from Table 8-8)
B₂ 11K (from Table 8-8)
U 5000
T 30 minutes (1800 seconds)

In this example, we see that this company will require 1.4 Mbps available bandwidth for MetaFrame Password Manager synchronization during the most intense time period of synchronization.

CAUTION: Performing synchronizations across a WAN link could cause a bottleneck between the synchronization point and MetaFrame Password Manager Agents.

File Share Server CPU Utilization

A File Share Server's CPU utilization was measured while an automated tool generated synchronization events from multiple MetaFrame Password Manager Agents. For this test, each synchronization event did not include any data changes. Figure 8-3 shows the results.

This test was performed on a 100Mb switched network with a gigabit backbone using the following hardware for the file server.

File Server Hardware Configuration　　The file server hardware configuration utilized for this test was as follows:

▼ Dell PowerEdge 2650

　■ Dual 2.4 GHz Xeon Processors with 512KB L2 Cache

　■ 16GB SCSI HD

　■ 1024MB RAM

　■ 2GB pagefile

File Server Software Configuration　　The file server software configuration utilized for this test was as follows:

▼ Windows 2000 w/ Service Pack 4 or Windows Server 2003 w/ Service Pack 1

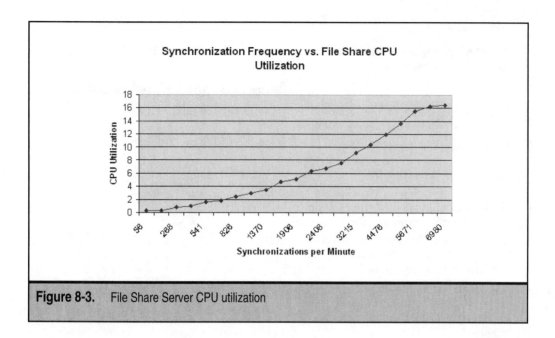

Figure 8-3.   File Share Server CPU utilization

MetaFrame Password Manager Agent Response Time   The time it takes for MetaFrame Password Manager to recognize a password protected application and provide its credentials can vary depending on the user's environment and MetaFrame Password Manager configuration. Some factors that may effect response time are the following:

▼   Network bandwidth availability

■   Use of roaming Windows profiles vs. local Windows profiles

■   Whether or not aggressive synchronization is enabled

■   MetaFrame server resource availability

■   Whether agent synchronization is installed

▲   Network latency between the synchronization point and the MetaFrame Password Manager Agent (e.g., LAN vs. WAN)

Tables 8-9 and 8-10 list agent response times with varying client configurations over a LAN for Windows 2000 and Windows Server 2003 respectively. Tables 8-11 and 8-12 list agent response times over a WAN for Windows 2000 and Windows Server 2003 respectively. All testing was done using a custom Win32 application, a custom web page, and NetManage Rumba Terminal Emulator (VM-370) running in an ICA session on a MetaFrame Presentation Server 3.0. For each configuration, the time between the application loading and the credentials being fully submitted by MetaFrame Password Manager is indicated.

Agent Response Time with File Share Synchronization over a LAN	Results Windows 2000 (in seconds)		
	Windows App	Web App	Terminal Emulator App
Single user operating on MetaFrame server with synchronization not installed	0.04	0.77	1.84
Single user operating on MetaFrame server with aggressive synchronization and local Windows profile	0.172	0.95	1.97
Single user operating on MetaFrame server with aggressive synchronization and roaming Windows profile	0.175	0.96	2.13
User operating on MetaFrame server that is at 65% CPU utilization with synchronization not installed	0.11	0.79	2.47
User operating on MetaFrame server that is at 65% CPU utilization with aggressive synchronization and local profile	0.539	1.67	2.69
User operating on MetaFrame server that is at 65% CPU utilization with aggressive synchronization and roaming profile	0.67	1.75	2.75

Table 8-9.   Agent Response Times over a LAN with Windows 2000

NOTE: Response times for Win32 and web credential requests were gathered using an automated test tool. Response times for Terminal Emulator Applications were gathered using a stop watch (times may not be accurate due to human error). Mainframe Host polling time was set to 700 milliseconds (ms), which may add to response time.

WAN Simulation Configuration   To simulate a connection to a file share synchronization over a WAN link, a Shunra Storm WAN Emulator box was used. The WAN emulator box was placed between the synchronization point and the MetaFrame Server. The following configuration was used:

▼   WAN Link type=T1

■   Latency: Avg. latency=230 ms, Std Deviation=20 ms

■   Packet Loss: Random loss of 1% of all packets

- Packet Effects: Out of Order Chance=1%
- Packet Offset=1%, Minimum=1, Maximum=1
- Fragmentation Chance=1%,
▲ Maximum Transmission Unit=512 Bytes

The WAN settings used were based upon data obtained by sampling a live WAN link between Fort Lauderdale, Florida and Sydney, Australia.

CAUTION: Having users perform credential synchronization with a file share accessed across a WAN link can cause excessive delays in agent response time. Care must be taken when planning such a deployment.

Agent Response Time with File Share Synchronization over a LAN	Results Windows 2003 (in seconds)		
	Windows App	Web App	Terminal Emulator App
Single user operating on MetaFrame server with synchronization not installed	0.05	0.36	1.99
Single user operating on MetaFrame server with aggressive synchronization and local Windows profile	0.19	0.52	2.13
Single user operating on MetaFrame server with aggressive synchronization and roaming Windows profile	0.176	0.53	2.21
User operating on MetaFrame server that is at 65% CPU utilization with synchronization not installed	0.08	0.53	2.09
User operating on MetaFrame server that is at 65% CPU utilization with aggressive synchronization and local profile	0.367	0.98	2.57
User operating on MetaFrame server that is at 65% CPU utilization with aggressive synchronization and roaming profile	0.406	0.98	2.57

Table 8-10. Agent Response Times over a LAN with Windows Server 2003

Agent Response Time with Synchronization over a WAN	Results Windows 2000 (in seconds)		
	Windows App	Web App	Terminal Emulator App
Single user operating on MetaFrame server with aggressive synchronization and roaming profile (stored on same network as MetaFrame Password Manager Agent)	14.06	15.30	16.20

Table 8-11.   Agent Response Times over a WAN with Windows 2000

Agent Response Time with Synchronization over a WAN	Results Windows 2003 (in seconds)		
	Windows App	Web App	Terminal Emulator App
Single user operating on MetaFrame server with aggressive synchronization and roaming profile (stored on same network as MetaFrame Password Manager Agent)	17.29	18.41	18.68

Table 8-12.   Agent Response Times over a WAN with Windows Server 2003

Credential Synchronization Using Microsoft Active Directory

The performance and scalability characteristics of using Microsoft Active Directory for credential synchronization include

▼   Active Directory replication network traffic

■   Network bandwidth utilization between MetaFrame Password Manager Agents and AD Domain Controllers

■   Active Directory Domain Controller CPU utilization

▲   MetaFrame Password Manager Agent response times

NOTE: In all Active Directory testing, the MetaFrame Servers and the AD synchronization point were in different domains but in the same forest. The two trusted domains had external nontransitive trust relationships.

> *IMPORTANT:*   MetaFrame Presentation session login time was not significantly impacted by the MetaFrame Password Manager Agent.

Active Directory Server Configuration

The Active Directory server hardware configuration utilized for this test was as follows:

▼ Dell PowerEdge 1400

- Dual 800 MHz Pentium III Processors with 256KB L2 Cache
- 8.4GB SCSI HD
- 512MB RAM
- 1GB pagefile

MetaFrame Server Hardware Configuration

The Terminal Server/MetaFrame Server hardware configuration utilized for this test was as follows:

▼ Dell PowerEdge 2650

- Dual 2.4 GHz Xeon Processors with 512KB L2 Cache
- 16GB SCSI HD
- 1024MB RAM
- 2GB pagefile

Client Hardware Configuration

The client hardware configuration utilized for this test was as follows:

▼ Compaq DL 320

MetaFrame Server Software Configuration

The Terminal Server/MetaFrame Server software configuration utilized for this test was as follows:

▼ Windows 2000 Server w/ Service Pack 4 or Windows Server 2003 w/ Service Pack 1

- MetaFrame Presentation Server 3.0
- MetaFrame Password Manager v 2.5
- Microsoft Office XP: Excel, Access, and PowerPoint

Client Software Configuration

The client software configuration utilized for this test was as follows:

▼ Windows 2000 Server w/ Service Pack 4

- Citrix ICA Program Neighborhood Version 8.00.24737
- 10 ICA sessions exist on each machine

Active Directory Server Software Configuration

The Active Directory server software configuration utilized for this test was as follows:

▼ Windows 2000 Server w/ Service Pack 4

Active Directory Replication Network Traffic

Using Active Directory for MetaFrame Password Manager Synchronization will cause an increase in AD replication traffic. The amount of additional traffic will depend on the frequency and type of events that will change data in the AD database.

Table 8-13 lists various events that will change data in the AD database. For each event, the amount of replication traffic associated with a single user is indicated. This data can be used to estimate the impact a MetaFrame Password Manager deployment may have on AD replication network traffic.

Event	Replication Data Size
User runs MetaFrame Password Manager for the first time with 20 apps (10 Win32, 10 Wed) defined in an FTU list.	22.5KB
User runs MetaFrame Password Manager for the first time without any apps defined.	6KB
User changes Windows logon password.	2KB
User configures a Windows app for use with MetaFrame Password Manager using the Agent.	3.6KB
User configures first web app for use with MetaFrame Password Manager using the Agent.	9.5KB

Table 8-13. Events Changing Data in the AD Database

NOTE: This data was captured using Microsoft Performance Monitor. The counters used were "DRA Inbound Bytes Not Compressed (Within Site)/sec" and "DRA Outbound Bytes Total/sec" located under the NTDS Performance Object. Replication was forced after each event using the "Active Directory Sites and Services" MMC Snap-in.

With the data listed in Table 8-13, the amount of replication data to be expected for a given period of time can be estimated with the following formula:

$$D = ((S_1 * B_1) + (S_2 * B_2) + \ldots + (S_n * B_n))$$

D   Amount of data that will be replicated during the time being considered
S_n For synchronization event type n, the expected frequency of the event (per user) during the time period being considered
B_n The expected number of KB transferred during AD replication for event n

The timing/frequency of replications will depend on whether replication takes place intrasite or intersite.

NOTE: Using an FTU list will reduce replication traffic on your network. If a user individually configures 10 Windows applications and 10 web applications after the initial user configuration of MetaFrame Password Manager, approximately 131KB of replication traffic will occur (3.6K for each Windows application, 9.5K for each web application). Using the FTU list during the initial configuration of the MetaFrame Password Manager Agent will cause approximately 22.5KB of data to be replicated.

Network Bandwidth Utilization Between MetaFrame Password Manager Agents and Active Directory Domain Controllers

Different events, such as logging on or changing a password, can trigger synchronization between the Password Manager Agent and the Active Directory. These synchronizations will put traffic on the network. The amount of network traffic between an agent and an Active Directory Domain Controller will depend on the following factors:

▼   Number of application definitions per user

■   Whether or not aggressive synchronization is enabled

▲   Frequency of synchronization events

Network Monitor was used to measure the amount of data passed between an Active Directory Domain Controller and the MetaFrame Password Manager Agent for various synchronization events. Each measurement was taken multiple times to obtain the average value for each event. The users were set up with 20 defined applications (10 Windows-based applications and 10 web-based applications). It is important to note that more or less application definitions could produce different results. Table 8-14 shows various synchronization events for Windows 2000 and Windows Server 2003.

Synchronization Event	Windows 2000	Windows 2003
User runs MetaFrame Password Manager for the first time with 20 apps defined in an FTU list.	153KB	155KB
User runs MetaFrame Password Manager for the first time without any apps defined.	110KB	111KB
User runs MetaFrame Password Manager (not first time) with no new app definitions or password changes to synchronize.	59KB	73KB
User changes Windows logon password.	60KB	57KB
User configures a Windows app for use with MetaFrame Password Manager using the Agent.	60KB	70KB
User configures a web app for use with MetaFrame Password Manager using the Agent.	140KB	14KB
User launches a MetaFrame Password Manager-defined Windows app with aggressive synchronization enabled.	15KB	15KB
User launches a web app. with aggressive synchronization enabled.	15KB	15KB
User opens the Agent's Logon Manager and hits the Refresh button.	84KB	55KB
Synchronization after MetaFrame Password Manager files in user's profile have been deleted.	76KB	71KB

Table 8-14.   Synchronization Events for Windows 2000 Server and Windows Server 2003

With the data from the table, the amount of network bandwidth required for synchronization over a given period of time can be estimated with the following formula:

$$N = \frac{((S_1 * B_1) + (S_2 * B_2) + \ldots + (S_n * B_n)) * 8 * U}{T}$$

N   Network bandwidth utilization measured in bits per second.
Sn   For synchronization event type n, the expected frequency of the event (per user) during time T.
Bn   For synchronization event type n, the expected number of bytes transferred between an agent and the Active Directory for event n. This value may be dependent on the number of applications defined for use with MetaFrame Password Manager. If this number is expressed in bytes, it must be multiplied by 8 as above.
U   Number of concurrent MetaFrame Password Manager users during time T.
T   Amount of elapsed time (in seconds) being analyzed.

Refer to the section of this chapter entitled "Network Bandwidth Utilization Between MetaFrame Password Manager Agents and the File Share Server" to see an usage example of this formula.

Active Directory Domain Controller Resource Impact

Citrix *e*Labs measured a Active Directory domain controller's CPU utilization while an automated tool generated synchronization events from multiple Agents. For this test, each synchronization event did not include any data changes. Figure 8-4 lists the results of this test.

The testing was done on a 100MB switched network with a gigabit backbone synchronizing to a single domain controller with the following configuration.

Active Directory Server Configuration   The Active Directory domain controller server hardware configuration utilized for this test was as follows:

▼   Dell PowerEdge 1400

■   Dual 800 MHz Pentium III Processors with 256KB L2 Cache

■   8.4GB SCSI HD

■   512MB RAM

■   1GB pagefile

Active Directory Server Software Configuration   The Active Directory domain controller server software configuration utilized for this test was as follows:

▼   Windows 2000 Server w/ Service Pack 4

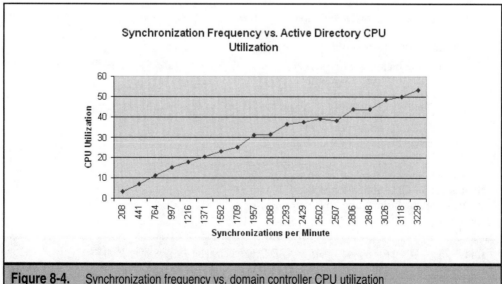

Figure 8-4.   Synchronization frequency vs. domain controller CPU utilization

Agent Response Time   The time it takes for MetaFrame Password Manager to recognize a password-protected application and provide its credentials can vary depending on the user's environment and MetaFrame Password Manager configuration. Some factors that may effect response time are the following:

- ▼ Network bandwidth availability
- ■ Use of roaming Windows profiles local Windows profiles
- ■ Whether aggressive synchronization is enabled or not
- ■ MetaFrame server resource availability
- ■ Whether agent synchronization is installed
- ▲ Network latency between the synchronization point and the MetaFrame Password Manager Agent (e.g., LAN vs. WAN)

Tables 8-15 and 8-16 list agent response times with varying client configurations for Windows 2000 and for Windows Server 2003 respectively. All testing was done using a

Agent Response Time with Active Directory Synchronization over a LAN	Results Windows 2000 (in seconds)		
	Windows App	Web App	Terminal Emulator App
Single user operating on MetaFrame server with synchronization not installed	0.05	0.80	2.07
Single user operating on MetaFrame server with aggressive synchronization and local Windows profile	0.266	0.969	2
Single user operating on MetaFrame server with aggressive synchronization and roaming Windows profile .	0.268	0.976	2.14
User operating on MetaFrame server that is at 65% CPU utilization with synchronization not installed	0.091	1.02	2.16
User operating on MetaFrame server that is at 65% CPU utilization with aggressive synchronization and local profile	0.561	1.685	2.61
User operating on MetaFrame server that is at 65% CPU utilization with aggressive synchronization and roaming profile	0.57	1.705	2.48

Table 8-15.   Agent Response Times with AD Synchronization for Windows 2000

Agent Response Time with Active Directory Synchronization over a LAN	Results Windows 2003 (in seconds)		
	Windows App	**Web App**	**Terminal Emulator App**
Single user operating on MetaFrame server with synchronization not installed	0.047	0.429	1.96
Single user operating on MetaFrame server with aggressive synchronization and local Windows profile	0.236	0.552	2.02
Single user operating on MetaFrame server with aggressive synchronization and roaming Windows profile .	0.236	0.561	2.12
User operating on MetaFrame server that is at 65% CPU utilization with synchronization not installed	0.087	0.583	2.08
User operating on MetaFrame server that is at 65% CPU utilization with aggressive synchronization and local profile	0.474	1.056	2.38
User operating on MetaFrame server that is at 65% CPU utilization with aggressive synchronization and roaming profile	0.587	1.043	2.53

Table 8-16.   Agent Response Times with AD Synchronization for Windows Server 2003

custom Win32 application, a custom web page, and NetManage Rumba Terminal Emulator (VM-370) running in an ICA session on a MetaFrame Presentation Server 3.0. For each configuration, the time between the application loading and the credentials being fully submitted by MetaFrame Password Manager is indicated.

NOTE: Response times for Win32 and web credential requests were gathered using an automated test tool. Response times for Terminal Emulator Applications were gathered using a stop watch (times may not be accurate due to human error). Mainframe Host polling time was set to 700 ms, which may add to response time.

Credential Synchronization Using Novell File Share

The scalability and performance characteristics related to using a Novell File Share for password synchronization include the following:

▼ Disk space utilization of the File Share Server

▲ MetaFrame Password Manager Agent response times

File Server Hardware Configuration

The file server hardware configuration utilized for this test was as follows:

▼ Dell PowerEdge 1400

■ Dual 800 MHz Pentium III Processors with 256KB L2 Cache

■ 8.4GB SCSI HD

■ 512MB RAM

▲ 1GB pagefile

MetaFrame Server Hardware Configuration

The Terminal Server/MetaFrame Server hardware configuration utilized for this test was as follows:

▼ Dell PowerEdge 2650

■ Dual 2.4 GHz Xeon Processors with 512KB L2 Cache

■ 16GB SCSI HD

■ 1024MB RAM

■ 2GB Pagefile

Client Hardware Configuration

The client hardware configuration utilized for this test was as follows:

▼ Compaq DL 320

File Server Software Configuration

The file server software configuration utilized for this test was as follows:

▼ Novell Netware 6.0 w/ eDirectory 8.7.3

MetaFrame Server Software Configuration

The Terminal Server/MetaFrame Server software configuration utilized for this test was as follows:

▼ Windows 2000 Server w/ Service Pack 4 or Windows Server 2003 w/ Service Pack 1

■ MetaFrame Presentation Server 3.0

■ Novell Client 4.9 Service Pack 1

■ MetaFrame Password Manager v 2.5

■ Microsoft Office XP: Excel, Access, and PowerPoint

Client Software Configuration

The client software configuration utilized for this test was as follows:

▼ Windows 2000 Server w/ Service Pack 4

■ Citrix ICA Program Neighborhood Version 8.00.24737

■ 10 ICA sessions exist on each machine

Disk Space Utilization of the Novell File Share Server

With file share synchronization, the file share includes a separate directory for each user. Within each user's directory, credential information is stored for each application defined for use with MetaFrame Password Manager. Table 8-17 shows the disk space utilized for a single user.

With the measurements shown in Table 8-17, the amount of disk space required on a File Share Server can be calculated with the following formula:

Disk Space required = (# of users) * (3.08 Kbytes + (# of defined apps * 0.68 Kbytes))

For example (using Windows 2000 as a MetaFrame Presentation Server), 1000 users, with 20 applications defined for each user would require 16,680KB, or, 16.9MB of disk space.

Disk Usage	Windows 2000	Windows 2003
Disk usage with no applications defined	3.08 Kb	3.08 Kb
Disk usage per application	0.68 Kb	0.64 Kb

Table 8-17.   Disk Utilization Measurement

MetaFrame Password Manager Agent Response Time

The time it takes for MetaFrame Password Manager to recognize a password protected application and provide its credentials can vary depending on the user's environment and MetaFrame Password Manager configuration. Some factors that may effect response time are the following:

▼ Network bandwidth availability

■ Use of roaming Windows profiles local Windows profiles

■ Whether or not aggressive synchronization is enabled

■ MetaFrame server resource availability

■ Whether agent synchronization is installed

▲ Network latency between the synchronization point and the MetaFrame Password Manager Agent (e.g., LAN vs.WAN)

Tables 8-18 and 8-19 list agent response times with varying client configurations for Windows 2000 and for Windows Server 2003, respectively. All testing was done using

Agent Response Time with Novell File Share Synchronization over a LAN	Results Windows 2000 (in seconds)		
	Windows App	Web App	Terminal Emulator App
Single user operating on MetaFrame server with synchronization not installed	0.046	0.805	1.96
Single user operating on MetaFrame server with aggressive synchronization and local Windows profile	0.191	1.0	2.15
Single user operating on MetaFrame server with aggressive synchronization and roaming Windows profile	0.219	1.02	2.12
User operating on MetaFrame server that is at 65% CPU utilization with synchronization not installed	0.089	1.09	2.20
User operating on MetaFrame server that is at 65% CPU utilization with aggressive synchronization and local profile	0.393	1.41	2.39
User operating on MetaFrame server that is at 65% CPU utilization with aggressive synchronization and roaming profile	0.457	1.46	2.49

Table 8-18. Agent Response Time with Novell File Share Synchronization over a LAN for Windows 2000

Agent Response Time with Novell File Share Synchronization over a LAN	Results Windows 2003 (in seconds)		
	Windows App	Web App	Terminal Emulator App
Single user operating on MetaFrame server with synchronization not installed	0.049	0.37	1.96
Single user operating on MetaFrame server with aggressive synchronization and local Windows profile	0.207	0.563	2.06
Single user operating on MetaFrame server with aggressive synchronization and roaming Windows profile	*	*	*
User operating on MetaFrame server that is at 65% CPU utilization with synchronization not installed	0.092	0.630	2.19
User operating on MetaFrame server that is at 65% CPU utilization with aggressive synchronization and local profile	0.451	0.974	2.65
User operating on MetaFrame server that is at 65% CPU utilization with aggressive synchronization and roaming profile	*	*	*

Table 8-19.   Agent Response Time with Novell File Share Synchronization over a LAN for Windows Server 2003

a custom Win32 application, a custom web page, and Rumba Terminal Emulator (VM-370) running in an ICA session on a MetaFrame Presentation Server 3.0 server. For each configuration, the time between the application loading and the credentials being fully submitted by MetaFrame Password Manager is indicated.

NOTE: Response times for Win32 and web credential requests were gathered using an automated test tool. Response times for Terminal Emulator Applications were gathered using a stop watch (times may not be accurate due to human error). Mainframe Host polling time was set to 700 ms, which may add to response time.

NOTE: Response time data for ICA sessions running on a Windows Server 2003 using roaming profiles are unavailable (see asterisks in Table 8-19) due to a documented issue with the Novell Client. Excerpt from Novell's support TID10087706: "Although the cause is unknown, it appears that the failure is around being unable to read terminal server-specific fields, such as TerminalServerProfilePath and TerminalServerHomeDirectory."

CHAPTER 9

MetaFrame Conferencing Manager 3.0

MetaFrame Conferencing Manager 3.0 is quickly generating enthusiasm from users by providing them with on-demand collaboration from anywhere at any time. Users range from salespeople collaborating on their forecasts to power users conducting ad hoc trainings for their peers. Enthusiasm from the IT staff is also prevalent since end users are able to plan and initiate meetings without requiring IT involvement.

In this chapter we discuss considerations for integrating MetaFrame Conferencing Manager 3.0 into the Network and Presentation Server environment, including architecture, communications, and sizing of Conferencing Manager Servers. We also cover the new Guest Attendee feature of MetaFrame Conferencing Manager 3.0 that allows external customers, vendors, and others to securely collaborate on documents along with employees.

METAFRAME CONFERENCING MANAGER ARCHITECTURE AND SCALABILITY

In order to properly deploy MetaFrame Conferencing Manager 3.0 into an existing MetaFrame environment, it is necessary to understand the core components in terms of how they interact and communicate with each other. MetaFrame Conferencing Manager 3.0 is broken up into five components and each of the components is necessary to start, join, leave, and end meetings. The five components are: Citrix MetaFrame Conferencing Manager (CMCM), also referred to as the MetaFrame Conferencing Manager User Interface, Conference Organizer, Conference Room, Conference Room Manager, and External Conference Service.

MetaFrame Conferencing Manager User Interface

The MetaFrame Conferencing Manager User Interface is a published application in the MetaFrame Presentation Server farm. Its main function is to allow conference participants access to the conference room.

In order to gain performance improvements, the Conferencing Manager User Interface can be load-balanced like any published application.

Conference Organizer

The main function of the Conference Organizer is to maintain meeting information for all meeting servers in the farm. The meeting information consists of created meetings, meeting starting times, servers the meetings are being held upon, and the attendee lists of those meetings. This information is stored in the registry on the Conference Organizer server.

The Conference Organizer also is responsible for load-balancing meetings across available meeting servers. It can be installed on a standalone server without MetaFrame Presentation Server installed, but it must be installed in the same domain where Conference Room and the Conferencing Manager User Interface are installed.

This is an important consideration for fault-tolerance purposes. Dual-*everything* (Mirrored Hard Drives (or RAID), dual power supplies, dual Network Interface Cards) on the server hosting the Conference Organizer service has been a typical Citrix Consulting Services recommendation.

NOTE: Only one instance of Conference Organizer is allowed per server farm.

Conference Room

Conference Room is the component that provides the actual shadowing session in which the users collaborate during a conference. It is installed as a hidden published application and can be load-balanced like any other published application. Conference Room is not visible to the user, but is automatically launched via Conferencing Manger User Interface when a meeting is started or joined.

CAUTION: It is important that the Conference Room Published Application is not renamed; otherwise, conferences cannot be started.

Conference Room Manager

Conference Room Manager maintains meeting information on a single server. It monitors the attendees and licensing information for the server and is responsible for meeting operations such as start, join, leave, and end meetings. It communicates information with the Conference Organizer service, such as when a meeting has started and the attendees currently in the meeting.

External Conference Service

The External Conference Service is only required if you are using the Guest Attendee feature and provides communication to the Conference Organizer from outside a firewall using the HTTP protocol. The External Conference Service must run on the same server as the Conference Organizer. It is also required to have Microsoft .NET 1.1 installed on this server.

GUEST ATTENDEE

MetaFrame Conferencing Manager 3.0 includes a new feature that enables users who do not have credentials for the internal network to easily and securely collaborate with internal users. Guest attendees access a locked down version of the published MetaFrame Conferencing Manager 3.0 application where they cannot create or start conferences or launch applications within a conference. The Guest Attendee feature can also be used to provide internal users with a controlled conference environment.

The components that comprise the Guest Attendee feature are the following:

▼ The Guest Attendee accounts

■ The Guest Attendee Web Interface

▲ The External Conference Service

NOTE: The Guest Attendee Web Interface requires Web Interface for MetaFrame Presentation Server 3.0 and IIS 5.0 or later installed on the same server. The Guest Attendee feature supports only Microsoft Internet Explorer, Version 5.5 or later. Guest Attendee accounts require domain accounts. This feature cannot be used in a workgroup.

See the *Administrator's Guide for MetaFrame Conferencing Manager 3.0* for installation and configuration instructions.

Guest Attendee Feature Deployment Considerations

This section discusses some internal workings, problems, and concerns with the Guest Attendee feature.

External Conference Service

The Guest Attendee feature uses guest accounts created by the External Conference Service. After a conference has ended, these accounts are disabled and their passwords are changed until they are needed again.

NOTE: Guests never know what their usernames or passwords are. They use their Guest ID and Conference ID to gain access to conferences.

Multiple Domain Controllers

In Windows Active Directory domains with more than one domain controller, there may be delays in the replication between domain controllers. This creates the potential for a guest attendee to be routed to the domain controller that has not yet been synchronized with new guest attendee account information.

If you encounter this delay in your environment, there are two possible resolutions: configure a domain controller for guest accounts, and implement a hotfix.

Create a Domain Controller for Guest Accounts   Administrators may configure or create a child domain with only one Domain Controller for the guest accounts. Create the Guest Attendee group and accounts in this child domain. With only one Domain Controller synchronization, issues are eliminated.

Implement a Hotfix   Contact Citrix Technical Support to request a *hotfix*, which allows the disable/enable/reset password features to be disabled for guest accounts, removing the need for replication to occur to update account information.

METAFRAME CONFERENCING MANAGER 3.0 COMMUNICATIONS

When deploying MetaFrame Conferencing Manager 3.0 into a MetaFrame Presentation Server environment, it is important to understand how MetaFrame Conferencing Manager 3.0 communicates with its various components. This is especially important when deploying MetaFrame Conferencing Manager 3.0 over a WAN. This section describes which MetaFrame Conferencing Manager 3.0 components communicate with each other, the protocols they use, and the amount of bandwidth that they consume.

Launch Conferencing Client

When MetaFrame Conferencing Manager 3.0 is idle, meaning no meetings in progress and no users creating or joining meetings, there is no bandwidth overhead. Figure 9-1 displays the three actions that result when a user launches the MetaFrame Conferencing Manager Client: 1) retrieves available meetings, 2) communicates with the Exchange server, and 3) retrieves a list of available published applications.

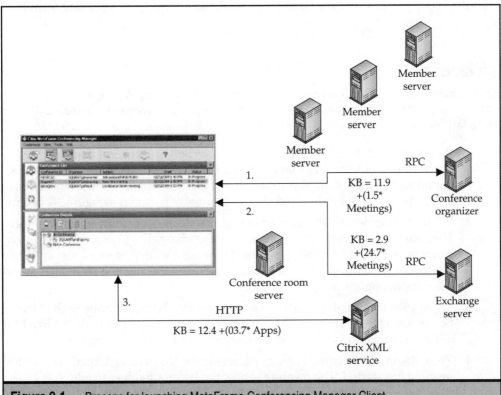

Figure 9-1.   Process for launching MetaFrame Conferencing Manager Client

Retrieve Available Meetings

When a user launches the MetaFrame Conferencing Manager Client, it communicates using Remote Procedure Call (RPC) with the Conference Organizer service. This communication retrieves a list of available meetings that the user can join. The formula used to determine the amount of bandwidth used during this action is the following:

$(KB = 11.9 + (1.5 * \# \textit{ of meetings}))$

Communicate with the Exchange Server

After retrieving the list of available meetings, the client then communicates to the Exchange server only if there is a valid Outlook profile. This also uses RPC, and the amount of bandwidth can be represented by the following:

$(KB = 2.9 + (24.7 * \# \textit{ of meetings}))$

Retrieve Available Published Applications

The client communicates with the configured Citrix XML Service to retrieve their list of available published applications on the Presentation Server farm. This communication uses the HTTP protocol and the bandwidth is calculated using the following formula:

$(KB = 12.4 + (0.3 * \# \textit{ of meetings}))$

Plan a Meeting

One of the most appealing features of MetaFrame Conferencing Manager 3.0 is the ability for users to create their own meetings without requiring IT involvement. Figure 9-2 displays the component interaction when a meeting is started.

1. A user connects to a MetaFrame Presentation Server farm and launches the MetaFrame Conferencing Manager User Interface published application. This communication uses the ICA protocol and is optimized for WAN connections. When the interface is initialized, the communication shown in Figure 9-2 begins.

2. When the user decides to create a meeting, the MetaFrame Conferencing Manager User Interface will contact the Conference Organizer. The Conference Organizer receives an ICA file directing the user to the least loaded meeting server. When the ICA file is launched, he will create a session on the meeting server and launch the CRoom application.

3. When CRoom initializes, the CRoom Manager will communicate to the License Server and check out a license for the meeting host. The bandwidth utilized for a license check-out is 1.3KB per license and uses the TCP protocol.

4. The CRoom Manager then communicates to the Conference Organizer that the meeting has started. The meeting is now ready for attendees to join.

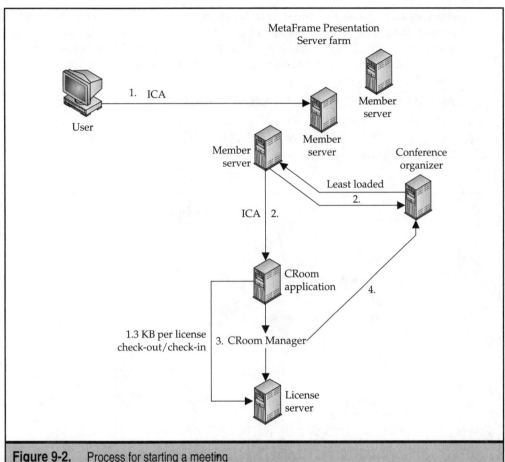

Figure 9-2. Process for starting a meeting

Join a Meeting

MetaFrame Conferencing Manager 3.0 makes it very simple for a user to join a meeting.
Figure 9-3 shows the component interaction when a meeting is started.

1. A user connects to a MetaFrame Presentation Server farm and launches the
   MetaFrame Conferencing Manager User Interface published application. This
   communication uses the ICA protocol and is optimized for WAN connections.
   When the interface is initialized, the communication shown in Figure 9-3 begins.
   The user decides to join a meeting displayed in the user interface.

2. When the user decides to join a meeting, the MetaFrame Conferencing Manager
   User Interface will contact the Conference Organizer. The Conference Organizer

receives an ICA file directing her to the meeting server where the conference is hosted. When the ICA file is launched, she will create a session on the meeting server and launch the CRoom application. The CRoom Manager will then communicate to the License Server and check out a license for the meeting attendee.

3. After the license acquisition, CRoom will shadow the host session and the attendee joins the meeting.

4. The CRoom Manager then communicates to the Conference Organizer that the current attendee has changed.

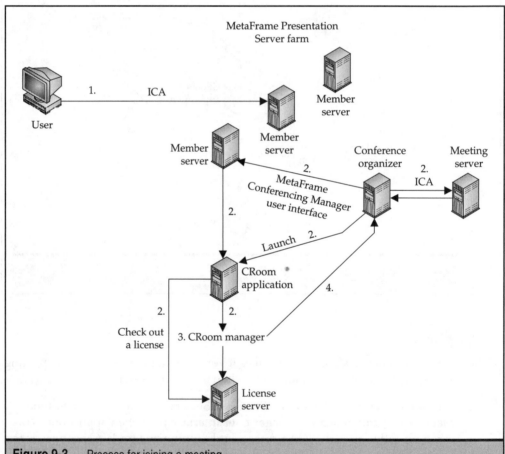

Figure 9-3. Process for joining a meeting

SIZE METAFRAME CONFERENCING MANAGER 3.0 SERVERS

MetaFrame Conferencing Manager 3.0 is particularly attractive from an economic stand-point. It is an inexpensive product that is sold on a concurrent usage basis, and concurrent MetaFrame Conferencing Manager 3.0 usage is typically far smaller than an organization's overall MetaFrame Presentation Server usage. It is important, however, not to dampen the growing enthusiasm for MetaFrame Conferencing Manager 3.0 by undersizing the servers and, consequently, giving MetaFrame Conferencing Manager 3.0 users a frustrating experience.

Correctly sizing the servers depends not only upon the hardware specifications of the MetaFrame Conferencing Manager Servers, but also on the resource requirements of the applications. This is why it is important to size your servers according to your environment before placing them into production.

Size for Memory Constraints

While processor, disk, and available network bandwidth all affect server sizing, memory is often the first bottleneck limiting acceptable performance. Acceptable performance can be described as *session latency*—how long it takes for all attendees to receive screen updates from the host session.

CAUTION: The number of attendees able to join a meeting with acceptable performance will also be decreased by applications that place a heavy load on the processor or consume large amounts of network bandwidth. For an acceptable end-user experience, CPU usage should not exceed 90%, and should not average more than 60% over any session period.

Size a Single MetaFrame Conferencing Manager Server

A single MetaFrame Conferencing Manager Server (where all components are installed on one server) includes the following components:

▼   MetaFrame Presentation Server 3.0
■   Citrix XML Service
■   Conference Organizer Service
■   Conference Room Manager Service
■   Conference Room Published Application
▲   MetaFrame Conferencing Manager User Interface

The formula for determining user capacity for a server is as follows:

$$\text{\# Users} = \frac{\text{TotalMemory (DesiredThreshold)} - (\text{SessionMemory} + \text{CRoom} + \text{MCM\_UI} + \text{Applications} + \text{OSOverhead})}{(\text{SessionMemory} + \text{MCM\_UI} + \text{CRoom} + \text{CShadow})}$$

TotalMemory   The amount of physical memory installed on the server.

DesiredThreshold   Maximum memory utilization desired. This should not exceed 80%.

SessionMemory   Memory cost of all the components required for an ICA session (*Winlogon.exe, WFShell.exe, Csrss.exe,* and *SSonSvr.exe*). This is the same for both the Host and Attendee sessions. The variable SessionMemory in the numerator refers to the organizer's session memory; the variable SessionMemory in the denominator refers to the attendee's session memory.

Applications   Memory cost for applications inside a meeting.

OSOverhead   Memory cost of the operating system and related services.

MCM_UI   Memory cost of the Citrix MetaFrame Conferencing Manager Client.

CRoom   Memory cost of the Conference Room Published Application.

CShadow   Memory cost of the *CShadow.exe* process (Attendee Only).

> **NOTE:** The following numerical data is intended only as a beginning point of reference. Citrix strongly recommends you perform your own sizing tests to properly determine your environment's capabilities.

Single Server Example   A server with 2GB of physical memory and a 2GB pagefile will have 4GB *TotalMemory*. The *DesiredThreshold* is 80% utilization. The session memory usage is 9.7MB, including all the processes associated with an ICA session. The size of the MetaFrame Conferencing Manager User Interface depends upon the number of published applications and meetings to which the user has rights, and will be around 24MB. The application used within the meeting is Microsoft PowerPoint, which utilizes 10MB. The O/S Overhead is 200MB. The denominator portion of the equation is the attendee's memory usage, which is 39.5MB. This includes all the processes associated with an ICA session, *MCM_UI, CRoom,* and *CShadow*.

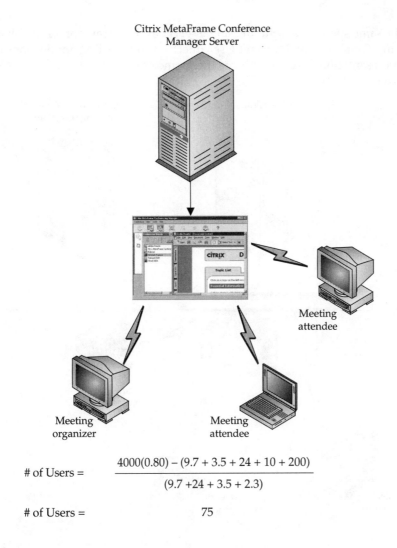

Citrix MetaFrame Conference
Manager Server

Meeting
attendee

Meeting
organizer

Meeting
attendee

$$\text{\# of Users} = \frac{4000(0.80) - (9.7 + 3.5 + 24 + 10 + 200)}{(9.7 + 24 + 3.5 + 2.3)}$$

$$\text{\# of Users} = 75$$

Size MetaFrame Conferencing Manager Server in a Multiple Server Environment

Overall memory utilization can be reduced by offloading the MetaFrame Conferencing Manager User Interface and applications to other MetaFrame Presentation Servers. The formula to accomplish this is simplified as follows:

$$\text{\# Users} = \frac{\text{TotalMemory (Desired Threshold)} - (\text{SessionMemory} + \text{CRoom} + \text{OS Overhead})}{(\text{SessionMemory} + \text{CRoom} + \text{CShadow})}$$

Using the same specifics as with the single server example (except for load-balancing the MetaFrame Conferencing Manager User Interface and meeting applications to other MetaFrame Presentation Servers) reduces the memory for each attendee by 24MB and each organizer by 34MB.

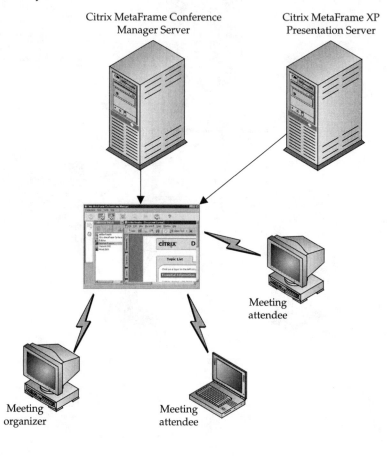

Citrix MetaFrame Conference
Manager Server

Citrix MetaFrame XP
Presentation Server

Meeting
attendee

Meeting
organizer

Meeting
attendee

$$\text{\# of Users} = \frac{4000(0.80) - (9.7 + 3.5 + 200)}{(9.7 + 3.5 + 2.3)}$$

$$\text{\# of Users} = 192$$

Multiple Server Example In the multiserver example we hit a limit of 192 users. This formula is accurate up to a certain number of users when based on memory alone. In practice, other considerations such as I/O bottlenecks, O/S limitations, and latency will prevent scaling this high. Testing in the Citrix *e*Labs shows that a server of this size can potentially support 90–100 users in a multiserver setup, depending on the type of applications in use.

Size for Applications

When sizing MetaFrame Conferencing Manager Servers, using the memory formula will not be sufficient to determine an accurate value for how many users a server can support. The types of applications in a meeting must also be taken into account, including the amount of user input and graphics being processed and displayed by the applications. Different applications will exhibit different amounts of latency depending on how much of the screen is changed with every action. The three types of applications are documents and spreadsheets, presentations, and highly intensive graphic and CAD applications.

Documents and Spreadsheets

Documents and spreadsheets update only small portions of the screen. When users collaborate using these applications, small amounts of session latency are sometimes unnoticeable. These types of meetings will be able to support the most users at the upper end of the memory formula spectrum.

Presentations

Presentations update the entire screen when slides are changed. When users collaborate they will notice a degree of session latency depending on the actions performed; changing the text will have little impact while adding pictures and transitions will be more intensive. These types of meetings will support the middle of the memory formula spectrum. Typical session latency on a meeting viewing a Microsoft PowerPoint presentation with 60 users is about 2 seconds per slide.

Highly Intensive Graphic and CAD Applications

These types of applications update the entire screen when changes occur and include complex shapes and colors. When users collaborate they will notice a (usually higher) degree of session latency depending on the actions performed, such as moving and resizing objects. These types of meetings will support the lower end of the memory formula spectrum.

Tune MetaFrame Conferencing Manager 3.0 Servers

The largest increase in performance will be seen when the MetaFrame Conferencing Manager User Interface and available applications are load-balanced across the servers in your MetaFrame Presentation Server farm. This will distribute the workload across multiple servers, thus reducing the memory and CPU consumption on the Conference server and allowing more users to participate in a meeting.

Disable Virtual Channels

When creating or joining a meeting, optimize the ICA Client by disabling any unneeded virtual channels. For example, if audio and printing are not needed in a conference, the administrator should disable these virtual channels for users connecting to that particular server. Not initializing these virtual channels during logon saves some memory and CPU resources. For ease in administration, virtual channels can be disabled through policies found in the Presentation Server Console.

Disable Windows Services

In order to maximize user capacity, disable all unneeded Windows services. Examples include IIS, Alerter, and the Spooler service, if printing is not needed.

It is important to disable any unnecessary processes that exist in every session. For example, if Microsoft Office is published on the server, processes such as Find Fast, Help Assistant, and automatic spell-checking should be disabled for each user.

Reduce Disk and Memory I/O

Many graphics applications tend to be I/O intensive, and when multiple users are viewing and potentially modifying information, I/O can bottleneck. The newer generation servers offer four times the bus speed of previous generations, and the latest RAID systems and SCSI drives are dramatically faster than previous generations. Additionally, new technology in the form of solid state drives can also be leveraged to further optimize the conferencing performance. It is important, when sizing servers and doing testing, to remember that processor capability and memory size are not the only variables that can have dramatic impacts on end-users' perceptions of performance.

CHAPTER 10

Security Issues and Guidelines

This chapter describes security issues that arise when particular third-party components are used with the MetaFrame Access Suite, as well as concepts relevant to implementing MetaFrame Password Manager. Additionally, baseline recommendations related to server hardening are addressed. The third-party components covered in this chapter are

▼ Databases (as used in the data store)

■ Proxy Servers

▲ Smart Cards

When necessary, specific steps can be taken to "harden" the servers hosting Citrix components against several types of network events (IP Stack Hardening) as well as steps to enforce additional security restrictions on access to MetaFrame management interfaces and OS features. These changes are often required to ensure compliance with U.S. Department of Defense (DoD) or Common Criteria security constraints. Generic hardening techinques, as identified in Microsoft or other vendor documentation, may or may not be compatible with MetaFrame Presentation Server and related components. Hardened configurations should be tested before being used in a production implementation. If you plan to use Presentation Server in the Common Criteria–evaluated configuration, refer to the detailed step-by-step instructions in the Common Criteria Evaluated Configuration Guide at http://www.citrix.com.

NOTE: This chapter is not intended to replace any documentation that is available through *readme.txt* documents, Knowledge Base articles, or Administrator's Guides for Citrix products, and it is assumed that the reader will refer to these documents as authoritative references. Other components of supporting infrastructure (such LAN, WAN, firewall, Windows domain, physical security, virus protection, and disaster recovery) security elements must also be secured. Best practices for these are discussed in Chapter 8 of *Citrix MetaFrame Access Suite for Windows Server 2003: The Official Guide* (McGraw-Hill/Osborne, 2003).

SECURING THE DATA STORE

Recommendations for data store security depend on the database used. In general, users who access MetaFrame Presentation Server do not require and should not be granted any access to the datas.

With direct mode access, all MetaFrame Presentation Server farm servers share a single user account and password for accessing the data store. Select a password that is not easily guessed. Keep the username and password secure and give it to MetaFrame Administrators for installation only.

If the user account for direct mode access to the database is changed at a later time, the IMA Service will fail to start on all MetaFrame servers configured with that account. To reconfigure the IMA Service password, use the **dsmaint config** command on each affected server. For information about the **dsmaint config** command, refer to the *MetaFrame Presentation Server Administrator's Guide*.

Microsoft Access

For an Access data store, the default username is "citrix" and the password is "citrix." If users have access to the data store server, change the password using **dsmaint config** and keep the information in a safe place.

NOTE: Microsoft Access is not recommended for production configurations. Because it is a flat-file and lacks true database check-pointing, an Access data store is easily corrupted.

Because it is a flat file and lacks true database check-pointing, an Access data store is easily corrupted.

IMPORTANT: Ensure you create a backup of your data store before using **dsmaint config** to change the data store password.

Microsoft SQL Desktop Edition, Service Pack 3 (MSDE)

Windows NT Authentication is supported for the MSDE database. For security reasons, Microsoft SQL Server authentication is not supported. For further information, please consult Microsoft documentation. In a default installation of MSDE, the username and password will typically be the local Administrator account, and MSDE will use the Local System account as a service account. If users have access to the data store server, change the password using **dsmaint config** and keep the information in a safe place. For added security, MSDE can be reconfigured to use a named Local User or a named Domain User as the MSDE service account.

Microsoft SQL Server

Microsoft SQL Server has two authentication modes: Windows Authentication Mode and Mixed Mode. Microsoft security recommendations are to use Windows Authentication Mode and avoid Mixed Mode. When Windows Authentication Mode is used, only Windows users and groups that have explicitly been mapped to SQL Server logins are valid. SQL Server accounts, such as the System Administrator (sa) account, are not valid in Windows Authentication Mode.

When Mixed Mode is used, SQL Server accounts, as well as mapped Windows users and groups, are valid.

The user account that is used to access the data store on Microsoft SQL Server has public and db_owner roles on the server and database.

TIP: Citrix recommends using only Windows Authentication Mode.

If the Microsoft SQL Server is configured for Mixed Mode security (with either Microsoft SQL Server Authentication or Windows NT Authentication), it is useful to create a Microsoft SQL Server user for the sole purpose of accessing the data store. Because the Microsoft SQL Server user account would access only the data store, there is no risk of compromising a Windows domain if the user's password is compromised.

After the initial installation of the database with db_owner permission, change the user account's permission to db_reader and db_writer.

CAUTION: Changing the user account's permission from db_owner might cause installation problems with future service packs or feature releases. Always change the account permission back to db_owner before installing a service pack or feature release.

Oracle

If the data store is hosted on Oracle, give the Oracle user account that is used for the MetaFrame Presentation Server farm only "connect" and "resource" permissions. System Administrator (system or sys) account permissions are not needed for data store access.

IBM DB2

If the data store is hosted on IBM DB2, give the DB2 user account that is used for the MetaFrame Presentation Server farm the following permissions:

▼ Connect database

■ Create tables

■ Register functions to execute to database manager's process

▲ Create schemas implicity

NOTE: System Administrator (DB2Admin) account permissions are not needed for data store access.

PROXY SERVER INTEGRATION

In many corporate environments, Proxy Servers are used to add an additional level of security and control. The MetaFrame Access Suite is compatible with most Proxy Server implementations, but additional configuration is necessary. This section covers some advanced concepts and configurations for MetaFrame Access Clients connecting via a Proxy Server, which support the SOCKS or Secure Proxy protocols. Many Proxy Server and firewall products support these protocols. This section assumes that the Proxy Server has already been configured, and that the default ports have been used.

MetaFrame Access Client Port Usage

The typical ports for connections are as follows:

ICA	1494
Common Gateway Protocol	2598
SOCKS	1080
Web Proxy	80 or 8080
Secure Proxy	443 or 563

NOTE: Some web proxy configurations may use Port 3128 as the default web proxy port.

Proxy Server Authentication Support

Some Proxy Servers can be configured to require authentication to the Proxy Server itself. Proxy Server authentication is similar to Web Server authentication, authentication methods include

▼ Basic

▲ NTLM (NT LAN Manager)

Basic authentication transmits the username and password to the Proxy Server. NTLM authentication uses a challenge/response protocol and does not transmit the actual password. Basic authentication is widely supported; NTLM authentication is supported by Microsoft Proxy Server 2.0 and Microsoft Internet Security and Acceleration (ISA) Server.

Proxy Server ICA/INI File Parameters

Various proxy parameters are used by the client's INI files (that is, *%userprofile%\Application Data\ICA Client\APPSRV.ini*) or ICA files (including the Web Interface for MetaFrame Presentation Server and Citrix Program Neighborhood *Template.ica*). See each product's Administration Guide for more information. The parameters can be placed in the [WFCLIENT] section of the INI/ICA file or in the [<APPLICATION>] section only if the DoNotUseDefaultCSL=ON parameter is set in the same section.

Parameters—ICA Client Version 6.20.986 and Earlier

Older versions of the ICA Client require slightly different settings:

▼ ICASOCKSProtocolVersion {-1|0|4|5}

  ■ **-1** (None) Do not use SOCKS

  ■ **0** Auto Detect

- ■ **4** Use SOCKS version 4
- ■ **5** Use SOCKS version 5
- ■ `ICASOCKSProxyHost` FQDN Proxy Address or IP Address
- ■ `ICASOCKSProxyPortNumber` Proxy Port
- ■ `ICASOCKSrfc1929UserName` SOCKSv5 Username
- ■ `ICASOCKSrfc1929Password` SOCKSv5 Username Password
- ▲ `ICASOCKSTimeout` Time in milliseconds after the client waits for initial response from the Proxy Server

Parameters—MetaFrame Access Client Version 6.30.1050 and Later

The INI file parameters include `ProxyType`, `ProxyHost`, `ProxyBypassList`, `ProxyAutoConfigURL`, `ProxyUsername`, `ProxyPassword`, and `ProxyTimeout`.

TIP: The 6.30 and above clients are able to read and understand the 6.20 parameters for backward compatibility.

- ▼ `ProxyType` None | Auto | SOCKS | SOCKSv4 | SOCKSv5 | Secure | Script
    - ■ **None** The client will always use a Direct Connection to the server; there will be no connection to the Proxy/Firewall server.
    - ■ **Auto** Auto uses the client machine's web browser settings (Microsoft Internet Explorer 4.*x* or later, Netscape Navigator 4.76 or later).
    - ■ **SOCKS** SOCKS creates a SOCKS connection to the server and autodetects the SOCKS version number used by the Proxy/Firewall.
    - ■ **SOCKSv4** SOCKSv4 creates SOCKS version 4 connections.
    - ■ **SOCKSv5** SOCKSv5 creates SOCKS version 5 connections.
    - ■ **Secure** Secure connects through a Secure Tunnel protocol, usually a High Encryption or SSL/TLS connection. You will have to configure your MetaFrame Server with SSL/TLS Relay or use Citrix Secure Gateway. It is recommended that you use SSL/TLS+HTTP connection protocol or use TCP/IP+HTTP and set the encryption to 128-bit.
    - ■ **Script** Script uses the JavaScript Proxy Auto-Configuration file (*.*PAC*) or the Microsoft Internet Explorer Internet Settings file (*.*INS*) to configure the proxy connection set in the mentioned formats. Set the `ProxyType` to Auto and use the client's web browser preferences for auto-configuration scripts. The path to the file is set in the `ProxyAutoConfigURL` parameter.
- ■ `ProxyHost` "Proxy Address:Proxy:Port:" or ":IP Address:Proxy Port." `ProxyHost` includes the address of the proxy host and port number. To set the IP address of the Proxy/ Proxy/Firewall server or use its Fully Qualified Domain Name (FQDN), enter the Proxy/Firewall port number at

the end of the address using the following sample formats: 192.168.0.1:8080 or proxy.citrix.com:1080.

■ `ProxyBypassList`   Domain names/IP addresses that the Proxy Server will ignore at connection time. `ProxyBypassList` allows the ability to include domain names that will be ignored during a proxy connection.

> **NOTE:**   The `ProxyBypassList` setting is used to connect to servers in the same subnet/network as the client machine without the use of the Proxy/Firewall servers. For example, a client machine may reside in the same corp.company.com domain where MetaFrame Presentation Servers reside. Therefore, instead of configuring each connection (connecting to the internal MetaFrame Presentation Server hosts) for direct connections, you can set `ProxyBypassList=*.corp.company.com` or `*.partner.company.com` and the client will ignore any Proxy Servers when connecting to these domains. You may use a semi-colon (;) or a comma (,) as a delimiter when specifying more than one domain.

■ `ProxyAutoConfigURL`   Address of HTTP server path of auto-configuration file. `ProxyAutoConfigURL` allows you to include an HTTP URL to a JavaScript Proxy auto-configuration file (*.*PAC*) or the Microsoft Internet Explorer Internet Settings file (*.*INS*).

> **NOTE:**   This setting is used when an administrator wants to centralize Proxy Server client configuration settings by using an autoconfiguration script file. The script file can be either a JavaScript PAC file or a Microsoft Internet Explorer INS file. For information on creating these files, follow these links:
>
> MSDN article on PAC files:
> http://www.microsoft.com/mind/0599/faq/faq0599.asp
> Internet Explorer Administration Kit Article:
> http://www.microsoft.com/windows/ieak/techinfo/deploy/60/en/default.asp?URL=/windows/ieak/techinfo/deploy/60/en/autodis.htm

■ `ProxyUsername`   NTLM/SOCKSv5/Secure Proxy Username. `ProxyUsername` provides the location to configure the NTLM, SOCKSv5 or Secure Proxy authentication credentials.

■ `ProxyPassword`   NTLM/SOCKSv5/Secure Proxy Password. Like `ProxyUsername`, `ProxyPassword` also provides the location to configure the NTLM, SOCKSv5, or Secure Proxy authentication credentials.

> **NOTE:**   If the `ProxyUsername`/`ProxyPassword` parameters are not set and the Proxy/Firewall configuration connects to a server configured for NTLM, SOCKSv5, or Secure Proxy with authentication, the ICA session will get prompted for user credentials. These user credentials are for proxy authentication only and need not be the same as the user's domain or network credentials. When these parameters are set, the MetaFrame Access Client will supply these credentials to the Proxy Server.

Basic authentication is not recommended due to security concerns.

IMPORTANT: If the Proxy Server negotiates basic authentication rather than NTLM, the username and password are passed in clear text. Citrix recommends not setting these parameters if there is a risk that unauthorized users can observe (sniff) network traffic.

▲ `ProxyTimeout` Time in milliseconds after the client waits for initial response from the Proxy Server. The minimum value is 1,000.

Proxy Server Parameters in ICA Clients

When connections are made via the Program Neighborhood or Program Neighborhood Agent, Proxy Server parameters can be configured within the client.

Program Neighborhood Client Parameters

When using the Program Neighborhood Client, the following parameters can be set from the Custom Connection Settings | Connection Properties | Application Set settings interface. In the Server Location dialog for any of the above, click the Firewalls button to set the parameters for web browser proxy settings: None, SOCKS, and Secure.

▼ **Use Web Browser Proxy Settings** Sets `ProxyType=Auto`

■ **None (direct connection)** Sets `ProxyType=None`

■ **SOCKS** Sets `ProxyType=SOCKS`. If a specific SOCKS version is required, edit the user's APPSRV.INI file to change the value for the `ProxyType` to the correct version parameter. This setting requires the proxy address and port fields to be entered.

▲ **Secure** Sets `ProxyType=Secure`. This setting requires the proxy address and port fields to be filled out, which sets the `ProxyHost` parameter.

NOTE: For more information, refer to the Client for 32-bit Windows Administrator's Guide.

Program Neighborhood Agent Client Parameters

In order to ensure Program Neighborhood Agent client connectivity via a proxy, follow the steps outlined later in this chapter in the section titled "Enabling Proxy Settings via the *Template.ica* File." Note that the *Template.ica* file that the Program Neighborhood Agent uses resides in a different directory than the standard client *Template.ica* file located under *%webroot%\Citrix\PNAgent*. If you use the Web Interface Administration Console to modify the settings for use of SOCKS connections only, there is no need to modify the *Template.ica* file for Program NeighborhoodAgent. The Program Neighborhood Agent *Template.ica* will read the parameters from the *WebInterface.conf* or *NFuse.conf* file.

If you edit the *Template.ica* file directly, you must ensure both the default copy and the Program Neighborhood Agent version are changed.

Default Installation of the *Config.xml* File   The default installation of the ***Config.xml*** file contains the NetBIOS name (as opposed to the FQDN) of the Web Server URL. To correctly support Internet connectivity, this value must be changed to the external IP address or to the FQDN of the Web Interface server. Additionally, the Web Interface must issue the configured alternate address of the MetaFrame Presentation Server for the Program Neighborhood Agent to connect. Certain Proxy Server configurations allow routing of HTTP traffic directly to a Web Server. Therefore, this tunneling configuration may be used if one Web Interface server receives all Internet traffic for the farm. The Program Neighborhood Agent client can connect to the external interface of the Proxy Server, while the configuration masks the internal network from being exposed through the XML traffic or configuration parameters.

NOTE: For more information on the Web Interface Administration Console, see the *Web Interface Administrator's Guide.*

Client-to-MetaFrame Presentation Server Proxy Configurations

Many Proxy Servers are configured to only permit standard web proxy connections, typically TCP Ports 443 and 80. MetaFrame Access Client proxy connections use destination ports based on the type of connection indicated in the ICA connection properties. For example, an ICA connection configured to use TCP/IP with a Proxy Server will attempt to proxy to Port 1494 when connecting to the MetaFrame Presentation Server. Many Proxy Servers would reject this connection attempt. If ICA Clients connect directly to the specified MetaFrame Presentation Server host, use Citrix Secure Sockets Layer (SSL) Relay to overcome this limitation.

Citrix SSL Relay Service

Citrix recommends that MetaFrame Presentation Servers are configured to run the Citrix SSL Relay service on the default port (TCP 443) to minimize problems with Proxy Server configuration. The MetaFrame Access Client should be configured to use SSL/TLS+ HTTP. This configuration forces the client to contact the Proxy Server with a destination port of 443 to the MetaFrame Presentation Server. If you do not use SSL/TLS, you will most likely need to configure your Proxy Server to allow TCP 1494 proxy sessions (if available) or bypass sessions destined for TCP 1494. With MetaFrame Presentation Server 3.0, you may also need to configure Port 2598 for the common gateway protocol (CGP), which is used for the session reliability feature.

Connecting to the MetaFrame Presentation Server Through the Proxy Server

Proxy servers may be configured to allow only outbound connections to an authorized set of IP addresses. In order to connect to the MetaFrame Presentation Server through the proxy server, modify the Proxy Server policy to ensure the FQDN or IP addresses of the MetaFrame Presentation Servers are permitted.

Client-to-Web Interface Proxy Connections

There are two ways to enable the MetaFrame Access Client to use the Web Interface to pass through a Proxy/Firewall server: use the Web Interface Console or edit the *.ICA* file manually. Both HTTP and SOCKS proxies are valid for configuration within these settings.

Enabling Proxy Settings Using the WI Console

Access the Web Interface Console at http(s)://*<server name>*/Citrix/MetaFrame/WIAdmin on the server running the WI.

Setting Default Proxy Parameters   To enable the default proxy parameters, follow these steps:

1. In the left menu, select Client-Side Firewall.
2. Select one of the following in the Default Proxy Setting section:
   - **Auto**   Allows the client to automatically detect the proxy settings.
   - **Client**   Sets client-configured proxy settings as the default.
   - **None**   Does not use any client-side proxies.
   - **Use Explicit Mapping**   Specifies the Proxy Server used. If this option is selected, you must enter the address of the Proxy Server in the Proxy Address field and the port number in the Proxy Port field. The proxy address can be an IP address or a DNS name. By default, the proxy port number is 1080.

Setting Specific Proxy Parameters   To configure specific proxy parameters, follow these steps:

1. In the left menu, select Client-Side Firewall.
2. In the Specific Proxy Settings section, enter an IP address or partial address in the Client Address Prefix field.
3. Select one of the following options:
   - **Auto**
   - **Client**
   - **None**
   - **Use Explicit Mapping**
4. Click Add to add proxy to the mapping list.
5. Using the Client-Side Firewall page, you can easily specify a proxy to specific clients connecting via the Web Interface. For example, you can set the default Proxy Settings to Auto or None for internal users, and force external users to use a specified proxy based on their IP address ranges.

NOTE: The Client Address Prefix field uses textual matching. For example, if you want to specify clients in the range 192.168.0.0 to 192.168.254.254, then the string *192.168* will match all clients within that range. Further, when multiple mappings are listed, they are matched in the sequence listed in the mapping list.

The Web Interface Console only enables the proxy parameters listed in the .ICA/.INI File Parameters section, and does not allow you to configure secure proxy settings. Additionally, SOCKSv5/Secure Proxy authentication parameters are not configurable using the Web Interface Console. For more information, see the "Proxy Server ICA/INI File Parameters" section earlier in this chapter.

Enabling Proxy Settings via the *Template.ica* File

You can edit the *Template.ica* file and add new parameters as needed. Citrix recommends that the parameters are added in both the [WFCLIENT] and [<APPLICATION>] sections of the *Template.ica* file. This will ensure proper connectivity for all client types.

Using Multiple Versions of MetaFrame Access Clients   If different versions of MetaFrame Access Clients are used to access the Web Interface, edit the *Template.ica* file and include all relevant Proxy Server parameters as described in the "Proxy Server ICA/INI File Parameters" section earlier in the chapter. This allows previous versions of ICA clients to connect using the parameters set for their client version and ensures correct connectivity for all versions of MetaFrame Access Clients.

Web browsers use their own proxy settings to connect to the Web Interface site. The *Template.ica* file enables the MetaFrame Access Client to connect by reading the proxy parameters.

Template.ica Parameters   The *Template.ica* parameters are not dependent on the version of the Web Interface being used. By using older versions and setting the new parameters in the *Template.ica* file, the client version determines which parameters will be read from the *Template.ica* file.

NOTE: The parameters can be placed in the [WFCLIENT] section of the .ICA/.INI file or in the [<APPLICATION>] section only if the DoNotUseDefaultCSL=ON parameter is in the same section.

Proxy Server Idle Timeout

Some Proxy Servers enforce timeouts for secure proxy HTTP protocol connections. For example, Microsoft Internet Acceleration and Security (ISA) Server has a default of 30 seconds. When using a secure HTTP protocol connection, ensure that the timeout is either disabled or set to a suitable value for a long-lived ICA session.

For more information about configuring the Web Interface, see the *Web Interface for MetaFrame XP Administrator's Guide.*

USING SMART CARDS WITH METAFRAME PRESENTATION SERVER

Smart card authentication provides increased security by requiring two factors: a physical device and a PIN. Smart cards can also increase application security—for example, for signing and encrypting e-mail.

MetaFrame Presentation Server itself can be easily configured to support smart cards. However, third-party components require additional configuration. This section assumes the following:

▼   Active Directory Service (ADS) Domains and Certificate Authorities (CA) have been set up correctly with smart card support. Refer to Microsoft documentation on ADS Domains and CA configuration. Refer to Microsoft Knowledge Base support articles 313274, 257480, and 231881 for smart card information.

■   Driver software for the smart card reader has been installed on client devices.

■   Smart card driver software, including a smart card CSP (Cryptographic Service Provider), has been installed on MetaFrame Presentation Server. If connecting via Program Neighborhood Agent or Web Interface, the same CSP must be installed on the client device as well.

▲   Smart cards are correctly configured per the vendor's specifications. Refer to documentation from your smart card vendor for details. For more information regarding smart cards on Windows 2000, refer to Microsoft Knowledge Base support articles 313557 and 227873.

Smart Card Deployment

Deploying smart cards requires enabling smart card support on the client and server, and establishing a certificate enrollment system. Consideration should also be given to smart card removal options, the smart card reader hardware, the smart cards themselves, PIN requirements, unloading smart cards, and to handling a situation where the Domain Controller is unavailable.

Smart Card Removal Options

There are two options that you can enable for smart card removal. The first option locks the computer when a smart card is removed. The second option logs you off the workstation when you remove a smart card. Additional information is available by referencing Microsoft Knowledge Base support article 227873.

To enable either of these options, set the data value of the `ScRemoveOption` value in the following registry key:

```
HKLM\SOFTWARE\Microsoft\Windows NT\CurrentVersion\Winlogon
     Value: ScRemoveOption (REG_SZ)
     Setting:     0 - No action
                  1 - Lock workstation
                  2 - Force logoff
```

Domain Controller Unavailability Errors

If a Domain Controller is not available, smart card logon fails even if the user has previously logged onto the computer using a smart card. If the Domain Controller is available but does not have a valid Certificate Revocation List (CRL) for the issuing CA, logon also fails. The error message in each of these cases is the same:

"The system could not log you on. Your credentials could not be verified."

USING SMART CARDS WITH THE WEB INTERFACE AND PROGRAM NEIGHBORHOOD AGENT

Additional configuration steps are required to use smart cards with Web Interface or Program Neighborhood Agent. There are also issues to be aware of regarding client operating systems, the CSP, specific smart card requirements, and USB readers.

Configuring Microsoft Internet Information Server (IIS)

To use smart cards with Web Interface, configure the Microsoft IIS Web Server and enable smart card authentication using the Web Interface Console. To use smart cards with Program Neighborhood Agent, only configure Microsoft IIS.

Microsoft IIS must be configured to have a CA, which can be set up in an Active Directory Domain.For further information, please refer to Microsoft's documentation on IIS and Certificate Authorities.

NOTE: It is assumed that the Web Interface Web Server is running Windows 2000 or above with Microsoft Internet Information Server (IIS).

Configuring IIS

IIS configuration involves three basic steps:

1. Enable the Windows Directory Mapper Service.

2. Install a server certificate.

3. Ensure that SSL is enabled on the Web Interface Web Server.

Enabling the Windows Directory Mapper Service   To configure the Windows Diretory Mapper, complete the following steps:

1. To open the Computer Management utility, right-click on My Computer and choose Manage.

2. Navigate down and expand Services and Applications.

3. Navigate down and expand Internet Information Services, right-click, and choose Properties.

4. Under the Internet Information Services tab, in the Master Properties box, click Edit.

5. Click the Directory Security tab.

6. Select the Enable the Windows Directory Service Mapper check box.

7. Click OK until the screen is back to Computer Management.

Installing a Server Certificate   Installing the Public Key Cryptography (PKI) Server Certificate on IIS consists of two major steps, generating the certificate request, and installing the resulting certificate.

To generate the certificate request, complete the following steps:

1. In the Computer Management utility under Internet Information Services, expand the tree until Default Web Site is displayed.

2. Right-click Default Web Site and choose Properties.

3. Click the Directory Security tab.

4. Click Server Certificate to begin the Web Server Certificate Wizard and click Next.

5. Choose Create New Certificate and click Next.

6. Choose one of the two options:

   a. Choose the Send The Request Immediately To The Certification Authority option and click Next. (This option is unavailable unless IIS has access to an Enterprise CA, which requires Certificate Server 2.0 to be installed in Active Directory.

   b. Choose the Prepare A New Request But Send It Later option and click Next. (Use this option if requesting a commercial certificate).

7. Type a friendly name for the certificate and click Next.

TIP: Use the server's FQDN name for the friendly name.

8. Choose the bit length of the key you want to use and whether you want to use SGC (Server Gated Cryptography), and then click Next. (For more information on bit length and SGC, see the IIS Help that is located on the server at the following address: http://<*servername*>/iishelp/iis/htm/core/iistesc.htm).

9. Type the corresponding organization and organizational unit and click Next.

10. For the Common Name, type the FQDN of the Web Interface Web Server and click Next.

11. Type State/Province and City/Locality and click Next.

12. The Certificate Authority should be automatically filled in. If not, select it from the drop-down list.

13. Click Next, Next, and Finish.

To install the certificate (response file), complete the following steps:

1. Repeat steps 1–3.

2. Under the Secure Communications section, click Server Certificate.

3. On the Web Site Certificate Wizard, click Next.

4. Choose to Process the Pending Request and Install the Certificate. Click Next.

5. Type in the location of the certificate response file (you may also browse to the file), and then click Next.

6. Read the summary screen to be sure that you are processing the correct certificate, and then click Next.

7. You will see a confirmation screen. When you have read this information, click Next.

Ensuring That SSL is Enabled on the Web Interface Web Server

In order to ensure that SSL is enabled on the Web Interface Web Server, follow these steps:

1. In the Computer Management utility under Internet Information Services, expand the tree until Default Web Site is displayed.

2. Right-click on Default Web Site and select Properties.

3. Choose the Web Site tab and make sure that SSL Port 443 is available for SSL connections.

4. Close the Computer Management utility.

Reenabling Smart Card Support after Installing a New Certificate on the IIS Server After IIS has been configured with a certificate, if that certificate needs to be removed and a new certificate installed, IIS removes some of the configured attributes that are required for both the Web Interface and the Program Neighborhood Agent clients to properly support smart card functionality. To reenable functionality, follow these steps:

1. In the Computer Management utility under Internet Information Services, expand the tree until Default Web Site is displayed.

2. Expand Default Web Site.

3. Expand Citrix.

4. Expand MetaFrame.

5. Right-click Certificate and select Properties.

6. Click the Directory Security tab.

7. Click Edit under Secure Communications.

8. Click Require Secure Channel (SSL).

9. Click Require Client Certificates.

10. Click Enable Client Certificate Mapping.

11. Click OK twice to close out the properties windows.

12. Click the PNAgent folder under the Citrix folder.

13. Right-click *smartcard_enum.asp* and select properties.

14. Repeat steps 6–11 for File Security.

15. Right-click *smartcard_launch.asp*.

16. Repeat steps 6–11 for File Security.

17. Right-click *smartcard_reconnect.asp* and select Properties.

18. Repeat steps 6–11 for File Security.

Enabling Smart Card Authentication Using the WI Console

To configure the Web Interface for smart card logons, follow these steps:

1. Open a browser and browse to http://*<your Web Interface server>*/Citrix/
   MetaFrame/WIAdmin.

2. Click the Authentication menu down the left side.

3. Enable the smart card option at the top of the screen.

4. Enable the smart card with Single Sign On option if you desire to allow Single
   Sign On.

5. Click Save.

6. Click the Apply Changes option on the bottom frame.

7. Exit from the Administration Console by closing the browser window.

Testing Web Interface Logons

To test the configuration, log onto the Web Interface Server (http//:*<your Web Interface Server>*) from an Access Client with a smart card and launch a published application.

Miscellaneous Smart Card Considerations

When using smart cards with Web Interface or with Program Neighborhood Agent, consideration should be given to the client operating system (OS), the CSP, and to specific smart card requirements.

Client Operating Systems

Smart cards using Single Sign On can only be enabled on Windows 2000, Windows XP, and Windows Server 2003 clients. They are the only clients that support logging on locally using a smart card.

Pre-installed (Native OS) Support for Smart Card Readers and Smart Cards   Windows 2000, Windows XP, and Windows Server 2003 have pre-installed support for some smart card readers. In order to check whether the reader is supported by default, attach the reader to the client and let the OS detect and install the drivers. If, after a restart of the system, there is not an option to logon using the smart card, the vendor's software drivers need to be installed.

Also, Windows 2000 Server, Windows XP, and Windows Server 2003 have pre-installed support for some Axalto (formerly Schlumberger) and Gemplus smart cards. On Windows XP, Axalto (Schlumberger) Cryptoflex 8K cards can be used without installing additional drivers whereas Axalto (Schlumberger) Cryptoflex 16K cards will require additional drivers.

Installing More Than One Type of Smart Card   MetaFrame Presentation Server generally supports more than one type of smart card. However, some types of smart cards will not function correctly if more than one type is installed. For example, the Axalto (formerly Schlumberger) and ActivCard smart card drivers may not function properly if they are both installed on the same server. However, either can be installed with the Gemplus smart card driver.

TIP: To test that a server is set up correctly for smart card logon over ICA, log on locally to the server using the smart card. If a local logon is successful, log on over an ICA session should also be successful.

METAFRAME PASSWORD MANAGER SECURITY

MetaFrame Password Manager is a Single Sign On solution that reconciles security and usability interests to allow for an effective security strategy. Users authenticate only once with a single primary password for domain authentication (Primary Authentication), possibly augmented with multifactor authentication devices. After the Primary Authentication is complete, MetaFrame Password Manager takes over the ongoing management of a user's secondary credentials to access enterprise, web- and host-based applications, or any other password-protected IT resource. MetaFrame Password Manager increases security by centralizing the definition and activation of password policies, enforcing strong passwords, applying uniform safeguards around credentials, and by imposing domain re-authentication parameters, such as to prevent walkaway breaches. This section addresses functional security within MetaFrame Password Manager and discusses considerations for using smart cards with MetaFrame Password Manager.

MetaFrame Password Manager Components

MetaFrame Password Manager consists of three primary software components: the agent, a central credential store, and the Administrator Console. Details on each component can be found in the *Citrix MetaFrame Password Manager Evaluator's Guide.*

MetaFrame Password Manager Agent

The MetaFrame Password Manager Agent acts on behalf of the end user, detecting and reacting automatically to password-related events. The user enters application credentials once at configuration time and then allows the agent to take over to perform all logon and password changes initiated by the applications. When a user attempts to access an application that requires authentication, the agent intercepts the application's request for authentication, retrieves the correct logon credentials from its encrypted local store, and supplies them to the application.

MetaFrame Password Manager Administrator Console

The console provides administrator's with control over all aspects of password management, but without providing any visibility to the actual user passwords. In particular, the console can activate individual applications for Single Sign On, define strong password policies, automate agent interactions, and publish agent settings on the central store. More specifically, the administrator can configure any number of password policies with granular controls to ensure the strongest password formation is enforced for every single application.

MetaFrame Password Manager Central Credential Store

All users' encrypted credentials are saved in a central store, deployed either as shared network folders, or in Microsoft Active Directory. In a File Share implementation, permissions are set so that only the valid user and administrator can access the credentials. The credential store (the "synchronization point") also contains the first-time-user (FTU) settings, application configurations, and administrative override settings as defined by the administrator. This is the central repository for all data necessary to configure generic software agents into user-specific password managers. At session startup, an agent accesses a user's settings and encrypted credentials from the central store and saves them locally. Then, the agent may update a number of credentials during the session. Upon termination, the agent performs a final synchronization with the central store assuring that the credentials are consistent between the local and central stores (optionally, depending on administrator configuration, the agent may also synchronize them during the course of the session). All updates are consolidated on the central store to let users reuse and maintain their credentials across sessions from any workstation within the domain.

Agent Security for MetaFrame Password Manager

Agent security is obviously extremely important for MetaFrame Password Manager in that the access security for an organization's on-demand enterprise must not be compromised. This section looks at the MMF file, including the method of encryption. It also discusses using `DeleteOnShutdown` and console settings to make the agent even more secure.

MMF File

The *Username.mmf* file is a binary file that stores the following agent information:

▼ Agent settings

■ Cached event IDs generated by the agent

- Application credentials
- Application credentials that have been deleted from the logon manager
- Excluded Web sites
▲ Transmit information

MMF File Location   Under Windows 2000, Windows Server 2003, and Windows XP, the MMF file can be found at the following location within the Window's user profile:

```
Documents and Settings\%Username%\Application Data\Citrix\MetaFrame
Password Manager
```

Under Windows NT4, the MMF file can be found at the following location within the Window's user profile:

```
%SystemRoot%\Profiles\%Username%\Application Data\Citrix\MetaFrame
Password Manager
```

MMF File Permissions   The permissions for the MMF file are the following:

▼ Administrators—Full control
- System Account—Full control
▲ The User—Full control

MMF File Synchronization   The agent updates the synchronization point with the information stored in the user's MMF file (and vice versa if Admin/Application overrides are pushed from the Administrator Console). If the MMF file is deleted from the user's Windows profile, the agent will use the data cached at the synchronization point to recreate the user-side MMF file. The latest information is always available at the synchronization point since the file cannot be deleted while the agent is running and while the agent synchronizes during shutdown.

MMF File Encryption   The agent encrypts the MMF file contents with Triple-DES (3DES) for encryption so that it is not man-readable.

Delete on Shutdown as a Security Mechanism

The DeleteOnShutdown option can be used by an administrator to make the agent more secure. When enabled, DeleteOnShutdown removes specific files and registry keys from a user's profile and from HKCU. Enabling DeleteOnShutdown should be considered when a high number of users use the same computer or when there are physical security concerns (access to client machines is not secured). As noted previously, files are stored in different locations based on the client OS (Windows 2000, Windows XP Pro, or Windows Server 2003).

Files Removed by the Agent During Shutdown   When `DeleteOnshutdown` is enabled, the agent removes the following files from the user's profile:

▼ *AEList.ini*   *AEList.ini* consists of merged *applist.ini* and *ENTList.ini* files. Agents use *AEList.ini* to identify and respond to credential and password change requests initiated by applications.

■ *ENTList.ini*   *ENTList.ini* contains the application definitions for Windows, Web, and Host applications.

■ *Username.mmf*   *Username.mmf* is the local storage file used by the agent to store user data.

▲ **Lock Folder**   Lock Folder contains a lock file that tracks changes made to the MMF file.

Registry Keys Removed by the Agent During Shutdown   `HKCU\Software\Citrix\MetaFrame Password Manager`

Using the Administrator Console Settings to Secure the Agent

Additional settings with regard to Force Re-Authentication, AutoLogin, End Timer, and the Windows Screensaver behavior can be enforced to secure the agent against a walk-away scenario or when using sensitive applications.

Force Re-authentication

Force Re-Authentication is an application-specific setting that instructs the agent to verify the user by requiring the user to re-enter their password (or PIN when smart cards are used). When enabled, the user is required to re-authenticate with the agent prior to the agent submitting credentials to an application.

AutoLogin

AutoLogin determines how long the user remains authenticated with the agent. By default, the timer is set to eight hours; however, it can be set to a shorter length of time. Shortening the length of time will force the user to re-authenticate frequently. The AutoLogin timer option is located in Access Manager under the Console's Agent Settings.

Windows Screensaver Interaction

The Windows Screensaver functionality (of the client workstation) is monitored by the agent and is used to trigger a lockdown event. Depending on how the screensaver options are set, the agent will behave differently during the lockdown process. The two common options in Windows NT 4.0 (or higher) either enable or disable password protection of the screensaver.

Windows Screensaver with Password Protected Option Enabled   When the screensaver activates, the workstation will be placed in a lockdown mode. Unlocking the workstation will also unlock the agent because the agent's GINA monitors the unlocking of the workstation and passes the same credentials to the agent.

Windows Screensaver with Password Protected Option Disabled   When the screensaver activates, the agent will not be placed in a lockdown mode and will not answer to any applications running in the background. Once input from the user is received and the screensaver is disabled, the agent will continue to function without the need to re-authenticate.

Using Smart Cards with MetaFrame Password Manager 2.5

Smart cards are particularly useful when combined with MetaFrame Password Manager 2.5 to provide users with access to their applications and data that is both secure and simple.

Smart Card Authentication

In smart card authentication, the user logs onto their computer using their Primary Authenticator (a smart card). The MetaFrame Password Manager Agent's GINA will detect the type of authenticator used and display the FTU wizard. The user will select an Identity Verification Question and provide an answer. The credentials will then be encrypted using one of two encryption schemes [Profile/DPAPI (Microsoft's Data Protection API) or Password/PIN] dependant upon the value of the `SmartCardSourceForKey` setting as discussed in the next section.

During subsequent logons, if the user continues to use the same Primary Authenticator, the agent will not ask the user to answer the Identity Verification Question. However, if the user decides to change his Primary Authenticator, the agent will ask the user to answer the Identity Verification Question. A detailed explanation of this behavior is discussed in the "Switching Between Authenticators" section later in this chapter.

SmartCardSourceForKey   Ordinarily, MetaFrame Password Manager derives the encryption keys that protect secondary credentials using the primary password. When a smart card is used for primary authentication, no primary password is available that can be used for this purpose. In this instance, the default behavior of the agent, the Profile/DPAPI option, is to use Microsoft's Data Protection API to derive encryption keys, which are used to protect secondary credentials. This encryption mechanism uses the user's Windows credentials to derive the encryption keys; however, it requires the use of roaming profiles and works only on Windows XP, Windows 2000 and later systems. If you use smart cards as the Primary Authenticator on a Windows NT 4.0 system, or you do not have roaming profiles, use the Password/PIN option.

When you select Password/PIN, the encryption keys used to protect secondary credentials are derived from the smart card PIN. In some enterprises, smart card PINs are four-digit numbers that do not provide an adequate level of protection, as compared to an eight-character password, and are more vulnerable to brute force attack.

NOTE: Citrix recommends using the Password/PIN option only if your organization enforces a smart card PIN policy that requires a mixture of letters and numbers, and that requires a minimum length of eight characters.

In order to switch from Profile/DPAPI to Password/PIN, the following registry value must be created on the client and the value `SmartCardSourceForKey` must be set to 1:

```
HKLM\SOFTWARE\Citrix\MetaFrame Password Manager\AUI
    Value: SmartCardSourceForKey (REG_DWORD)
    Setting:
        0 - Profile/DPAPI
        1 - Password/PIN
```

NOTE: The agent will not accept this setting as an "admin override." It will only lower the encryption level when the above registry key and value are present in the registry. This can be done by manually creating the registry key and values or by including the setting in a Custom MSI Package for the agent installation.

Re-authentication

When using MetaFrame Password Manager Agent, there may be times when the user might need to re-authenticate with the agent in order to regain access to the credential store. For example, if the user performs a shutdown of the agent and then restarts it, the next action the user performs that requires access to the credential store will require the user to re-authenticate. Another example would be when the user attempts to "Reveal" passwords for stored credentials and the `reauthonreveal` setting requires re-authentication.

The agent handles re-authentication by locking the user's workstation—this gives control of the workstation over to the WinLogon process (and thereby the original security GINA) and requires the user to authenticate to the workstation using the Primary Authenticator. Once the user has re-authenticated to Windows, the Agent's GINA will be informed and the user will regain access to the credential store.

Determining Type of Authenticator from the Client Registry

Depending on the type of Primary Authenticator used, MetaFrame Password Manager Agent will populate different areas of the registry. Although you can determine the type of authenticator used by simply asking the user, the registry can also be used to determine the authenticator type.

In the registry, the `MSAuth` key will contain values if the user is using a password-based authenticator or if the `SmartCardSourceForKey` has been set to 1 (Password/ PIN). It is not the presence of the `SmartCardSourceForKey` value but its setting that determines if MetaFrame Password Manager Agent will use the `MSAuth` key. The `SmartCardSourceForKey` registry value must be examined first. See the previous "SmartCardSourceForKey" section for the registry key location and values.

```
HKCU\SOFTWARE\Citrix\MetaFrame Password Manager\AUI\MSAuth
Value: Context (REG_BINARY)
Value: CSP (REG_DWORD)
```

```
Value: Usage (REG_BINARY)
Value: Ver (REG_BINARY)
```

The `Reset` key will contain values no matter what type of authenticator is used. Values contained in this key are related to the Identity Verification Question.

```
HKCU\SOFTWARE\Citrix\MetaFrame Password Manager\AUI\MSAuth\Reset
Value: Context (REG_BINARY)
Value: CSP (REG_DWORD)
Value: Usage (REG_BINARY)
Value: Ver (REG_BINARY)
```

The `StrongAuth` key will contain values if the user is using a smart card and the `SmartCardSourceForKey` is set to 0 (use Profile/DPAPI).

Switching Between Authenticators

MetaFrame Password Manager Agent supports multiple authenticators, but also allows the user to switch between them. When a user attempts to switch the Primary Authenticator (for example, changing from smart card with `SmartCardSourceForKey` set to Profile/DPAPI to Windows Password Authentication), MetaFrame Password Manager will ask the user to answer the Identity Verification Question. Once answered by the user, the agent will clear the registry values associated with the old Primary Authenticator and populate the registry values associated with the new Primary Authenticator.

Detecting Primary Authenticator Change

How does the agent know that the Primary Authenticator has changed and why does it ask the Identity Verification Question? The MetaFrame Password Manager Agent will populate different registry keys according to the type of authenticator used. The following registry keys are used:

Password-Based Authenticator   When using a password-based authenticator, the following registry key is used:

```
HKCU\SOFTWARE\Citrix\MetaFrame Password Manager\AUI\MSAuth
```

Smart Card Authenticator and SmartCardSourceForKey   When using a smart card authenticator and `SmartCardSourceForKey` is set to 1, the following registry key is used:

```
HKCU\SOFTWARE\Citrix\MetaFrame Password Manager\AUI\MSAuth
```

Smart Card Authenticator   When using a smart card authenticator and `SmartCardSourceForKey` is set to 0, the following registry key is used:

```
HKCU\SOFTWARE\Citrix\MetaFrame Password Manager\AUI\StrongAuth
```

Log On with a Password-Based Authenticator

If you are using a password-based authenticator, during logon the agent will verify that the password-based authenticator registry key is populated. If the registry key is populated, the agent will authenticate the user and not prompt the user to answer the Identity Verification Question.

Table 10-1 provides a summary of changes made by the agent when switching between the supported authenticators.

From Authenticator	To Authenticator	Identity Verification Question	Registry Key Action
Novell	Novell	No	None
Novell	Windows	No	None
Novell	Smart Card with `SmartCardSource ForKey` set to Profile/DPAPI	Yes	Clear Values: `HKCU\Software\Citrix\ MetaFrame Password Manager\ AUI\MSAuth` Set Values: (Usage) `HKCU\Software\Citrix\ MetaFrame Password Manager\ AUI\StrongAuth`
Novell	Smart Card with `SmartCardSource ForKey` set to Password/PIN	Yes	Re-create Values: (values are re-created since the encryption method has change) `HKCU\Software\Citrix\ MetaFrame Password Manager\ AUI\MSAuth`
Windows	Windows	No	None
Windows	Novell	No	None
Windows	Smart Card with `SmartCardSource ForKey` set to Profile/DPAPI	Yes	Clear Values: `HKCU\Software\Citrix\ MetaFrame Password Manager\ AUI\MSAuth` Set Values: (Usage) `HKCU\Software\Citrix\ MetaFrame Password Manager\ AUI\StrongAuth`
Windows	Smart Card with `SmartCardSource ForKey` set to Password/PIN	Yes	Re-create Values: (values are re-created since the encryption method has change) `HKCU\Software\Citrix\ MetaFrame Password Manager\ AUI\MSAuth`

Table 10-1.   Switching Between Authenticators

From Authenticator	To Authenticator	Identity Verification Question	Registry Key Action
Smart Card with `SmartCardSource ForKey` set to Profile/DPAPI	Novell	Yes	Clear Values: HKCU\Software\Citrix\ MetaFrame Password Manager\ AUI\StrongAuth Set Values: (Context, CSP, Usage, Ver) HKCU\Software\Citrix\ MetaFrame Password Manager\ AUI\MSAuth
Smart Card with `SmartCardSource ForKey` set to Profile/DPAPI	Windows	Yes	Clear Values: HKCU\Software\Citrix\ MetaFrame Password Manager\ AUI\StrongAuth Set Values: (Context, CSP, Usage, Ver) HKCU\Software\Citrix\ MetaFrame Password Manager\ AUI\MSAuth
Smart Card with `SmartCardSource ForKey` set to Profile/DPAPI	Smart Card with `SmartCardSource ForKey` set to Profile/DPAPI	No	None
Smart Card with `SmartCardSource ForKey` set to Profile/DPAPI	Smart Card with `SmartCardSource ForKey` set to Password/PIN	Yes	Clear Values: HKCU\Software\Citrix\ MetaFrame Password Manager\ AUI\StrongAuth Set Values: (Context, CSP, Usage, Ver) HKCU\Software\Citrix\ MetaFrame Password Manager\ AUI\MSAuth
Smart Card with `SmartCardSource ForKey` set to Password/PIN	Smart Card with `SmartCardSource ForKey` set to Profile/DPAPI	Yes	Clear Values: HKCU\Software\Citrix\ MetaFrame Password Manager\ AUI\MSAuth Set Values: (Usage) HKCU\Software\Citrix\ MetaFrame Password Manager\ AUI\StrongAuth
Smart Card with `SmartCardSource ForKey` set to Password/PIN	Smart Card with `SmartCardSource ForKey` set to Password/PIN	No	None

Table 10-1.   Switching Between Authenticators *(continued)*

From Authenticator	To Authenticator	Identity Verification Question	Registry Key Action
Smart Card with `SmartCardSource ForKey` set to Password/PIN	Windows	Yes	Re-create Values: (values are re-created since the encryption method has change) `HKCU\Software\Citrix\ MetaFrame Password Manager\ AUI\MSAuth`
Smart Card with `SmartCardSource ForKey` set to Password/PIN	Novell	Yes	Re-create Values: (values are re-created since the encryption method has change) `HKCU\Software\Citrix\ MetaFrame Password Manager\ AUI\MSAuth`

Table 10-1. Switching Between Authenticators *(continued)*

Supported Authentication Devices Tested with MetaFrame Password Manager 2.5

Table 10-2 shows the smart cards, biometrics, and proximity tokens that were tested with MetaFrame Password Manager 2.5.

Hardware/Readers			
Product [Cryptographic Service Provider (CSP)]	Software	Hardware/Readers	Description
Axalto–Schlumberger Cyberflex Access V2	Java 2.1 Cards, 32K V2 Cards, COVE configuration–Windows GINA and the Schlumberger GINA	ReFlex USB Version 2 Reader for Schlumberger Cyberflex V2 Cards	Multi-application card for digital credential security.
Gemplus	Gemplus Logon Software	GemSAFE 16K Smart Card Serial GemPC410 Reader or USB GemPC430 Reader	

Table 10-2. Supported Smart Cards, Biometrics, and Proximity Tokens Tested with MetaFrame Password Manager 2.5

Gemplus	GemSAFE Software Libraries 3.2.2 (To be used with GemSAFE Smart Card)	GemSAFE 16K Smart Card Serial GemPC410 Reader or USB GemPC430 Reader	With GemSAFE Libraries, users can store their identity and confidential information on a smart card.
Ensure Technologies–Xyloc	XyLoc Solo or Enterprise Software	Proximity Card	XyLoc Enterprise works just like XyLoc Solo.
Identix–Fingerprint Logon	BioLogon for Windows, BioLogon for Thin Client	Identix Fingerprint Reader	Biometric logon for Windows, or Thin Clients.
SAFLINK Workstation Edition	SAFLINK Workstation Software	Precise Biometrics Fingerprint/Smart Card Reader	Windows 2000/NT/XP Professional.
SAFLINK Enterprise Edition	SAFLINK Enterprise Software	Precise Biometrics Fingerprint/Smart Card Reader	Integrates with MS Active Directory.
SAFremote Authenticator (developed for MetaFrame Presentation Server)	Add-on Software to SAFLINK base software		Add-on product to SAFLINK base products that enables terminal and remote end users to benefit from the same SAFLINK secure authentication framework that is available on local workstations.
ActivCard	Trinity software framework (For MetaFrame Password Manager 2.5 Windows was tested. Novell was not tested.)	ActivKey Token ActivCard Tokens ActivReader USB–Smart Card Reader	Citrix NFuse and MetaFrame Support Windows 2000/Windows XP.
Panasonic Iris Camera	SAFLINK Workstation/Enterprise Software	Panasonic BM–ET100US Authenticam Iris Recognition Camera	
SecureComputing	SafeWord	SafeWord TokenID	Developed for Citrix Systems.

Table 10-2.   Smart Cards Tested with MetaFrame Password Manager 2.5 *(continued)*

PART II

MetaFrame Access Suite: Administration, Maintenance, and Troubleshooting

CHAPTER 11

Application Publishing and Deployment

M etaFrame Presention Server 3.0 provides access flexibility by enabling users to utilize published applications and content redirection within Program Neighborhood, Program Neighborhod Agent, and within a web browser. Handling application publishing according to the environment and adopting appropriate techniques can simplify maintenance and improve performance. This chapter contains recommendations for publishing application packages [Microsoft System Installer file (MSI) or Installation Manager's application deployment format (ADF)] with Installation Manager as well as for the application deployment considerations with Installation Manager. It also covers working both with Content Redirection and enhanced content and publishing in the Web Interface for MetaFrame Presentation Server 3.0.

INSTALLATION MANAGER

Citrix Installation Manager is designed to automate the application installation process and facilitate application replication across MetaFrame Presentation Servers throughout the enterprise. Through the use of Installation Manager, applications, files, service packs, and Microsoft Software Patches (MSP) can be distributed across multiple servers in minutes rather than days or weeks. Installation Manager is available as a part of MetaFrame Presentation Server, Enterprise Edition only. Installation Manager is fully integrated into the Presentation Server Console.

Installation Manager is especially useful in organizations utilizing more than three MetaFrame Presentation Servers, or having numerous and frequently updated applications. In these environments, the automation offered by Installation Manager can yield significant cost and administrative time savings.

Installation Manager contains two components: the Packager and the Installer. With the Installer deployed to all MetaFrame Presentation Servers in the enterprise, the Packager makes replicating applications a simple two-step "package and publish" process.

The Packager runs on its own server, while the Installer runs as a background service on each MetaFrame Presentation Server and is transparent to the user.

The Packager provides the administrator with a wizard that supports the step-by-step process of installing and configuring an application. The result is a "package" that contains all application files and a "script" (that is, the ADF file, which uses the extension *.wfs*) that describes the application setup process.

NOTE: With applications that can be deployed from an MSI file, it is not necessary to create an Installation Manager package. You only need to use the MSI and any desired Microsoft Transform Files (MST).

To "push" an application to MetaFrame Presentation Servers equipped with the Installation Manger, publish the script or MSI file to those servers. The application will then be distributed, automatically installed, and published onto MetaFrame Presentation Servers across the enterprise.

Installation Manager also helps to sort out un-install issues associated with many applications. For example, with many un-install programs, application components can be left behind on the server. With Installation Manager, the Installer component tracks every application component installed and completely un-installs the components when the administrator elects to "unpublish" the application on a specific server. This simplifies the relocation of applications from one server to another.

Both MSI and application deployment considerations are important to effectively deploy Installation Manager.

MSI Considerations

Things to be considered when using MSI files during deployment of applications using Installation Manager include MST files, MSP files, forced reinstall, Installation Manager interoperability, interaction with Load Manager, and un-installing Application Deployment File (ADF) packages.

Microsoft Software Patches Packages

It is not necessary to record MSP packages. You can browse through the Installation Manager node in the Presentation Server Console, and add the *.msp* file.

You may remove a MSP package from the target server; however you will be unable to un-install the patch from the server it was deployed to. If you need to apply another patch to the application installed on the target server, un-install the application on the target server first, deploy the application, and then apply the new MSP package.

CAUTION: When installing many MSI packages with or without Installation Manager, a memory leak may be detected in *msiexec.exe*. To avoid this issue, install the latest Windows 2000 Service Pack delivered by Microsoft.

Force Reinstall Option

When a package is scheduled to deploy to a target server, Installation Manager will detect if the package is already installed. If the application is detected, Installation Manager will abort the new installation and return an "Already Installed" status. If you need to overwrite an existing installation, set the Force Reinstall option from the properties screen of the already installed package. This new installation can be used to fix any previously damaged installations or overwrite the existing application of the same version, with changes.

After you Force Reinstall the same package, the Installed Packages tab of the target server will report two records for the same package.

NOTE: After you Force Reinstall a package, the previous package cannot be used to un-install the application from the target server. Un-install can only proceed from the newly installed package.

Installation Manager Interoperability

The version of Installation Manager shipped with MetaFrame Presentation Server 3.0 supports installing packages made using previous versions of Installation Manager. However, some applications may cause incompatibility issues. Consequently, Citrix recommends that you re-create the packages using the latest version of Installation Manager. Packages created with earlier versions may have been packaged on servers that did not have the operating system and other updates your MetaFrame Presentation Server farm contains. When recording a package, the source server should have similar configuration to that of the target servers.

Interaction with Load Manager and Application Publishing

Use the Application Publishing wizard to add the Installation Manager package to the farm through the Applications node of the Presentation Server Console. The wizard allows you to automatically install, publish, and load balance the applications. Additionally, the command line utility `apputil` can be used to add and remove servers from these published packages via scripting, further automating the application installation process. If you use Installation Manager without the wizard, applications are not automatically published or load balanced. For more information about `apputil`, please see the *MetaFrame Presentation Server Administrator's Guide*.

NOTE: Packages created by earlier versions of Installation Manager may not allow access to this feature.

Uninstall Behavior

By default, a deployed package can only be uninstalled from the original package. You cannot directly uninstall an ADF package that has a status of "Already installed." Instead, perform another full installation using the Force Reinstall option, which can be used to uninstall the same package. The application can also be uninstalled from target servers locally without Installation Manager using Add/Remove Programs.

NOTE: If you uninstall from the "Already Installed" package, the target server will not detect the un-install and still will report that the MSI package is installed.

APPLICATION DEPLOYMENT CONSIDERATIONS WITH INDEPENDENT MANAGEMENT ARCHITECTURE

In order to effectively utilize Published Applications, application deployment variables must be considered including publishing in Active Directory Domains that contain thousands of objects.

Publish in Domains that Contain Thousands of Objects

MetaFrame Presentation Server was tested in domains with over 10,000 objects in a single directory services container. A directory services or domain environment that contains a large number of objects, such as Novell Directory Service or Microsoft Active Directory Service, has factors to be considered. Recommendations for this type of environment include using groups to categorize and assign permissions, publishing applications with less than 1,000 users or group objects, and using the Add List of Names button.

Use Groups to Categorize and Easily Assign Permissions to Large Numbers of Users

An application published to one group of 1,000 users requires MetaFrame Presentation Server to validate only one object for all 1,000 users. That same application published to 1,000 individual user accounts requires the IMA service to validate 1,000 objects.

Publish Applications with Less than 1,000 Users or Group Objects

Application publishing time is decreased since all user and group accounts must be verified. Publishing an application with 10,000 objects may take up to 41 minutes to complete. Although the Presentation Server Console may time out after 5 minutes, the IMA service continues to publish the application in the background.

Use the Add List of Names button

Using the Add List of Names button is much faster than scrolling to locate a user when the users container holds thousands of objects.

WORK WITH THE CONTENT REDIRECTION FEATURE

The Content Redirection feature of MetaFrame Presentation Server 3.0 allows PC users running local applications to seamlessly access content from the server, as well as for users running server sessions to seamlessly access local applications. An example of content redirection is when a user running Microsoft Outlook on the local PC opens a Visio file attached to an e-mail using Visio from the MetaFrame Presentation Server farm. Another example is when a user running Internet Explorer from the server farm clicks on a URL and that URL is opened in the user's local web browser. Both of these examples are very common in environments where only some of the applications are deployed from the server farm.

Redirect Content from Client to Server

When configuring Content Redirection from client to server, users running the Program Neighborhood Agent open all files of the associated type encountered in locally running applications with applications published on the MetaFrame Presentation Server. The Web

Interface for MetaFrame Presentation Server must be used as the server configuration tool to configure the Program Neighborhood Agent to allow users to connect to published applications.

NOTE: Content Redirection from client to server is available only with MetaFrame Presentation Server Advanced and Enterprise editions.

The Program Neighborhood Agent

The Program Neighborhood Agent gets updated properties for published applications from the server running the Web Interface. When publishing an application and associating it with file types, the application's file type association is changed to reference the published application in the client device's Windows registry.

Run Local Applications   If users run applications, such as e-mail programs, locally, MetaFrame Presentation Server's Content Redirection capability can be used in conjunction with the Program Neighborhood Agent to redirect application launching from client device to MetaFrame Presentation Server. When users double-click attachments encountered in an e-mail application running locally, the attachment opens in an application that is published on the MetaFrame Presentation Server, associated with the corresponding file type, and assigned to the user.

IMPORTANT: You must enable client drive mapping to use this feature. You can enable client drive mapping for the entire server farm, for specific servers, or for specific users with user policies. For more information about user policies, see the *MetaFrame Presentation Server Administrator's Guide.*

If you do not want this to occur for *any* Program Neighborhood Agent users, do not associate the published application with any file types. If you do not want this to occur for *specific* Program Neighborhood Agent users, do not assign those users to the published application associated with the file type.

Configuration of Content Redirection from Client to Server

The following procedure enables configuration of Content Redirection from client to server:

1. Determine which users connect to published applications using the Program Neighborhood Agent. Content Redirection from client to server applies only to those users connecting with the Program Neighborhood Agent.

2. Verify that client drive mapping is enabled. You can enable client drive mapping for a specific connection using Citrix Connection Configuration or for specific users, servers, client IP addresses, or client names by creating user policies.

3. Publish applications you want the Program Neighborhood Agent users to open on the MetaFrame Presentation Server.

4. When you publish the application, associate it with file types on the last page of the Application Publishing wizard.

Redirect Content from Server to Client

Enabling Content Redirection from server to client causes embedded URLs to be intercepted on the MetaFrame Presentation Server and sent to the client using the ICA Control virtual channel. The user's locally installed browser is used to play the URL. Users cannot disable this feature.

For example, users may frequently access web and multimedia URLs they encounter when running an e-mail program published on a MetaFrame Presentation Server. If you do not enable Content Redirection from server to client, users open these URLs with web browsers or multimedia players present on MetaFrame Presentation Servers.

NOTE: Only URLs that are addressable from the client will be redirected. If a link points to a site that is inaccessible from the client, the URL will open with Internet Explorer on the server.

Reduce Server Processing Requirements

In order to free servers from processing these types of requests, application launching can be redirected for supported URLs from the MetaFrame Presentation Server to the local client device (a PC or a thin client with a web browser).

NOTE: If the client device fails to connect to a URL, the URL is redirected back to the server.

The following URL types are opened locally on Windows 32-bit and Linux clients when this type of content redirection is enabled:

- ▼ HTTP (Hypertext Transfer Protocol)
- ■ HTTPS (Secure Hypertext Transfer Protocol)
- ■ RTSP (Real Player and QuickTime)
- ■ RTSPU (Real Player and QuickTime also use this URL type)
- ■ PNM (Legacy Real Player)
- ▲ MMS (Microsoft's Media Format)

TIP: If Content Redirection from server to client is not working for some of the HTTPS links, verify that the client device has an appropriate certificate installed. If the appropriate certificate is not installed, the HTTP ping from the client device to the URL fails and the URL is redirected back to the server. Content Redirection from server to client requires Internet Explorer Version 5.5 with Service Pack 2 on systems running Windows 98.

Configuration of Content Redirection from Server to Client

The following procedures enable Content Redirection from server to client:

1. Determine if Content Redirection from server to client will apply for the entire server farm, for specific servers, or for specific users only.

2. To apply the behavior to the entire server farm, right-click the farm name in the Presentation Server Console and select Properties. Select MetaFrame Settings in the left pane of the farm's Properties page. Select the option "Enable Content Redirection from server to client."

3. To apply the behavior to a specific server, right-click the server in the Servers node in the Presentation Server Console and select Properties. Select MetaFrame Settings in the left pane of the server's Properties page. Ensure "Use farm settings" is not checked and Select the option "Enable Content Redirection from server to client."

4. To apply the behavior to specific users, create a user policy and enable the rule "Content Redirection from server to client." Assign the policy to only those users you want to open supported URL file types on client devices. For more information about user policies, see the *MetaFrame Presentation Server Administrator's Guide*.

ENHANCED CONTENT PUBLISHING AND REDIRECTION IN THE WEB INTERFACE FOR METAFRAME PRESENTATION SERVER

This section provides further information about Web Interface support for the Enhanced Content Publishing and Redirection features available in MetaFrame Presentation Server.

Published content can be associated with a published application in a server farm. With MetaFrame XP Feature Release 2 and previous editions, users could open published content only with locally installed applications. With MetaFrame Presentation Server 3.0, when published content is accessed, content redirection now allows the clients to automatically launch a connection to a MetaFrame Presentation Server and open that content.

For applications to work with Enhanced Content Publishing and Redirection they must be capable of accepting command line arguments, and the appropriate command line argument syntax must be used. For example, Notepad accepts UNC addresses but not URLs—so the command line syntax must be stated as a UNC.

To associate an application with content, the application must be published appropriately on the MetaFrame Presentation Server. When an application is published, a %* (percentage and asterisk) must be included at the end of the command line, for example:

C:\Program Files\Office\WINWORD.EXE "%*"

For more information about Content Publishing and Redirection, see the *MetaFrame Presentation Server Administrator's Guide*. For more information about the Web Interface, see Chapter 16 of *Citrix MetaFrame Access Suite for Windows Server 2003: The Official Guide* by Steve Kaplan, Tim Reeser, and Alan Wood (McGraw-Hill/Osborne, 2003), and the *Web Interface Administrator's Guide*.

CHAPTER 12

SpeedScreen Browser Acceleration and Multimedia Optimization

MetaFrame Presentation Server 3.0 provides significant enhancements to access infrastructure by dramatically improving the speed and subsequent usefulness of multimedia applications. The software also, for the first time, enables bidirectional audio. This chapter covers the optimization of SpeedScreen Browser Acceleration, both with Internet Explorer and with the MetaFrame Presentation Server Client. It also covers optimization of audio playback as well as MetaFrame Presentation Server's new audio recording capabilities.

OPTIMIZING SPEEDSCREEN BROWSER ACCELERATION WITH INTERNET EXPLORER

SpeedScreen Browser Acceleration improves the responsiveness of HTML pages when using Microsoft Outlook, Outlook Express, and Internet Explorer 5.5 or higher as published applications. With SpeedScreen Browser Acceleration enabled, version 7.0 or later of the MetaFrame Presentation Server Clients for Win32, and a MetaFrame Presentation Server connection with a color depth of High Color (16 bit) or greater, the user can scroll the pages and use the Back and Stop buttons immediately while image files download in the background. The following sections provide methods for the MetaFrame Administrator to further optimize the user's experience by controlling the default behavior of SpeedScreen Browser Acceleration through the use of registry value modifications and ICA file settings.

Play Animations in Web Pages

When this feature is enabled, animated GIF images are rendered as animations, and SpeedScreen Browser support for GIF images is disabled. Citrix recommends disabling "Play Animations in web pages." When this feature is disabled, SpeedScreen Browser Acceleration support for GIF images is enabled. The secondary benefit is a further bandwidth reduction due to the absence of animations, which consume significant bandwidth.

MetaFrame Presentation Server, by default, disables the "Play animations in web pages" option for all users on the server. The feature is disabled when the user logs in for the first time following the installation of MetaFrame Presentation Server. If a user subsequently enables the setting, it will not be modified again unless the MetaFrame Administrator changes specific values in the registry. For information about the necessary registry changes, see the section "Advanced Configuration Information," next.

This feature can be accessed by opening Internet Explorer and selecting Tools | Internet Options | Advanced or by navigating to Internet Options under Control Panel.

Advanced Configuration Information

MetaFrame Presentation Server will disable the IE feature "Play animations in web pages" the first time a user logs in following the installation of MetaFrame Presentation Server. This feature is only disabled following the first login.

Value Name	Default Value (if not present)	Description
DisablePlayAnimations	1	Disables the Play animations in web pages feature in IE

Table 12-1.   MetaFrame Presentation Server IE SpeedScreen Registry Value

The disabling of this feature is controlled through a registry entry. The registry value is contained in the registry key HKCU\Software\Citrix. The registry value is defined in Table 12-1.

If this value is not present in the registry at login or is set to 1, the IE option will be automatically disabled for the user. If the value is set to 0, the server does not attempt to disable the feature in the user's session at login, despite whether the feature is currently enabled or disabled in the user's profile.

Administrators may find this information useful when designing logoff scripts. It may be useful to have this option always disabled at login, in which case a logoff script can be used to set the registry value to 1.

CONFIGURING SPEEDSCREEN BROWSER ACCELERATION ON THE ICA CLIENT

There is no client-side user interface control for SpeedScreen Browser Acceleration. SpeedScreen Browser Acceleration settings must be configured in the ICA files. The preferred configuration method is through Web Interface. By default, SpeedScreen Browser Acceleration is enabled on the ICA Client for all connections.

NOTE: If either the server or the client has SpeedScreen Browser Acceleration configured to OFF, it will be disabled for that connection.

This section describes the ICA file parameters that can be used to configure SpeedScreen Browser Acceleration. It is divided into two sections: Basic settings and Advanced settings.

Basic SpeedScreen Browser Acceleration ICA File Settings

Typically, administrators will only need to use the Basic settings for configuring SpeedScreen Browser Acceleration in the *Template.ICA* file in Web Interface. Usage is as follows:

```
SpeedScreenBA=[ON | OFF]
```

SpeedScreenBA

Setting **SpeedScreenBA=On** enables SpeedScreen Browser Acceleration for a connection. Note that the server settings may override this setting. Disabling SpeedScreen Browser Acceleration on the server will cause this setting to be ignored for a connection.

Setting **SpeedScreenBA=Off** disables SpeedScreen Browser Acceleration for a connection. This will be disabled even if the server setting specifies that SpeedScreen Browser Acceleration is to be enabled.

SpeedScreenBACompressionEnabled

Setting **SpeedScreenBACompressionEnabled=On** enables SpeedScreen Browser Acceleration JPEG image compression for a connection. If the server has disabled JPEG image compression, the server setting will override the client setting.

Setting **SpeedScreenBACompressionEnabled=Off** disables SpeedScreen Browser Acceleration JPEG compression for a connection. This will be disabled even if the server setting specifies that JPEG compression is to be enabled.

Advanced SpeedScreen ICA File Settings

Administrators may utilize the advanced cache file and compression settings of SpeedScreen to optimize SpeedScreen Browser Acceleration for very slow connections, servers with limited memory or drive space, or servers with an overabundance of memory or drive space. Usage within the ICA File is as follows:

```
SpeedScreenBACompressedCacheSize=value
SpeedScreenBADecompressedCacheSize=value
SpeedScreenBAMaximumCompressionLevel=value
```

Using the SpeedScreenBACompressedCacheSize Setting

SpeedScreen uses a compressed cache to store JPEG and GIF data sent from the MetaFrame Presentation Server. With this data cached on the ICA Client, pages that are revisited will display faster because the server will not retransmit the cached images to the client. The size of the cache determines how long images will remain inside the cache, and also generally the number of images that will fit into the cache. When the cache is filled, images previously added to the cache are removed. The least recently used image is deleted from the cache first. Initially, the cache is empty and does not consume memory. As images are added to the cache, it grows to accommodate the images. If an image exceeds the maximum compressed cache size, it will not be displayed through SpeedScreen.

value Parameter   The **value** parameter is the maximum memory consumption that SpeedScreen will use to store JPEG and GIF image data, measured in KB. The default value for this parameter is 16384KB (16MB). Administrators can use this setting either to limit the maximum memory consumption of the ICA Client or to allow higher maximum memory consumption when this is required.

NOTE: Increasing the memory consumption may provide some benefit on very slow connections, where the transmission time for images is very high. If images remain on the client for longer, the probability that a retransmit of an image will need to occur is reduced.

Using the SpeedScreenBADecompressedCacheSize Setting

SpeedScreen stores the bitmap representations of JPEG and GIF images in a decompressed cache. Using a decompressed cache means that the JPEG and GIF images do not need to be decompressed each time they are drawn. Using a decompressed cache provides a significant performance boost when a page is scrolled because a scroll operation results in a number of drawing operations on the same image.

When an image needs to be drawn, it is decompressed and added to the decompressed cache. Images remain in the decompressed cache until more space is required in the cache. Images are deleted from the decompressed cache when the operation of adding a new image could exceed the maximum decompressed cache size. Images can be added and removed from the decompressed cache any number of times while the image is in the compressed cache.

The maximum size of the decompressed cache will determine the maximum dimensions of an image that can be displayed through SpeedScreen. JPEG images require 24bpp (bits per pixel), whereas GIF images require 8bpp. A larger decompressed cache size will allow images with a larger dimension to be displayed. Reducing the size of the decompressed cache will reduce the maximum image dimensions that can be displayed.

NOTE: Images that will exceed the maximum decompressed cache size when decompressed are not downloaded to the client at all, and are displayed in Legacy mode.

Using the SpeedScreenBAMaximumCompressionLevel Setting

The **SpeedScreenBAMaximumCompressionLevel** ICA file parameter defines the maximum SpeedScreen compression level for a connection. The valid values for this parameter are shown in Table 12-2.

The default value for this parameter is 2 (high compression).

SpeedScreen JPEG Image Recompression performs a lossey compression on the JPEG images transferred to the ICA Client. A higher compression level will result in reduced bandwidth consumption, but will have the most significant impact on image quality.

0	Low Compression
1	Medium Compression
2	High Compression

Table 12-2.   SpeedScreen Maximum Compression Level Settings

The lower of the two compression levels specified on the client and the server is used as the maximum compression level for a connection. Therefore, if the client specifies medium compression and the server high, the maximum compression level used for the connection will be medium compression.

NOTE: This parameter is ignored if either the client or server indicates that compression is not enabled for a connection.

SpeedScreen Browser Acceleration Limitations and Known Issues

There are two known limitations with SpeedScreen Browser Acceleration:

▼   No support for transparent GIF images

▲   No support for HTML image resizing

No Support for Transparent GIF Images

SpeedScreen Browser Acceleration does not support transparent GIF images. Transparent GIF images are rendered in Legacy mode.

Images Resized in HTML

The HTML that describes a Web page can also specify the width and the height that an image may use. This may be different from the actual width and height of the image. In this case, Internet Explorer grows or shrinks the image as required to fit it into the size specified in the HTML.

SpeedScreen Browser Acceleration does not support images that are resized using this technique. Images that are resized in HTML are drawn in Legacy mode.

This feature is not the same as the Automatic Image Resizing feature described previously. Automatic Image Resizing refers to the scaling of an image that is larger than the browser display area so that it fits into the display area of the browser.

SpeedScreen Multimedia Acceleration

SpeedScreen Multimedia Acceleration was introduced in MetaFrame Presentation Server 3.0 to better support Citrix environments with multimedia delivery requirements. This feature effectively accelerates multimedia playback on a PC or Windows XP embedded client by utilizing the codec on the local client machine to decode the multimedia rather than utilizing the codec on the MetaFrame Presentation Server and streaming the results to the client. SpeedScreen Multimedia Acceleration is enabled by default and is controlled through the Presentation Server Console in the properties of the farm or in the individual server's properties.

This section describes the range of multimedia playback support for SpeedScreen Multimedia Acceleration. Table 12-3 lists a few of the media types that were tested successfully using Windows Media Player 6.4/8.0/9.0 and RealOne Player. In general, SpeedScreen

Media Type (Media Encoding Format)	File Format (File Extension)	Microsoft Media Player 6.4/8.0/9.0	RealOne Player	QuickTime	DirectShow-Based Media Players
DIVX Video	AVI MPEG MPG ASF	√	√	X	√
XVID Video		√	√	X	√
Microsoft Video 1		√	√	X	√
MPEG-1 Video		√	√	X	√
MPEG-4 Video		√	√	X	√
Indeo Interactive Video		√	√	X	√
MPEG-1 Audio		√	√	X	√
AC3 Audio		√	√	X	√
Fraunhofer MPEG Layer-3 Codec		√	√	X	√
MP3	MP3	√*	X	X	X
WMA	WMA	√*	X	X	X
WMV	WMV	X	X	X	X
Real Media	RM	X	X	X	X
QuickTime	MOV	X	X	X	X

√ – Supported through SpeedScreen Multimedia Acceleration.
X – Not supported through SpeedScreen Multimedia Acceleration.
* – Supported through SpeedScreen Multimedia Acceleration only when playing through Windows Media Player 9.0. Data is transferred in uncompressed format.

Table 12-3.   Media Types and File Formats

Multimedia Acceleration supports all media types that can be decoded by a DirectShow-based codec, regardless of file format. SpeedScreen Multimedia Acceleration is supported when connecting to Windows 2000 and Windows 2003 servers from Windows 9*x*, Windows 2000, and Windows XP clients.

Media Formats Supported By SpeedScreen Multimedia Acceleration

It is important to note that media type differs from the file format. Some examples of file formats are

▼ AVI

■ MPEG

■ MPG

- ASF
- WMV
- WMA
▲ MP3

These file formats can encapsulate various media types, such as those listed in Table 12-3. For example, a single AVI file could contain a DIVX Video stream and an AC3 Digital Audio Stream, and it would need both the DIVX and AC3 DirectShow codecs for proper playback.

NOTE: Table 12-3 only describes some of the more popular media types and file formats. In general, SpeedScreen Multimedia Acceleration supports all media types that can be decoded by a DirectShow-based codec, regardless of file format.

Best Practices

Citrix recommends upgrading the client devices to use the latest version of Microsoft's DirectX software. Citrix also recommends keeping the server's version of Microsoft Windows Media Player upgraded to the latest version/update.

SpeedScreen Multimedia Acceleration INI File Options

The SpeedScreen Multimedia Acceleration parameters have default values and descriptions, as shown in Table 12-4. These settings can be inserted into ICA files and the *Appsrv.ini* and *PN.ini* files on the local client machine. If there is no setting in the respective file, the default setting applies.

Parameter	Default Value	Description
SpeedScreenMMAVideoEnabled	TRUE	Enables/disables video playback through RAVE.
SpeedScreenMMAAudioEnabled	TRUE	Enables/disables audio playback through RAVE.
SpeedScreenMMASecondsToBuffer	10	Approximate amount of seconds of buffer in the client. Values range from 1–10. The server and client both have this value set, and the connection will be set up with the smaller of the values (i.e., the server sets 5 seconds, the client sets 4 seconds, and then the connection will be set up with a 4-second buffer).
SpeedScreenMMAMaximumBufferSize	30240	Maximum size in KB of the media queue that the client can create. This is per stream, so the client could create a 30,240KB queue for audio, and 30,240KB queue for video.

Table 12-4.   SpeedScreen Multimedia Acceleration ICA File Options

Parameter	Default Value	Description
SpeedScreenMMAMinBufferThreshHold	10	Percent value with a range of 5–15. When the data in the media queue reaches this value, the client will request a burst from the server to replenish its media queue.
SpeedScreenMMAMaxBufferThreshHold	90	Percent value with a range of 85–95. When the data in the media queue reaches this value, the client will request that the server stop sending data until the level of data in the queue levels off.
SpeedScreenMMAPlaybackPercent	35	Percent value with a range of 25–45. This is the percent of the media queue that needs to be filled before playback on the client end begins.

Table 12-4.   SpeedScreen Multimedia Acceleration ICA File Options *(continued)*

RECORDING SOUND IN A METAFRAME SESSION

One of the new features of MetaFrame Presentation Server 3.0 is the ability to record sound inside an ICA session. One of the primary uses for this is for professionals to be able dictate a recording in one session and then have that data transcribed at a later date.

Enabling recording of sound inside of an ICA session requires a MetaFrame Presentation Server, version 3.0, and a MetaFrame Presentation Server Client of version 8.0 or higher. The process is usually facilitated by third-party software vendors, such as WinScribe, with their Internet Author and Internet Typist software. Usually software like this is used in conjunction with Philips SpeechMike devices or similar hardware.

Optimizing Audio for Playback

Most of the existing audio settings are optimized for playback and not recording. This entails buffering up several seconds of data sent to the client. This is done to avoid drops in playback, much like when Windows Media Player or Real Player buffer data before sending it.

Playback can take advantage of the new SpeedScreen Multimedia Acceleration when playing MP3 or other such audio. In this case, MetaFrame Presentation Server doesn't actually play the data and send WAV out data to client, but instead streams the compressed codec data to the client and allows the client to decompress and play the data.

Optimizing Audio for Recording

When the primary focus of using audio is for recording, users can experience synchronization errors between what they hear and what is visible inside a session. This is due to the queued-up data in the buffer mentioned before. Several things can be done to reduce these delays, and recommended settings are outlined as follows.

CAUTION: Changing these settings can cause quality degradations in the playback of audio. Only make these changes if the primary use of audio is for recording.

The settings that control SpeedScreen Multimedia Acceleration are totally separate from the settings that control the recording of audio; a user can use SpeedScreen Multimedia Acceleration for playback and then optimize their settings for recording without degrading playback quality.

Configuring the Server

By default, MetaFrame Presentation Server requires no special configuration for audio recording to work. The default settings will allow users to record audio using a standard microphone. In order to use a device whose driver is not automatically installed on Windows 2000 Server or Windows Server 2003, such as the Philips SpeechMike devices, the drivers must be installed on all servers that are to have sessions that will record audio. We recommend that the drivers be installed after the operating system and prior to MetaFrame Presentation Server.

WinScribe Software   If using WinScribe's software, the Internet Author and/or the Internet Typist programs will need to be installed on the servers. Refer to the WinScribe documentation for any setup instructions.

Published Desktops or Recording Applications   Published desktops or published recording applications should be configured to use legacy audio. The client connection's ICA Settings Audio Quality should be set to medium or high. Medium is the default and should be satisfactory for most applications.

Configuring the Client

The client PC (or Windows XP embedded thin client) must have an audio playback device, such as a sound card, and an audio recording device, such as a microphone. The Philips SpeechMike devices often serve both purposes.

Audio Quality Setting   Audio needs to be enabled in the Program Neighborhood, Program Neighborhood Agent, or Web Interface client, depending on which is used. (The feature will work with all of them.)

Audio Security Settings   Ensure that the audio security settings, available from the connection center or via a session's system menu, are configured to allow the recording of audio. These settings work in the same manner as the preexisting file security dialogs.

Using the Philips SpeechMike

Using a Philips SpeechMike is a relatively straightforward process. Ensure that the drivers for the device are installed correctly on both the client and server. Make sure the recorder works correctly on the local client. Do this by loading the recorder utility that comes with the drivers. Ensure that audio records and plays back locally.

MetaFrame Presentation Server supports using the SpeechMike controls and foot pedal devices as well. Before attempting to use them in a session, however, once again, test them locally in the Philips recording utility. If everything is working fine locally on the client device, there should be no problems using the same devices inside an ICA session.

SpeechMike controls may also have to be enabled inside the applications. This is currently true for Internet Author and Typist. See the specific application documentation for details. Additionally, Citrix testing has experienced issues with configured USB foot pedals in Internet Author and Typist. It is recommended that if you're using these devices that the settings for them be left at their default or none.

Optimizing Audio Settings for Recording

If making recordings is the primary task for which audio will be used, several settings can be modified to improve performance. The settings detailed here are all located in the *Module.ini* file, which is typically located in %Program Files%\Citrix\ICA Client. These settings are primarily intended for a standard LAN environment. The settings should be satisfactory for a WAN as well, but there is a much greater likelihood that audio will drop if the settings are set too low in a WAN environment. If that is a problem, the values can be increased, but this will cause delay to be reintroduced.

CAUTION: Making changes to these settings can cause playback quality to degrade, especially on low-bandwidth, high-latency connections.

PlaybackDelayThresh   On the client, open the *Module.ini* file located in the main install folder, which is usually %Program Files%\Citrix\ICA Client. Go to the **ClientAudio** section. Change **PlaybackDelayThresh** to 1 or 2. This will cause the data to be played almost immediately, rather than being queued up on the client. Change **NumDataBuffers** to a small value such as 4 or 5. This will cause fewer buffers to be allocated so less data can be queued up on the client. A lower value can be tried, but network latency is usually too great to allocate enough data and you will get a lot of dropped packets on playback.

NumDataBuffers   The values will have to be balanced based on what applications the users will be running. If playback is of little importance, use the preceding recommendations. If playback is more important, increase the **NumDataBuffers** setting to around 10, but accept that this will cause a higher delay time from what is visually depicted on the screen and what is actually heard. Continue to increase this number for WAN connections until you're satisfied with the resulting playback quality.

NOTE: We recommend that the **NumDataBuffers** value be manipulated before **Play-backDelayThresh** when experimenting on high-latency networks. This is because the **PlaybackDelayThresh** value causes more discontinuity on the server side with respect to synchronization issues. The higher this value is set, the more likely playback will jump ahead inappropriately, causing the recording to start playing at a later spot than when it was stopped.

Client Audio Mapping Virtual Driver

This section describes the Client Audio Mapping Virtual Driver configuration settings and the best practices for changing these settings in the *Module.ini* file located in %Program Files%\Citrix\ICA Client.

NumCommandBuffers = 64

This setting defines how many commands can be buffered going from server to client.

Maximum Limit: 65000   It is not advisable to increase this value higher than 64 commands for the best performance of the server and client.

Minimum Limit: 0   If you set this value to 0, the performance of the server and client will be affected. The client will slow down or may not respond to the commands sent by the server. It is necessary to have proper buffers defined because after executing a command sent by the server, the client will look in the buffer for the next command. Also, with no buffers, the commands sent to the client by the server might not be stored on the client and executed. The best practice is to use the setting 64.

NumDataBuffers = 32

This setting defines how many data buffers are available on the client to store the sound data sent by the server to the client.

Maximum Limit: 65000   It is not advisable to set this value to the maximum because this might lead to memory hogging on the client, eventually resulting in the degraded performance of the client. The best practice is to set **NumDataBuffers** to 32 for the best performance of the server and the client.

Minimum Limit: 0   When this value is set to 0, there will be no data buffers available on the client. Also, the sound data being sent from the server to the client will not be stored, and eventually will not play. The best practice is to use the setting 32. These 32 buffers are defined to store a maximum of 2048 bytes of sound data.

MaxDataBufferSize = 2048

This setting defines the size of the Data Buffer and also defines how many bytes of sound data can be sent to the client from the server.

Maximum Limit : 2048 bytes   Out of 2048 bytes, 10 bytes are reserved for the sound packet header, while the remainder is the actual sound that gets played on the client.

Minimum Limit: 1000 bytes   Best practice is to set **MaxDataBufferSize** to 2048 bytes for the best sound performance on the client.

CommandAckThresh = 10

This setting specifies that the client will wait for ten commands to be sent by the server before it sends an acknowledgement to the server for all the commands received.

Maximum Limit   The maximum limit depends on the `NumCommandBuffers` setting. If **NumCommandBuffers** is set to 64, `CommandAckThresh` should not be set to more than 64 because the client will not acknowledge more than 64 commands. Best practice is to set `CommandAckThresh` to 10 for the best performance of the client and server.

Minimum Limit: 10   Anything less than 10 might degrade the performance of the client because it will start acknowledging the server's commands too often, which will interfere in the execution of the commands from the server.

DataAckThresh = 10

This setting specifies that the client will wait for ten sound data/packets to be sent by the server before it sends an acknowledgement to the server for all the sound data/packets received.

Maximum Limit   The maximum limit depends on **NumDataBuffers**. If **NumDataBuffers** is set to 32, **DataAckThresh** should not be set higher than 32 because the client will not acknowledge more than 32 sound data/packets. Best practice is to set **DataAckThresh** to 10 for the best performance of the client and server.

Minimum Limit: 10   Anything less than 10 might degrade the performance of the client because it will send acknowledgements to the servers too often, which will interfere in the playing of the sound data/packets from the server.

AckDelayThresh = 350

This setting specifies that the client will wait for 350 milliseconds before it sends an acknowledgement to the server for all the commands received from the server.

Maximum Limit: 350   `AckDelayThresh` and `CommandAckThresh` are not interdependent. Say, for example, `CommandAckThresh` is set to 10 and `AckDelayThresh` is set to 350. If 350 milliseconds have not yet passed since the client last sent an acknowledgment, but ten commands have been sent by the server to the client, the client will still send the acknowledgment. The same holds true if 350 milliseconds have passed but the server has not sent ten commands. The client will send the acknowledgement to the server without waiting for ten commands.

Minimum Limit: 350   Anything less than 350 milliseconds might degrade the performance of the client because it will start acknowledging the server regularly, which will interfere with executions of the commands from the server.

PlaybackDelayThresh = 250

This setting specifies that the client will wait for 250 milliseconds before it sends an acknowledgement to the server for all the sound data/packets received from the server.

Maximum Limit: 250   `PlaybackDelayThresh` and `DataAckThresh` are not interdependent. For example, suppose that `DataAckThresh` is set to 10 and `PlaybackDelayThresh` is set to 250. If 250 milliseconds have passed after the client has sent an acknowledgment but ten sound data/packets have not been sent by the server to the client, the client will still send the acknowledgment. The same holds true if 250 milliseconds have not yet passed but the server has already sent ten sound data/packets; the client will send the acknowledgement to the server without waiting for 250 milliseconds.

Minimum Limit: 250   Anything less than 250 milliseconds might degrade the performance of the client because it will send acknowledgements to the server too often, which will interfere in the playing of the sound data/packets from the server.

CHAPTER 13

Printer Management

ince the inception of networking, printing has been a primary concern during the design and implementation phases of building a network. Whether the issue is the quality of the print job, bandwidth needs, performance requirements, paper tray demystification, or simply determining a print job went, administrators have struggled with providing secure, fast, and simple printing solutions to their users.

Because we covered, in detail, Windows printer management, configuration, troubleshooting, and the use of third-party tools in *Citrix MetaFrame Access Suite for Windows Server 2003: The Official Guide,* we will focus in this chapter on the centralized printer management features in the Presentation Server Console of MetaFrame Presentation Server. Also, the new features built into MetaFrame Presentation Server 3.0. Printer Driver replication are discussed in depth, and printer optimization using the MetaFrame Presentation Server tools is addressed. Some of the new MetaFrame Presentation Server 3.0 features discussed include automatic installation of print drivers for autocreated printers and enforced printer compatibility.

THE METAFRAME PRESENTATION SERVER PRINT ARCHITECTURE

Users connecting to a MetaFrame Presentation Server environment can print to the following types of printers:

▼ Printers connected to ports on the user's client device on Windows, Windows CE, DOS, Linux, UNIX, or Mac OS platforms

■ Virtual printers created for tasks such as printing from a PostScript driver to a file on a Windows client device

■ Shared printers connected to print servers on a Windows network

▲ Printers connected directly to MetaFrame Presentation Servers

The printer objects that MetaFrame Presentation Server clients use can be categorized by connection types. There are three kinds of printer connections in a MetaFrame Presentation Server farm: client connections, network connections, and local connections. This chapter refers to printers in a server farm as client printers, network printers, or local printers, depending on the type of connection they have in the farm.

Client Printers

Client printers are defined differently depending on the MetaFrame Presentation Server Client platform:

▼ On DOS-based and Windows CE client devices, a client printer is physically connected to a port on the client device by a cable.

■ On UNIX and Macintosh client devices, a PC or PostScript printer connected to a serial port (or a USB port for newer Macintoshes) is considered a client printer.

▲ On 32-bit Windows platforms (Windows 9*x*, Windows NT, Windows 2000, and Windows XP), any printer that is set up in Windows is a client printer (these printers appear in the Printers folder on the client device). Locally connected printers, printers that are connected on a network, and virtual printers are all considered client printers.

Network Printers

Printers that are connected to print servers and shared on a Windows network are referred to as *network printers*. In Windows network environments, users can set up a network printer on their computers if they have permission to connect to the print server. In a MetaFrame Presentation Server environment, administrators can import network printers and assign them to users based on group membership. When a network printer is set up for use on an individual Windows computer, the printer is a client printer on the client device.

Local Printers

A local printer is created by an administrator on the MetaFrame Presentation Server using the Add Printer Wizard from within the Printers applet in the Control Panel. As with a network printer, print jobs printed to a local printer bypass the client device and can be sent either to a Windows print server or directly to a printer, depending on how the printer has been created on the server. If the printer is added to the MetaFrame Presentation Server with the port pointing to a share such as *printserver**sharename*, the print job is sent to the print server before heading to the printer.

The print queue can be Windows, NetWare, or UNIX based. If the printer is added and the port specifies the actual printer itself (such as an lpr queue to the printer's IP address), the MetaFrame Presentation Server is essentially the print server, and the job is sent directly to the printer. Local printers are not typically utilized in an enterprise MetaFrame Presentation Server environment because of the need for the MetaFrame administrator to set up every printer in the environment on each MetaFrame Presentation Server. However, local printers can be utilized successfully in smaller MetaFrame Presentation Server farms (three or fewer servers).

PRINTER DRIVER REPLICATION

Printer driver replication was introduced in MetaFrame Presentation Server to reduce the management nightmare of ensuring that all MetaFrame Presentation Servers in the farm have the required printer drivers for an environment.

Printer driver replication is designed to copy printer driver files and registry settings across the server farm. You can install all required printer drivers on one MetaFrame Presentation Server in the farm and then replicate the files and registry settings to all other servers in the farm. Management of printer driver replication is performed through the Presentation Server Console. Printer driver replication does not replicate printer properties such as paper size and print quality.

> **TIP:** Printer driver replication can be CPU intensive on the source server. To improve performance, avoid replicating drivers while the farm is under heavy load, such as when many users are logging on.

Managing the Printer Driver Replication Queue

Each printer driver/server combination creates an item in the printer replication queue. For best performance, this queue should not exceed 1,500 entries in length. To determine the queue size, use the following formula:

$$QueueSize = Drivers * Servers$$

where *Drivers* is the number of printer drivers and *Servers* is the number of servers to which the printer drivers are being replicated.

Using this formula, the queue can include 30 drivers for replication to 50 servers (30*50=1,500) or three drivers for replication to 500 servers (3*500=1,500) without exceeding the queue size recommendation.

The replication queue items can be monitored with the **qprinter /replica** command. For more information on the **qprinter** command, see the next section, "qprinter Command."

qprinter Command

The **qprinter** command is a utility designed to allow administrators to monitor the progress of the printer driver replication queue and import printer name–mapping parameters into the data store. The syntax of the **qprinter** command is

```
qprinter [/replica]
qprinter [/imprmapping mappingfilename]
```

where *mappingfilename* specifies the full path to the text file containing the printer-mapping parameters to import. The filename cannot have more than 256 characters and cannot contain quotation marks.

Here are the options for the **qprinter** command:

▼ **/replica** Displays all the replication entries queued for distribution but not yet completed. The **/replica** switch displays all events in the queue, including broken or failed events.

▲ **/imprmapping** *mappingfilename* Imports printer mappings from the file specified by *mappingfilename* into the data store. The file format can be in either the *Wtsprnt.inf* format or the *Wtsuprn.txt* format. The **/imprmapping** switch allows central administration of all printer name mappings. The file can be imported once from any server in the farm and is available for all servers in the farm. The **/imprmapping** switch does not process an improperly formatted file and does not return an error when provided with an invalid file format. To verify that the information is correctly imported into the data store, use the Citrix Management Console.

NOTE: Only MetaFrame administrators can execute this command.

The MetaFrame Presentation Server installation first attempts to import the *Wtsuprn.txt* file, followed by the *Wtsprnt.inf* file. If the two files fail to import, no error is returned. Use the **/imprmapping** switch to manually import either file.

Qprinter is not installed by default. It is in the \support\debug\W2K folder (for Windows 2000 Servers) or the \support\debug\W2K3 folder (for Windows 2003 Servers) on the MetaFrame Presentation Server CD.

TIP: You can determine the success or failure of printer driver replication by checking the Application log in Event Viewer on the target servers.

Driver Replication and Performance Issues

The number of printer drivers installed on or replicated to each server in the farm can affect server performance and the IMA service response time. The following sections provide recommendations for minimizing potential performance issues when installing or replicating printer drivers.

Driver Replication and Server Performance

The time required to complete printer driver replications depends on network traffic and server load. The replication distribution queue is handled by the IMA service.

The printer driver replication subsystem can process an average of 50 entries a minute in a 50-server farm under a light user and network load. A 500-server farm under the same conditions can process an average of 20 entries a minute.

The distribution subsystem monitors the load on the MetaFrame Presentation Server that is replicating the print drivers while they are distributed across the server farm.

To complete printer driver replication as quickly as possible, Citrix recommends that it be executed during off-peak hours, when higher-priority network traffic is at a minimum.

TIP: The progress of the replication jobs can be monitored by running **qprinter /replica**.

Driver Replication and IMA Performance

The data store holds one record for each printer driver, one record for each farm server, and one record for each printer driver/server combination. The more printer drivers installed on farm servers, the larger the printer driver tables in the data store, thus requiring more time to query information from the data store at startup. Introducing a large number of printer drivers to MetaFrame Presentation Server—whether they are manually installed or replicated—will slow IMA response time.

The best practice is to limit the number of printer drivers in the farm using the following guidelines:

▼ Install printer drivers only for printers that will be used by MetaFrame Presentation Server Clients in the farm.

■ Install printer drivers only on servers that will host users who need access to the printers.

■ Install printer drivers that work for multiple printer types, if possible.

■ Remove unnecessary printer drivers from cloned images.

■ In WAN environments where a large number of printer drivers are installed, use a replicated data store if better performance is necessary.

▲ Use the Citrix Universal Print Driver instead of the native Windows drivers, if possible.

Using Autoreplication

Every MetaFrame Presentation Server maintains a list of drivers that it received through autoreplication under `HKLM\SOFTWARE\Citrix\IMAPrinter:AutoReplicate`. This registry value contains IMA UIDs for each driver that is configured for autoreplication. During IMA service startup, the IMA service's Printer subsystem checks if a driver's UID is already present in the registry. If a driver is already registered as being replicated to a server, that driver will not be reinstalled, even if the "overwrite" option is checked.

For "regular" replication (when autoreplication is not selected), when the replication job is started, if "overwrite" is not selected, the target server is checked to verify whether the server already contains the necessary files needed to install the driver. If the files exist, the server is told to install the driver. If the driver files are not already available on the target server, they are sent from the source server to the target server and installed. If "overwrite" is selected, the drivers are always sent from the source server to the targets.

This behavior ensures every server has the same version of the driver installed.

When an autoreplication job is scheduled, if the driver is not already detected as replicated in the aforementioned registry key, the IMA service attempts to download it during IMA service startup. If several printer replication jobs are destined for a server, the IMA service may take an extended period of time to start. If autoreplication must be used, keep the number of printer drivers to be replicated to a minimum.

OPTIMIZING PRINTER CREATION

Network printer shares that reside on the client system can cause an increase in client login times because the printers are created and deleted during each logon and logoff. Using autocreated network printers instead of client network printer shares can reduce login times because the connections to the network printers remain persistent. If the network printer is on the MetaFrame Presentation Server, no other action is required; otherwise, you need to perform the following steps to import the required network print servers into the farm.

To add network printers to a MetaFrame Presentation Server farm, follow these steps:

1. Open the Presentation Server Console and select the Printer Management node.

2. Right-click Printer Management and select Import Network Print Server.

3. Specify the network print server to import and add any necessary authentication credentials.

4. When the operation finishes, the print server appears on the Network Print Servers tab.

5. Install the printer drivers for your network printers on a MetaFrame Presentation Server in the server farm.

6. Within the Presentation Server Console, expand the Printer Management node, right-click Drivers, and select Auto Replication to distribute the drivers to all MetaFrame Presentation Servers in the farm. This also maintains the replication job in the data store so that these drivers can be added to any new servers added to the farm in the future. Use the guidelines outlined previously in the section "Using Autoreplication" when performing replication.

To allocate network printers to users, follow these steps:

1. Within the Presentation Server Console, expand the Printer Management node.

2. Select the Printers node and then select a printer.

3. Right-click on a printer and select Auto-Creation.

4. Specify a domain and select the groups and users who need to use the printer.

When a specified user logs onto a MetaFrame Presentation Server in the farm, the printer becomes available in the user's ICA session as if the printer were installed on the user's client device.

Controlling the Behavior of Autocreated Network Printers

By default, if a client machine's network printers are allowed to be autocreated in a session, during client logon the MetaFrame Presentation Server will determine if it can contact the print server directly. If the MetaFrame Presentation Server can contact the print server directly, then it will create the user's network printer as if the network printer were configured on the MetaFrame Presentation Server. When a print job is sent to this printer, instead of being sent back to the client through the ICA printer virtual channel, the print job will be sent directly from the MetaFrame Presentation Server to the print server.

In certain scenarios (such as when the print server is located across the WAN) or if you wish to control client printing bandwidth, this can cause performance issues. With previous versions of MetaFrame Presentation Server, a registry modification was required to control whether network printers were created with a direct connection from the server to the printer or as client printers that print through the ICA client device. With MetaFrame Presentation Server 3.0, you can configure a print job–routing policy to control how printing requests to network printers are processed. For more information about using policies, see *MetaFrame Presentation Server Administrator's Guide* and the Presentation Server Console online help.

Changing the Autocreated Printer Setting to Allow Only Local Client Printers

To change the autocreated printer setting to allow only local client printers to be mapped, perform the following steps:

1. Using the Presentation Server Console, right-click on Printer Management and select Properties.

2. Within the Printer Management Properties window, highlight Printers in the left window.

3. Under "Auto-Create these client print devices," select the radio button "Local (non-network) client printers only."

4. Click OK to finish.

Updating Printer Properties at Logon

Updating an autocreated client printer's properties and an autocreated network printer's properties at logon can cause increases in login times. When these settings are enabled, communication must occur between the server and the client systems to update the printer property settings at each client logon. If these settings are not used, the settings are read once when the client first logs onto the server and then are saved in the user's profile and restored the next time they log on.

Here are the steps to follow to verify that autocreated client printers and autocreated network printers are not updating printer properties at each logon (the default setting is that properties are not updated):

1. In the Presentation Server Console, right-click the Printer Management node and select Properties.

2. Within the Printer Management Properties window, highlight Printers in the left window.

3. Verify in the Auto-Created Client Printers frame that the check box labeled "Update printer properties at each logon" is not selected.

METAFRAME PRESENTATION SERVER 3.0 CLIENT ENHANCEMENTS

The 8.*x* version of the MetaFrame Presentation Server Client for 32-bit Windows contains improvements in the PCL renderer that will reduce the size of the spool files compared to earlier versions of the client. Additionally, the 8.*x* client, when matched to a MetaFrame Presentation Server 3.0 farm, provides for three new features, as detailed next.

Autoinstalling Drivers for Autocreated Printers

This new feature automatically installs the administrator-approved user's printer drivers during login. You can limit which drivers are installed by using the driver compatibility list. This feature does not disable the autocreation of client and network printers; it only disables the installation of any drivers that are not currently on the server.

An administrator can enable or disable autoinstallation of printer drivers for any (network and client) autocreated printers in the Presentation Server Console, under Printer Management | Drivers by checking or unchecking "Automatically install native drivers for auto-created client and network printers."

NOTE: Once a driver is automatically installed on the server, it is the same as if the driver were manually installed. The driver remains on the server unless it is manually removed. Therefore, to properly test the functionality of the check box "Automatically install native drivers for auto-created client and network printers," use a printer whose drivers are not already installed on the server. One way to check for the installed drivers on the server is to open the server's Printers applet from the Control Panel (on Windows Server 2003, open Printers and Faxes). From the File menu select Server Properties and click on the Drivers tab. The drivers installed on the server are listed here.

This feature can dramatically reduce an administrator's workload and reduce the chance of server instability/crashing due to bad printer drivers in smaller environments.

NOTE: Because the installation of the printer driver for networked printers will occur at login if the driver is not already installed, there may be an impact when the user firsts logs in. This issue will resolve itself once the driver is installed and the user logs in a second time.

In most enterprise environments though, the driver replication feature discussed in the section "Print Driver Replication," earlier in this chapter, is a more efficient and complete method to control the print driver deployment.

NOTE: Printers can be autocreated only on servers where their drivers can be found. A primary set of native printer drivers is provided with Windows. You must manually install third-party drivers that are not provided in this set or replicate them from another server in the farm.

Enforce Printer Compatibility

A persistent problem in MetaFrame Presentation Server environments has been the instability caused by the installation of unsupported printers into the environment. The Enforce Printer Compatibility feature allows administrators to disallow specific printer drivers from being used, thus solving this problem.

NOTE: Ensure that you check the list of allowed/denied printer drivers prior to enabling this feature.

During login, the autocreated client printers are checked against a banned list of printers restricted by the administrator. This allows the administrator to enforce banning print drivers, which may cause issues on the MetaFrame Presentation Servers.

The administrator can configure drivers that are either allowed or banned using the Presentation Server Console. This is accomplished by performing the following steps:

1. Open the Presentation Server Console and expand the Printer Management node.
2. Right-click Drivers and select Compatibility.
3. In the Driver Compatibility window, you have two options:

   ■ **Allow only drivers in the list**   The farm uses only the drivers included in this list and excludes all others.

   ■ **Allow all drivers except those in the list**   The farm excludes only the drivers in the compatibility list and accepts all others.

Select the radio button for the type of compatibility desired and use the Add, Edit, and Remove controls to customize the list to your needs.

During logon time, the client printers are automatically mapped into the session and verified against the print driver compatibility list to either be created or denied. If printer autocreation is denied, an event will be generated in the event log on the server for any banned client printer drivers.

Controlling the Behavior of the Universal Driver

The version of the universal driver installed with MetaFrame Presentation Server 3.0 supports color printing by default. This additional functionality may cause print jobs to complete more slowly than in previous versions of MetaFrame Presentation Server. If you want users to print in black and white while using the universal driver, follow these steps:

1. In the registry, navigate to HKLM\SOFTWARE\Citrix\UniversalPrintDrivers.
2. Double-click the value Driver List and delete PCL5c.

If you do not want the universal driver to be used on a specific server, rename or remove the Driver List value in the registry key. This will disable all universal drivers on that server.

CHAPTER 14

Farm Maintenance

This chapter covers best practices, recommendations, and maintenance issues that might be encountered while administering a MetaFrame Presentation Server farm, including cyclic booting, renaming of MetaFrame Presentation Servers, Presentation Server Console usage, use of the Management Console for the MetaFrame Access Suite, Installation Manager, Resource Manager, Network Manager, and Associators. Additional information organized by daily, weekly, and monthly administrative tasks can be found in Chapter 21 of *Citrix MetaFrame Access Suite for Windows Server 2003: The Official Guide*.

CYCLIC REBOOTING METAFRAME PRESENTATION SERVERS

MetaFrame Presentation Servers do not require a regular restart cycle to run effectively. However, some applications have memory leaks or programming errors that build upon themselves, thus requiring regular reboots. In order to provide consistently good performance for these applications in a MetaFrame Presentation Server environment, a good solution is to simply reboot the MetaFrame Presentation Servers on a consistent cycle. This section covers the methodology and steps for configuring a MetaFrame Presentation Server to be rebooted on a consistent cycle.

A simple reboot script such as the one shown in Figure 14-1 can be used as a scheduled task to reboot servers with MetaFrame Presentation Server. MetaFrame Presentation Server, Enterprise Edition has a built-in reboot functionality that can be scheduled from the server properties in the Presentation Server Console.

```
change logon /disable
msg * Please log off and save your work. The server is going down in 5 mins.
sleep.exe 5
net stop spooler
sleep.exe 30
del c:\WINNT\System32\spool\PRINTERS\*.* /q
REM ** unremark the next three lines if you are using Microsoft Access as
the IMA datastore.
REM net stop "independent management console"
REM sleep.exe 30
REM copy C:\Program Files\Citrix\Independent Management Architecture\mf20.bak
\\backupserver\share
sleep.exe 30
tsshutdn.exe /REBOOT
```

Figure 14-1.   Sample reboot script

When the IMA Service starts after a reboot, it establishes a connection to the data store and performs various reads to update the local host cache. These reads can vary from a few hundred kilobytes of data to several megabytes of data, depending on the size and configuration of the server farm.

To reduce the load on the data store and to reduce the IMA Service start time, Citrix recommends maintaining cycle boot groups of no more than 100 servers. In large server farms with hundreds of servers, or when the database hardware is not sufficient, you should restart servers in groups of approximately 50, with at least 10-minute intervals between groups.

TIP: If the Service Control Manager reports that the IMA Service could not be started after a restart of a MetaFrame Presentation Server, but the service eventually starts, ignore this message. The Service Control Manager has a timeout of 6 minutes. The IMA Service can take longer than 6 minutes to start because the load on the database exceeds the capabilities of the database hardware. In order to eliminate this message, try restarting fewer servers at the same time.

CHANGING THE FARM MEMBERSHIP OF SERVERS

MetaFrame Presentation Servers require the use of the **chfarm** command to change farm membership.

CAUTION: Misuse of **chfarm** can corrupt the data store. Before running the **chfarm** command on any server in the farm, you should back up the data store.

Using the chfarm Command

The **chfarm** command can be executed from %ProgramFiles%\Citrix\system32\citrix \ima, the installation CD, or a network image of the CD.

CAUTION: If **chfarm** reports any errors, continuing the process can corrupt the data store. Instead, click Cancel and troubleshoot the unresponsive server.

Executing chfarm

The **chfarm** command performs the following tasks on the host server:

▼   It attempts to remove the server from the farm.

■   It stops the IMA Service.

■   It configures the data store.

▲   It restarts the IMA Service.

Important chfarm Considerations

Running **chfarm** on a server hosting the data store (MS Access, MSDE) deletes the current data store database. Do not use **chfarm** on the server hosting the MS Access or MSDE database until all other servers in that farm are moved to a new server farm. Failure to follow this process causes errors when **chfarm** is executed on those servers that no longer have a valid data store.

Creating an MS Access Data Store on a New Server Farm

When creating a MS Access data store on a new server farm, you have three steps to follow in running the **chfarm** command:

1. Run **chfarm** first on the server hosting the new data store.
2. Execute **chfarm** on other servers to be added to the new server farm.
3. Run **chfarm** on any servers that hosted the data store for the previous farm.

Close all connections to the Presentation Server Console on the local server before executing the **chfarm** command. Execute **chfarm** only on a functioning MetaFrame Presentation Server. Do not execute **chfarm** on a server that was removed from a server farm.

IMPORTANT: Using **chfarm** does not migrate published applications or any server settings to the new server farm.

Using chfarm with MSDE   When using the Chfarm utility to change a MetaFrame Presentation Server's farm membership or to create a new farm that will use Microsoft SQL Server 2000 Database Engine (MSDE) for the server farm's data store, you must install a named instance of MSDE on the server on which you run **chfarm**.

The default named instance that **chfarm** uses is CITRIX_METAFRAME. Running **chfarm** does not automatically install MSDE; it must be installed manually using the MSDE Windows Installer installation package included on the MetaFrame Presentation Server CD, located in the Support\MSDE\MSDE folder.

Creating and Installing a Named Instance of MSDE   You can run *SetupMsdeForMetaFrame.cmd*, located in the Support\MSDE folder, to automatically create a named instance properly configured with the preconfigured instance name "CITRIX_METAFRAME." This is the instance name used by default for MetaFrame Presentation Server farm installations.

To install MSDE with a different instance name, refer to the *ReadmeMSDE2000A.htm* file located in the Support\MSDE\MSDE folder.

chfarm Options when Using MSDE   Use the **/instancename** and **/database** options when running **chfarm** to create a new farm with MSDE as the data store. Here is the syntax of the command options:

```
/instancename:<name>
```

The default value is **CITRIX_METAFRAME**.

```
/database:<name>
```

The default value is **MF20**.

NOTE: You cannot migrate a database to a named instance of MSDE that is already in use. If you are already using MSDE and you want to migrate to a new farm using MSDE, you must either migrate to another database (Microsoft Access or a third-party database) and then back to MSDE or install another named instance of MSDE and then launch **chfarm** with the **/instancename** option.

Moving a Server to a New Server Farm Using MSDE as the Data Store   In order to move a server to a new server farm using MSDE as the data store, follow these steps:

1. Create a named instance of MSDE by installing MSDE on the first server in the new farm.

2. Run **chfarm** on the server that you want to use to create the new farm using the **/instancename:<name>** option, where **<name>** is the name of the instance of MSDE created in Step 1.

NOTE: If there is already a named instance of MSDE called CITRIX_METAFRAME, it is not necessary to use the **/instancename** option.

Backup/Restore of the MSDE Database   Use **DSMAINT BACKUP** to back up the MSDE database. Specify a local path for the location of the database backup files. Essentially, this command uses a default OSQL script to back up the database (OSQL is a utility that can be run interactively to execute Transact-SQL statements in a command prompt window). Use **DSMAINT RECOVER** to restore a previously backed up copy of the MSDE database for use as the IMA data store.

To create customized OSQL scripts for backup, refer to Microsoft Knowledge Base article 241397, "How to Back Up a Microsoft Data Engine Database with Transact-SQL," for further details.

NOTE: If you are moving the MSDE database to a different server in the farm, you will need to perform **DSMAINT FAILOVER** on all indirect servers in order to point them to the new database server. This action is similar to the directions found in the section "To move or restore an Access data store" of Citrix Knowledge Base article CTX677542.

RENAMING A METAFRAME PRESENTATION SERVER

The name and security ID given to a server when it is installed and added to a server farm generally remains unchanged, but the server can be renamed if necessary (due to a change in naming convention, for example).

Renaming a Server in a Server Farm

The ten steps for renaming a server in a server farm are as follows:

1. In the Presentation Server Console, select the check box in the Add Administrators Wizard to add local administrators to the MetaFrame Administrators node and then select Full Administration from the Select Tasks screen.

2. Use **chglogon /disable** to prevent users from logging into the server.

3. Remove the server to be renamed from published applications assigned to that server.

4. Stop the IMA Service.

5. Change the name of the server.

6. Restart the server.

7. Log onto Presentation Server Console using the local administrator account.

8. Expand the Servers folder.

9. Remove the old server name from the Presentation Server Console's list of servers.

10. Add the new server name to the list of configured servers for published applications.

UNINSTALLING METAFRAME PRESENTATION SERVERS IN INDIRECT MODE

If MetaFrame Presentation Server is removed from a server with a direct connection to the data store, indirect servers will no longer be able to access the data store. Information such as published applications, MetaFrame administrators, and anything else in the data store will be lost. Citrix recommends uninstalling the indirect servers first and uninstalling the direct server last. Uninstalling the direct server first prevents any other servers from being uninstalled from the data store.

Uninstalling when the Data Store Cannot Be Accessed

In order to force an uninstall of a MetaFrame Presentation Server when the data store cannot be accessed, use the following command:

```
msiexec /x mps.msi CTX_MF_FORCE_SUBSYSTEM_UNINSTALL=YES
```

where **mps.msi** is the full path location, including the name of the MSI package for MetaFrame Presentation Server.

For more on how to pass properties to the Windows Installer, refer to the *MetaFrame Presentation Administrator's Guide.*

THE PRESENTATION SERVER CONSOLE

This section offers recommendations for using the Presentation Server Console in an enterprise environment.

Using Server and Application Folders

The Presentation Server Console provides the ability to group servers and applications into folders. There is no correlation between the Presentation Server Console folders and the Program Neighborhood folders that appear in application sets.

The Presentation Server Console folders help to manage a large number of servers and applications and increase performance because the Presentation Server Console only queries for data for the servers or applications in the current folder view. One way to increase response time of the console is to divide the list of servers into folders based on their zones.

TIP: Viewing server details on large groups of servers may result in incomplete information being gathered for all the servers. Grouping servers in folders under the Servers node of the Presentation Server Console can reduce the likelihood of this happening.

Configuring Data Refresh

By default, the automatic refresh of data is disabled in the Presentation Server Console. Enabling automatic refresh increases CPU utilization by the console and increases TCP traffic on the network. Opening multiple Presentation Server Console instances in the same farm with automatic refresh enabled increases network congestion.

In some cases, though, automatic refresh might be useful. For example, automatic refresh can be enabled to view real-time data on client connections and disconnections.

Enabling Automatic Data Refresh in the Presentation Server Console

Automatic refresh settings are saved on the server on which the Presentation Server Console is running. In order to enable automatic data refresh in the console, launch the Presentation Server Console, log into the farm, and then follow these three steps:

1. Choose the View | Preferences | User Data tab.

2. Select the automatic refresh options and enter the refresh rate. Choices include automatic refresh for server data, server folders, and application user data.

3. Click OK to apply the settings.

Performance Considerations

The Presentation Server Console queries the data collector and the member servers for information such as running processes, connected users, and server loads. Depending on the size of the server farm, the Presentation Server Console might affect performance in the server farm.

Very Large MetaFrame Presentation Server Deployments

In MetaFrame Presentation Server deployments with hundreds of servers and thousands of users, connect only one instance of the Presentation Server Console to the farm for each zone.

Direct Data Query

Connect the Presentation Server Console to a data collector so that the Presentation Server Console can query data directly, rather than through an intermediate MetaFrame Presentation Server.

Presentation Server Console Refresh Time

In large farms, the Presentation Server Console can take a long time to refresh. The refresh time depends on the number of servers in the zone, the number of clients requesting connections, and the number of Presentation Server Console instances requesting information. If the refresh query takes longer to complete than the specified automatic refresh interval, the data collector becomes overloaded. Set the automatic refresh interval for users and applications as long as is practical. Using the minimum refresh interval of 10 seconds is not recommended. For best performance, disable automatic refresh and manually refresh the data as needed.

Managing a Farm Across a Congested WAN

When managing a farm across a congested WAN, run the Presentation Server Console within an ICA session to a remote server rather than running it locally. Running the Presentation Server Console from within an ICA session reduces the amount of bandwidth consumed across the WAN and provides better performance from the Presentation Server Console.

Adding a Server to Multiple Published Applications

In customer environments with hundreds or thousands of published applications, adding a new server to all the published applications can be cumbersome. To add multiple applications to a server, launch the Presentation Server Console and select the existing published applications to be published to the new server. Drag the selected applications to the server to be published to in the left side of the console. This will automatically add all the selected applications to the server, as shown in Figure 14-2.

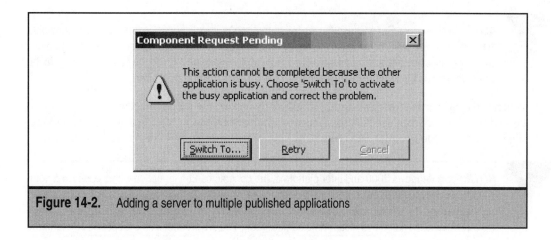

Figure 14-2. Adding a server to multiple published applications

CAUTION: Make sure the new server has access to the user accounts for which the applications are published. If the machine does not have permissions for the existing user accounts, the accounts will be reset and replaced with the Built-in User accounts.

MICROSOFT MANAGEMENT CONSOLE INTEGRATION WITH THE MANAGEMENT CONSOLE FOR THE METAFRAME ACCESS SUITE

The Access Suite Console extends the ability to centrally manage a MetaFrame Access Suite deployment by integrating consoles with the Microsoft Management Console (MMC).

Platform Support

The Access Suite Console is supported on Windows 2000 Server, Windows 2000 Professional, Windows XP, and Windows Server 2003.

IMPORTANT: Microsoft .NET Framework version 1.1, available in the Support folder of the MetaFrame Presentation Server CD, is required to install the Citrix MetaFrame Access Suite Console.

Discovery

While the discovery process is being run, only one server name is required for the farm. Once the discovery process is run for a certain farm, the discovered objects can be saved by saving the MSC (Microsoft Management Console) file.

NOTE: The Access Suite Console uses "pass-through" authentication. Ensure you are logged onto the client machine (where the console is installed) as a MetaFrame administrator for the farm. To avoid problems with credentials, it's advisable to ensure that the machine running the console belongs to the same domain as the MetaFrame Presentation Server farm member machines.

When the MSC file is launched again, it will know about the discovered objects. When you launch the console from the ICA toolbar or from the Start Menu, the choice to save the MSC file is not available because the console is saved automatically every time it is closed.

NOTE: On Windows 2000 and later platforms, the console can be launched with the **runas** command to specify the proper credentials. For example, you can execute **runas /u:*<DOMAIN>* *username* C:\\Program Files\\Citrix\\MMCPlugins\\CMILaunch.exe**, where **username** is the name of a MetaFrame administrator. You are prompted for the specified MetaFrame administrator's password, and the console launches in the context of that user.

Web-Based Tools

Several Web-based tools, such as the Web Interface Console, Program Neighborhood Agent Console, and License Management Console, can be launched from the Access Suite Console. In order to launch each tool using a separate Internet Explorer window, follow these steps in Internet Explorer:

1. Choose **Tools | Internet Options | Advanced.**
2. Under the Browsing section, uncheck "Reuse windows for launching shortcuts."

TIP: Use My Views to create custom views of frequently used applications and servers.

Update of Published Applications

The updating of published applications doesn't happen automatically for the Applications node of the Access Suite Console. The discovery process must be rerun for the update to take effect.

NOTE: If the MetaFrame Presentation Server Client is not installed on the machine, the option to shadow from the console will not be available.

MetaFrame COM Server Service

The Access Suite Console communicates with the server farm using the MetaFrame COM server service. When troubleshooting, ensure that this service is running on the MetaFrame Presentation Server.

NOTE: If you upgrade from MetaFrame XP Feature Release 1 to MetaFrame Presentation Server 3.0, the MetaFrame COM server service fails to start. The workaround to this issue is to unregister and then reregister the MFCOM service. From a command line, execute the following:

```
mfcom   /unregserver
mfcom   /regserver
```

INSTALLATION MANAGER FOR METAFRAME PRESENTATION SERVER

You must understand various design and architecture topics before using MetaFrame Installation Manager to deploy applications to a MetaFrame Presentation Server farm in an enterprise environment. These topics include data store usage, group size considerations, WAN recommendations, and application deployment recommendations. Before we discuss some of these advanced topics, a quick review of Installation Manager's capabilities may be worthwhile.

Installation Manager is designed to automate the application installation process and facilitate application replication across MetaFrame Presentation Servers throughout the enterprise. Although Installation Manager does not facilitate the initial server building and configuration process, it is quite handy for software installation and maintenance. Through the use of Installation Manager, applications can be distributed across multiple servers in minutes rather than days or weeks. MetaFrame Installation Manager is bundled with MetaFrame Presentation Server, Enterprise Edition and cannot be purchased separately. Installation Manager is fully integrated into the Presentation Server Console.

Installation Manager creates a central repository for software application packaging and distribution. Having a central repository that packages, distributes, and inventories applications aids administrators by

- ▼   Allowing all software to be managed in a single location
- ■   Allowing scheduling of application deployment/distribution during low server load times
- ▲   Allowing retention/tracking of all applications/versions contained in each server in the server farm

If the farm is configured using an application load-balanced architecture, Installation Manager allows for the rapid tuning and placement of applications onto the server groups, as well as ensuring consistency across all server types.

Data Store Usage when Deploying Applications with Installation Manager

Group size considerations, network setup considerations, and WAN considerations are all important to optimizing data store usage for deploying applications with Installation Manager.

Group Size Considerations

Installation Manager permits the installation of applications to predefined groups of servers. A group allows a MetaFrame administrator to install applications to a specific set of servers quickly and efficiently so that individual servers do not have to be selected with every installation (the Accounting department, for example).

When you're creating a server group for application deployment, it is important to plan how to use and create the server group. It is also important to keep the group size reasonable, as shown in Table 14-1.

Installation Manager deploys applications to servers simultaneously, but it does not use multicasting. Each target server reads the data from the location where the installation package is stored. Large installation packages, such as Microsoft Office XP, copy more than 200MB of data from the package server to the target server. The amount of data transferred across the network is

$$D = I \times N$$

where D is the amount of data, I is the size of the installation, and N is the number of target servers.

Smaller group sizes (see Table 14-1) are needed when installing applications that require a server to restart. Installations occur simultaneously, and the MetaFrame Presentation Servers can be forced to restart at nearly the same time. Because of this, a transient load is placed on the data store. The data store server, the internetworking infrastructure, and the performance of the network can be greatly affected during application deployment and server restarting.

Clustering Groups   It is important to cluster groups logically. Deployment is more efficient if several logical groups are created that match the schema of the overall enterprise.

	Small	Medium	Large
Application size	< 5MB	5–20MB	> 20MB
Recommended group size	< 100	< 80	< 50

Table 14-1.   Recommended Server Group Size

One group might contain servers that host standard business applications, another group can host engineering applications, and so on.

Network Setup Recommendations

The network setup recommendations for MetaFrame Presentation Server also apply to Installation Manager. The more efficient and capable the network, the quicker and easier applications are to install. The use of Layer 3 switches, high-speed backbones, and high-speed disk drives greatly enhance the ability of Installation Manager to install applications to large server farms efficiently. Chapter 17 of *Citrix MetaFrame Access Suite for Windows Server 2003: The Official Guide* provides very deep detail on optimal network configuration.

WAN Recommendations

Do not install applications to target servers across a WAN. The amount of bandwidth and time required to install an application over a WAN can congest the network for extended periods of time, which can result in network timeouts.

Creating a New Application Package for Remote Sites   One way to avoid installing applications across a WAN is to create a new application package at the remote site where the application is to be deployed.

Multiple Target Servers   If there is more than one remote target server, copy the package and the associated installation files over the WAN once; then deploy the package on that segment.

Installation Manager Application Deployment Recommendations

Application deployment considerations when using Installation Manager in conjunction with MetaFrame Presentation Server include package server recommendations, deployment server recommendations, the network share account, job scheduling and staggered installation, package group deployment, user-specified restart, and recording applications requiring restarts during installation. If these considerations are ignored, the corruption of applications or servers and the failure of the network are very likely.

Package Server

The package server is used to record an application's installation. The package server can be used to generate packages for applications that do not have MSI installations. The generated package is then deployed to the MetaFrame Presentation Servers.

Package Server Configuration   Keep the package server as similar in configuration (both hardware and software) as possible to the target server.

Make the Package Server "Clean"   Make the package server as "clean" as possible. Previously installed applications should be rolled back or uninstalled before recording. For additional information, see the *Installation Manager Administrator's Guide*.

Running Applications While an Image Is Recording   Do not run other applications while an image is recording.

Background Processes   Any unnecessary background processes should be stopped before recording an installation using the Installation Manager Packager, including the IMA Service, especially if a manual install needs to be performed. Background processes and file changes may be recorded by the Packager and could overwrite important files such as the local access database files used by the IMA Service.

Application Packaging   Do not package applications through an ICA session.

Deployment Server

The deployment server is the server where the package and installation files reside. All target servers communicate with this server to get the files and information they need to install the application. The following two recommendations offer helpful information about deploying packages.

Put the Deployment Server on a Server Grade Machine   Each target server requests the same file set from the deployment server. The load on the deployment server can be high. The deployment server must be capable of handling the combined load of the servers connecting and requesting information simultaneously in a deployment group.

Put the Deployment Server on the Fastest Switched Ethernet Port Available   Running the deployment server in a shared collision domain increases latency. Connections can be refused due to timeout or server overload. This problem increases on a busy network and when many servers are targeted for a single installation. Therefore, it is critical to put the deployment server on a 100Mb Switched port (at minimum), preferably on a Layer 3 Virtual LAN Gigabit port. For best results, the other servers that will be receiving the application deployment should be the only servers on the virtual LAN with the deployment server(s).

Network Share Account

The network share account allows the target server to have access rights to the network share point where the package is located.

Setting Up a Network Shared Account   In order to set up a network share account, follow these three steps:

1. Right-click the Installation Manager node in the Presentation Server Console.
2. Select Properties.
3. Enter the domain account and password that will be used to access network shares.

When an unattended install is being performed, the network share account must have administrator privileges on the target server.

IMPORTANT: Installation Manager only supports Windows Domain Authentication models, not Workgroups.

Job Scheduling

The following recommendations can lower bandwidth consumption, allowing the farm to function without a loss of performance:

▼ Schedule the installation of packages during times of low network usage.

▲ Avoid installations during scheduled server backups or restorations.

Staggered Installations

Installation Manager supports staggered installations of package groups. Installation window options and multiple dates can be used for package groups to schedule the installation job during a certain time period within specific days.

Installation Window Options   Schedule the installation window during times of low network usage.

Multiple Dates   Select multiple dates if the installation of the packages in a package group requires multiple dates for installation. The packages that haven't been installed will begin installation in the same installation window on the selected dates.

IMPORTANT: A staggered installation of a single package is not supported.

Package Group Deployment

Package groups are used to deploy multiple packages to the same target server or server groups in one schedule.

Package Group Creation   Create package groups with similar packages to simplify deployment.

Changes to the Package Group Contents   After scheduling an installation of a package group, do not make changes to the package group contents, because this may result in temporarily inaccurate Job Result information. Refresh the Presentation Server Console to correct this behavior.

Changing the Package Group   After the package group has been deployed, do not make changes to the package group (that is, don't add or delete packages to/from the package group). This will cause unnecessary uninstall errors. If you need to deploy new packages, create a new package group and then deploy it.

User-Specified Reboot

The server restart behavior during package deployment is affected by three options:

▼ Do not reboot servers if any user sessions are open

■ Delay reboot until the end of job

▲ Force reboot after job

Each of these is explained in more detail in the sections that follow.

Do Not Reboot Servers If Any User Sessions Are Open   Set the option "Do not reboot severs if any user sessions are open" before deploying packages. The target server will not restart if a user connection to the target server is detected, even though the package deployment requires a restart. The target server will be restarted after the user logs off to finish the deployment. This can be overwritten if the "Force reboot after job" option is selected during the scheduling of the package installation.

Delay Reboot Until the End of Job   If a package group is deployed and one or more of the applications require a restart at the end of the deployment, set the "Delay reboot until the end of job" option while scheduling the installation to postpone the restart until the end of the entire package group deployment.

Force Reboot After Job   If "Force reboot after job" is set, the server will restart after the package has been deployed. Any active user sessions will receive a message from the server, asking them to log off. The messages will be sent in 5-minute intervals for 15 minutes (this is the default setting and can be changed). Any active sessions will be terminated, and then the server will restart.

Recording Applications Requiring Reboot During Installation

The Installation Manager's Packager cannot resume a package recording after a reboot during an application's installation. To support applications that require a reboot during the installation process, follow the instructions in the next four sections.

Application Recording   When recording an application that prompts the user for a restart, cancel the restart and stop the recording on the Packager.

Applications Forcing Restarts That Cannot be Canceled by the User   Installation Manager's Packager cannot record an application that forces a restart that cannot be canceled by the user.

Applications Requiring Multiple Server Restarts   Installation Manager's Packager cannot record an application that requires multiple server restarts during installation.

Application Unattended Installation Programs   If an application has an unattended installation program, the Packager will create a package from the unattended installation program only.

The Packager will not record the actual installation. When you're using the Packager to package the application, select the "Package an Unattended Program" option to package the unattended install program and any other necessary files. This method allows applications that require one or more restarts during installation to be packaged.

USER POLICIES BEST PRACTICES

With user policies, select MetaFrame Presentation Server settings can be applied to specific users or user groups, servers, MetaFrame Presentation Server client names, and client IP addresses. Policies available include shadowing permission settings, printer autocreation settings, and client device mapping settings. Using policies, any environment can be tailored all the way down to the user level.

Assign User Policies to User Groups Rather Than Individual Users

Assigning policies to groups rather than individual users dramatically reduces administrative overhead. When user policies are assigned to user groups, assignments are updated automatically when users are added or removed from the groups.

Disable Unused Policies

Policies with all the rules set to Not Configured create unnecessary processing. Disable any unused policies to avoid this unnecessary processing overhead.

Avoid Conflicting Settings in Citrix Connection Configuration or in the Farmwide Settings of the Presentation Server Console

Several policy rules can be set both in Citrix Connection Configuration and in the farmwide settings in the Presentation Server Console. When possible, keep all settings consistent (enabled or disabled) for ease of troubleshooting.

Use the Search Functionality to See Which Policy Rules Are Being Applied to Users or User Groups

Use the Search function to determine the effective policy being applied to users. The resultant policy that is returned from a search allows an administrator to determine which rules are in effect for users.

Use the Drag-and-Drop Feature of User Policies to Quickly Assign the Correct Priority to a User Policy

To move a policy up or down in priority, drag the policy above or below the policy that currently has the desired rank.

User-to-User Shadowing Policies Best Practices

Users can shadow other users without having administrator rights. Similar to MetaFrame Conferencing Manager, multiple users from different locations can view presentations and training sessions, allowing one-to-many, many-to-one, and many-to-many online collaboration.

NOTE: Although it is possible for users to shadow each other for collaboration, training, and other tasks, MetaFrame Conferencing Manager is a more suitable solution for performing these tasks because it automates the setup and configuration of conferences.

Administrator Group Shadow Rights

Members of the administrators group do not necessarily have shadow rights by default. Although local administrators may have shadowing rights enabled in Citrix Connection Configuration, they are not able to shadow users who have been assigned to the policy by default. In order to allow an administrator to shadow, add the members of the local administrators group to the list of people with shadow rights in the user policy.

User Policies Precedence

Although, in general, user policies take precedence over settings configured in other MetaFrame Presentation Server utilities, shadowing is an exception. If shadowing was disabled during MetaFrame Presentation Server installation or disabled in Citrix Connection Configuration for a particular connection, user policies with shadowing enabled have no effect.

Controlling Shadow Settings

Because the *most* restrictive of the three shadow settings (settings in the Citrix Connection Configuration, settings specified during the MetaFrame Presentation Server installation, and settings in shadow policies) go into effect, avoid unnecessary administrative headache by using shadow policies as the central control to manage shadow settings. An exception to this rule is the need to adhere to local governmental laws that stipulate certain privacy requirements.

ENHANCED DELEGATED ADMINISTRATION

MetaFrame Presentation Server delegated administration allows administrators to assign custom roles to individual users or groups to facilitate management of the MetaFrame Presentation Server environment. In MetaFrame Presentation Server 3.0, this support has been enhanced to include the ability to delegate permissions on Server and Application folders, thus allowing an administrator to delegate administrative capabilities at a much more granular level.

Most enterprise environments will benefit from utilizing this delegated administrative functionality to relieve the head administrator from performing all tasks as well as having to make users administrators who should not have administrative privileges over the entire farm. When creating the custom MetaFrame administrators, simply select the group instead of the user(s) from within the NDS, Active Directory, or Windows NT domain. Configuring the group instead of the user allows the administrator to add and remove users to these preconfigured groups without having to reconfigure all the permissions.

Assigning a Server to a Published Application

One capability that is new to the delegated administration feature of MetaFrame Presentation Server 3.0 is the ability to assign a server to a published application.

NOTE: In order to assign a server to a published application, the lead administrator must not only grant the Assign Applications To Servers permission on the server folder that contains the servers that the custom administrator will be allowed to assign, but they also must grant at least **view** permissions on the application folder(s) that contains the application(s) for which the custom administrator will be allowed to manage the server list.

This means that without any view or edit permissions to the server and without edit permissions to a published application, a user can still be granted rights to manage the addition and removal of the servers that are assigned to run this published application.

IMPORTANT: Proper design is very important when configuring this feature. If an application is published on a server, but the custom administrator has not been granted the Assign Applications To Servers permission on the folder containing the server, they will not be able to see the server in the published application properties. This could potentially lead to confusion for the administrator as well as complexities if servers are assigned that have different domain trust relationships.

Another capability that is new for MetaFrame Presentation Server 3.0 is the ability to assign permissions to a custom MetaFrame administrator to manage sessions at the Application level only. This means that they would only be able to see and manage the users who are using a particular published application and not all users logged onto the server.

IMPORTANT: Multiple published applications may be launched within the same session using the sharing feature of MetaFrame Presentation Server. Therefore, if a custom administrator attempts to use the **logoff**, **disconnect**, or **reset** session management options on a user running a particular published application, they will affect all other session-shared applications that are running within that session. Proper design is very important because if a custom administrator has the rights to reset one published application that a user is running but does not have any rights over another published application, they will still implicitly have rights over the other application if both applications run in the same session.

Delegated Administrator Tips

The following three tips will help with delegated administration.

Edit License Server   In MetaFrame Presentation Server 3.0, in order to assign the right to edit the farm's license server to a custom administrator, the lead administrator must assign the Edit License Server privilege to at least one server folder.

Shadowing Through the Presentation Server Console   In order to allow a user to shadow through the Presentation Server Console, enable the following permissions at a minimum:

▼ **MetaFrame Administrators**   Log on to Presentation Server Console

■ **Servers**   View Server Information

▲ **Sessions**   View Session Management

Shadowing Permissions   In order to enable shadowing for the user, either shadowing permissions must be granted in the Citrix Connection Configuration tool or a MetaFrame Presentation Server policy must be configured.

CITRIX RESOURCE MANAGEMENT

Resource Manager is a component of MetaFrame Presentation Server, Enterprise Edition and is not available in the MetaFrame Presentation Server Advanced or Standard Editions. The version of Resource Manager included with MetaFrame Presentation Server 3.0 is improved in the areas of performance, usability, stability, and scalability. Resource Manager also includes the Summary Database, which allows historical data of metrics and servers to be stored and reports to be produced on the stored data.

Resource Manager Database and Metric Server

Resource Manager stores all its configurations, settings, thresholds, and metrics in the data store and in the local host cache. Previous versions of Resource Manager contained a local Resource Manager database and a Farm Metric Server. Feature Release 2 introduced a Database Connection Server that is used with the Summary Database.

Local Resource Manager Database

Each MetaFrame Presentation Server with Resource Manager installed has a local database in which it stores its individual metric information.

RMLocalDatabase.mdb   The local Resource Manager database is a Microsoft Access Jet database named *RMLocalDatabase.mdb*, located in the %ProgramFiles%\Citrix\Citrix Resource Manager\LocalDB folder by default.

Accessing the Local Resource Manager Database   The local Resource Manager database is accessed when creating real-time graphs, displaying system snapshots, running reports on that specific server, and writing server metrics. Administrators can view real-time graphs, server snapshots, and current reports.

Server Metric and Process Data   Server metric and process data is written to the local Resource Manager database. The local Resource Manager database holds metric values and application information for the previous 96 hours.

Compacting the Resource Manager Database   This database is compacted when the IMA Service is started and once per day while the IMA Service is running.

Farm Metric Server

The Farm Metric Server is used for application and server monitoring. The Farm Metric Server gathers its information from the data collector. Because the Farm Metric Server accesses the data collector every 15 seconds to obtain published application counters and every 30 seconds to determine if machines are offline, configuring data collectors to also perform the roles of Farm Metric Servers and backup Farm Metric Servers can improve performance. The Farm Metric Server may also perform the role of the Database Connection Server.

TIP: Although Resource Manager can track any Performance Monitor counter as a server metric, Citrix recommends that you limit the total number of metrics tracked on a server to fewer than 50.

Alerts

Resource Manager has the ability to send alerts to users or groups of users using either e-mail or Microsoft System Management Server. It can also send alerts to a SNMP management console.

TIP: If the e-mail service is not sending alerts, the MetaFrame administrator should confirm that they are able to access the e-mail server using the configured account. Also, the administrator should verify that the e-mail client being used (Microsoft Outlook, for example) is the default mail client for the server and that no additional password is required to connect to the mail server. In order to enable Resource Manager to send SNMP traps for Application Alerts, SNMP must be set up on the primary and backup Farm Metric Servers.

Summary Database

The Summary Database is used for storing historical data from servers in the farm. MetaFrame administrators may produce reports, such as billing, based on the stored data. These can be based on several criteria, such as CPU usage and application usage.

Database Connection Server   Each farm that requires the Summary Database must have a Database Connection Server (DCS), which writes the metric information from other farm servers to the Summary Database.

A System Data Source Name (DSN) called RMSummaryDatabase defines the connection between the DCS and the database where the metric information is stored.

Updating Summary Files   Data is stored on each individual server in summary files. Summary files are updated whenever a session or process terminates, whenever an event occurs, and once an hour for metrics.

Recording Summary Data   Each Resource Manager server in the farm records its own summary data locally for 24 hours and then transmits it to the Database Connection Server at a configurable time of day.

TIP: Report templates for the popular Crystal Reports tool are available from the Citrix Web site. Visit http://www.citrix.com.

Additional Functionality of Resource Manager in MetaFrame XP FR3 and Newer

The following additional functionality has been added to Resource Manager with the release of MetaFrame Presentation Server Feature Release 3:

▼ Folder and zone support

■ Oracle 7 and 8 seamless support without the need for a hotfix

■ Improved efficiency for some stored procedures

▲ Additional process information for processes taking more than 5% of memory or CPU

TIP: By default, metrics are stored in the Summary Database. This can be changed on the Threshold Configuration screen. It is also possible to specify the time of day or week that metrics are recorded in the Summary Database on a per-server basis.

Folders and Zones

With MetaFrame Presentation Server, you can record which folders and zone a server is in at the time of writing data to the summary file. This information can be used to group servers when creating reports outside of the Presentation Server Console. By default, the summary period for server metrics is 1 hour.

If either the folder or zone has changed for a server, just before the next set of server metric records are written to the summary file, a new Folder and Zone record will be written. All following server metric records will be associated with this new Folder and Zone record. The result of this is that if the folder or zone changes multiple times within the summary period, only the one record will be written prior to writing the new server metric records to the summary file. All other folder and zone changes will go unnoticed.

Billing Reports   The sdb_scratch table is used with the generation of billing reports to store information about the reports currently opened so that the records being displayed in the report can be marked as billed. One record exists in the sdb_scratch table per open billing report in the farm. When a report is closed, the record will be deleted from the table.

Data Purging   The Summary Database allows administrators to control how long data is stored by purging the database at set periods. It is also possible to turn purging off, in which case all data will be kept for an indefinite period. If a purge is missed (for example, if the DCS is not online at the purge time), a purge will be initiated when the DCS next starts up.

NOTE: Active sessions, and the processes associated with them, will not be purged from the database whether they are billed or not. Processes are purged only if their "parent" session record is purged (i.e., to maintain data integrity, it is not desirable to purge only process records).

Uploads to the Database Connection Server

Uploads to the Database Connection Server are initiated by the individual servers in the farm based on the Upload time. The following sequence of events occurs each day when the Upload time occurs for every MetaFrame Presentation Server with Resource Manager enabled:

1. MetaFrame Presentation Server closes the current summary file and begins a new file.

2. MetaFrame Presentation Server sends a notification to the Database Connection Server stating it has a summary file to be uploaded; there is one notification per summary file ready to be uploaded.

3. Database Connection Server maintains a list of all notifications.

4. Database Connection Server requests files to be copied to it. The number of concurrent uploads is limited to reduce congestion.

5. When files are available on the Database Connection Server, the import starts. Imports are limited to a maximum concurrent amount.

6. For each file being imported, a new file is uploaded, such that there are ten files either being copied or ready to be imported.

7. When the import succeeds, a message is sent to the originating host informing it that the summary file can be safely deleted. The file is also deleted from the Database Connection Server.

8. This process continues until there are no further summary files to be uploaded or imported.

Database Connection Server Upload Considerations

The following sections discuss some design and administrative concerns to keep in mind with the Database Connection Server uploads.

Inactive Summary Files   Only summary files that are not currently active will be uploaded to the Database Connection Server.

Request to Upload a Second Summary File   If the Database Connection Server receives another request to upload a summary file, it will log a duplicate request and the old request will be deleted from the list. This can occur if updates are taking longer than 24 hours.

Default Setting for Concurrent Uploads   The default setting for concurrent uploads is 10. The default setting for concurrent imports is 1. This reduces the required database connection licenses.

Duplicate Entries   Importing a record into the Summary Database twice will not cause duplicate entries.

Transfer Time   If a summary file takes longer than 30 minutes to transfer, the Database Connection Server will assume it has timed out and delete any record of requesting it. This file will not be retransmitted until the next update period, 24 hours later (unless a manual update is invoked). If the uploaded summary file eventually reaches the Database Connection Server after it has timed out, it will be ignored and deleted.

Upload Time Synchronization   The server performing the upload will compare its time to the server it is uploading to. The main server's time zone is used to determine if uploads should begin. For example, a MetaFrame Presentation Server farm with the majority of its machines in the East Coast of the U.S. and a smaller zone in the U.K. has an upload time set to 1:00 A.M. The servers in the U.S. will begin to upload files at 1:00 A.M. EST, whereas machines in the U.K. will start their uploads at 1:00 A.M. GMT (8:00 pm EST).

Duplicate Upload Request   A "Duplicate upload request" message in the DCS Server log is an indicator of problems in the system but is not an error. The duplicate request will not cause any invalid or duplicate data to be thrown out in the Summary Database and should be treated as an informational message. Examples of events that could result in a "Duplicate upload request" message would be a manual upload requested when an upload is already under way (either a timed update or a previously requested manual request) and an upload that is taking more than 24 hours to complete, resulting in the next daily upload beginning before the previous one has completed.

Resource Manager Summary Files

Summary files are only written when the Summary Database has been enabled in the MetaFrame Presentation Server farm. Each file is given a random name when it is created. At creation time, a header is written to the file. This header contains the following fields: Schema Version, Server's Name, Server's Domain, and Farm Name

Additional records are written to the file based on these events:

▼ When a process terminates, a process record is written to the file.
■ Every 60 minutes a metric record is written for each metric configured to store summary data.
■ When a session is started, a session record is written.

- When a session ends, a session record is written.

▲   When an event is generated, an event record is written.

> **NOTE:**   Summary files can be manually copied to the Database Connection Server or other servers before the daily update is started. The header information in the summary file will ensure the records are associated with the correct server.

Metric Records

Metric records store data in the following fields: Object Name, Counter Name, Instance Name, Update Time, Server UTC Bias (in minutes), Sample Period (in seconds), Data Count, Min Value, Max Value, Mean Value, and Std Dev value.

Application Metric Records

Application metric records store data in the following fields: Application Name, Application Type, Farm Name, Object name, Update time, Sample period (in seconds), Data Count, Min Value, Max Value, Mean Value, and Std Dev value.

Process Records

Process records store data in the following fields: User Name, Client Name, Client Address Family, Client Address, App name, App Type, Path Name, Process Name, Version, Product Date, Type, PID, Exit Code, Affinity, Start Time, End Time, Total Time, Active Time, Kernel Used, User Used, User Active, Kernel Active, Memory, Memory Active, Working Set, Page File, Page Faults, Paged Pool, Non Paged Pool, SessionID, Server UTC Bias (in minutes), User Domain, and Session Start time.

Session Records

Session records store data in the following fields: User Name, Client Name, Client Address Family, Client Address, App Name, App Type, Winstation, Protocol, Session Start, Session End, Duration (in milliseconds), Server UTC bias (in minutes), Session UTC bias (in minutes), SessionID, and User Domain.

Event Records

Event records store data in the following fields: Server Name, NetDomain Name, Farm Name, Event Time, Server UTC Bias (in minutes), and Event Code.

Folder Records

Folder records store only Folder Name data.

Zone Records

Zone records store only Zone Name data.

NOTE: Only Server Up and Server Down events are stored. The Server Down event is generated by the Farm Metric Server upon detecting a server can no longer be contacted. The Server Up event is generated by the server as the IMA Service is started.

SDB_HEURISTICS Table

With large amounts of data in a Summary Database (1GB or more), an administrator generating reports may encounter a situation in which the Presentation Server Console is unable to display reports that are many megabytes in size. The sdb_heuristics table in the Summary Database is used by Resource Manager to ensure that any summary report to be generated can be displayed within the Presentation Server Console. By default, it will contain the entries and values in Table 14-2.

When the administrator specifies various report options in the summary report–generation dialogs, Resource Manager performs calculations based on these options and the entries in the SDB_HEURISTICS table to estimate the size of the report that will be returned. If this estimated value is greater than MAXIMUM_PRACTICAL_HTML_BYTES, in the case of Process, User, and Server Summary reports, and BILL_HTML_MAX, in the case of billing reports, a warning message will be displayed stating that the report may be too large to be displayed within the Presentation Server Console. In such a case, the administrator has the option to cancel the report generation or continue. If the administrator continues and the report is too large to be displayed, an error message will be displayed within the report window. The administrator then has the option of saving the report directly to disk for viewing in another application that can display HTML (such as Internet Explorer).

NOTE: If the Summary Database is not available, all reports (Current Process, Current User, and Server Snapshot) will make use of a hard-coded default value of 1048576 bytes (which equals 524,288 characters).

Depending on the usage of servers in the farm, an administrator may want to configure the values in this table to more accurately reflect the amount of data that may be displayed in reports.

PK_HEURISTIC	HEURVALUE
BILL_HTML_MAX (characters)	72500
MAXIMUM_PRACTICAL_HTML_BYTES (bytes)	1048576
PROCESSES_PER_SESSION	10
SESSIONS_PER_USER_PER_DAY	5
USERSUM_HTML_BYTES_PER_PROCESS	128

Table 14-2. SDB_HEURISTICS Table

NOTE: The ability of the Presentation Server Console to display reports is dependent on the number of report windows currently open. Each time a report is returned to the console, a calculation is performed that subtracts the size of the report (in bytes for Summary reports and characters for Billing reports) from the respective maximum values in the table, thus producing an "available size" figure for subsequent Management reports. Accordingly, an administrator is more likely to receive a warning in the report windows that the report cannot be displayed if they have multiple reports open. Once a report is closed, its "size" is returned to the "available size" figure for future reports.

Report Center in the MetaFrame Access Suite Console

The Report Center in the MetaFrame Access Suite Console extends the reporting capabilities in Resource Manager and allows you to easily generate reports from a variety of real-time and historic data sources. A wizard helps you select the type of report, the data to be displayed, and the schedule for running the report. You can view the status of your scheduled reports and adjust the report parameters.

This section provides information about the different reports available, the data sources for these reports, and how to copy reports and report specifications to other servers.

Copying Report Center Reports and Specifications to a Different Console

The Access Suite Console provides a Report Center extension that enables MetaFrame administrators to generate HTML and CSV reports from a variety of real-time and historic data sources. Commands are available to view the reports from within the console and to make the reports more widely available by copying them to other locations or e-mailing them to selected recipients.

Each successful report and a copy of the specification used to generate it is stored locally on the machine running the console. For reports that administrators plan to run regularly, named specifications, recording report formats, farm information, data source details, required time period, and other report parameters can be generated. These can then be run manually or scheduled to run when required.

If an administrator, therefore, wants to generate reports from an Access Suite Console on a different machine, neither previous reports (and their associated specifications) nor any named specification will be available from the new console. However, it is possible to copy the necessary files across to the machine running the new console and then use them from there, without editing anything, provided the second machine has access to the same farm and Resource Manager Summary Database as the first machine.

User-Configured Report and Specification File Locations

Report Center stores its user-configurable data on the machine running the Access Suite Console. Consequently, a Citrix administrator logged onto a Windows 2003 server will find the report and specification files in

%USERPROFILE%\Local Settings\Application Data\Citrix\ReportCenter

Specifications are stored as .spec files in appropriately named folders within

%USERPROFILE%\Local Settings\Application Data\Citrix\ReportCenter
\CustomSettings\Specifications

Generated reports (and their associated unique specifications) are stored under

%USERPROFILE%\Local Settings\Application Data \Citrix\ReportCenter
\DataSets

with each set of related files in a folder with a unique system-generated name (for example, 4C7F885E0EF72F30).

NOTE: Each report folder's set of files will always include a *Results.xml* file containing the raw data used to generate the necessary HTML reports, graphs, and CSV files when the user requests them. Because the HTML and CSV folders and their contents are only generated when required, they may not be present when you examine the folders within DataSets. This is by design, and both types of reports can always be generated when required.

In order to move previously created specifications and reports to the new console, the administrator should copy all the relevant folders to their corresponding location on the new machine. Once the discovery process has been run and the Specifications and Jobs displays have been refreshed, all the transferred items should be listed as before. Administrators can then view previous reports and generate new ones as required.

WARNING: In the Jobs display, the Elapsed Time values for the copied reports will be incorrect after they are copied to another machine. This is due to the fact that Report Center calculates Elapsed Time by using the creation time of the files, which changes when they are copied to the new machine.

Available Report Center Reports and Their Data Sources

There are many Report Center reports with various data sources. We will discuss several of the more popular reports in the next several sections.

Application Availability Report   The Application Availability report determines if applications were always available for clients to connect. It also determines if applications were unavailable for clients to connect. Its data source is the SDB_APPHISTORY table in the Summary Database.

The Application Availability report displays the percentage of time that the application was available in the farm during the reporting time period. It determines when the application was available for connection across any of the servers onto which it has been published. "Unavailable" is defined as no servers online to be able to service the application to clients.

Application Report   The Application report lists settings for selected applications in the farm. It provides a way to get all application settings quickly in one view. Its data source is MFCOM, via servers selected at the time of specification.

The Application report displays the settings for each published application selected. It details the configured users, servers, application location, working directory, appearance, client options, and current status in the farm (whether it is enabled or disabled).

It only provides information for applications that are published to clients. This includes published desktops and published content. The Application report also provides information regarding the unused applications in the farm.

Application Usage Report   The purpose of the Application Usage report is to view the usage of applications across selected servers over a period of time. It also enables you to view a list of applications that were unused across selected servers over a period of time. Its data source is the SDB_SESSION table in the Summary Database.

The Application Usage report displays the total number of sessions and maximum concurrent number of sessions for each application selected. It displays a table of the most heavily used applications out of the list of selected applications. "Heavily used" is defined by the highest values for maximum concurrent users. The total number of applications the reports displays is configurable.

This report optionally displays a table of unused applications. These are applications that have no sessions during the reporting period. It also optionally displays a graph of time versus concurrent sessions for each application selected.

Client Type Report   The purpose of the Client Type report is to view different types of clients that have connected to the servers. Its data source is the SDB_SESSION, SDB_CLIENTHISTORY table in the Summary Database.

The Client Type report displays the client type and version for connections made to the selected servers. It also includes a graph of the different client types and the percentage of connections made to each.

Disconnected Sessions Report   The purpose of the Disconnected Sessions report is to display the number of disconnected sessions across a selection of servers over a period of time. Its data source is the DB_CONNECTIONHISTORY table in the Summary Database.

This report shows a graph displaying the number of disconnected sessions across the specified servers over the period of time being reported. It also displays a trend line of these disconnected sessions.

Policy Report   The Policy report lists all policies defined in the farm and displays the details of the policies. Policies that are not set to either enabled or disabled can be excluded from the report using the Hide Unconfigured Policies check box. Unchecking this box will include all details of the policies even if they are set to Unconfigured. Its data source is MFCOM.

Server Availability Report   The Server Availability report determines the percentage of time the selected servers were available to service connections. It also can determine the period of time for which servers were down due to scheduled reboots. The report also enables you to determine the period of time for which servers were down due to unexpected reboots. Its data source is the SDB_EVENTLOG table in the Summary Database.

The Server Availability report displays a table with the percentages of uptime, unscheduled downtime, and scheduled downtime. A graph is also displayed with a separate bar for each server selected. The bar is color coded to show the uptime, scheduled downtime, and unscheduled downtime during the reported time period.

Server Performance Report The Server Performance report determines the heaviest used server across a selection of servers based on CPU load, available memory, or maximum concurrent sessions. Its data source is the SDB_METRICS, SDB_CONNECTIONHISTORY table in the Summary Database.

The Server Performance report displays load information for all the selected servers. The report also shows three separate tables detailing the servers that had the highest load. These tables only show servers that have been selected for inclusion in the report.

The number of servers listed in these tables can be configured using the "Number of servers to display" setting. The tables contain data based on the report period for the following three criteria:

▼ Highest CPU load

■ Lowest available memory

▲ Highest maximum concurrent sessions

Server Reboot Report The Server Reboot report determines when servers have been rebooted. It also determines which servers shut down but were not restarted. Its data source is the SDB_EVENTLOG table in the Summary Database.

The Server Reboot report shows, in table format, the times at which servers started up, the time at which they were available to handle client connections, and the time at which they were rebooted.

Server Utilization (CPU) Report The CPU report lists processes across servers that take more than a defined average percentage of the CPU. It also displays the average percentage of the server's CPU for the reported time period. Its data source is the SDB_PROCESS, SDB_METRICS tables in the Summary Database.

This report displays the servers in the selection that have the highest average CPU utilization during the reported time period. The number of servers to be displayed is configurable, allowing the server selection to be the entire farm, but only the heaviest used servers to be displayed in the table.

There is a separate table for each server in the list to show all the processes with high CPU usage during the reported time period. The criterion for "high CPU usage" is configurable.

Server Utilization (Memory) Report The Server Utilization report displays the servers with the least available memory. It also displays the processes consuming the most memory on individual servers. Its data source is the SDB_PROCESS, SDB_METRICS table.

The Server Utilization report displays servers that have had the least available memory within the server selection and reported time period. For each server listed, a separate table shows the processes that consumed the most memory during the reported time period. The number of servers and processes to be displayed is configurable.

Session Statistics Report   The Session Statistic report displays the number of concurrent sessions made to a selection of servers. It also displays the servers that have received the most concurrent sessions. Its data source is the SDB_SESSION tables in the Summary Database.

The Session Statistic report lists, in table format, the servers that have the highest number of concurrent sessions during the reported time period. The number of servers to be included in this table is configurable. A scatter graph showing the highest number of concurrent sessions across the server selection based on time is also displayed.

NETWORK MANAGER FOR METAFRAME PRESENTATION SERVER

Network Manager is a component of MetaFrame Presentation Server, Enterprise Edition and is not available in MetaFrame Presentation Server's Advanced and Standard Editions.

Known Issues with Network Manager (NM)

Network Manager has known issues working with Tivoli NetView, HP Network Node Manager, and Unicenter.

Tivoli NetView

In Tivoli NetView, the server icon is sometimes green, whereas the subsystem icons are light blue. In this case, highlight the green server icon and perform a Status Update to update the status of the subsystem icons. This is a Tivoli NetView IP Map issue that occurs while running for extended periods of time.

Trapd.exe Process   When you're using Tivoli NetView, if the *Trapd.exe* process is killed while the *Metadis.exe* and *Metalan.exe* services are running, each service acquires 50% CPU utilization. The services do not return to normal CPU levels until *Trapd.exe* is restarted. This is a known issue with Tivoli NetView.

HP Network Node Manager

In HP Network Node Manager, a link-down status is represented by a blue icon. This happens only if the server cannot be contacted by the console when the Status Update is performed. In Tivoli NetView, on the other hand, a link-down status is displayed in red.

Uninstalling Network Manager from an SNMP Management Console   When Network Manager is uninstalled from one of the SNMP management consoles, by default the Network Manager icons stay in the IP Map until they are deleted and the nodes are rediscovered. The icons can be deleted, prior to uninstalling in NetView, by going to Properties in the Edit pull-down menu, selecting the application Network Manager, and then clicking the Properties button. In Openview, the icons can be deleted prior to uninstalling by selecting Properties in the Map pull-down menu, clicking the Application tab, selecting Network Manager, and then clicking the "Configure for this map" button.

Unicenter

In order for Unicenter to reclass Windows servers as MetaFrame servers, it is necessary that Security Management (secadmin) be configured and enabled; otherwise, a message similar to

Security authorization failure. The action has been denied.

will appear in the Unicenter event log (conlog).

Network Manager SNMP Agent Issues

This section will discuss known SNMP Agent issues and recommendations for resolving them.

Windows 2000 Default Security for SNMP

In Windows 2000, the default security for the SNMP service is Read Only. Network administrators cannot perform SET operations (Logoff, Disconnect, Send Message, and Terminate Process) from Network Management consoles unless security is Read/Create.

Recommendation   Change security to Read/Create.

Windows 2003 SNMP Messages

For Windows 2003 Server, the SNMP service will, by default, only accept SNMP messages from Local Host. Windows 2000 and previous operating systems allow any SNMP messages from any host from the start.

Recommendation   Add more servers to the list of allowed hosts (recommended) or allow messages from any host (not secure).

Older Network Manager Versions

Older versions of Network Manager had the ability to shut down or restart a MetaFrame server. To comply with Microsoft SNMP security, these options have been removed in newer versions of the plug-ins. Any attempt to reboot a MetaFrame server with an older version of a Network Manager plug-in will be denied.

TIP: Enable or disable the SNMP Agent only when farm activity is low.

USING VBSCRIPT AND METAFRAMECOM TO ADD OR REMOVE A USER FROM A PUBLISHED APPLICATION

MetaFrameCOM (MFCOM) is a COM server that exposes some of the MetaFrame Presentation Server control and monitoring functions through defined objects and interfaces.

MFCOM is a programming interface to the functions provided by the Presentation Server Console. MFCOM is a COM object that meets the requirements defined in the Microsoft Component Object Model specification. It is a COM server, not a COM client. It exposes objects that can be accessed from a COM client, is a free threading COM server, and supports automation. It is also a DCOM server; that is, a COM client can remotely connect to a MetaFrame Presentation Server.

Using MFCOM

In most cases, MFCOM can be used on MetaFrame Presentation Servers with no additional configuration. MFCOM is installed and registered by the installation of MetaFrame Presentation Server. The *C:\Program Files\citrix\system32\mfreg.exe* program can be used to register or unregister MFCOM manually on the server.

In order to use MFCOM remotely, a utility program (*%Program Files%\citrix\mpssdk \utils\mfreg.exe*) must be used to register MFCOM as a remote server. To obtain the *mfreg.exe* program, download the MetaFrame Presentation Server SDK (MPSSDK) from the downloads section of the Citrix Web site (http://www.citrix.com). Installing the MPSSDK package will provide a prompt to register the MetaFrame Presentation Server. To register or unregister the DCOM client manually, use the *C:\Program Files\citrix\mpssdk\utils\mfreg.exe* program. Additionally, you may have to use the Microsoft tool *DCOMCNFG.EXE* to change the default impersonation to "impersonate." This change will require a reboot. For additional information, visit the Citrix Developer Network at http://apps.citrix.com/cdn/.

MetaFrameCOM VBScripting

Although MFCOM can be used with any COM-compliant programming language, such as Visual Basic 6.0, Visual C++, Perl, VB.NET, C#.NET, and C++.NET, it is very convenient to use VBScript. This is because VBScript is included in most versions of Microsoft Windows. VBScript is a perfect programming tool for MetaFrame Presentation Server administrators who want to take advantage of scripting to overcome the difficult tasks of server maintenance. The following example can be used to add or remove an Active Directory (ADS) domain user or group to or from a published application, and it demonstrates how a simple VBScript can be created. With modification to the script, other tasks applicable to the published applications can be automated as well.

Using a Script to Automate "Add/Remove Users or Groups" Functions

Using the Presentation Server Console to add or remove domain users and groups can be a tedious task for an administrator of published applications. If your farms have just a few published applications, using a script to add or remove a couple user accounts may not seem beneficial, but if you have a large number of published applications, you'll save a lot of time. Scripts can be used to batch the process of adding or removing accounts from published applications.

In order to run the following script, execute the command **cscript addacct.wsf** from a CMD window.

```
<package>
  <job  id="AddAcct">
    <comment>
    File:addacct.wsf
    Description:Example  of  how  to  add  a  ADS  user  or
  group  to  a  published  application.
    Requirements:WSH  5.5  or  higher.
        Copyright  (c)  2004  Citrix  Systems,  Inc.
        </comment>
        <runtime>
            <description>
        Add  a  user  or  group  to  an  application.
            </description>
            <example>
            CScript  //nologo  USAGE:  Addacct.wsf
DOMAIN  NAME,  USER|GROUP  NAME
Example:  Addacct.wsf  MYADS  Domain  Users
Use  Double  Quotes  for  names  such  as  Domain  Users
  Example:  Addacct.wsf  MYADS  JONDOE
            </example>
        </runtime>
        <reference  object="MetaFrameCOM.MetaFrameFarm"/>
        <script  language="VBScript">

        Option  Explicit

      Dim  AAName,  AcctName,  theFarm,  anApp,  MFUser,  aWinApp


        if  WScript.Arguments.Count  <>  2  Then
                WScript.Echo  "USAGE:  Addacct.wsf  DOMAIN  NAME,  USER|GROUP  NAME"
                WScript.Echo  ""
                WScript.Echo  "Example:  Addacct.wsf  MYADS  Domain  Users"
        WScript.Echo  "Use  Double  Quotes  for  names  such  as  Domain  Users"
                WScript.Echo  "Example:  Addacct.wsf  MYADS  JONDOE"
                WScript.Quit  0
        Else
      AAName  =  WScript.Arguments(0)
          AcctName  =  WScript.Arguments(1)
wscript.echo  AAName,  ACCTNAME
          End  If
   ''
```

```
            Set theFarm = CreateObject("MetaFrameCOM.MetaFrameFarm")
            if Err.Number <> 0 Then
                WScript.Echo "Can't create MetaFrameFarm object"
                WScript.Echo "(" & Err.Number & ") " & Err.Description
                WScript.Echo ""
                WScript.Quit Err.Number
            End if


''
''   Initialize the farm object.
''

            theFarm.Initialize(MetaFrameWinFarmObject)
            if Err.Number <> 0 Then
                WScript.Echo "Can't Initialize MetaFrameFarm object"
                WScript.Echo "(" & Err.Number & ") " & Err.Description
                WScript.Echo "quiting "
                WScript.Quit Err.Number
            End if
''          Are you Citrix Administrator?
            if theFarm.WinFarmObject.IsCitrixAdministrator = 0 then
                WScript.Echo "You must be a Citrix admin to run this script"
                WScript.Echo ""
                WScript.Quit 0
            End If
''          Display all applications in the farm.
            For Each anApp In theFarm.Applications
                if Err.Number <> 0 Then
                    WScript.Echo "Can''t enumerate applications"
                    WScript.Echo "(" & Err.Number & ") " & Err.Description
                    WScript.Echo ""
                    WScript.Quit Err.Number
                End if

''     Create the user object
            Set MFUser = CreateObject("MetaFrameCOM.MetaFrameUser")
            MFUser.initialize MFAccountAuthorityADS,
AAName,MFAccountDomainUser, AcctName
''
''          Add the user or group to all published applications
''

                anApp.LoadData(TRUE)
                if anApp.AppType = MetaFrameWinAppObject Then
                    ' MetaFrameWinApp object.
                    Set aWinApp = anApp.WinAppObject
                    anApp.Adduser MFAccountAuthorityADS, AAName, MFAccountDomainUser, AcctName
        anApp.SaveData
                end if
            Next


    </script>
  </job>
</package>
```

Modifying one line of code in the preceding Windows script file can produce an entirely different result.

For example, replacing the line:

```
anApp.Adduser  MFAccountAuthorityADS,  AAName,  MFAccountDomainUser,  AcctName
```

with

```
anApp.removeuser  MFAccountAuthorityADS,  AAName,  MFAccountDomainUser,  AcctName
```

will remove an Active Directory user or group from all the published applications.

In this simple functional VBScript, the **MFAccountAuthorityADS** and **MFAccountDomainUser** enumerations are coded into the calls to add and remove AD users and groups. If you are adding or removing users and groups to or from other account authorities, such as NDS, NT, or the local machine, you will have to change these parameters (enumerations) at a minimum. For additional information, visit the Citrix Developer Network at http://apps.citrix.com/cdn/.

CHAPTER 15

MetaFrame Password Manager Administration

T he increasing number and complexity of passwords that the average user has to memorize frequently leads to both increased help desk calls and to security workarounds such as maintaining a list of passwords.

The Single Sign On capability enabled by MetaFrame Password Manager is a valuable component to an access infrastructure. The software, though, is by design very sophisticated in order to accommodate a wide range of applications—from Windows to Web to mainframe. This chapter covers the administration and maintenance tasks for keeping MetaFrame Password Manager working smoothly, including working with Windows, Java, and .NET applications, working with ActiveX, file synchronization points, Logon Manager, and dealing with attempted user workarounds.

NOTE: The following information is not a replacement for the information contained in the Administrator's guide. If you intend to use MetaFrame Password Manager, you should familiarize yourself with the information in the Administrator's guide.

CONFIGURING WINDOWS APPLICATIONS WITH DYNAMIC WINDOWS CLASS IDS

The MetaFrame Password Manager Agent uses class IDs to identify configured applications. When an administrator, however, configures an application definition for a Windows application that uses a dynamic Windows class ID, the application is not detected by the MetaFrame Password Manager Agent.

Class IDs

The agent fails to recognize a Windows application as a MetaFrame Password Manager–configured application when the class ID changes every time the application is loaded. This occurs because when an administrator uses the Password Manager wizard to define an application, the wizard configures the application to use the Windows class ID at the time of detection. Each time this Windows application is loaded, its class ID is different and is therefore not recognized.

Class ID Examples

Figure 15-1 shows two examples of a class ID. The highlighted sections of the class ID are dynamic.

When an application is loaded, the MetaFrame Password Manager Agent checks its list of class IDs that are allowed against the class ID of the running application. If the specific class ID is not found, the agent ignores this application.

The Windows class does not have a user interface in the console. You can obtain or modify this information by viewing or editing the application definition file. The attribute key in the application definition file for a Window class name is

```
AllowClassName=
```

AllowClassName=ClassID11:37:25	AllowClassName=ClassID11:38:35

Figure 15-1.   Examples of a class ID

In order to work around this limitation, export the definition from the console to an INI file and change the Window class definition to the following:

```
AllowClassName=ClassID*
```

Then import the application definition to the console and synchronize it to the agents.

In order for the applications represented in Figure 15-1 to be detected by the MetaFrame Password Manager Agent, the application definition should be edited as follows:

```
AllowClassName=ClassID11*
```

This edited configuration enables the agent to continue to monitor the applications. It is also now able to recognize the class IDs. Even if the last portion of the class IDs changes, the agent will now submit the credentials.

HOW TO CONFIGURE JAVA APPLETS, JAVASCRIPT, OR ACTIVEX WEB PAGES

MetaFrame Password Manager supports Web pages that have embedded Java applets, JavaScript, or ActiveX controls. There are four primary steps to follow in order to configure such a Web page for MetaFrame Password Manager: determining Send Keys, configuring a Web application, configuring a Windows application, and editing the INI file.

NOTE: Before you begin, you must install the latest version of the Java Runtime Environment (JRE) from http://www.java.com.

Step 1: Determine Send Keys

Browse to the Web page you wish to configure. Using only the keyboard, map out the key combination necessary to navigate to the login fields. For more information on Send Keys, see the section later in this chapter titled "Using Send Keys for .NET and Java Applications in MetaFrame Password Manager."

Step 2: Configure a Web Application

The three steps to configuring the Web application are as follows:

1. In the MetaFrame Password Manager console, configure a new Web application.
2. Configure the Web application with the URL of the Web page.
3. Under the fields section, click Add and then OK to take the default field values.

NOTE: In this scenario, these fields are not significant because the Web application is only used to determine the URL. The Windows application is what will be used to fill in the logon fields.

Step 3: Configure a Windows Application

The six steps to configuring a Windows application are as follows:

1. Return to the Web page you wish to configure and leave it open.
2. From the console, create a new Windows application.
3. Click on the Detect Fields Wizard and choose the Internet Explorer window that is displaying the desired site.
4. Click Next.
5. Select the check box to use Send Keys and then click Next, then Finish.
6. Click on the Fields tab and define the Send Keys identified in Step 1.

Step 4: Edit the INI File

There are six steps to editing the INI file:

1. On the MetaFrame Password Manager console, right-click on the Applications node and choose Export.
2. Export both the Windows and Web applications you defined earlier to an INI file.
3. Open the INI file and locate the section for the defined Web application.
4. Add **RedirectToWinApp=1** to the Web application, as shown in Figure 15-2.
5. Save the INI file and import it back into the console, replacing the old definitions.
6. Save the application to the central credential store and synchronize with the agent.

Troubleshooting

When you're configuring a Web page for MetaFrame Password Manager, three primary areas may require troubleshooting: lack of application detection, the incorrect entering of the characters, and receiving an error during the INI import.

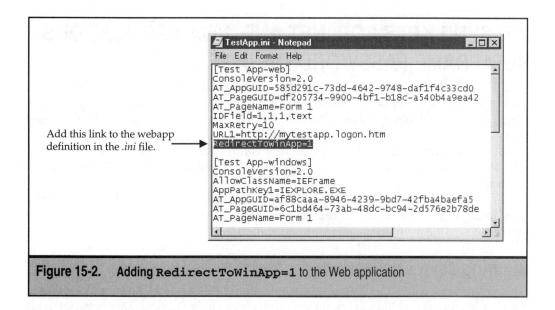

Add this link to the webapp definition in the *.ini* file. ⟶

Figure 15-2.   Adding `RedirectToWinApp=1` to the Web application

The Application Is Not Detected

Verify that `RedirectToWinApp=1` is included in the Web application definition. If you have multiple forms in your definition, verify you have placed `RedirectToWinApp=1` in the form's definition rather than in the overall Web definition.

The Characters Are Being Entered Incorrectly

Verify that you have the latest version of the JRE installed. With older versions of the JRE, keyboard navigation may not work properly. Also, the page may take some time to load, so it is recommended that you add delays to the Send Keys configuration. Using the ALT-D combination to begin the Send Keys configuration is also helpful because it guarantees the cursor begins in the Internet Explorer address bar.

Error During INI Import

Check the syntax and location if you get the following error message:

Unknown key-value-pair

Verify that the `RedirectToWinApp=1` value is set (see the section "Step 4: Edit the INI File," earlier in this chapter).

USING SEND KEYS FOR .NET AND JAVA APPLICATIONS IN METAFRAME PASSWORD MANAGER

MetaFrame Password Manager currently has a somewhat limited mechanism for dealing with .NET and Java applications. MetaFrame Password Manager uses the application's fingerprint (executable, window title, and control IDs) to detect and handle the logon process.

Both Java and .NET applications present control ID issues. MetaFrame Password Manager cannot detect the control IDs within Java applications. In .NET applications, control IDs change at run time.

In order for MetaFrame Password Manager to handle Java and .NET applications, they must be first configured in the MetaFrame Password Manager Console and then pushed out to the agent.

Configuring Java Applications for MetaFrame Password Manager

The recommended setup for Java applications is to configure the application definition to locate fields using Send Keys in conjunction with the use of hot keys to move between fields in a single dialog. Hot keys increase reliability by verifying that the correct field is chosen. Without hot keys, the assumption is the same field has focus each time the application requests credentials.

Creating a Java Application Definition

In order to create a Java application definition, open the Java application to be added to the application list. Then go to its Authentication page and leave it open.

On the Applications tab, perform the following steps:

1. On the console, click Applications in the left pane and click Add in the right pane. (Right-click the Applications node and click New Windows Application. The Add Application dialog opens.)

2. Enter the application name.

3. Select Windows as the Application Type and click Finish. The application's definition dialog appears.

Follow these steps on the General tab (you'll go through the General tab of the application's definition dialog to link the keys and actions to define the form):

1. Click the Detect Fields Wizard button.

2. Click the Logon button in the Form Type dialog.

3. Select the appropriate window title from the Application Window list and click Next. This list contains the window title, module, and window class for each application running on your system.

NOTE: A flashing border appears around the application you choose from the list.

4. Click to select the option "Use "SendKeys" for this form; do not use Control IDs."
   Click Next, then Finish.

Follow these steps on the Fields tab (you'll go through the Fields tab of the application's definition dialog to link the keys and actions to define the form):

1. Click the Edit button to open the SendKeys dialog. Select the Special Keys tab.

2. Click to select Modifier Keys from the Category Panel and ALT from the Keys Panel. Click the Insert button to insert the modifier keys.

3. Click the Text tab in the SendKeys window.

4. Enter a single letter into the text box and click Insert. The hot key modifier applies only to a single character.

5. Click the Fields tab in the SendKeys dialog.

6. Select Username/ID and click Insert.

7. Repeat these steps until all fields for the application have been assigned a key. Click OK to close the SendKeys dialog.

8. Click OK to close the application's definition dialog.

9. Push out the newly created application definition to the synchronization point.

Configuring .NET Applications for MetaFrame Password Manager

MetaFrame Password Manager can be configured to detect and handle .NET applications by creating standard Windows application definitions using control IDs. See the *MetaFrame Password Manager Administrator's Guide* for more information on creating application definitions.

Both control IDs and Send Keys can be used to configure the credential field matching for a .NET application. However, MetaFrame Password Manager uses the order of the credential fields to keep track of where the objects are within the application. This is due to the control ID runtime changes that occur in .NET applications.

CAUTION: The order matching for .NET applications may cause problems with dynamic application forms. If the application's tab order is changed, the order of the credential fields is no longer valid and MetaFrame Password Manager will cease to work for the application.

HOW TO MOVE FILE SYNCHRONIZATION POINTS BETWEEN DOMAINS

It will sometimes be necessary to move a file synchronization point from one Active Directory domain to another, while preserving the user's credential data. For example, this may happen if a migration is planned from an existing domain to a new domain. A file synchronization point will exist on a server in the old domain. The file synchronization point on the old domain will be deleted when all users are using the new domain and the old domain is no longer in use.

The procedure for performing the migration necessitates the following primary steps:

1. Migrate users from Domain A to Domain B.
2. Create a new file synchronization point on Domain B.
3. Move the agent settings, FTUlist, and Entlist from Domain A's file synchronization point to Domain B's file synchronization point.
4. Create a new registry file to import to client workstations.
5. Copy the People folder from Domain A's file synchronization point to Domain B's file synchronization point.
6. Rename users' folders under Domain B's People folder.
7. Clean MMF files from users' local and roaming profiles.
8. Import new agent settings into the workstations' registry.
9. Move the workstations' membership from Domain A to Domain B.
10. Log in the users to the workstations on Domain B and answer the user-verification question.

Step 1: Migrate Users from Domain A to Domain B

The migration of users from Domain A to Domain B can be done any way you wish, as long as the user accounts have identical user account names in both domains and the SID history is preserved for all migrated user accounts.

SID History

The new domain must have an "SID history" for each user that will contain the user's SID (Security Identifier) from the old domain. This is due to the fact that each user's folder on the synchronization point contains special permissions for CREATOR OWNER. If the SID history is not preserved, the users will not be able to access their folders, and they will not be able to get their credential information from the synchronization point.

NOTE: For more information on file share permissions, see the section titled "Securing the File Synchronization Folder Manually" in the *MetaFrame Password Manager Administrator's Guide.*

Active Directory Migration Tool

Microsoft's Active Directory Migration Tool (ADMT) can be used to migrate the user accounts from the old domain to the new domain while preserving the SID history.

NOTE: Although we do not address it in this chapter, it is possible to perform the migration if the SID history is not preserved. In order to accomplish this, you must modify the permissions or ownership of *each* user's folder either by changing the ownership of each folder to that of the appropriate user or by adding the appropriate user to the ACL of each folder and granting Modify permissions to that user.

Step 2: Create a New File Synchronization Point on Domain B

To create the new file synchronization point in the new domain, create a new file synchronization point on a server in the new domain using the ctxfilesyncprep tool on the MetaFrame Password Manager installation CD.

On the new server, you should now have a file share with the following structure:

```
<file-share name (e.g. CITRIXSYNC$)>
+--People
```

NOTE: Instructions for creating a file share can be found in the *MetaFrame Password Manager Administrator's Guide.*

Step 3: Move Agent Settings, FTUlist, and Entlist from Domain A's File Synchronization Point to Domain B's File Synchronization Point

The eight steps for moving objects to Domain B's file synchronization point are as follows:

1. Launch the MetaFrame Password Manager Console and connect to the old domain's synchronization point.
2. Right-click on the Adminoverride object and select Bring to Console.
3. Right-click on the Entlist object and select Bring to Console.
4. Right-click on the FTUList object and select Bring to Console.
5. Connect to the new domain's synchronization point.

6. Go into the Adminoverride agent settings node. Reconfigure the synchronizer to point to the new synchronization point (instead of the old synchronization point).

7. Configure the synchronization point with the aforementioned settings and objects (Adminoverride, Entlist, and FTUList).

8. Do not close the console or clear the Adminoverride settings. You will need them for the next primary step of creating a new registry to import to client workstations.

WARNING: If the FTUList object from the old synchronization point is not pushed to the new synchronization point, any user who answers an identity-verification question other than the default question will *not* be able to access their credential data. The identity-verification questions from the old domain are contained in the FTUList object and must be preserved in the new domain. All the users being migrated will be asked to answer their identity-verification question.

Step 4: Create a New Registry File to Import to Client Workstations

To create the new registry file, keep the console open, with the Adminoverride setting configured in Step 3. The Adminoverride setting contains the new synchronization point. Export these agent settings to a REG file. You will be importing this REG file to client workstations, so you may want to put this file on removable media or a network file share.

Step 5: Copy the People Folder from Domain A's File Synchronization Point to Domain B's File Synchronization Point

The People folder (and its subfolders) must be copied from the file synchronization point on Domain A to the file synchronization point on Domain B. This must be done with care in order to preserve the permissions and ownership that apply to each user's folder. If the permissions and ownership are not preserved, the users will not be able to access their folders.

File, Folder, and Subfolder Ownership

Each subfolder must be owned by its respective user. Special NTFS permissions are set for the CREATOR OWNER of the folder, subfolder, and files. If the user loses ownership of the file and/or subfolders, they will no longer be able to access the folder.

File, Folder, and Subfolder Copying

Most copy operations (and copy programs, such as xcopy) do not copy a folder while keeping NTFS permissions and ownership intact. For example, if a user in the Administrators group performs the copying, the Administrators group becomes the new CREATOR OWNER. For the purpose of this task, the Robocopy utility will be used to perform the file copy. It is possible to use any other file copy program that allows NTFS permissions (and file/folder ownership) to be copied over from source to destination.

When copying, use the **/E** and **/COPYALL** flags to ensure that all subfolders and files are copied and that the NTFS ownership information is preserved for all subfolders and files. Here's an example:

```
"robocopy "\\DomainASyncPointServer\citrixsync$\people
"\\DomainBSycnPointServer\citrixsync$\people "*.* "/e "/z "/COPYALL
```

NOTE: Robocopy is available for download from Microsoft as part of the Windows Server 2003 deployment kit, in the Resource Kit Tools for Windows Server 2003. This kit is available for download at http://www.microsoft.com/windowsserver2003/techinfo/reskit/deploykit.mspx. Some older versions of Robocopy do not support copying of the ownership attributes for files and folders. Be sure to use an up-to-date version of Robocopy (Robocopy XP010 or a later version should work).

Step 6: Rename Users' Folders Under Domain B's People Folder

The domain portion of each user's folder name must be changed to the new domain. The MetaFrame Password Manager Agent locates the user's data by joining the user's domain name with the username.

Joining the User's Domain Name with the Username

As an example, the user's domain name and username are joined as follows:

DomainA.*username*

In this scenario, the user *username* will move from Domain A to Domain B. The user will log into Domain B for the first time, and the MetaFrame Password Manager Agent will search the file synchronization point for the following folder:

DomainB.*username*

If the user is in DomainB and the folder is still named "DomainA.*username*," the agent will fail to find the user's data because the folder "DomainB.*username*" does not exist. The agent will assume that there is no data for the user on the synchronization point and will prompt the user to configure their credentials again.

The names of the folders on the destination file share must therefore be changed to reflect the new domain.

Changing Folder Names

For a very small number of users, the folder names can be changed easily. For a large number of users, this can be done automatically using a Visual Basic script as described next:

1. Using a text editor (such as Notepad), copy the following Visual Basic script into a file. Give the filename a *.vbs* extension (such as *MigrateMPM.vbs*).

```
Option Explicit
Dim objFSO, objLogFile, objPeople, objFolder
Dim strOldDomain, strNewDomain
Dim strInputPath, strNewFolder, strOldFolder
Dim strMsg, strTitle, strDefault
Dim intPos

' Check that script was executed with CScript, else notify user and quit. '
' Script makes extensive use of WScript.Echo method, which is bad for
WScript.exe.
If UCase(Right(WScript.FullName,11))  "CSCRIPT.EXE" Then
       Wscript.Echo "Please use Cscript.exe to launch this script instead of " &
Right(WScript.FullName,11) _
       & "." & vbCrLf & "For example: 'Cscript.exe " & WScript.ScriptName & "'."
       Wscript.Quit 1
       End If
' Create a file system object
Set objFSO = CreateObject("Scripting.FileSystemObject")

' Create log file
Set objLogFile = objFSO.CreateTextFile("MigrateMPM.log", True)

strMsg = "Please specify the fully qualified path to the People folder."
strTitle = "Where is the People folder?"
strDefault = "C:\FileSync\People"
strInputPath = InputBox (strMsg, strTitle, strDefault)

'A little input validation
If strInputPath = "" Then
     DisplayAndLog "You must enter the fully qualified path to the People folder!"
     WScript.Quit 1
End If

strMsg = "Please specify the old domain name."
strTitle = "What is the old domain name?"
strDefault = "DOMAINA"
strOldDomain = InputBox (strMsg, strTitle, strDefault)
'A little input validation
If strOldDomain = "" Then
     DisplayAndLog "You must enter the old domain name!"
     WScript.Quit 1
End If
strOldDomain = strOldDomain & "."
```

```
strMsg = "Please specify the new domain name."
strTitle = "What is the new domain name?"
strDefault = "DOMAINB"
strNewDomain = InputBox (strMsg, strTitle, strDefault)
'A little input validation
If strNewDomain = "" Then
      DisplayAndLog "You must enter the new domain name!"
      WScript.Quit 1
End If
strNewDomain = strNewDomain & "."
On Error Resume Next
Set objPeople = objFSO.GetFolder(strInputPath)
If Err.Number  0 Then
      DisplayAndLog "Unable to locate the folder " & strInputPath
      DisplayAndLog "Error: " & Err.Number
      DisplayAndLog "Description: " & Err.Description
      WScript.Quit 2
End If

For Each objFolder In objPeople.SubFolders
      If Err.Number  0 Then
            DisplayAndLog "Failure enumerating subfolders of " & strInputPath
            DisplayAndLog "Error: " & Err.Number
            DisplayAndLog "Description: " & Err.Description
            WScript.Quit 3
      End If
      strOldFolder = objFolder.Name
      intPos = InStr(1, objFolder.Name, strOldDomain, 1)
      If intPos  0 Then
            strNewFolder = Replace(objFolder.Name, strOldDomain, strNewDomain,1 , 1, 1)
            objFolder.Name = strNewFolder
            If Err.Number  0 Then
                  DisplayAndLog vbTab & "Error renaming subfolder " & strOldFolder
                  DisplayAndLog vbTab & "Error: " & Err.Number
                  DisplayAndLog vbTab & "Description: " & Err.Description
            Else
                  DisplayAndLog "Successfully renamed: " & objFolder.Name
            End If
      Else
            DisplayAndLog "Not renaming      : " & objFolder.Name
      End If
      Err.Clear
Next

' Cleanup
objLogFile.Close
Set objFolder = Nothing
Set objPeople = Nothing
Set objLogFile = Nothing
Set objFSO = Nothing
```

```
Private Function DisplayAndLog(strMessage)
    WScript.Echo strMessage
    objLogFile.WriteLine(strMessage)
End Function
```

2. Use the **cscript** command to execute the script. Here's an example:

```
cscript migratempm.vbs
```

3. At the execution of the script, a pop-up window will request the path to the People folder of the synchronization point:

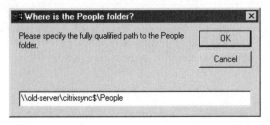

> **NOTE:**   You may specify a UNC path or a local path to the People folder.

4. Next, provide the name of the old domain:

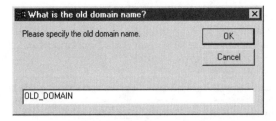

5. Provide the new domain name:

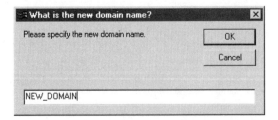

6. A success (or failure) message will appear on the command line. Here's an example:

```
T:\OS utils>cscript migratempm.vbs
Microsoft (R) Windows Script Host Version 5.6
Copyright (C) Microsoft Corporation 1996-2001. All rights reserved.
Successfully renamed: NEW_DOMAIN.administrator
```

At the end of the script, the tool will display the names of all user folders that were renamed.

NOTE: The names on the folders on the new synchronization point no longer match the names of the respective folders on the old synchronization point. This makes it impossible for file-copying tools such as xcopy to "refresh" data on the new synchronization point with newer data from the old synchronization point. For that reason, we warn users not to make any updates until the migration has finished and their workstations have been migrated to the new domain.

Step 7: Clean MMF Files from Users' Local and Roaming Profiles

When a user logs into the new domain, even though the user's username is the same, the domain is different and therefore a new user profile will be loaded. The user's local keys and credentials (in the MMF file) will be left behind in the user's old profile and will not be accessible.

Deleting Old MMF Files

The MMF files in the user's old profile will not be updated, and the information in these files will become outdated. Therefore, it is advisable to delete all MMF files on a workstation that will be moved to the new domain in order to ensure that these files are never accidentally used. To ensure that the old MMF files are not used in error, perform the following two steps on all user workstations and any file shares that hold roaming profiles that will result in removal of the files.

1. Stop the agent if it is running.

2. Remove the directory "MetaFrame Password Manager" from all user profiles on the workstation. They will be found in the following path:

    %SystemDrive% \Documents and Settings\%UserName%\Application Data\Citrix\

WARNING: Performing this step will remove *all* users' local keys and credentials from their roaming and local profiles. After this step, any keys and credentials that are not already on the *new* synchronization point will be lost.

Step 8: Move Workstations' Membership from Domain A to Domain B

There are three steps to follow:

1. Disjoin all user workstations from Domain A.

2. Restart the user workstations.

3. Rejoin all user workstations to Domain B.

Step 9: Import New Agent Settings into the Workstations' Registry

The following two steps enable importing new agent settings into the workstations' registry:

1. Shut down the agent if it is started.

2. Import the REG file created in Step 4 into the user workstations' registry. The workstations' registry will now contain a key that specifies the new synchronization point.

When the agent starts up for the first time in Domain B, it will use this key to find the synchronization point.

Step 10: Log in the Users to Their Workstations on Domain B and Answer the User-Verification Question

When a user logs into the new domain, the MetaFrame Password Manager Agent will attempt to determine the location of the synchronization point. It will check two locations, in the following order:

▼ The MMF file in the user's profile (%SystemDrive%\Documents and Settings \%Username%\Application Data\Citrix\ MetaFrame Password Manager)

▲ The registry (HKEY_LOCAL_MACHINE\SOFTWARE\Citrix\ MetaFrame Password Manager\Extensions\SyncManager\Syncs\fs\Servers\Server1)

If there is a synchronization point specified in the MMF file, it will be used, and the synchronization point specified in the registry (if there is one) will be ignored. In the case of switching domains, the user will have to log in for the first time to the new domain. When this happens, a new profile will be created on the machine, so there will not be an MMF file. Therefore, the agent will be forced to use the synchronization point specified in the registry. The agent will then go to the synchronization point, download the information that was migrated from the old synchronization point, and prompt the user for the answer to their identity-verification question. Once the user correctly submits the answer to the identity-verification question, the user' credential information will be accessible and the agent can proceed with submitting credentials for previously configured applications.

Warnings when Performing the Active Directory Domain Switch

The administrator needs to take care that users do not lose either their credentials or data. Care also must be taken with accessing the new file share.

Identity-Verification Question and User Access to Credentials

Because the file synchronization point is being moved from Domain A to Domain B, users will need to remember their initial MetaFrame Password Manager configuration identity-verification question and the answer to it. When they log on to the new domain, the MetaFrame Password Manager Agent will ask them to answer their identity-verification question because parts of their domain credentials have changed (the domain name changed). If they cannot answer their identity-verification question, they will *not* have access to their credentials. The administrator should warn all users that this will happen. Users who cannot remember their identity-verification question will have to set up their MetaFrame Password Manager account again, losing all configured credentials that were migrated from the old file synchronization point, and they will have to reenter all their credentials.

Synchronization and Potential Data Loss

All users should synchronize prior to the migration. They should be warned that any changes they make after the file synchronization point has been migrated will be *lost* as soon as their workstation is moved to the new domain and the MetaFrame Password Manager Agent has been configured to use the new synchronization point. Users who work offline have a higher risk of losing data because they do not synchronize as often. Special care must be taken to make sure these users synchronize prior to the migration.

Waiting to Access the New File Share Until Steps 1 Through 6 Are Complete

Do not configure any machines to access the new file share until the primary steps (1 through 6) are completed. If any of the files on the new file share are being accessed during Steps 1 through 6, the migration may fail.

Additional Information

For more information on SID history, refer to the following Microsoft article, in the section titled "Sid History":

http://www.microsoft.com/resources/documentation/WindowsServ/2003/all/deployguide/en-us/Default.asp?url=/resources/documentation/windowsserv/2003/all/deployguide/en-us/dssbh_rera_utek.asp

For more information on the Active Directory Migration Tool, refer to the following Microsoft article:

http://www.microsoft.com/windows2000/techinfo/planning/activedirectory/admt.asp

PREVENTING USERS FROM DISABLING THE METAFRAME PASSWORD MANAGER AGENT

In order for MetaFrame Password Manager to have optimal effectiveness, all users should be forced to use the MetaFrame Password Manager Agent. This prohibits users from going around the system in order to access their applications. A MetaFrame administrator can enforce this policy by preventing users from disabling the agent.

Do Not Give Users Administrative Privileges

The users should not have administrative privileges and should not be part of the Administrators, Power Users, Server Operators, or Domain Administrators group, or any other group that gives the user administrative rights. Without these privileges, the users will not be able to alter any program files, system files, or registry keys that may affect the behavior of the agent.

Disable Access to Unnecessary Capabilities

Disable access to the Add/Remove Control Panel applet, the Command Prompt, the Task Manager, and the Run command, and disable the ability to create/modify shortcuts. An efficient approach is to create a Group Policy with the following settings and apply it to the OU or group that contains the user accounts.

Add/Remove Control Panel

Disabling access to this applet prevents the users from being able to remove the agent or other components that the agent may rely on to operate. In order to apply this setting, open the Group Policy and enable the following policy:

User Configuration | Administrative Templates | Control Panel | Add/Remove Programs | Disable Add/Remove Programs

Command Prompt

Prohibiting user access to the Command Prompt prevents the execution of any commands that may delete or alter files, shut down programs, or cause other results that would disable the agent. In order to apply this setting, open the Group Policy and enable the following policy:

User Configuration | Administrative Templates | System | Disable the command prompt

Disabling the Command.com File   The Command Prompt policy has a limitation: It only disables the *CMD.exe* file. In the WINNT\System32 folder is another command-line utility, called *command.com*, that the users can still run to disable the agent. To avoid this, restrict users from running the *command.com* file by enabling and editing one of the two following policies:

▼ User Configuration | Administrative Templates | System | Don't run specified Windows applications.

   For this policy, click on the Show button and add **command.com**.

▲ Computer Configuration | Windows Settings | Security Settings | Software Restriction Policies | Additional Rules

   For this policy, create a new Hash Policy to prohibit the execution of *command.com*.

Run

Similar to the Command Prompt, removing the **Run** command prevents the execution of any commands that may delete or alter files, shut down programs, or cause other results that would disable the agent. To apply this setting, open the Group Policy and enable the following policy:

   User Configuration | Administrative Templates | Start Menu & Taskbar | Remove Run menu from Start Menu

Task Manager

If a user can access the Task Manager, the user has the ability to end processes and tasks relevant to the agent, thus causing the agent to stop. You can enforce a policy that prohibits the user from accessing Task Manager. To apply this setting, open the Group Policy and enable the following policy:

   User Configuration | Administrative Templates | System | Logon/Logoff | Disable Task Manager

Ability to Create/Modify Shortcuts

Although we have restricted the users from being able to execute any command-line commands, they are still able to create a shortcut and modify the properties of that shortcut to add the switch **/shutdown**, which would disable the agent. In order to prevent this occurrence, disable all users' ability to create and modify shortcuts. There are two policies to modify in order to make this restriction secure. In order to apply these settings, open the Group Policy and enable the following policies:

▼ User Configuration | Administrative Templates | Windows Components | Windows Explorer | Disable Windows Explorer's default context menu.

▲ User Configuration | Start Menu & Taskbar | Disable drag-and-drop context menus on the Start Menu.

Hide the MetaFrame Password Manager Agent Tray Icon

A user with access to the MetaFrame Password Manager Agent tray icon can easily right-click on the icon and choose to shut down the agent. As a MetaFrame Password Manager administrator, you can configure the agent to hide the tray icon while it still functions normally. To configure this setting, in Agent Settings | Shell set ShowTrayIcon to "Do not show the Tray Icon," as shown in Figure 15-3.

Force Credential Storage

By default, if a user opens an application requiring authentication, the agent asks if they would like to store their credentials in Logon Manager. Simply clicking No would avoid storing the user's credentials in Logon Manager.

By enabling ForceCredStorage, users are not prompted with the question but rather are directly prompted to store their credentials in Logon Manager. In order to configure this setting, in Agent Settings | AccessManager, set ForceCredStorage to Enabled, as shown in Figure 15-4.

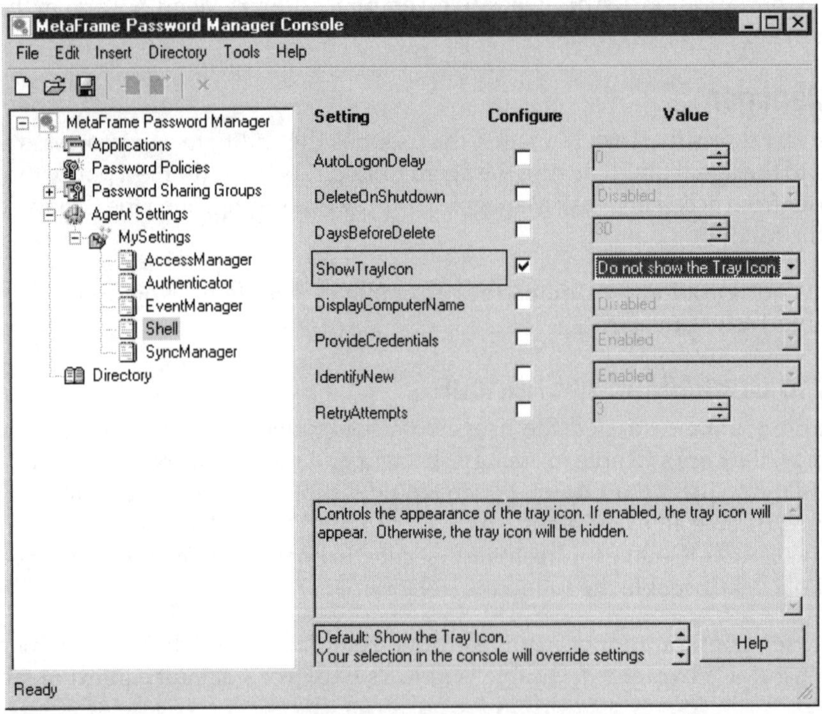

Figure 15-3. ShowTrayIcon

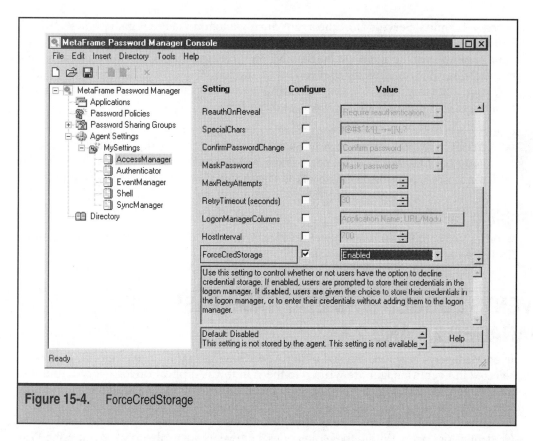

Figure 15-4.   ForceCredStorage

There may be some legitimate reasons why users should not be forced to store their credentials, so we recommend thorough user testing prior to using this feature.

ACCESSING LOGON MANAGER WITH A DISABLED TRAY ICON

In MetaFrame Password Manager 2.5, the administrator can choose whether or not to display the agent's tray icon on a per-deployment basis. This setting can be deployed as a registry setting or as an agent setting using the MetaFrame Password Manager 2.5 Console.

NOTE: Changing the tray icon display behavior will not affect the agent until the agent is restarted either by logging out or by shutting down the agent manually.

The default installation configures the agent to be run with the **/background** flag, which does not invoke the Logon Manager on startup but only starts the background process. Terminal Servers start the agent during a logon via the registry entry HKLM\ Software\Microsoft\Windows NT\Current Version\winlogon\appsetup. Desktop operating systems start the agent via the Start Menu's startup folder. Once the user has logged in and the agent is running, the user can invoke Logon Manager by double-clicking on the tray icon. If the tray icon is disabled, an administrator can still invoke Logon Manager by running *ssoshell.exe* without the **/background** flag.

NOTE: The shortcut installed in the Start Menu contains the **/background** flag and will not invoke Logon Manager if the tray icon is disabled. In a MetaFrame Presentation Server environment, you can choose to publish *ssoshelll.exe* with no arguments to allow users to access the Logon Manager.

Disabling the Tray Icon

In order to disable the tray icon, set ShowTrayIcon to "Do not show the tray icon" under Shell | Agent Settings in the console.

EVENTS LOGGED BY METAFRAME PASSWORD MANAGER 2.0 AND 2.5

EventManager settings are enabled under Agent Settings in the console. Specific LogEvents selected in EventManager are written to the Windows Application log every 15 minutes and at agent startup. Figure 15-5 shows a screen capture of the LogEvents settings found in the console.

The LogEvents fall into one of three Windows Application log categories: Feature, Credential, or Logon. Within these categories, LogEvents are further broken out using Windows Event log event IDs. Table 15-1 lists the LogEvents and their corresponding Windows Application log category, event ID, and description. Table 15-2 describes what the individual LogEvents record.

Known Limitations

There are some known limitations as to what the LogEvents record in regard to event time, event limit, event IDs, failed login attempts, and installation.

Event Time Discrepancy

There can be a discrepancy in time between the actual agent-generated event and the Windows Application event. The discrepancy happens because the agent only writes events to the Windows Application logs once every 15 minutes and whenever the agent is restarted.

Event Limit

The agent can cache a maximum of 1000 events and writes them to the Windows Application log every 15 minutes. Events waiting to be written to the Windows Application log are cached in the users' encrypted credential store, known as the MMF file.

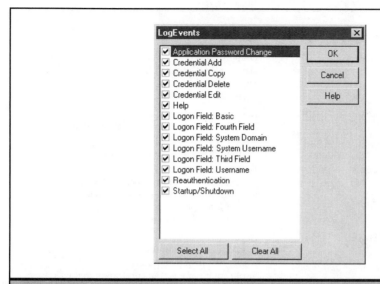

Figure 15-5.   LogEvents settings

LogEvents	Category	ID	Description
Application Password Change	Feature	102	Logon: PWChange – done application name – (application that changed password appears here) event time – date/time here (e.g., 12/5/2003 4:04:16 PM)
Credential Add	Credential	103	Credential: add – (the application that was added to Logon Manager appears here) event time – date/time
Credential Copy	Credential	103	Credential: copy – (the application that was copied in Logon Manager appears here) event time – date/time
Credential Delete	Credential	103	Credential: delete – (the application that was deleted in Logon Manager appears here) event time – date/time
Credential Edit	Credential	103	Credential: edit – (the application that was edited in Logon Manager appears here) event time – date/time

Table 15-1.   Event Viewer LogEvents Table

LogEvents	Category	ID	Description
Help	Feature	111	Help used: (The Agent tab that Help was launched from appears here) event time – date/time
Logon Field: Basic	Logon	101	Logon: application name – (the application name appears here) event time – date/time
Logon Field: Fourth Field	Logon	101	Logon: FourthField – (the fourth field value appears here) application name – (the application that was logged into appears here) event time – date/time
Logon Field: System Domain	Logon	101	Logon: SysDomain – (Windows Domain of MetaFrame Server or Client Computer) application name – (the application that was logged into appears here) event time – date/time
Logon Field: Third Field	Logon	101	Logon: ThirdField – (the third field value would display here) application name – (the application that was logged into appears here) event time – date/time
Logon Field: System Username	Logon	101	Logon: SysUser – (Authenticator, a.k.a. Windows, username) application name – (the application that was logged into appears here) event time – date/time
Logon Field: Username	Logon	101	Logon: username – (application username appears here) application name - (the application that was logged into appears here) event time – date/time
Reauthentication	Feature	109	Reauthentication: MSAuth SUCCESS (indicates successful authentication to agent) event time – date/time *or* Reauthentication: MSAuth CANCEL (failed or unsuccessful authentication to agent) event time – date/time
Startup/Shutdown	Feature	106/107	Startup or shutdown event time – date/time

Table 15-1. Event Viewer LogEvents Table *(continued)*

Event Viewer LogEvent	Event Trigger or Description
Application Password Change	Successful/Failed Password Changes Include Domain and Regular Password Sharing Groups
Credential Add	Whenever an application is added to Logon Manager in the agent
Credential Copy	Whenever an application is copied in Logon Manager in the agent
Credential Delete	Whenever an application is deleted in Logon Manager
Credential Edit	Whenever an application's properties are modified in Logon Manager
Help	Whenever Help in the agent is used/accessed (excluding the Host/Mainframe tab)
Logon Field: Basic	Whenever an application is logged into successfully
Logon Field: Fourth Field	Displays an application's Fourth Field value in event Description
Logon Field: System Domain	Displays the Windows domain of the MetaFrame Server or Client computer
Logon Field: Third Field	Displays an application's Third Field value in event Description
Logon Field System Username	Displays thse Windows username in event Description
Logon Field: Username	Displays an application's username in event Description
Reauthentication	Displays successful/failed attempts to authenticate to the agent
Startup/Shutdown	Displays the startup and shutdown of the agent

Table 15-2.   Event Viewer LogEvents Explanation Table

Event IDs Lack a Username

Many of the events do not report the username that generated them. This makes trouble-shooting difficult in multiuser environments (like MetaFrame Presentation Server farms).

Failed Login Attempts to Applications Not Logged

There is no event generated for failed application login attempts.

Installation

The agent does not log any warning or error events, either while running or during installation.

CHAPTER 16

Tuning and Optimizations

Although the default installation of MetaFrame Presentation Server performs adequately in most environments, a number of optimization and tuning changes can be made to further increase performance. Many of the recommendations are derived from Microsoft Knowledge Base articles. For the purposes of this chapter, we assume that the reader has a fundamental understanding of MetaFrame Presentation Server and Windows Terminal Services, and has reviewed the relevant Microsoft references to better understand the ramifications and expected results from any system changes.

CLIENT OPTIMIZATIONS

Many of the settings and optimizations available for connecting over WAN links involve the MetaFrame Presentation Server Client software. This section will discuss how to configure the client settings to improve the user experience over highly latent connections, slow connections, and inconsistent connections.

Improving Connectivity over Inconsistent WAN Links

Clients connecting over the Internet or via TCP/IP over WAN links that exhibit inconsistent latency may experience session disconnects. The Internet has, by design, nondeterministic bandwidth—the number of hops and the amount of available throughput between any two points is dynamic and may change from moment to moment. WAN links as part of a private network are often relatively deterministic in terms of hop count (a finite number of paths exists between any two endpoints), but throughput and path latency may change rapidly when the path changes or even when a single-hop path becomes saturated with traffic. Increasing latency is common when connecting through an Internet Service Provider (ISP), particularly when the connection is opened in the morning and maintained throughout the day. Similarly, for the first user to connect via a heavily loaded WAN link, the TCP/IP stack will establish a low-latency benchmark for roundtrip delay. A user connecting when the link is fully loaded will start with a much higher latency roundtrip time.

Clients connecting over certain media types such as satellite or wireless WAN will always experience high latency connections due to the nature of the media (relatively low throughput and higher physical path delay). For example, a connection over a geosynchronous satellite link will have a minimum roundtrip delay of 480 milliseconds:

$$(22{,}400 \text{ miles} \times 4 \text{ hops})/186{,}000 \text{ miles/second}$$

The larger the TCP segment size (in bytes), the longer the delay. To test this, ping across a WAN link with a default ICMP packet (100 bytes) and compare the roundtrip time to the same path for a 1000-byte ping.

By default, TCP uses the initial packet roundtrip time when the session is initiated to determine what is "normal" for that connection. Note that TCP does not measure speed per se, but imputes speed from roundtrip delay. Because this establishes the benchmark for all remaining packets in the session, it is better to have a consistently slow WAN connection than to have a connection that starts out fast and then becomes slow. Once this "benchmark" is established, TCP uses a dynamically adjustable retransmission timer to compensate for path changes. See the section titled "Selecting Nonstandard TCP Packet Sizes" for more information on specifying a smaller TCP packet size to address the impact of high latency.

For more information about optimizing Citrix technology for operation over wireless wide area networks, review the Citrix Knowledgebase articles CTX104742, CTX101602, and CTX101879.

Retransmission Behavior

TCP starts a retransmission timer when each outbound segment is handed down to IP. If no acknowledgment is received for the data in a given segment before the timer expires, the segment is retransmitted up to the number of times specified in the following registry key as the value name **TcpMaxDataRetransmissions**.

```
HKLM\SYSTEM\CurrentControlSet\Services\Tcpip\Parameters\
```

The default value for this parameter is 5.

The retransmission timer is initialized to 3 seconds when a TCP connection is established; however, it is adjusted dynamically to match the characteristics of the connection using Smoothed Round Trip Time (SRTT) calculations, as described in RFC 793. The timer for a given segment is doubled (from the initial value described earlier) after each retransmission of that segment. Using this algorithm, TCP tunes itself to the normal delay of a connection. Because the default number of retries is five, the roundtrip time can double four times (in other words, become 16 times slower than its initial value) before the session is dropped. By increasing this number to 10, you allow the roundtrip time to double nine times instead of four, which allows the connection quality to erode up to 512 times its original value before being dropped. For example, a connection that begins with a roundtrip time of 20 milliseconds would have to erode to in excess of 10,240 milliseconds before being dropped by the server. The same session would be dropped when it exceeds 320 milliseconds using the default value.

To compensate for this behavior, add or modify the **TcpMaxDataRetransmissions** registry value on the server and, if possible, the client as follows (see Microsoft Knowledge Base articles 120642 and 170359 for more information):

1. Open **HKLM\SYSTEM\CurrentControlSet\Services\Tcpip\Parameters** with the registry editor.

2. Highlight "**Parameters**". From the Edit menu choose Add Value.

3. Type **TcpMaxDataRetransmissions** in the Value Name box.

4. Select REG_DWORD in the Data Type box. Click OK.

5. Select Decimal from the Radix options.

6. Type **10** in the Data box. Click OK.

Selecting Nonstandard TCP Packet Sizes

By default, ICA sessions connecting over TCP will use maximum-sized TCP packets (up to 1460 bytes of data) for the transmission of large amounts of data. However, there are a small number of network types, most likely particular wireless or satellite-based networks, where better performance can be achieved by using smaller maximum-sized packets.

For MetaFrame Presentation Server 3.0, the normal maximum size (1460) can be overridden on a server by setting the following registry entry:

```
HKLM\System\CurrentControlSet\Control\TerminalServer\Wds\icawd\
MaxICAPacketLength
```

If required, the entry should be defined as a DWORD parameter (for example, 1000) and the server should be restarted for this registry value to take effect.

If the entry is undefined, has a value of zero, or a value greater than 1460, it will have no effect. Any value in the range 1–1460 will cause the server and its clients to use a smaller maximum length for all packets sent after connection time.

CAUTION:　Setting this registry value to enforce a lower maximum will have a significant negative effect on performance on all normal networks, and it should therefore only be used in special situations.

Monitoring ICA Session Latency

New functionality has been introduced in MetaFrame Presentation Server that allows an administrator to determine whether latency is occurring in the client's session (and the amount of latency) without requiring client interaction/input. The Windows Performance Monitor (PerfMon) counter ICA Session Performance Counter | Latency | Last Recorded represents the last recorded latency measurement for a session. The default function of this counter requires active user input (keystrokes, mouse movements) to determine the latency occurring on a session. To change the functionality of this counter to dynamic (on-demand), edit the registry as follows:

1. Open **HKLM\SYSTEM\CurrentControlSet\Control\Terminal Server\ Wds\icawd** with the registry editor.

2. From the Edit menu choose Add Value if no **ActiveLatencyPeriodInSeconds** value exists.

   a. Type **ActiveLatencyPeriodInSeconds** in the Value Name box.

   b. Select REG_DWORD in the Data Type box. Click OK.

   c. Select Decimal from the Radix options.

   d. Type the decimal value for the desired refresh interval in seconds in the Data box. Click OK.

DISK OPTIMIZATIONS

Several registry settings can be modified to increase disk performance and throughput. Enhancements include increasing I/O locks and disabling last file access updates.

I/O Locks

For Windows Server 2000, the registry setting **IoPageLockLimit** specifies the limit of the number of bytes that can be locked for I/O operations. Because RAM is being sacrificed for increased disk performance, determining the optimal setting for this value should be accomplished through pilot tests. Changing this setting from the default can speed up file system activity. Use Table 16-1 as a guide for changing the registry setting.

Modify the registry setting for **IoPageLockLimit** as follows:

1. Open **HKLM\SYSTEM\CurrentControlSet\Control\Session Manager\ Memory Management** with the registry editor.

2. From the Edit menu choose Add Value if no **IoPageLockLimit** value exists.

   a. Type IoPageLockLimit in the Value Name box.

   b. Select REG_DWORD in the Data Type box. Click OK.

   c. Select Decimal from the Radix options.

   d. Type the value from Table 16-1 in the Data box (0 = 512KB is used). Click OK.

For additional information on the **IoPageLockLimit** registry setting, refer to *Windows 2000 Server Resource Kit Supplement 1: Technical Reference to the Registry*, located on Microsoft's Web site.

Last Access Update

With both Windows 2000 Server and Windows Server 2003, the NTFS file system stores the last time a file is accessed, whether it is viewed in a directory listing, searched, or opened.

Server RAM (MB)	IoPageLockLimit (Decimal)	IoPageLockLimit (Hex)
64–128	4096	1000
256	8192	2000
512	16384	4000
1024+	65536	10000

Table 16-1. **IoPageLock**Limit Settings

In a multiuser environment, this updating can cause a small performance decrease. To disable this feature, modify the registry as follows:

1. Open **HKLM\SYSTEM\CurrentControlSet\Control\FileSystem** with the registry editor.
2. From the Edit menu choose Add Value.
   a. Type NtfsDisableLastAccessUpdate in the Value Name box.
   b. Select REG_DWORD in the Data Type box. Click OK.
   c. Select Decimal from the Radix options.
   d. Type **1** in the Data box. Click OK.

MEMORY OPTIMIZATIONS

This section describes configurations for optimizing memory usage by adjusting the system paging file and system page table entries.

Paging File

The paging file is temporary storage used by the operating system to hold program data that will not fit into the physical RAM of the server. The ratio of physical memory to paged memory is the most important factor when determining the size of a paging file. When configuring the paging file, follow these guidelines:

▼ A proper balance between physical memory and paged memory prevents thrashing. Verify that more memory is in physical RAM than paged to disk.

■ Place the paging file on its own disk controller or on a partition that is separate from the OS, application, and user data files. If the paging file must share a partition or disk, place it on the partition or disk with the least amount of activity. Performance gains from a paging file on the same disk controller as the other active partitions are negligible.

■ To prevent disk fragmentation of the paging file, always set the paging file initial size to be the same as the maximum size.

■ The optimal size of a paging file is best determined by monitoring the server under a peak load. Set the paging file to be three to five times the size of the physical RAM and then stress the server while observing the size of the paging file. To conserve resources, set the paging file to a value slightly larger than the maximum utilized while the server is under stress.

▲ If the server is short on physical RAM, use the paging file to provide additional memory at the expense of performance.

NOTE: For debugging purposes (i.e., to support memory dumps), create a paging file on the root partition that is slightly larger than the amount of RAM installed.

Page Table Entries

You can improve single-server scalability (the number of users on a server) by manually adjusting the page table entries (PTE) in the registry. The Windows kernel uses PTE values to allocate physical RAM between two pools of memory. By manually setting the maximum space allocated to the system PTE, you can use the remaining space to increase the number of users supported on the server.

Determining the optimal configuration for PTE values is a complex task. For detailed information, see the Microsoft Knowledge Base article 247904. A Kernel Tuning Assistant for Windows 2000 Server is also available from Microsoft.

NETWORK OPTIMIZATIONS

Some simple changes to network settings can often improve network performance. This section covers a few common issues that can be remedied by adjusting the default Windows network configuration.

Network Cards

Most 10/100-based network cards autosense the network speed by default. Manually setting these cards (preferably to 100 Mbps full-duplex) prevents the autosensing process from interfering with communication and forces the desired speed. If the server is connected to an autosensing device, such as a switch, apply these same speed and duplex settings to this device as well.

Network Protocols

Verify that only the necessary protocols are installed and that the binding order of those protocols to the network interface card lists the most commonly used protocol first. For Windows 2000 or Windows Server 2003, only TCP/IP and NetBIOS over TCP/IP (NBT) are enabled by default. Other protocols such as IPX/SPX, NETBEUI, DLC, and AppleTalk generate excess network broadcast traffic and, if such broadcasts come from other devices on the network, excess network-driven CPU interrupts on the server.

Refused Connections

The server can refuse connections due to self-imposed limits specified by the **MaxMpxCt** and **MaxWorkItem** registry values. If this happens, users see the following errors:

System could not log you on because domain <domainname> is not available.

or

You do not have access to logon to this session.

The default registry values can be modified to more appropriate values (such as 1024 for MaxMpxCt and 4096 MaxWorkItems). Before adding these values, read the Microsoft Knowledge Base article 232476. Here's how to change the registry values:

1. Open **HKLM\SYSTEM\CurrentControlSet\Services\LanManServer\ Parameters** with the registry editor.

2. From the Edit menu choose Add Value if no MaxMpxCt value exists.

   a. Type **MaxMpxCt** in the Value Name box.

   b. Select REG_DWORD in the Data Type box. Click OK.

   c. Select Decimal from the Radix options.

   d. Type the value **1024** in the Data box. Click OK.

3. From the Edit menu choose Add Value if no **MaxWorkItems** value exists.

   a. Type **MaxWorkItems** in the Value Name box.

   b. Select REG_DWORD in the Data Type box. Click OK.

   c. Select Decimal from the Radix options.

   d. Type the value **4096** in the Data box. Click OK.

TCP/IP and ICA KeepAlives

In networks that are subject to periodic intervals of high network latency, client connections may time out when connected to a session. When users attempt to reconnect to a dropped session, they receive a new session instead of being reconnected to their previous session because the server is not aware that the previous session was dropped.

To remedy this problem, enable TCP KeepAlives for ICA sessions over TCP. Modifying the **TCPKeepAlive** parameter helps the host server become aware of any sessions dropped due to network problems sooner. For more information about TCP parameters, see the Microsoft Knowledge Base article 120642. For more information on configuring TCP and ICA KeepAlive values, see the Citrix Knowledge Base article CTX708444.

Enable TCP KeepAlives for ICA sessions over TCP as follows:

1. Open **HKLM\SYSTEM\CurrentControlSet\Services\Tcpip\ Parameters** with the registry editor.

2. From the Edit menu choose Add Value if no **KeepAliveTime** value exists.

   a. Type **KeepAliveTime** in the Value Name box.

   b. Select REG_DWORD in the Data Type box. Click OK.

   c. Select Hex from the Radix options.

   d. Type the value **0000ea60** in the Data box. Click OK.

3. From the Edit menu choose Add Value if no **KeepAliveInterval** value exists.

   a. Type **KeepAliveInterval** in the Value Name box.

   b. Select REG_DWORD in the Data Type box. Click OK.

c. Select Hex from the Radix options.

d. Type the value **000003e8** in the Data box. Click OK.

> **IMPORTANT:**   Aggressive parameters may cause TCP/IP-based communications to time out prematurely. Adjust these parameters as necessary to prevent this behavior.

MetaFrame also has an ICA KeepAlive packet that is not protocol specific. To configure ICA KeepAlives, edit the registry as follows:

1. Open **HKLM\SYSTEM\CurrentControlSet\Control\Citrix** with the registry editor.

2. From the Edit menu choose Add Value if no **ICAEnableKeepAlive** value exists.

   a. Type **ICAEnableKeepAlive** in the Value Name box.

   b. Select REG_DWORD in the Data Type box. Click OK.

   c. Select Decimal from the Radix options.

   d. Type the value **1** in the Data box (the default is 0, which equals Off). Click OK.

3. From the Edit menu choose Add Value if no **ICAKeepAliveInterval** value exists.

   a. Type **ICAKeepAliveInterval** in the Value Name box.

   b. Select REG_DWORD in the Data Type box. Click OK.

   c. Select Decimal from the Radix options.

   d. Type the preferred interval value in seconds in the Data box (the default is 60 seconds). Click OK.

> **IMPORTANT:**   Enabling ICA KeepAlives may keep demand-dial links up in a WAN environment.

SERVER OPTIMIZATIONS

Correctly configuring Windows services and applications for use in a multiuser environment improves performance and prevents system problems. Relatively simple changes to key services, error-handling, and event-logging options can prevent minor events from impacting application delivery to users.

Auto-End Tasks

When an application does not properly exit when closed or upon server shutdown, the OS can terminate the application using Auto-End Tasks, which terminates any task that does not respond to a shutdown notice within the default timeout period. Enabling Auto-End Tasks affects all applications on the server and can cause issues with some applications that require a shutdown time period that is longer than the default timeout period. The default timeout period must be greater than the time required for the longest successful shutdown for any server application. Before enforcing Auto-End Tasks, thoroughly investigate "normal" application shutdown performance for installed applications. To enable Auto-End Tasks and set the default timeout period, modify the registry as follows:

1. Open **HKU\.DEFAULT\Control Panel\Desktop** with the registry editor.

2. From the Edit menu choose Add Value if no **AutoEndTasks** value exists.

   a. Type **AutoEndTasks** in the Value Name box.

   b. Select REG_SZ in the Data Type box. Click OK.

   c. Type the value **1** in the Data box (the default is 0, which equals Off). Click OK.

3. From the Edit menu choose Add Value if no **WaitToKillAppTimeout** value exists.

   a. Type **WaitToKillAppTimeout** in the Value Name box.

   b. Select REG_SZ in the Data Type box. Click OK.

   c. Type the value in milliseconds to wait before killing a task in the Data box (the default is 20000). Click OK.

For more information, see the Microsoft Knowledge Base article 191805 and refer to *Windows 2000 Server Resource Kit Supplement 1: Technical Reference to the Registry*, located on Microsoft's Web site.

Processes Preventing a Graceful Logoff

When a process does not terminate within a MetaFrame Presentation Server session, it may prevent the session from logging off gracefully, and the session will still appear active in the Presentation Server Console. In the Presentation Server Console you can see the processes running in the session, and killing the responsible process will allow the logoff to complete. One example of such a process is *Wisptis.exe*. Wisptis is an acronym for "Windows Ink Services Platform Tablet Input Subsystem." It is a pen input device tool for the Microsoft Tablet PC platform and can sometimes be observed in a session running Windows Office 2003. The registry can be modified to allow the logoff process to ignore such processes and successfully complete a graceful logoff. To add a process to the ignore list, follow these steps:

1. Open the registry and navigate to **HKEY_LOCAL_MACHINE\SYSTEM\ CurrentControlSet\Control\Citrix\wfshell\TWI**.

2. From the Edit menu choose Add Value if no **LogoffCheckSysModules** value exists.

   a. Type **LogoffCheckSysModules** in the Value Name box.

   b. Select REG_SZ in the Data Type box. Click OK.

   c. Type the name of the processes' executable in the Data box. Click OK.

   d. Enter the list of executable names with a comma and no spaces between them.

For more information about **LogOffCheckSysModules**, see Citrix Knowledge Base article CTX891671.

Dr. Watson

If you're using Dr. Watson, run the Dr. Watson Application Compatibility script to prevent stability problems. Citrix recommends that you disable the Visual Notification option available on the main screen of *Drwtsn32.exe*.

Dr. Watson can be disabled completely by clearing the following registry key value:

```
HKLM\SOFTWARE\Microsoft\Windows NT\CurrentVersion\AeDebug\Debugger
```

You can restore Dr. Watson as the default debugger by executing the command **drwtsn32.exe -i**.

For more information regarding Dr. Watson, see the Citrix Support Knowledge Base article CTX103209.

Configuring the Event Log

Change the default event log configuration to prevent log files from running out of space, which generates errors.

To change event log settings on Windows 2000 Server (or later), follow these steps:

1. Launch Event Viewer.
2. Right-click System Log and choose Properties.
3. Set Maximum Log Size to at least 1024KB.
4. Choose "Overwrite events as needed."
5. Click OK to save the settings.
6. Repeat Steps 3–5 for the Application log.

Configuring Print Job Logging

By default, each print job logs two informational messages to the System log. On MetaFrame Presentation Servers with many users, this feature generates numerous events and fills up the log faster. If these messages are not desired, disable them through the Printers Control Panel applet (select File | Server Properties | Advanced and clear the Log spooler Information events checkbox) or by changing the registry as follows:

1. Open **HKLM\SYSTEM\CurrentControlSet\Control\Print\Providers** with the registry editor.
2. From the Edit menu choose Add Value if no Event Log value exists.
   a. Type **Event Log** in the Value Name box.
   b. Select REG_DWORD in the Data Type box. Click OK.

    c. Select Decimal from the Radix options.

    d. Type the value **0** in the Data box. Click OK.

Restart the server after making either of these changes to invoke the new behavior. Removing the Event Log value from the registry and restarting the server reenables the logging of all print events.

RPC (Remote Procedure Call) Services

When RPC-aware applications such as Windows Explorer and Control Panel are opened, delays of several minutes can be the result of incorrect service startup settings. Verify that the RPC service Startup type is set to Automatic and the RPC Locator service Startup type is set to Manual.

USER OPTIMIZATIONS

Correctly setting up users can provide additional performance gains. Where possible, modify the Default User profile to include the recommendations listed in this section.

TIP: When making changes to the Default User profile, you might need to restart the server before the changes take effect because the *Ntuser.dat* file is in use and unavailable to new users.

Windows Policies

System and Group Policies should be used to control the user environment and behavior where possible. In an Active Directory environment, Group Policies provide a dynamic means of manipulating potions of the user environment. For more information about configuring policies, see Microsoft Knowledge Base article 260370. For Citrix-specific Group Policy guidance, refer to Chapter 15 of *Citrix MetaFrame Access Suite for Windows Server 2000: The Official Guide*.

Profiles

Users require an initial setup when logging on for the first time. This setup time is minimized by the use of roaming or mandatory profiles. For more information about configuring roaming profiles, see the Microsoft Knowledge Base article 142682 and Chapter 15 of *Citrix MetaFrame Access Suite for Windows Server 2003: The Official Guide*.

Observe the following when you set up roaming profiles:

▼   Configure a dedicated server to host the profiles. If it is not possible to place the profiles on a dedicated server, place them on an isolated disk or partition.

■   When using a server or drive dedicated to profiles and temp files, change the users' profile and temp directories to point to the dedicated location.

- Configure profile size quotas to ensure that profiles do not grow too large.
- ▲ Delete locally cached copies of the users' profiles via the following Registry key:

`HKLM\Software\Policies\Microsoft\Windows\System\DeleteRoamingCache (DWORD)`

Set the value to 1 to delete the locally cached copy of the user's profile upon logoff.

Menu Refresh

You can change the menu refresh rate to expedite menu response time by modifying the registry as follows:

1. Open **HKU\.Default\Control Panel\Desktop** with the registry editor.
2. From the Edit menu choose Add Value if no **MenuShowDelay** value exists.
   a. Type **MenuShowDelay** in the Value Name box.
   b. Select REG_SZ in the Data Type box. Click OK.
   c. Type the value **10** in the Data box. Click OK.

NOTE: In some cases it may be desirable to increase the **MenuShowDelay** setting to avoid a situation where a user causes a submenu to display by inadvertently scrolling over a menu, sending extraneous data through the MetaFrame Presentation Server session.

REMOVING UNNECESSARY FEATURES

To conserve ICA bandwidth, you can adjust or eliminate a number of features appropriate for desktop users. Areas of concern include ICA feature mappings, Windows and Microsoft Office features, scrolling behavior, and application behavior. Additional changes, such as suppressing the default Internet Explorer and Windows "splash" screens, can be enforced via Group Policies.

Default Windows and Microsoft Office Features

The following features are generally unnecessary and can degrade performance in a MetaFrame Presentation Server environment and should be disabled or removed:

- ▼ Active Desktop on Windows 2000. This can be disabled through Terminal Services Configuration.
- Desktop wallpaper. In addition, remove any BMP files found in the %SystemRoot% directory to prevent users from selecting them.
- Screensavers.

- Microsoft Office FindFast.
- Microsoft Office Assistants.
- ▲ Microsoft Office features such as active spell and grammar checking.

Default ICA Channels

Remove any unnecessary drive mappings, printers, or ports. This includes COM and LPT port mapping and client audio mapping. All these channels, even if no ports or drives are mapped and no audio is transported, still consume some resources because they must be monitored for activity.

Smooth Scrolling

Many applications have smooth scrolling or other features that increase the frequency of updates sent to the client workstation. If applications exhibit poor performance, disable these features to improve performance. Two common settings are animation in Microsoft Excel and smooth scrolling in Microsoft Internet Explorer. The following steps will disable these two features:

- ▼ Microsoft Excel 97/2000:
    1. Choose Tools | Options.
    2. Select the Edit tab.
    3. Clear the "Provide feedback with Animation" option.

- ▼ Microsoft Internet Explorer 5:
    1. Choose Tools | Internet Options.
    2. Select the Advanced tab.
    3. Clear the Use Smooth Scrolling option in the Browsing section.

TIP: Place the server in install mode (**change user /install**), before changing application settings. This applies the changes to all future users. When finished, place the server back into execute mode (**change user /execute**).

Microsoft Internet Explorer Wizard

On the first launch of Microsoft Internet Explorer, the Internet Connection Wizard requests the connection type. If the connection type is a LAN connection, this dialog can be by-passed by editing the Default User's registry settings as follows:

1. Open **HKU\.Default\Software\Microsoft\Internet Connection Wizard** with the registry editor.
2. From the Edit menu choose Add Value.

a. Type **Completed** in the Value Name box.

b. Select REG_DWORD in the Data Type box. Click OK.

c. Select Hex from the Radix options.

d. Type the value **0x1** in the Data box. Click OK.

Disable the Windows Network Status Icon

Windows 2000 Server and Windows 2003 Server have an available option to show the network icon in the system tray. When this option is selected, a network icon is displayed in the system tray within the session, and this network icon blinks each time network traffic occurs. Because the network icon blinks for each update, an infinite feedback loop occurs. When the network icon in the system tray blinks, it causes the ICA session to update, and because the ICA session is being updated, network traffic occurs, which causes the network icon to blink, thus causing the infinite loop.

To turn off the network status icon, follow these steps:

1. Open Control Panel | Network and Dial-up Connections.

2. Right-click Local Area Connection and select Properties.

3. Uncheck "Show Icon in notification area when connected." (In Windows 2000 Server the option reads "Show Icon in taskbar when connected".)

4. Repeat these steps for each network adapter or connection on every server in your farm.

ICA PRIORITY PACKET TAGGING

The Citrix ICA protocol includes a feature that identifies and tags ICA data based on the virtual channel from which the data originated. This feature, referred to as *ICA Priority Packet Tagging,* lays the foundation for a more granular Quality of Service (QoS) solution by providing the ability to prioritize ICA sessions based on the virtual channel data being transmitted. This section describes virtual channel priorities and how ICA data is tagged with these priorities when sent over the network using TCP/IP. QoS solutions that take advantage of ICA Priority Packet Tagging will provide QoS benefits that are more granular than prioritizing ICA traffic based only on application name or username. This section assumes the reader is generally familiar with ICA virtual channels, the TCP/IP protocol, and QoS solutions.

Virtual Channel Priorities

ICA Priority Packet Tagging provides the ability to prioritize ICA sessions based on the virtual channel data being transmitted. TCP/IP must be the protocol used. This is accomplished by associating each virtual channel with a two-bit priority. This two-bit priority is included as part of each ICA framing header (the ICA framing header is described in more detail in the section titled "Quality of Service (QoS) Solutions." The two priority bits combine to form four priority values:

- ▼ **00 (0)** High priority
- ■ **01 (1)** Medium priority
- ■ **10 (2)** Low priority
- ▲ **11 (3)** Background priority

Table 16-2 lists the default ICA channel-to-priority mappings.

The priority settings for all virtual channels are stored in the registry under the key **HKLM\System\CurrentControlSet\Control\Terminal Server\Wds\icawd\ Priority** as a **REG_MULTI_SZ** value. This registry key will contain one line for each virtual channel in the format

VirtualChannelName, Priority

Virtual Channel	Default Priority	Description
CTXTW	0	Remote Windows screen update data (Thinwire)
CTXTWI	0	Seamless Windows screen update data (Thinwire)
CTXCLIP	1	Clipboard
CTXCAM	1	Client audio mapping
CTXLIC	1	License management
CTXVFM	1	Video server video (i.e., not Thinwire video)
CTXPN	1	Program Neighborhood
CTXCCM	2	Client COM port mapping
CTXCDM	2	Client drive mapping
CTXCM	3	Client management (Auto Client Update)
CTXLPT1	3	Printer mapping for non-spooling clients (i.e., WinTerms)
CTXLPT2	3	Printer mapping for non-spooling clients (i.e., WinTerms)
CTXCOM1	3	Printer mapping for non-spooling clients (i.e., WinTerms)
CTXCOM2	3	Printer mapping for non-spooling clients (i.e., WinTerms)
CTXCPM	3	Printer mapping for spooling clients
OEMOEM	3	Used by OEMs
OEMOEM2	3	Used by OEMs

Table 16-2. ICA Virtual Channel Priorities

where *VirtualChannelName* is the standard virtual channel abbreviation, as specified in Table 16-2. *VirtualChannelName* must be seven characters, so trailing spaces must be added before the comma when necessary. *Priority* is one of the following numeric priority values: 0, 1, 2, or 3.

The Thinwire virtual channels (CTXTW and CTXTWI) are the only high-priority virtual channels by default, thus ensuring that time-sensitive user interface data is sent ahead of all other data.

ICA Data Transmission

The implementation details of ICA Priority Packet Tagging are better understood by examining the different layers of the ICA protocol and how the ICA protocol interacts with TCP/IP to send ICA data over a network. The priority bits used for ICA Priority Packet Tagging are determined and set within this data-transmission process.

Figure 16-1 depicts the flow of ICA data through each protocol layer as it is generated by the client application (or server) and packaged for delivery to a server (or client application) over a TCP/IP network.

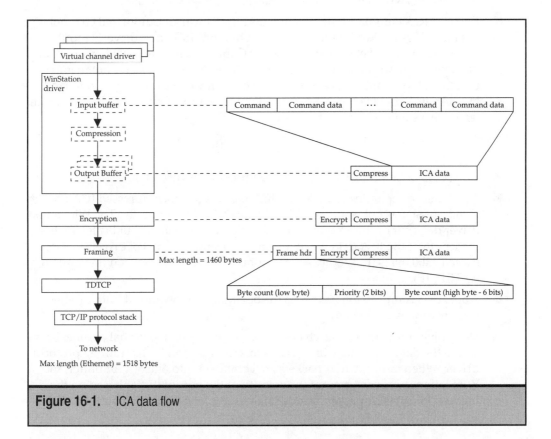

Figure 16-1.   ICA data flow

ICA data travels through the same protocol layers but in the reverse direction when received at the destination (client or server). All ICA protocol layers reside at the Presentation layer of the OSI networking model. The ICA protocol layers depicted in Figure 16-1 are described further in the following sections.

Virtual Channel Drivers

Each virtual channel has its own virtual channel driver that sends virtual channel data to the WinStation driver (described in the following section). The format of the virtual channel data is not standardized because it depends completely on the virtual channel implementation.

WinStation Driver   The WinStation driver receives ICA virtual channel data from multiple virtual channel drivers and packages the data for receipt by lower network layers. The WinStation driver works at the Application, Presentation, and Session layers of the OSI networking model. The WinStation driver performs the following functions:

▼   Establishes the ICA session between the client and the server, and maintains session information such as whether compression and encryption are turned on as well as whether ICA Priority Packet Tagging will be used.

■   Encodes ICA command information and transforms input virtual channel data into ICA packets, which are placed in the WinStation driver's input buffer. An ICA packet consists of a single Command byte followed by optional variable-length Command Data, as shown here. An ICA packet is not required to contain Command Data and therefore may only contain a single Command byte. An ICA packet contains data from only one virtual channel. The maximum length of a single ICA packet cannot exceed 2048 bytes (2KB).

Command	Command data

■   Compresses the ICA packets (when compression is turned on).

■   Combines or separates compressed ICA packets (or uncompressed ICA packets if compression is not being used) into an available output buffer. The WinStation driver determines the amount of data to include in each output buffer so that the length of the ICA data when leaving the framing protocol driver does not exceed 1460 bytes (to keep ICA data from being broken up when transmitted by TCP/IP).

■   Appends a compression header to the beginning of the output buffer (when compression is turned on).

■   Determines the priority of each output buffer, based on the virtual channel from where the data originated, and passes this information to the framing protocol driver. When multiple ICA packets are combined into one output buffer, the WinStation driver determines the priority of the output buffer based on the highest priority ICA packet included. For example, if the output buffer contains

Thinwire (priority 0) and printing (priority 3) ICA packets, the output buffer is given a priority of 0 based on the included Thinwire data.

▲   Forwards the output buffer to the encryption protocol driver (when encryption is turned on).

Encryption Protocol Driver   When encryption is turned on, the encryption protocol driver adds an encryption header to the output buffer data passed from the WinStation driver. All data after the encryption header is encrypted, including the compression header (if included).

Framing Protocol Driver   The framing protocol driver calculates the byte count of the output buffer and adds a framing header. In addition to the byte count, the framing header includes a two-bit priority value as determined by the WinStation driver. For example, if the total byte count of the output buffer is 1320 bytes and the packet is high priority, the binary value of the framing header is as follows:

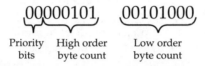

| Priority | High order | Low order |
| bits | byte count | byte count |

The low-order and high-order bytes are reversed for network transmission, and the framing header is as follows:

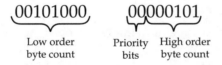

| Low order | Priority | High order |
| byte count | bits | byte count |

TCP Transport Driver (TDTCP)   The ICA protocol transfers control to the TCP/IP protocol stack through TDTCP, the TCP transport driver. TDTCP is ICA's (and RDP's) interface to the TCP/IP protocol stack. TDTCP does not append any additional header or trailer information to the ICA data.

TCP/IP   Once TDTCP transfers control to the TCP/IP protocol stack, the TCP/IP protocol drivers prepare the ICA data for network transmission. Detailed information on the TCP/IP standards and how TCP/IP encapsulates data for network transmission can be found in the Request for Comments (RFC) and Standards (STD) documents available on the Internet (http://www.faqs.org/).

Quality of Service (QoS) Solutions

QoS solutions prioritize ICA traffic against all other traffic on the network. These solutions are able to identify network traffic as ICA traffic either based on the TCP port (1494 by default) or by identifying the ICA initialization handshake that occurs when a new session is established (this is safer than using the TCP port because the TCP port number is configurable). Some QoS solutions can also identify ICA traffic based on other information, such as published application or source IP address. This identification allows ICA sessions to be prioritized against each other across the entire network. For example, all PeopleSoft ICA sessions can be given a higher priority than sessions performing less critical tasks.

ICA Priority Packet Tagging provides QoS policing mechanisms with the opportunity to identify virtual channel priorities within an ICA session so that ICA sessions transmitting higher priority data are delivered first. ICA Priority Packet Tagging requires a QoS solution to consider the following:

▼ TCP and IP are stream-oriented protocols. When ICA data is received by TCP and then by IP, it may be combined or broken up differently than how it was packaged by the ICA protocol drivers. The ICA output buffers are specifically limited to 1460 bytes so that they remain intact when delivered to the TCP/IP protocol stack. However, it is not guaranteed that the output buffers will remain intact. Therefore, the priority bits in the ICA framing header may not always be in the same place in the TCP segment or IP packet. This prevents QoS solutions from relying on a data offset to identify the priority bits at the TCP or IP layers. To circumvent this potential issue, QoS solutions must verify that the TCP packet contains the complete contents of an ICA output buffer. When aligned correctly, the first two bits of ICA data in the IP packet can be treated as priority bits. When the byte counts do not match, the ICA output buffers are most likely not intact within the TCP segments; therefore, the first two bits of ICA data in the IP packet should not be interpreted as priority bits.

■ ICA Priority Packet Tagging is implemented at the Presentation Layer (Layer 6 of the OSI networking model). Most routers read data at lower layers (Layers 2 through 4). Therefore, routers don't generally have access to the ICA Priority Packet Tagging information. When IP packets are sent through a router, the packets may be fragmented. If this is the case, the first packet will contain the framing header, including the priority bits and a now *incorrect* byte count (because the packet has been fragmented). Subsequent packet fragments will *not* have a framing header and therefore will *not* include the priority bits (or a byte count). Therefore, if QoS solutions receive the ICA traffic after fragmentation by a router, not all IP packets will have the priority bits. Verifying the byte counts between the IP layer and the ICA framing header as described previously ensures that the priority bits are interpreted correctly.

■ TCP requires an acknowledgement of receipt for each TCP segment in the TCP buffer before sending additional segments. This prevents QoS solutions from being able to implement functionality that holds back printing ICA data and forwards on Thinwire ICA data within a single ICA stream (which is also a single TCP stream). TCP would report a failure of receipt for the TCP segments being held because they were not received by the destination in a timely manner. QoS solutions must implement ICA Priority Packet Tagging in such a way that the transmission speed of each TCP stream is dynamically altered based on the priority bits of the ICA data being transmitted, instead of attempting to hold back individual pieces of data within the stream.

▲ Program Neighborhood clients and MetaFrame Presentation Servers running a software version prior to MetaFrame 1.8 Feature Release 1 will establish ICA sessions without ICA Priority Packet Tagging. Unless QoS solutions detect the Citrix software version in use by the ICA session, all ICA traffic in these sessions will be treated as high priority (priority 0) because the two bits that are now used for ICA Priority Packet Tagging were not used (and thus set to 0) in previous versions of MetaFrame.

SESSION MONITORING AND CONTROL (SMC)

Session Monitoring and Control is an additional server-side module that adds functionality to enhance MetaFrame Presentation Server session-monitoring and control capabilities. Session Monitoring and Control includes:

▼ Monitoring session bandwidth usage down to the virtual channel level. Bandwidth statistics are provided in both server-to-client and client-to-server directions.

■ Monitoring compression ratios in both directions for

   ■ The MetaFrame Presentation Server as a whole.

   ■ Individual sessions on the server.

■ Monitoring session latency.

■ Real-time control of session bandwidths.

■ Real-time control of virtual channel bandwidths.

▲ Real-time control of virtual channel priorities.

An example of a Session Monitoring and Control console is available within the MetaFrame Presentation Server Software Development Kit (MPSSDK). The MPSSDK can be downloaded from the Citrix Developer Network Web site (http://www.cdn.citrix.com). For additional information about the use of Session Monitoring and Control, see the Citrix Knowledge Base articles CTX101754 and CTX103213.

CHAPTER 17

MetaFrame Presentation Server Troubleshooting and Tips

This chapter covers more advanced troubleshooting techniques for MetaFrame Presentation Server, including troubleshooting the Independent Management Architecture (IMA) Service, Resource Manager, Novell NDS Integration, connectivity issues, and SQL Replication. It also contains tips and information on common problems and guidance on collecting data for Citrix Technical Support information.

TROUBLESHOOTING THE IMA SERVICE

The IMA Service is the core of MetaFrame Presentation Server and runs on all farm servers. As such, many general failures or problems related to farm operation and stability are traceable to problems with the IMA Service. The solutions presented in this section can help resolve most production IMA issues.

NOTE: The IMA Service executable called by Windows as a service is *ImaSrv.exe* (*%SystemDrive%\ Program Files\Citrix\System32\Citrix\Ima\ImaSrv.exe*).

IMA Service Fails to Start

If the IMA Service fails to start, values contained in the registry indicate the nature and cause of the failure. The actual plug-ins to be loaded and the load sequence are version-specific and are contained in **HKLM\Software\Citrix\IMA\RUNTIME**. The values listed in `RequiredPlugins` and `ProductPlugins` constitute the ordered load sequence for plug-ins. The plug-ins listed in `RequiredPlugins` are loaded first, then the plug-ins listed in `ProductPlugins` are loaded. Examine the following registry setting:

```
HKLM\SOFTWARE\Citrix\IMA\Runtime\CurrentlyLoadingPlugin
```

Blank Registry Value

If the IMA Service fails to start and the registry value is blank, either the IMA Service could not connect to the data store or the local host cache is missing or corrupt.

Specific Registry Value

If a registry value exists, the IMA Service successfully connected to the data store but a subsequent subsystem failed to load. The value displayed is the name of the subsystem that failed to load. For additional information about subsystem troubleshooting, see the "IMA Service Logging" section, later in this chapter.

NOTE: During the normal startup process of the IMA Service, this value cycles through the names of the subsystems as they are loaded. Once the IMA Service has started successfully, the value will be blank.

Troubleshooting Actions to Start the IMA Service

The following actions should be taken in order to troubleshoot the reason for IMA Service startup failures.

Data Store Connectivity   If you're using a *direct* connection to the data store (that is, the server has its own ODBC connection), verify that ODBC connectivity exists. For more information, see the "ODBC Connection Fails" section, later in this chapter. If you're using an *indirect* connection to the data store (that is, server is pointed to another farm server to aggregate queries), verify that the IMA Service is running on the direct server.

IMA Service Error Code   Review the entries in the event log for the IMA Service error code that is returned. See "IMA Error Codes" in Appendix A for a detailed listing of errors.

Print Spooler Service   Verify that the Print Spooler service is started in the context of Local System rather than as a user.

"IMA Service Failed" Message   When restarting a server, if you get an "IMA Service Failed" message, with error code 2147483649, the local system account may be missing a temp directory. Change the IMA Service startup account to the local administrator. If the IMA Service starts under the local administrator's account, check for a missing temp directory. Switch the service back to the local system account and try manually creating the temp directory %systemroot%\temp. Verify that both the TMP and TEMP environment variables point to this directory. For more information, see Microsoft Knowledge Base article 251254.

IMA Service Eventually Starts Despite Error Message

If the Service Control Manager reports that the IMA Service could not be started, but the service eventually starts, ignore this message. The Service Control Manager has a timeout of six minutes. The IMA Service can take longer than six minutes to start if either the load on the database exceeds the capabilities of the database hardware or the network has high latency.

IMA Service Fails to Stop

Microsoft's Systems Management Server (SMS) Netmon2 client utility is not supported on MetaFrame Presentation Servers. The IMA Service fails to stop when this utility is installed on the MetaFrame Presentation Server. If present, the Netmon2 client should be uninstalled.

ODBC Connection Fails

If the server uses a direct connection to the data store, ODBC connectivity is required for proper operation of the IMA Service. If ODBC issues are suspected, verify that the database server is online, attempt to connect to the database using the DSN file with an ODBC Test utility, verify that the correct username and password are being used, reinstall MDAC 2.6 SP1 (or later), and then enable ODBC tracing for further troubleshooting.

Verify That the Database Server Is Online

Verify the name of the DSN file the IMA Service is using by looking in the registry at **HKLM\SOFTWARE\Citrix\IMA\DataSourceName**. Then check to ensure the target server is accessible over the network.

ODBC Test Utility

Attempt to connect to the database using the DSN file with an ODBC Test utility (such as Oracle ODBC Test, DB2 Client Configuration Assistant Test, or SQL Server ODBC Test).

Username and Password

Verify that the username and password are correct for database connectivity. The username and password can be changed using the **dsmaint config** command. For more information, see the *MetaFrame Presentation Server Administrator's Guide*.

Reinstall MDAC 2.6 SP1 or Later

Reinstall MDAC 2.6 SP1 (or later) to verify that the correct ODBC files and drivers are installed.

Further Troubleshooting

Enable ODBC tracing for further troubleshooting. For more information, see the "ODBC Tracing" section later in this chapter.

SERVER FAILS TO CONNECT TO THE DATA STORE

If basic ODBC connectivity has been verified using the previous procedures and the server still fails to connect, this can indicate a corrupt local host cache. To correct the problem, follow these steps:

1. Copy *imalhc.mdb* to another directory for backup purposes.
2. Stop the IMA service. This can be accomplished from the Services control panel or from a command prompt by typing **net stop imaservice**.
3. From the command prompt, re-create the local host cache using the **dsmaint recreatelhc** command.
4. Restart the server.

Failed to Initialize Permanent Storage During Installation

This error usually indicates that the IMA Service is unable to create objects in the data store. If basic ODBC connectivity has been verified using the previous procedures and this error occurs, follow these steps:

1. Verify that the user account for the database has permissions to create tables, stored procedures, and index objects. For Microsoft SQL Server, the permission is "db_owner." For Oracle, the permission is "resource." For IBM DB2, the permission is "database administrator authority" or the equivalent list of permissions specified in the *MetaFrame Presentation Server Administrator's Guide*.

2. In the case of an Oracle data store, verify that the system tablespace is not full on the Oracle server.

IMA Service Logging

For advanced troubleshooting of the IMA Service, logging can be enabled at the server level. The following steps enable logging for either debug output (viewed using a debug hook utility such as DBGVIEW from SysInternals) or a text file. To enable logging of IMA events, modify the registry as detailed in the following subsections.

NOTE: Table A-2 in Appendix A provides a cross reference of MetaFrame Presentation Server systems to the relevant IMA subsystems so that tracing can be focused on specific areas rather than globally enabled.

Enabling Server Logging of IMA Events

Enabling logging and tracing of IMA events requires two sets of registry-based changes: First to enable logging globally, and second to enable logging for each subsystem to be debugged.

Enabling Logging To enable logging, modify the registry as follows:

1. Open **HKLM\SOFTWARE\Citrix\IMA\Tracer** with the registry editor.

2. Edit the value for "Log to Debugger" as a hex value (REG_DWORD). Enter **0x0** (the default value) to disable debug output or **0x1** to enable debug output.

3. Edit the value for "Log to File" as a hex value (REG_DWORD). Enter **0x0** (the default value) to disable file output or **0x1** to enable file output.

4. Edit the value for "Log File Name" as a text value (REG_SZ). Change the default value (\MF20) to reflect the desired full path and filename of the output file.

Enable Per-Subsystem Logging/Tracing The registry key **HKLM\SOFTWARE\Citrix\IMA\Tracer** contains subkeys for each subsystem that can have information traced. Tracing for all subsystems is on by default, but the specific types of messages for the subsystems are off, as shown in Figure 17-1. To enable tracing for a subsystem, both the default value and the message value (such as Error or Info) must have a value of 1.

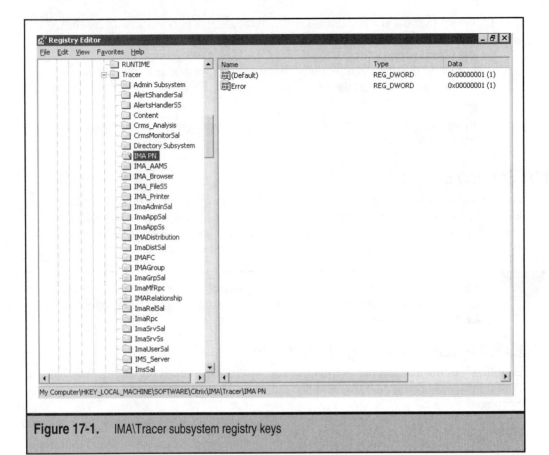

Figure 17-1. IMA\Tracer subsystem registry keys

CAUTION: The default value for each subsystem *must* be 1 and should never be changed. Default values are displayed as (Default) in regedit or as <No Name> in regedt32. Other values within each key correspond to types of messages to log and are set to 0 by default.

Recovering from a Failed Installation

If the installation of a MetaFrame Presentation Server into the farm fails, there is a possibility that the data collector will continually attempt to contact the failed/uninstalled server.

After a failed installation, the list of servers in the Presentation Server Console should be compared to the list of servers returned by the **queryhr** command-line utility. Use the command **queryhr -d *hostID*** to remove any server listed in the queryhr results that is not listed in the Presentation Server Console.

CAUTION: Do not use the **−d** switch on farm servers that are functioning properly. This switch removes the server from the farm. The server must be reinstalled into the farm in order to regain functionality.

Recovering an Unresponsive Server

If a farm member server is no longer responding to IMA requests and the IMA Service cannot be started, the server is considered to be unresponsive. The **chfarm** command cannot be used with an unresponsive server because the command requires connectivity to the data store.

The following steps can be used to rejoin an unresponsive server to the farm:

CAUTION: The original state of the server cannot be recovered after performing this procedure. Before using this technique, first attempt all other solutions presented in the "Troubleshooting the IMA Service" section.

1. Uninstall MetaFrame Presentation Server on the unresponsive server.

2. Remove the unresponsive server from the farm using the Presentation Server Console.

3. Reinstall MetaFrame Presentation Server on the unresponsive server and rejoin it to the farm during installation.

RESOURCE MANAGER CONSIDERATIONS AND TROUBLESHOOTING

The following information applies to Resource Manager for MetaFrame Presentation Server in regard to the Database Data Source Name, alerts for high context switches, the zone elections counter, certain error messages when using Oracle, and multiple duplicate import request messages.

Resource Manager Summary Database Data Source Name (DSN)

The RMSummaryDatabase DSN is *not* case sensitive; any case can be used for the summary database DSN.

Resource Manager Alert "High Context Switches/Second"

When Resource Manager is installed with default metrics configured on the server, Resource Manager may report alerts for "high context switches/second," although the server seems to be functioning normally. These "default metric" threshold values are intended as baseline configuration values to be tuned by the MetaFrame administrator. The values are based on a minimal server configuration. Although most metric defaults such as Processor – %Processor Time are suitable as a "one size fits all" solution, some metrics, such as System – Context Switches / Sec, need to be tuned for the actual environment.

MetaFrame administrators can achieve more realistic threshold values by using the Visual Threshold Configuration graph in a test-bed or production environment. An administrator can see where the peaks and troughs exist for up to 96 hours' worth of sampled data and then estimate, based on real data, what the threshold value should be for the environment.

Resource Manager Zone Elections Counter

The Citrix MetaFrame Presentation Server – Zone Elections counter monitors the number of Data Collector elections that have occurred in the server's zone since the IMA Service was last started. Data Collectors store dynamic data about the zone, which can create a considerable amount of data if many active connections exist (users, published applications, servers, and so on). Monitoring this metric can determine whether or not excessive Data Collector elections are taking place due to intermittent network connectivity, IMA Service restarts, Data Collector failures, or elections requested by another MetaFrame Presentation Server. Elections can take place when there is a communications failure between any MetaFrame Presentation Server in any zone.

TIP: Proactively monitor Zone Elections to ensure that excessive data transfer between zones is not occurring. In particular, monitor the Citrix MetaFrame Presentation Server – Zone Elections Won metric and the Citrix MetaFrame Presentation Server – Zone Elections metric and set the appropriate alert thresholds. Alternatively, you can use the Microsoft Operations Manager (MOM) to monitor excessive election rates.

Resource Manager Error: Oracle Cannot ROLLBACK in a Distributed Transaction

When using Resource Manager with Oracle, the system may continually generate messages about ROLLBACK of distributed transactions. This can occur if the Disable MTS (Microsoft Transaction Server) Support option in the Oracle ODBC driver workaround's configuration is not set. If the workaround is not enabled (the default on most Oracle ODBC configurations), this leads to a unique key violation that terminates the SQL transaction and generates the following Resource Manager server log entry:

```
[Oracle][ODBC][Ora]ORA-02074: cannot ROLLBACK in a distributed transaction.
```

Resource Manager Error: Oracle Must Reparse Cursor to Change Bind Variable Datatype

After you reboot the Resource Manager Database Connection Server, the system may generate an Oracle ODBC error in the Resource Manager server log, such as this:

```
14 June 2003 11:32:26 - System - [Oracle][ODBC][Ora]ORA-01475: must
reparse cursor to change bind variable datatype.
```

To resolve this error, set the Oracle ODBC workaround for Enable Closing Cursors.

Resource Manager Error: Failed to Create Summary Database (Oracle)

If summary database creation fails, the system may generate an error indicating schema deployment problems for the summary database. Here's a typical "Failed to create summary database" error in the Resource Manager server log:

```
11 July 2002 12:26:02 - System - Failed to create summary database.
```

Error Message Common Causes

This error is typically generated in Resource Manager when a database problem occurs while the summary database schema is being created or if the database user has insufficient privileges to create the schema.

Database Problem Creating the Summary Database Schema Initially   When an Oracle database configuration such as the rollback segment is too small and "non-autoextending," schema creation, and hence summary database creation, can fail. This can prevent the successful deployment of the Resource Manager schema when Resource Manager is creating some or all of the packages. To correct the problem, follow these steps:

1. Check the Oracle or SQL Server configuration settings to ensure that there is enough space in the database to create the schema. Several megabytes should be enough space to create the schema.

2. Check that all the rollback segments are autoextending; these can be tuned after the database is created.

Database User Has Insufficient Privileges to Create the Schema   When the database user lacks sufficient privileges to allow Resource Manager to insert data into tables or create packages, summary database creation will fail. To correct the problem, ensure that the user has rights to the database and can successfully communicate with the database server.

Resource Manager Error: Multiple Duplicate Import Request Messages

The Resource Manager server log may show multiple duplicate import request messages. These informational messages may appear in the Resource Manager server log in response to multiple duplicate import requests. Many messages similar to the following may be observed in the Resource Manager server log file:

```
22 November 1978 00:02:10 - System - Ignoring duplicate import request for
  file "C:\Program Files\Citrix Resource Manager\SummaryFiles\1C2865FABC926CA"
from host "XXXXXXX".
```

These messages usually appear because the Update Now button has been activated multiple times or there are spurious network conditions that cause the server to request an import more than once. The messages are normal and summary file imports are unaffected.

TROUBLESHOOTING NOVELL DIRECTORY SERVICES INTEGRATION

Integration of MetaFrame Presentation Server into a Novell Directory Services (NDS) environment presents additional challenges. This section lists some of the known NDS integration issues and relevant troubleshooting tips.

NDS Credentials

Inability to log on or to assign rights to published applications using NDS credentials is a common problem and can usually be resolved by verifying NDS settings for the farm, verifying correct logon, verifying the correct Novell client configuration, and finally by verifying the Novell Workstation Manager component of the Novell client.

Verifying NDS Settings for the Farm

Verify that NDS is enabled for the farm. Right-click the farm name in the Presentation Server Console and choose Properties. Navigate to the MetaFrame Settings tab and verify that the Novell Directory Services Preferred Tree is set correctly.

Verifying Correct Logon

Verify that the username, password, context, and tree name are correct by logging on from another computer using the same settings.

Verifying Novell Client Configuration

Verify that the Novell Client is correctly configured by logging on from the console (the actual physical desktop) of the MetaFrame Presentation Server and browsing the NDS.

Verifying the Novell Workstation Manager Component

If the ZENworks Dynamic Local User (DLU) policies are not being applied on some MetaFrame Presentation Servers, check the Novell Workstation Manager component of the Novell Client. To check the Novell Workstation Manager component in Windows 2000, follow these steps:

1. Right-click the My Network Places icon on the MetaFrame Presentation Server's desktop and select Properties.

2. In the Network and Dial-up Connections window, right-click Local Area Connection and select Properties.

3. Select Novell Workstation Manager from the components list and click the Properties button.

4. Verify the following:

   ■ Workstation Manager is enabled.

   ■ The tree name is set to the tree that has the DLU policies applied.

   ■ All other options have the default settings applied.

Failure to Delete Volatile User Accounts

If the DLU policy in NDS is set to delete users after they log out (the Volatile User option) and the volatile user accounts are not automatically deleted, ensure that the Enable Volatile User Caching option is disabled.

Autologon Problems

If autologon problems occur (with or without the ZENworks Dynamic Local User (DLU) feature as the Windows authentication method), start troubleshooting with the following three steps:

1. *Make a desktop connection.* Make a desktop connection using an ICA Custom Connection with the Autologon feature enabled.

2. *Specify user credentials.* Specify user credentials as follows:

   ■ **Username**   A valid Distinguished Name, such as ".SampleUser.company"

   ■ **Password**   A valid password

   ■ **Domain**   Contains the NDS tree name

3. *Launch the connection.* Perform troubleshooting based on the result of launching the connection.

IMPORTANT: The following troubleshooting actions are not always true if the custom connection is not created exactly as described in the previous three steps.

Troubleshooting the Connection

The results of the preceding connection test determine the next step. The following paragraphs identify troubleshooting steps and fixes for the most common errors.

Novell Client Error Message If the Novell client displays an error message about an invalid username, server, or tree, log onto the console of the MetaFrame Presentation Server as the same user. If the logon is not successful, the Novell client is not configured properly.

Microsoft Client Error Message If the Microsoft client prompts you to reenter your credentials or displays an error message, click Cancel to return to the Novell logon dialog box. On the NT/2000 tab, view and verify the user information.

Username Field Contains a Distinguished Name If the Username field in the NT/2000 tab field contains a Distinguished Name (*.username.context*), upgrade to Novell Client 4.81 or later. (Older Novell clients do not parse the username from the Distinguished Name.)

Blank Domain Name with ZENworks DLU If the domain name is blank or set to the local machine name and ZENworks DLU is being used, then troubleshoot DLU policies IAW Novell procedures. (DLU is not functioning properly.)

Blank Domain Name without ZENworks DLU If the domain name is blank or is set to the local machine name and ZENworks DLU is not being used, locate or create the following the registry value:

```
HKLM\Software\Citrix\NDS\SyncedDomainName (REG_SZ or String Value)
```

Set the registry key value to the name of the Windows domain that is synchronized with the NDS tree.

NOTE: For additional information regarding the use of the **SyncedDomainName** value, see Citrix Knowledge Base articles CTX103252, CTX737605, and CTX582798.

Domain Field Contains NDS Tree Name If the Domain field contains the name of the NDS tree, enable NDS integration.

Domain Field Contains Windows Domain Name If the Domain field contains the name of a Windows domain and you are not using ZENworks DLU functionality for Windows authentication, verify that the server has a valid trust relationship between the server's domain and the user's domain (Windows Domain Trust).

Known Issues and Workarounds

Several known issues exist regarding ZENworks, MetaFrame Presentation Server not accepting NDS credentials, session sharing, and dial-up ICA connections. Workarounds for these issues are discussed in this section.

ZENworks Failure to Distinguish Between Identical Usernames

ZENworks for Desktops 3 does not distinguish between users with the same username, even if they are in different contexts in the tree. If the first user is still logged in when the second user logs on, the profile of the first user is reused by the second user. Ideally, usernames should be globally unique in the tree. If the tree already includes users with the same username, aliases are required to differentiate between objects (users). See the section "Creating Aliases" in Chapter 6.

Logon Failure after Removing Novell Client

Uninstalling the Novell Client from a MetaFrame Presentation Server also removes the relevant Novell logon GINA registry entries. Unfortunately, the uninstall process will not reset the default Microsoft and Citrix GINA entries in the registry. The registry must be modified back to the "default" state using the following steps:

CAUTION: If you uninstall the Novell Client from a MetaFrame Presentation Server, do *not* restart the server until the required registry entries have been repopulated.

1. Open **HKLM\SOFTWARE\Windows NT\CurrentVersion\Winlogon** with the registry editor.

2. From the Edit menu choose Add Value.

   a. Type **GinaDLL** in the Value Name box.

   b. Select REG_SZ in the Data Type box. Click OK.

   c. Type **Ctxgina.DLL** in the String Value box.

   d. Click OK.

3. From the Edit menu choose Add Value.

   a. Type **CtxGinaDLL** in the Value Name box.

   b. Select REG_SZ in the Data Type box. Click OK.

   c. Type **MSgina.DLL** in the String Value box.

   d. Click OK.

Session-Sharing Feature Unsupported

The session-sharing feature is not supported for the MetaFrame Presentation Server Client for 32-bit Windows custom ICA connections that are configured for NDS user credentials. In order to work around this issue, use session sharing for custom ICA connections in Program Neighborhood; do not specify user credentials on the Login Information tab in the Properties dialog.

TROUBLESHOOTING FREQUENTLY ENCOUNTERED PROBLEMS

Some common problems relate to misconfigurations or misconceptions. Issues in this category include a protocol driver error when connecting to Secure Gateway with the Program Neighborhood Agent, the inability to launch the Secure Web Interface through Internet Explorer, folders missing in Program Neighborhood, cross-domain printer importing, servers not taking product license counts, USB redirection problems, and content-redirection issues.

Program Neighborhood Agent Cannot Connect Through Secure Gateway

If a client receives a "Cannot connect to the Citrix server: Protocol driver error" pop-up message when attempting to connect to Secure Gateway from the Program Neighborhood Agent, the cause is most likely that the client machine does not have the proper encryption level installed. The client must have 128-bit encryption installed. The required high-encryption pack is included as part of IE 5.5 SP2 and later.

Cannot Launch Published Application Through Secure Web Interface Site

Users connecting through a secure Web interface site (HTTPS) may receive an error message of "ICA file not found." This can occur if Internet Explorer prevents saving of encrypted pages to disk. To check or change this setting, follow these steps:

1. Open Internet Explorer.
2. Click on Tools | Internet Options.
3. Click on the Advanced tab.
4. Scroll all the way down to Security.
5. Ensure there is no check in the box next to "Do not save encrypted pages to disk."
6. Click on OK to close this process.

Folders Do Not Appear in Program Neighborhood

Folders created to organize applications in the Presentation Server Console are not related to application folders that appear in Program Neighborhood on the client side. To specify application folders for Program Neighborhood, use the Program Neighborhood Settings tab in the Properties dialog box for the published application to set the PN folder as follows:

1. Right-click the published application in the Presentation Server Console and choose Properties.

2. On the Program Neighborhood Settings tab, type the folder name in the Program Neighborhood Folder box.

USB Redirection Does Not Work

MetaFrame Presentation Server supports USB printers installed on the server. MetaFrame Presentation Server Client for 32-bit Windows supports installed USB printers when the client platform is Windows 98, Windows 2000, or Windows Me. Other USB devices, including scanners and cameras, are not currently supported by MetaFrame Presentation Server.

Content Redirection (File Type Association) Not Available

File type association for client-to-server content redirection may be unavailable for an application if the application is installed and then published *after* MetaFrame Presentation Server is installed. The file type association in each server's registry must be updated. To update the associations, follow these steps:

1. Open the Presentation Server Console.

2. Expand the Servers node in the left window pane.

3. Right-click a server the application is published to and select "Update File Types from Registry."

Once the file type updates have taken place, go back to the properties of the published application. The content redirection options should no longer be disabled.

WINDOWS SERVER 2003 ISSUES AND WORKAROUNDS

There are known Windows Server 2003 issues regarding Active Directory forest trusts and user access to Terminal Services.

Forest Trusts

Windows Server 2003 Active Directory introduces a new trust called a "forest trust." Forest trusts make it easier to manage multiple forests because a forest trust can be configured such that all domains in one forest transitively trust all domains in a second forest. The Presentation Server Console is unable to display or browse the trusted forest when enumerating domain objects. If you need to access objects from a trusted forest within the Presentation Server Console, there are two possible workarounds.

The recommended solution is to create a domain local group in the server farm's domain and then populate this domain local group with universal or global groups from one or more trusted domains. When publishing applications, use the domain local group from the server farm's local domain. All servers in the farm must be members of the same domain in order for this solution to be viable.

Another solution is to create one or more explicit trusts between the MetaFrame Presentation Server farm's domain and one or more domains in the trusted forest. Then you can use security principals directly, such as global groups from the trusted domain, when configuring published application access.

User Access to Terminal Servers

By default on Windows Server 2003, members of the Administrators and Remote Desktop Users groups can connect via Terminal Services. The default Remote Desktop Users group contains no users; you must manually add any users or groups that will require Terminal Services access. If the users are not already members of the computer's local security groups (usually established with the domain "Domain Users" or "Authenticated Users" group as a member of the local "Users" group), it is also necessary to add them. Unlike Windows 2000 Server policies, the Computer Local Policy under User Rights, "Allow log on locally," no longer provides access to Terminal Services connections. For additional information, refer to Windows Server 2003 online documentation and Citrix Knowledge Base articles CTX103221 and CTX102892.

WORKING WITH CITRIX TECHNICAL SUPPORT

If, after trying the solutions outlined earlier in the "Troubleshooting the IMA Service" section of this chapter, you have not resolved your problems, you can contact Citrix Technical Support for assistance. Before contacting Citrix Technical Support, there are established methods and baseline requirements for collecting information to use for debugging purposes.

Obtaining Installation/Uninstallation Logs

If the MetaFrame Presentation Server installation fails to complete, Citrix Technical Support will require an installation log file in order to troubleshoot the problem. MetaFrame Presentation Server is a Windows Installer package (.msi file). Therefore, the Windows Installer must be invoked with the **/l** option to create the necessary installation log file. Citrix recommends that if the MetaFrame Presentation Server installation fails, a second installation be attempted using the following command line in order to create a log file:

```
Msiexec /i <CD>\MF\MPS.msi /l*v %SystemDrive%\msi.log
```

Replace *<CD>* with the CD drive letter containing the MetaFrame Presentation Server installation CD. If the installation CD has been copied to a hard drive or network share, *<CD>* could instead be replaced with the full path to the CD image. This command line will create a log file named *msi.log* in the root of the system drive. Additional information about the Windows Installer can be found at http://www.microsoft.com/windows2000/docs/wininstaller.doc.

Capturing Management Console Debug Output

In order to capture debug output from the Presentation Server Console, the Presentation Server Console must be launched with the **–debugFile** command line option. Create a shortcut for this startup option as follows:

1. Right-click on the desktop and select New | Shortcut from the context menu.

2. The Create Shortcut Wizard will start. In the "Type the location of the item" field enter **%SystemRoot%\system32\java.exe**. When prompted to type a name for this shortcut, enter descriptive text such as "Console Debugging" and click Finish.

3. Right-click on the new shortcut and select Properties from the context menu.

4. In the **Shortcut** tab, enter the following text in the Target field (the text is word-wrapped here, but it must be entered as one line):

   ```
   java.exe -Djava.ext.dirs="ext;%ProgramFiles%\Java\ jre1.4.1\lib
   \ext" -jar Tool.jar -debugFile:output.log
   ```

5. Change the Start in field to **%ProgramFiles%\Citrix\Administration**.

6. Click the Change Icon button and enter **%ProgramFiles%\Citrix\Administration\ctxload.exe**.

7. In the Layout tab, configure the Screen buffer size properties to **9999** lines.

8. Click OK to save the shortcut.

When the shortcut is launched, two windows will display. The first window is a command window containing the debug messages output by *java.exe*. The second window is the Presentation Server Console user interface. If the Presentation Server Console hangs or otherwise fails, press CTRL-BREAK in the command window to view the stack trace.

Obtaining Installation Manager Debug Files

Obtain the following Installation Manager files before calling Citrix Technical Support for Installation Manager troubleshooting questions:

▼ WFS (the package script)

■ AEL (the recorder log file)

■ AEP (the packager project file)

▲ LOG (the Windows Installer log file)

Obtaining System Information

Citrix Technical Support may request information about the state of the system when troubleshooting an issue. The easiest way to obtain such information is to execute **winmsd**, which launches the System Information tool on Windows 2000. From the MMC Action menu, select "Save as System Information File." The file may then be sent to Citrix Technical support if necessary.

ODBC Tracing

Additional ODBC tracing information might be requested by Citrix Technical Support or the database vendor support team. Be prepared to execute ODBC traces. The procedure to enable ODBC tracing depends on the database server software being used.

To activate Microsoft SQL Server ODBC tracing, follow these steps:

1. Launch the ODBC Data Source Administrator.
2. Select the Tracing tab.
3. Enter a path for the log file in the Log File Path box.
4. Click Start Tracing Now to begin tracing. Click Stop Tracing Now to end tracing.

Here's how to activate Oracle ODBC tracing:

1. Launch the Net8 Assistant.
2. Select Configuration | Local | Profile.
3. Select General from the drop-down box in the right pane.
4. Use the Tracing and Logging tabs to configure ODBC tracing as needed.

Finally, to activate IBM DB2 ODBC tracing, follow these steps:

1. Launch the DB2 Client Configuration Assistant.
2. Select Client Settings | Diagnostics.
3. Set the diagnostic error capture level to **4** (meaning all errors, warnings, and information messages).

CHAPTER 18

MetaFrame Access Suite Troubleshooting and Tips

W hereas Chapter 17 covered troubleshooting MetaFrame Presentation Server, this chapter covers troubleshooting tips for the remaining three MetaFrame Access Suite products: MetaFrame Secure Access Manager, MetaFrame Conferencing Manager, and MetaFrame Password Manager (including issues with Java, .NET, and guest users).

METAFRAME SECURE ACCESS MANAGER

This MetaFrame Secure Access Manager troubleshooting section includes discussions on the Java client, uninstalling the Secure Gateway Secure Ticket Authority, registering the .NET framework, and the Secure Gateway Client internal server list.

Java Archives Do Not Download when Using the Secure Gateway Client

When using the Secure Gateway Client, a scenario can arise where none of the archive files for the Java client are downloaded. This happens because the applet and CAB files are seen as unsigned by the Java Virtual Machine (JVM). By default, unsigned Java files run in the "sandbox." When the JVM tries to resolve the name of the host from where the files are being downloaded, the hostname seen by the client will be an internal server name. This internal server name cannot be resolved, which generates a security error.

The best way to approach this problem is to prevent the hostname check by changing the security settings for the JVM to allow connections to all network addresses. This enables downloading of the archives.

The steps for changing the JVM security settings are as follows:

1. Go to Internet Explorer properties.
2. Click the Security tab.
3. Click Custom Level to change the settings for the Internet zone.
4. Scroll down to the section for the Microsoft JVM.
5. Select the radio button Custom.
6. A button appears to the bottom left labeled Java Custom Settings. Click it.
7. Click the Edit Permissions tab.
8. Under Unsigned Content, enable access for all network addresses.

NOTE: During the testing of the Release Candidate version of Microsoft Windows XP Service Pack 2, Citrix *e*Labs identified some potential conflicts with the Secure Gateway Client. For more details see the Citrix Knowledge Base articles CTX104760, CTX103896, and CTX103897.

Uninstalling the Secure Gateway Secure Ticket Authority (STA)

The Secure Gateway Secure Ticket Authority (STA) is installed by default on all MetaFrame Secure Access Manager Web Servers. With versions prior to MetaFrame Secure Access Manager 2.2, uninstalling the STA must be done from the registry because the Control Panel applet Add/Remove Programs does not contain an uninstall for this item.

The steps for uninstalling the STA installed by MetaFrame Secure Access Manager are as follows:

1. Open the registry and go to HKLM\SOFTWARE\Classes\Installer\Products.

2. Search for *CSG_STA.msi*.

3. Remove the key that contains this reference (it's usually 21A2384414AD5864A8E7ABEC5EFAA2E5).

4. From a command prompt, navigate to the STA installation MSI file and run the following command:

```
msiexec /i csg_sta.msi
```

NOTE: The MetaFrame Secure Access Manager 2.2 STA can be uninstalled from the Add/Remove Programs applet in Control Panel. If the installation was an upgrade, however, doing so will *not* uninstall the previous STA installation; it will merely cause the system to revert to the earlier installed version.

Registering the .NET Framework Prior to Internet Information Services Installation

Difficulties in accessing the Authentication Service test page may arise from the *.asmx, .aspx,* or *.config* extension not being correctly registered in Internet Information Services (IIS). This can happen if IIS was installed after the installation of the .NET Framework. There are two resolutions to this problem. The first is simply to uninstall and then reinstall the .NET Framework. The second is to register the appropriate extensions in IIS by doing the following:

1. Open the Internet Services Manager.

2. Right-click on the Authentication Service virtual directory (located underneath the access center virtual directory) and select Properties.

3. On the Virtual Directory Tab, click the Configuration button.

4. Under Application Mappings, click Add.

5. For the executable, enter the location of the .NET Framework *aspnet_isapi.dll* file. This is generally located under %SystemRoot%\Microsoft.NET\FrameWork\ v1.1.*xxx.*

6. For the extension, enter **.asmx**.

7. Limit Verbs to GET,HEAD,POST,DEBUG.

8. Check the box for the script engine.

9. Repeat these steps, as needed, adding the same entry for the *.aspx* and *.config* extensions.

NOTE: Lack of proper registration may cause problems with other file extensions.

Secure Gateway Client Internal Server List

If Secure Gateway users are having trouble accessing internal servers, check to ensure that the requests are actually being sent to the Secure Gateway server. If they aren't, there may be a problem with the internal server list.

METAFRAME CONFERENCING MANAGER TROUBLESHOOTING

MetaFrame Conferencing Manager users may experience problems associated with the Active Directory environment. In this section we discuss issues concerning the Citrix Conference Room component, guest users, and users who are members of 200 or more Active Directory groups.

MetaFrame Conferencing Manager's Conference Room Component

During the installation of the Citrix Conference Room, a published application is automatically created with the name "Citrix Conference Room." This published application is hidden from the browse list of published applications but is necessary for the Citrix MetaFrame Conferencing Manager to work properly. If the published application "Citrix Conference Room" is renamed or deleted in the Presentation Server Console for any reason, MetaFrame Conferencing Manager will no longer work. If the published application is deleted or renamed and someone attempts to create a conference, they may receive the following error message: "An error occurred while processing your request. Try again. If you continue to receive this message, contact your MetaFrame Presentation Server administrator." You may also see the following event in the server's application event log:

```
Event Type:Error
Event Source: Citrix MetaFrame Conferencing Manager
Event Category: None
Event ID: 1541
User: N/A
```

```
Computer: <name of MetaFrame Presentation Server where error occurred>
Description: The Citrix XML Service returned error code unspecified.
```

In order to resolve this issue, perform a repair installation of the Citrix MetaFrame Conferencing Manager.

Perform a Repair Installation of the Citrix MetaFrame Conferencing Manager

To perform a repair installation of Citrix MetaFrame Conferencing Manager, follow these steps:

1. Navigate to Control Panel | Add/Remove Programs.

2. Highlight the program Citrix MetaFrame Conferencing Manager and select Change.

3. On the screen titled Citrix MetaFrame Conferencing Manager Setup – Application Maintenance, select the radio button next to Repair and then click Next.

4. On the next screen titled MetaFrame Presentation Server Administrator Credentials, select either "Use my current credentials" if the current user is a MetaFrame administrator or "Use my MetaFrame Presentation" "Server administrator credentials," if it is necessary to specify another MetaFrame administrator's credentials.

5. Enter the appropriate credentials and then click Next.

6. Once you are certain all options have been correctly configured, click Next on the Ready to Repair the Application screen.

7. When the repair installation has completed, click Finish.

Error: "Citrix Conference Room" Failed to Start

When initiating a meeting, you may receive the following error:

"Citrix Conference Room" failed to start. The Citrix server is unable to process your request to start this published application at this time. Please try again later. If the problem persists, contact your administrator.

This error can occur if the initial published application specified for the meeting and the Conference Room are published on separate servers. In order to avoid this message, increase the amount of time Conference Room will wait before starting the specified initial published application by creating the following registry value:

```
HKLM\Software\Citrix\CMCM
Value: ConferenceDelay (REG_DWORD) :< number in milliseconds>
```

Initially, configure the delay time to be 5000 (5 seconds). Increase or decrease this value to avoid the error message and minimize the delay. Adding or modifying this registry value does not require a reboot.

Error when Running *InstallAddIn.cmd* to Install the Outlook Add-in DLL

When using *InstallAddIn.cmd* to manually install *CMCMOL.dll* on a client machine, you may see the following messages during the execution of the file:

```
C:\>xcopy /y /f CMCMOL.dll "C:\Program Files\Citrix\CMCM\Outlook"
File not found - CMCMOL.dll
0 File(s) copied
C:\>xcopy /y /f Resources*.txt "C:\Program Files\Citrix\CMCM\Outlook"
File not found - Resources*.txt
0 File(s) copied
```

After executing the file and launching Outlook, you may also notice that you do not see the MetaFrame Conference button on the Outlook menu bar. It may be necessary at the command prompt to change directory locations to the directory that contains *InstallAddIn.cmd* and its supporting files before running the file. By default, these files are located in the Outlook folder on the MetaFrame Conferencing Manager CD-ROM.

Guest Users

In environments with more than one Active Directory domain controller, guest attendees may not be able to log on. The Guest Attendee feature uses guest accounts created by the External Conference Service. Currently, after a conference has ended, these accounts are disabled and their passwords are changed until they are needed again.

In Active Directory domains with more than one domain controller, there may be delays in the synchronization between domain controllers. This creates the potential for a guest attendee to be routed to a domain controller that has not yet been synchronized with new Guest Attendee account information.

NOTE: Guest users never know the actual username and password. They use a guest ID and conference ID to gain access to conferences.

Resolution

To resolve this issue, administrators can configure a new single domain controller as a subdomain of the domain to which MetaFrame Presentation Server users log on and then create the Guest Attendee group and accounts in this subdomain. For additional solutions, contact Citrix Technical Support.

Users Are Members of 200 or More Active Directory Groups

If a user is a member of 200 or more Active Directory groups, when attempting to start a conference they may not be able to see all of their published applications. Also, they may see the following error message:

> An error occurred while processing your request. You do not currently have access to any published applications. If you continue to receive this message, contact your MetaFrame Administrator.

Resolution

A hotfix was created for MetaFrame Conferencing Manager 2.0 for this issue; see Citrix Knowledge Base article CTX102891 for more details. Although this hotfix has been incorporated into MetaFrame Conferencing Manager 3.0, it is still necessary to modify the registry.

In order to allow users to see their published applications, create the following values in the registry:

```
HKLM\SOFTWARE\Citrix\XML Service
Name: MaxRequestSize
Type: DWORD
Data: 0032000


HKLM\SYSTEM\CurrentControlSet\Services\CtxHttp
Name: MaximumIncoming
Type: DWORD
Data: 0032000
```

You can increase the data value to a larger number if the user is a member of more than 200 Active Directory groups. Increase the data value by intervals of 4000 until the error message disappears.

METAFRAME PASSWORD MANAGER

Several troubleshooting tips for MetaFrame Password Manager are included in Chapter 15, which covers MetaFrame Password Manager administration. In this section we cover enabling advanced logging for the MetaFrame Password Manager 2.5 Agent.

Activating Advanced Logging for the MetaFrame Password Manager 2.5 Agent

Citrix recommends enabling logging only during troubleshooting because it adds considerable overhead to the MetaFrame Password Manager process. Do not allow logging to remain enabled during normal use; after the log has been collected, disable logging.

In order to activate the Advanced Logging capability included in the MetaFrame Password Manager 2.5 Agent, add the following registry keys:

```
HKLM\SOFTWARE\Citrix\MetaFrame Password Manager\Log
"Enabled"=dword:00000001
"Filter"=dword:ffffffff
"MaxSizeInBytes"=dword:000c8000
```

The enabled registry key controls the activation and deactivation of the logging information for all MetaFrame Password Manager sessions on the machine. Tables 18-1 through 18-3 show the advanced logging registry key control settings and the resultant behavior.

The Filter Setting

The Filter setting is a bitmask that can be used to enable and disable different types of log information. For example, if you only want Windows and Web application detection, use the value 0x00000003.

The MaxSizeInBytes Setting

The MaxSizeInBytes setting controls the maximum size of the logging file, which can be found in the user profile directory with the following format:

sso_<*userName*>.log

NOTE: If the log goes over the size limit, it will be reinitialized and start from 0KB.

Notes on Dynamic Windows Class IDs

If an application using dynamic Windows class IDs is executed, the debug log does not show this application's executable and the debug log is not able to provide information on the application. This is a known issue caused by the debug tool's Windows filtering sequence. However, the debug tool identifies the time when the application started and indicates that the MetaFrame Password Manger agent ignored the application because the Windows class ID is not the same as the application definition. If there is an application with a Windows class ID that has a number in it, it is possible that this number will change each time the application starts. Another useful tool that can be used to track these types of applications is SPY++ from Microsoft.

NOTE: For additional information about configuring definitions for applications with dynamic Windows class IDs, refer to the section in Chapter 15 titled "Configuring Windows Applications with Dynamic Windows Class IDs."

Setting	Behavior
0	Disables logging (default)
1	Enables logging

Table 18-1. Advanced Logging Registry Key Control Settings

Setting	Behavior
0xFFFFFFFF	Enables all logging
0x00000001	Logs information about Windows application detection only
0x00000002	Logs information about Web application detection only
0x00000004	Logs only password filling events for both Windows and Web applications
0x00000020	Logs information about Terminal Emulator detection only
0x10000000	Logs information about the *SSOSHELL.EXE* process only

Table 18-2. The Filter Setting

Setting	Behavior
819200	8KB (default)

Table 18-3. The MaxSizeInBytes Setting

PART III

Appendixes

APPENDIX A

Error Messages

This appendix includes text and tables detailing IMA error codes, IMA subsystem tracing, Presentation Server console error codes, Resource Manager billing error codes, and event log (*imamsgs.dll*) warning and error messages intended to help in troubleshooting and resolving problems with MetaFrame Presentation Server.

IMA ERROR CODES

Table A-1 lists the IMA service error codes that might appear in the Event Viewer.

Hex Value	Signed Value	Unsigned Value	Mnemonic
00000000h	0	0	IMA_RESULT_SUCCESS
00000001h	1	1	IMA_RESULT_OPERATION_ INCOMPLETE
00000002h	2	2	IMA_RESULT_CALL_NEXT_ HOOK
00000003h	3	3	IMA_RESULT_DISCARD_ MESSAGE
00000004h	4	4	IMA_RESULT_CREATED_NEW
00000005h	5	5	IMA_RESULT_FOUND_ EXISTING
00000009h	9	9	IMA_RESULT_CONNECTION_ IDLE
00130001h	1245185	1245185	IMA_RESULT_DS_NOT_ INSTALLED
00130002h	1245186	1245186	IMA_RESULT_SECURITY_INFO_ INCOMPLETE
002D0001h	2949121	2949121	IMA_RESULT_ALREADY_ MASTER
80000001h	-2147483647	2147483649	IMA_RESULT_FAILURE
80000002h	-2147483646	2147483650	IMA_RESULT_NO_MEMORY
80000003h	-2147483645	2147483651	IMA_RESULT_INVALID_ARG
80000004h	-2147483644	2147483652	IMA_RESULT_UNKNOWN_ MESSAGE

Table A-1.   IMA Error Codes

Hex Value	Signed Value	Unsigned Value	Mnemonic
80000005h	-2147483643	2147483653	IMA_RESULT_DESTINATION_ UNREACHABLE
80000006h	-2147483642	2147483654	IMA_RESULT_REFERENCE_ COUNT_NOT_ZERO
80000007h	-2147483641	2147483655	IMA_RESULT_ENTRY_NOT_ FOUND
80000008h	-2147483640	2147483656	IMA_RESULT_NETWORK_ FAILURE
80000009h	-2147483639	2147483657	IMA_RESULT_NOT_ IMPLEMENTED
8000000Ah	-2147483638	2147483658	IMA_RESULT_INVALID_ MESSAGE
8000000Bh	-2147483637	2147483659	IMA_RESULT_TIMEOUT
8000000Ch	-2147483636	2147483660	IMA_RESULT_POINTER_IS_ NULL
8000000Dh	-2147483635	2147483661	IMA_RESULT_UNINITIALIZED
8000000Eh	-2147483634	2147483662	IMA_RESULT_FINDITEM_ FAILURE
8000000Fh	-2147483633	2147483663	IMA_RESULT_CREATEPOOL_ FAILURE
80000010h	-2147483632	2147483664	IMA_RESULT_SUBSYS_NOT_ FOUND
80000013h	-2147483629	2147483667	IMA_RESULT_PS_UNINITIALIZED
80000014h	-2147483628	2147483668	IMA_RESULT_REGMAPFAIL
80000015h	-2147483627	2147483669	IMA_RESULT_DEST_TOO_ SMALL
80000016h	-2147483626	2147483670	IMA_RESULT_ACCESS_DENIED
80000017h	-2147483625	2147483671	IMA_RESULT_NOT_SHUTTING_ DOWN
80000018h	-2147483624	2147483672	IMA_RESULT_MUSTLOAD_ FAILURE
80000019h	-2147483623	2147483673	IMA_RESULT_CREATELOCK_ FAILURE

Table A-1.   IMA Error Codes *(continued)*

Hex Value	Signed Value	Unsigned Value	Mnemonic
8000001Ah	-2147483622	2147483674	IMA_RESULT_SHUTDOWN_FAILURE
8000001Ch	-2147483620	2147483676	IMA_RESULT_SENDWAIT_FAILURE
8000001Dh	-2147483619	2147483677	IMA_RESULT_NO_COLLECTORS
8000001Eh	-2147483618	2147483678	IMA_RESULT_UPDATED
8000001Fh	-2147483617	2147483679	IMA_RESULT_NO_CHANGE
80000020h	-2147483616	2147483680	IMA_RESULT_LEGACY_NOT_ENABLED
80000021h	-2147483615	2147483681	IMA_RESULT_VALUE_ALREADY_CREATED
80000022h	-2147483614	2147483682	IMA_RESULT_UID_EXCEEDED_BOUNDS
80000023h	-2147483613	2147483683	IMA_RESULT_NO_EVENTS
80000024h	-2147483612	2147483684	IMA_RESULT_NOT_FOUND
80000025h	-2147483611	2147483685	IMA_RESULT_ALREADY_EXISTS
80000026h	-2147483610	2147483686	IMA_RESULT_GROUP_ALREADY_EXISTS
80000027h	-2147483609	2147483687	IMA_RESULT_NOT_A_GROUP
80000028h	-2147483608	2147483688	IMA_RESULT_GROUP_DIR_ACCESS_FAILURE
80000029h	-2147483607	2147483689	IMA_RESULT_EOF
8000002Ah	-2147483606	2147483690	IMA_RESULT_REGISTRY_ERROR
8000002Bh	-2147483605	2147483691	IMA_RESULT_DSN_OPEN_FAILURE
8000002Ch	-2147483604	2147483692	IMA_RESULT_REMOVING_PSSERVER
8000002Dh	-2147483603	2147483693	IMA_RESULT_NO_REPLY_SENT
8000002Eh	-2147483602	2147483694	IMA_RESULT_PLUGIN_FAILED_VERIFY
8000002Fh	-2147483601	2147483695	IMA_RESULT_FILE_NOT_FOUND

Table A-1.   IMA Error Codes *(continued)*

Hex Value	Signed Value	Unsigned Value	Mnemonic
80000030h	-2147483600	2147483696	IMA_RESULT_PLUGIN_ENTRY_ NOT_FOUND
80000031h	-2147483599	2147483697	IMA_RESULT_CLOSED
80000032h	-2147483598	2147483698	IMA_RESULT_PATH_NAME_ TOO_LONG
80000033h	-2147483597	2147483699	IMA_RESULT_ CREATEMESSAGEPORT_FAILED
80000034h	-2147483596	2147483700	IMA_RESULT_ALTADDRESS_ NOT_DEFINED
80000035h	-2147483595	2147483701	IMA_RESULT_WOULD_BLOCK
80000036h	-2147483594	2147483702	IMA_RESULT_ALREADY_ CLOSED
80000037h	-2147483593	2147483703	IMA_RESULT_TOO_BUSY
80000038h	-2147483592	2147483704	IMA_RESULT_HOST_ SHUTTING_DOWN
80000039h	-2147483591	2147483705	IMA_RESULT_PORT_IN_USE
8000003Ah	-2147483590	2147483706	IMA_RESULT_NOT_SUPPORTED
80040001h	-2147221503	2147745793	IMA_RESULT_FILE_OPEN_ FAILURE
80040002h	-2147221502	2147745794	IMA_RESULT_SESSION_ REQUEST_DENIED
80040003h	-2147221501	2147745795	IMA_RESULT_JOB_NOT_FOUND
80040004h	-2147221500	2147745796	IMA_RESULT_SESSION_NOT_ FOUND
80040005h	-2147221499	2147745797	IMA_RESULT_FILE_SEEK_ FAILURE
80040006h	-2147221498	2147745798	IMA_RESULT_FILE_READ_ FAILURE
80040007h	-2147221497	2147745799	IMA_RESULT_FILE_WRITE_ FAILURE
80040008h	-2147221496	2147745800	IMA_RESULT_JOB_CANNOT_ BE_UPDATED
80040009h	-2147221495	2147745801	IMA_RESULT_NO_TARGET_ HOSTS

Table A-1.   IMA Error Codes *(continued)*

Hex Value	Signed Value	Unsigned Value	Mnemonic
8004000Ah	-2147221494	2147745802	IMA_RESULT_NO_SOURCE_FILES
80060001h	-2147090431	2147876865	IMA_RESULT_ATTR_NOT_FOUND
80060002h	-2147090430	2147876866	IMA_RESULT_CONTEXT_NOT_FOUND
80060003h	-2147090429	2147876867	IMA_RESULT_VALUE_NOT_FOUND
80060004h	-2147090428	2147876868	IMA_RESULT_DATA_NOT_FOUND
80060005h	-2147090427	2147876869	IMA_RESULT_ENTRY_LOCKED
80060006h	-2147090426	2147876870	IMA_RESULT_SEARCH_HASMORE
80060007h	-2147090425	2147876871	IMA_RESULT_INCOMPLETE
80060008h	-2147090424	2147876872	IMA_RESULT_READEXCEPTION
80060009h	-2147090423	2147876873	IMA_RESULT_WRITEEXCEPTION
8006000Ah	-2147090422	2147876874	IMA_RESULT_LDAP_PARTIALINSTALL
8006000Bh	-2147090421	2147876875	IMA_RESULT_LDAP_NOTREADY
8006000Ch	-2147090420	2147876876	IMA_RESULT_BUFFER_TOO_SMALL
8006000Dh	-2147090419	2147876877	IMA_RESULT_CONTAINER_NOT_EMPTY
8006000Eh	-2147090418	2147876878	IMA_RESULT_CONFIGURATION_ERROR
8006000Fh	-2147090417	2147876879	IMA_RESULT_GET_BASEOBJECT
80060010h	-2147090416	2147876880	IMA_RESULT_GET_DERIVEDOBJECT
80060011h	-2147090415	2147876881	IMA_RESULT_OBJECTCLASS_NOTMATCH
80060012h	-2147090414	2147876882	IMA_RESULT_ATTRIBUTE_NOTINDEXED

Table A-1. IMA Error Codes *(continued)*

Hex Value	Signed Value	Unsigned Value	Mnemonic
80060013h	-2147090413	2147876883	IMA_RESULT_OBJECTCLASS_VIOLATION
80060014h	-2147090412	2147876884	IMA_RESULT_ENUMFAIL
80060015h	-2147090411	2147876885	IMA_RESULT_ENUMNODATA
80060016h	-2147090410	2147876886	IMA_RESULT_DBCONNECT_FAILURE
80060017h	-2147090409	2147876887	IMA_RESULT_TRUNCATE
80060018h	-2147090408	2147876888	IMA_RESULT_DUPLICATE
80060019h	-2147090407	2147876889	IMA_RESULT_PS_NOTINITIALIZED
8006001Ah	-2147090406	2147876890	IMA_RESULT_USING_ORACLE_7
8006001Bh	-2147090405	2147876891	IMA_RESULT_USING_ORACLE_8
8006001Ch	-2147090404	2147876892	IMA_RESULT_USING_ORACLE_UNKNOWN
8006001Dh	-2147090403	2147876893	IMA_RESULT_LOAD_DAO_ENGINE_FAILED
8006001Eh	-2147090402	2147876894	IMA_RESULT_COMPACT_DB_FAILED
80060033h	-2147090381	2147876915	IMA_RESULT_ODBC_NO_CONNECTIONS_AVAILABLE
80060034h	-2147090380	2147876916	IMA_RESULT_CREATE_SQL_ENVIRONMENT_FAILED
80060035h	-2147090379	2147876917	IMA_RESULT_SQL_EXECUTE_FAILED
80060036h	-2147090378	2147876918	IMA_RESULT_SQL_FETCH_FAILED
80060037h	-2147090377	2147876919	IMA_RESULT_SQL_BIND_PARAM_FAILED
80060038h	-2147090376	2147876920	IMA_RESULT_SQL_GET_COLUMN_DATA_FAILED
80060039h	-2147090375	2147876921	IMA_RESULT_REPLICATED_DATA_CONTENTION
8006003Ah	-2147090374	2147876922	IMA_RESULT_DB_TABLE_NOT_FOUND

Table A-1. IMA Error Codes *(continued)*

Hex Value	Signed Value	Unsigned Value	Mnemonic
8006003Bh	-2147090373	2147876923	IMA_RESULT_CONNECTION_EXIST
8006003Ch	-2147090372	2147876924	IMA_RESULT_QUERY_MAX_NODEID_FAILED
8006003Dh	-2147090371	2147876925	IMA_RESULT_SQL_FUNCTION_SEQUENCE_ERROR
8006003Eh	-2147090370	2147876926	IMA_RESULT_DB_CONNECTION_TIMEOUT
8006003Fh	-2147090369	2147876927	IMA_RESULT_SQL_INVALID_TRANSACTION_STATE
80060040h	-2147090368	2147876928	IMA_RESULT_DB_NO_DISK_SPACE
80110104h	-2146369276	2148598020	LMS_RESULT_NO_SERVER_AVAILABLE
80110105h	-2146369024	2148598272	IMA_RESULT_FULL_SERVER_OR_APP_LOAD_REACHED
80130001h	-2146238463	2148728833	IMA_RESULT_MORE_ITEMS
80130002h	-2146238462	2148728834	IMA_RESULT_INVALID_ACCOUNT
80130003h	-2146238461	2148728835	IMA_RESULT_INVALID_PASSWORD
80130004h	-2146238460	2148728836	IMA_RESULT_EXPIRED_PASSWORD
80130005h	-2146238459	2148728837	IMA_RESULT_GROUP_IGNORED
80130006h	-2146238458	2148728838	IMA_RESULT_BUILTIN_GROUP
80130007h	-2146238457	2148728839	IMA_RESULT_DC_NOT_AVAILABLE
80130008h	-2146238456	2148728840	IMA_RESULT_NW_CLIENT_NOT_INSTALLED
80130009h	-2146238455	2148728841	IMA_RESULT_ACCOUNT_LOCKED_OUT
8013000Ah	-2146238454	2148728842	IMA_RESULT_INVALID_LOGON_HOURS

Table A-1.   IMA Error Codes *(continued)*

Hex Value	Signed Value	Unsigned Value	Mnemonic
8013000Bh	-2146238453	2148728843	IMA_RESULT_ACCOUNT_ DISABLED
8013000Ch	-2146238452	2148728844	IMA_RESULT_PREFERRED_ TREE_NOT_SET
80160001h	-2146041855	2148925441	IMA_RESULT_NODE_NOT_ FOUND
80160002h	-2146041854	2148925442	IMA_RESULT_NODE_NAME_ INVALID
80160003h	-2146041853	2148925443	IMA_RESULT_NODE_NOT_ EMPTY
80160004h	-2146041852	2148925444	IMA_RESULT_NODE_MOVE_ DENIED
80160005h	-2146041851	2148925445	IMA_RESULT_NODE_NAME_ NOT_UNIQUE
80160006h	-2146041850	2148925446	IMA_RESULT_NODE_RENAME_ DENIED
80160007h	-2146041849	2148925447	IMA_RESULT_CONSTRAINT_ VIOLATION
80160008h	-2146041848	2148925448	IMA_RESULT_LDAP_ PROTOCOL_ERROR
80160009h	-2146041847	2148925449	IMA_RESULT_LDAP_SERVER_ DOWN
8016000Ch	-2146041844	2148925452	IMA_RESULT_NODE_DELETE_ DENIED
8016000Fh	-2146041841	2148925455	IMA_RESULT_ CANNOTCHANGE_PASSWORD
80160010h	-2146041840	2148925456	IMA_RESULT_ CANNOTCHANGE_LAST_RW
80160011h	-2146041839	2148925457	IMA_RESULT_LOGON_USER_ DISABLED
80160012h	-2146041838	2148925458	IMA_RESULT_CMC_ CONNECTION_DISABLED
80160013h	-2146041837	2148925459	IMA_RESULT_INSUFFICIENT_ SERVER_SEC_FOR_USER

Table A-1. IMA Error Codes *(continued)*

Hex Value	Signed Value	Unsigned Value	Mnemonic
80160014h	-2146041836	2148925460	IMA_RESULT_FEATURE_ LICENSE_NOT_FOUND
80160015h	-2146041835	2148925461	IMA_RESULT_DISALLOW_ CMC_LOGON
80260001h	-2144993279	2149974017	IMA_RESULT_NW_PRINT_ SERVER_ALREADY_PRESENT
80260002h	-2144993278	2149974018	IMA_RESULT_SERVER_ ALREADY_PRESENT
802D0001h	-2144534527	2150432769	IMA_RESULT_TABLE_NOT_ FOUND
802D0002h	-2144534526	2150432770	IMA_RESULT_NOT_TABLE_ OWNER
802D0003h	-2144534525	2150432771	IMA_RESULT_INVALID_QUERY
802D0004h	-2144534524	2150432772	IMA_RESULT_TABLE_OWNER_ HAS_CHANGED
802D0005h	-2144534523	2150432773	IMA_RESULT_SERVICE_NOT_ AVAILABLE
802D0006h	-2144534522	2150432774	IMA_RESULT_ZONE_MASTER_ UNKNOWN
802D0007h	-2144534521	2150432775	IMA_RESULT_NON_UNIQUE_ HOSTID
802D0008h	-2144534520	2150432776	IMA_RESULT_REG_VALUE_ NOT_FOUND
802D0009h	-2144534519	2150432777	IMA_RESULT_PARTIAL_LOAD
802D000Ah	-2144534518	2150432778	IMA_RESULT_GATEWAY_NOT_ ESTABLISHED
802D000Bh	-2144534517	2150432779	IMA_RESULT_INVALID_ GATEWAY
802D000Ch	-2144534516	2150432780	IMA_RESULT_SERVER_NOT_ AVAILABLE
80300001h	-2144337919	2150629377	IMA_RESULT_SERVICE_NOT_ SUPPORTED
80300002h	-2144337920	2150629378	IMA_RESULT_BUILD_SD_ FAILED

Table A-1. IMA Error Codes (continued)

Hex Value	Signed Value	Unsigned Value	Mnemonic
80300003h	-2144337921	2150629379	IMA_RESULT_RPC_USE_ ENDPOINT_FAILED
80300004h	-2144337922	2150629380	IMA_RESULT_RPC_REG_ INTERFACE_FAILED
80300005h	-2144337923	2150629381	IMA_RESULT_RPC_LISTEN_ FAILED
80300006h	-2144337924	2150629382	IMA_RESULT_BUILD_FILTER_ FAILED
80300007h	-2144337925	2150629383	IMA_RESULT_RPC_BUFFER_ TOO_SMALL
80300008h	-2144337926	2150629384	IMA_RESULT_REQUEST_ TICKET_FAILED
80300009h	-2144337927	2150629385	IMA_RESULT_INVALID_TICKET
8030000Ah	-2144337928	2150629386	IMA_RESULT_LOAD_ TICKETDLL_FAILED

Table A-1.   IMA Error Codes *(continued)*

IMA SUBSYSTEM TRACING

Table A-2 can be used with IMA Service Logging to determine which registry keys need to be activated for the various MetaFrame Presentation Server systems.

MetaFrame Presentation Server System	Subsystems to Trace
Application Management, Application Folders	ImaAdminSal
COM/SDK, Citrix Management Console	Remote Access
Common Application settings (LM, IM, MF, UNIX)	ImaAppSal, ImaAppSs
Common Server (common farm server properties and server enumeration)	ImaSrvSal, ImaSrvSs

Table A-2.   IMA Subsystem Tracing

MetaFrame Presentation Server System	Subsystems to Trace
Data store (including LHC)	Directory Subsystem, System\DataStoreDriver, Profiling\DataStore, Profiling\LHC, Runtime\PersistentStore
Dynamic Store	Runtime\DynamicStore, Profiling\DynamicStore
File Browsing	IMA_FileSS
Folder Enumeration	ImaGrpSal, IMAGroup
Host Resolver	Runtime\HostResolver
IMA Browser	IMA_Browser
IMA Program Interface (Terminal Services, other software)	ImaRpc, ImaLicRpc, ImaMfRpc
IMS	ImsSal
Load Management	LmsSal, LMS_Subsystem
MetaFrame Applications (enumeration and properties)	MfAppSal, MFApp
MetaFrame Server Properties (ICA Display, MetaFrame Settings)	MfSrvSal, MFSrvSs
Policy	Policy
Printer Management and Printer Drivers	MfPrintSal, IMA_Printer, ImaRelSal, IMARelationship
Printer Replication	ImaDistSal, IMADistribution
Program Neighborhood	MfPNSal
Remote Access	RemoteAccess, Remote Access
Runtime	Runtime\Runtime
Service Locator	Runtime\ServiceLocator
Subscription Manager	Runtime\SubscriptionManager
User Management (User Lists, Viewing, Launching Applications, and Network Printer Autocreation)	ImaUserSal, IMA_AAMS, WinDrvSS, NDSDrvSS
Zone Manager	Runtime\ZoneManager

Table A-2.   IMA Subsystem Tracing *(continued)*

MetaFrame Presentation Server Console Error Codes

Table A-3 displays the MetaFrame Presentation Server Console error codes. Information in the "Error Comes From" column refers to a plug-in module or a subsystem call. This information may be required by Citrix Technical Support if you place a call for support.

Error Code (Decimal)	Error Code (Hex)	Error Message	Error Comes From
	c0160a96	An error occurred while attempting to retrieve the backup Farm Metric Server details. The error returned was: ~0~.	ResourceMgr
	c0160a97	An error occurred while attempting to set the Farm Metric Servers. The error returned was: ~0~.	ResourceMgr
	c0160a98	The backup Farm Metric Server may not be identical to the primary Farm Metric Server. Please choose a different backup Farm Metric Server.	ResourceMgr
	c0160a99	No alarm objects have been returned from the monitor.	ResourceMgr
	c0160a9a	Cannot retrieve counter instance names.	ResourceMgr
	c0160aaa	Could not retrieve the list of ignored processes.	ResourceMgr
	c0160aab	Could not save the new list of ignored processes.	ResourceMgr
	c0160aac	Could not save the new list of ignored processes: ~0~.	ResourceMgr

Table A-3.   MetaFrame Presentation Server Console Error Codes

Error Code (Decimal)	Error Code (Hex)	Error Message	Error Comes From
	c0160abe	The application name is invalid. It cannot contain any of the following characters: ~0~.	ResourceMgr
	c0160abf	There was no response from Resource Manager.	ResourceMgr
	c0160ac0	An error occurred when attempting to create the application. The error returned was: ~0~.	ResourceMgr
	c0160ac3	You must specify an application name.	ResourceMgr
	c0160ac4	You must specify the full path and filename of the application.	ResourceMgr
	c0160ac5	You must select at least one server.	ResourceMgr
	c0160ac6	You have not provided a new application name.	ResourceMgr
	c0160ac7	This application name already exists. Please enter a different application name.	ResourceMgr
	c0160ac8	An error occurred when attempting to update the application properties. The error returned was: ~0~.	ResourceMgr
	c0160ac9	Error sending request for counter list from Farm Metric Server.	ResourceMgr
	c0160aca	Error talking to the monitor subsystem.	ResourceMgr

Table A-3.   MetaFrame Presentation Server Console Error Codes *(continued)*

Error Code (Decimal)	Error Code (Hex)	Error Message	Error Comes From
	c0160acc	Error updating application properties. Confirm that the data store can be accessed.	ResourceMgr
	c0160acd	An object with the same name already exists in the target folder!	ResourceMgr
	c0160ace	An unexpected error occurred when trying to move the application. The error returned was: ~0~.	ResourceMgr
	c0160acf	The application name can be no longer than ~0~ characters.	ResourceMgr
	c0160ad2	Error reading application metric properties information.	ResourceMgr
	c0160ad3	Error retrieving metric properties.	ResourceMgr
	c0160ad4	Error writing application metric properties information.	ResourceMgr
	c0160ad5	Error writing server metric properties information.	ResourceMgr
	c0160ad6	An error occurred while updating the application metrics.	ResourceMgr
	c0160ad7	An error occurred while updating the application metric properties.	ResourceMgr
	c0160ad8	SERVER_ADD_ REMOVE_METRICS_ WRITE_ERROR	ResourceMgr

Table A-3. MetaFrame Presentation Server Console Error Codes *(continued)*

Error Code (Decimal)	Error Code (Hex)	Error Message	Error Comes From
	c0160ad9	SERVER_RESTORE_ METRICS_WRITE_ ERROR	ResourceMgr
	c0160ae3	An unknown error occurred while trying to get the log for ~0~.	ResourceMgr
	c0160add	An unexpected error occurred retrieving the reboot message details. The error returned was: ~0~.	ResourceMgr
	c0160ade	An unexpected error occurred setting the reboot message details. The error returned was: ~0~.	ResourceMgr
	c0160af1	Error sending request for counter list from Farm Metric Server.	ResourceMgr
	c0160af2	The Farm Metric Server(s) cannot be contacted. This will cause Resource Manager to function incorrectly. Check that the Farm Metric Server(s) are running and can be contacted.	ResourceMgr
	c0160afb	Failed to set alerts configuration.	ResourceMgr
	c0160b00	Failed to set SNMP alerts configuration: ~0~.	ResourceMgr
	c0160b10	Must supply a gateway name.	ResourceMgr
	c0160b11	Must supply a username.	ResourceMgr

Table A-3.   MetaFrame Presentation Server Console Error Codes *(continued)*

Error Code (Decimal)	Error Code (Hex)	Error Message	Error Comes From
	c0160b12	Must supply a group name.	ResourceMgr
	c0160b13	Gateway "~0~" already exists.	ResourceMgr
	c0160b14	User or group name "~0~" already exists	ResourceMgr
	c0160b15	Illegal character(s) in phone number.	ResourceMgr
	c0160b16	Cannot add a user—configure a gateway first.	ResourceMgr
	c0160b17	Cannot add a group—configure a user first.	ResourceMgr
	c0160b18	Cannot delete gateway while a user item still refers to it.	ResourceMgr
	c0160b19	Illegal character(s) in prefix.	ResourceMgr
	c0160b22	Failed to retrieve report: ~0~.	ResourceMgr
	c0160b24	The report could not be saved. Check that the server is online, the location that the file is to be saved to exists, and that you have the necessary permissions to save files in that location.	ResourceMgr
	c0160b25	Failed to convert report: ~0~.	ResourceMgr
	c0160b4a	Resource Manager is not licensed.	ResourceMgr

Table A-3.   MetaFrame Presentation Server Console Error Codes *(continued)*

Error Code (Decimal)	Error Code (Hex)	Error Message	Error Comes From
	c0160b4b	Unable to contact IMA service running on ~0~.	ResourceMgr
	c0160b4c	Unable to contact IMA service running on ~0~.	ResourceMgr
	c0160b4d	Received an invalid packet from the IMA service running on ~0~.	ResourceMgr
	c0160b54	Failed to generate Server Summary report. Check that the DBMS and Database Connection Servers and the IMA connection to the Database Connection Server are working properly.	ResourceMgr
	c0160b55	Failed to generate User Summary report. Check that the DBMS and Database Connection Servers and the IMA connection to the Database Connection Server are working properly.	ResourceMgr
	c0160b56	Failed to generate Process Summary report. Check that the DBMS and Database Connection Servers and the IMA connection to the Database Connection Server are working properly.	ResourceMgr

Table A-3.   MetaFrame Presentation Server Console Error Codes *(continued)*

Error Code (Decimal)	Error Code (Hex)	Error Message	Error Comes From
	c0160b57	Failed to create Server Snapshot report.	ResourceMgr
	c0160b58	Failed to create Current User report.	ResourceMgr
	c0160b59	Failed to create Current Process report.	ResourceMgr
	c0160b5a	Unable to communicate with the Resource Manager Database Connection Server. Summary reports will not be available.	ResourceMgr
	c0160b5b	Unable to communicate with the Resource Manager Database Connection Server. Summary reports will not be available.	ResourceMgr
	c0160b5c	Unable to communicate with the Resource Manager Database Connection Server. Summary reports will not be available.	ResourceMgr
	c0160b5d	Unable to communicate with the Resource Manager local database. Current reports will not be available.	ResourceMgr
	c0160b5e	Unable to communicate with the Resource Manager local database. Current reports will not be available.	ResourceMgr

Table A-3.   MetaFrame Presentation Server Console Error Codes *(continued)*

Error Code (Decimal)	Error Code (Hex)	Error Message	Error Comes From
	c0160b5f	Unable to communicate with the Resource Manager local database. Current reports will not be available.	ResourceMgr
	c0160b60	The Summary Database does not contain enough information to generate a Process Summary report.	ResourceMgr
	c0160b61	The Summary Database contains no server information.	ResourceMgr
	c0160b62	The Summary Database does not contain enough information to generate a User Summary report.	ResourceMgr
	c0160b63	Failed to save reports.	ResourceMgr
	c0160b64	Unable to identify the Summary Database software versions. Summary Database functionality may not operate correctly in the Management Console.	ResourceMgr
	c0160b65	Unable to identify any Resource Manager summary database servers in the farm.	ResourceMgr
	c0160b66	All start times should be less than the stop times.	ResourceMgr
	c0160adc	Summary Database functionality cannot be enabled without a Database Connection Server being set.	ResourceMgr

Table A-3.   MetaFrame Presentation Server Console Error Codes *(continued)*

Error Code (Decimal)	Error Code (Hex)	Error Message	Error Comes From
	c0160b67	Unable to identify Database Connection Server.	ResourceMgr
	c0160b68	Error saving file ~0~. Check access permissions.	ResourceMgr
	c0160b69	Error setting the method of sending e-mail alerts.	ResourceMgr
	c0160b6a	Failed to read SMTP server configuration.	ResourceMgr
	c0160b6b	Failed to set SMTP server configuration.	ResourceMgr
	c0160b6c	Failed to set SMTP recipient addresses.	ResourceMgr
	c0160b6d	Failed to read SMTP recipient addresses.	ResourceMgr
500	1F4	A timeout has occurred! Please try again!	AdminMgr
510	1FE	A folder name cannot contain any of the following characters: \ / : * ? " < >		AdminMgr
511	1FF	Please enter a folder name!	AdminMgr
512	200	An object with the same name already exists in the target folder!	AdminMgr
513	201	Can't rename folder!	AdminMgr
514	202	The selected folder is not empty. A folder cannot be deleted until it is empty.	AdminMgr

Table A-3.   MetaFrame Presentation Server Console Error Codes *(continued)*

Error Code (Decimal)	Error Code (Hex)	Error Message	Error Comes From
515	203	Can't delete folder!	AdminMgr
516	204	The selected folder is not empty. A folder cannot be moved until it is empty.	AdminMgr
517	205	Can't move folder!	AdminMgr
518	206	A folder name cannot contain more than 256 characters!	AdminMgr
500	1F4	A timeout has occurred! Please try again!	ServerGrpMgr
512	200	Action failed!	ServerGrpMgr
1100		An unknown error occurred while loading <plugin name>. Its features will not be available during this session.	PluginMgr
1110		Farm Logon Error.	PluginMgr
1111		Pass-through Authentication failed; failed to connect to server <server>.	PluginMgr
1300	514	The ICA Display settings could not be changed.	ServerMgrNew
1301	515	The product code you entered was invalid. The server's product code has not been changed.	ServerMgrNew
1302	516	The product code you entered was invalid. None of the servers' product codes have been changed.	ServerMgrNew

Table A-3.   MetaFrame Presentation Server Console Error Codes *(continued)*

Error Code (Decimal)	Error Code (Hex)	Error Message	Error Comes From
1305	519	The product code could not be changed.	ServerMgrNew
1306	51A	The value entered for "maximum memory to use for each session's graphics" is invalid. Please enter a value between 150 kilobytes and 8192 kilobytes.	ServerMgrNew
1307	51B	Failed to change the listening TCP port for the Citrix XML Service!	ServerMgrNew
1308	51C	Some servers' product codes were changed, but some could not be.	ServerMgrNew
1309	51D	None of the servers' product codes could be changed.	ServerMgrNew
1311	51F	Please make sure that the Reset value is greater or equal than the Set value.	ServerMgrNew
1312	520	Session information is not available for this session. User information will be refreshed.	ServerMgrNew
1313	521	Failed to disconnect session. User information will be refreshed.	ServerMgrNew
1314	522	Failed to connect session. User information will be refreshed.	ServerMgrNew

Table A-3.   MetaFrame Presentation Server Console Error Codes *(continued)*

Error Code (Decimal)	Error Code (Hex)	Error Message	Error Comes From
1314	522	Wrong password. Letters in passwords must be typed using the correct case. Make sure that Caps Lock is not accidentally on.	ServerMgrNew
1315	523	Failed to reset session. User information will be refreshed.	ServerMgrNew
1316	524	Unable to send message to the selected session. User information will be refreshed.	ServerMgrNew
1317	525	Status information is not available for this session. User information will be refreshed.	ServerMgrNew
1318	526	Unable to collect process data for this server. The request timed out.	ServerMgrNew
1319	527	Unable to collect session data for this server. The request timed out.	ServerMgrNew
1320	528	The Auto Client Reconnect settings could not be changed.	ServerMgrNew
1330	532	Please choose a Feature Release level.	ServerMgrNew
1331	533	The Feature Release level could not be changed.	ServerMgrNew

Table A-3. MetaFrame Presentation Server Console Error Codes *(continued)*

Error Code (Decimal)	Error Code (Hex)	Error Message	Error Comes From
1340	53C	The File Type Association settings could not be changed.	ServerMgrNew
1341	53D	The Enable Logon settings could not be changed.	ServerMgrNew
1350	546	The ICA KeepAlive settings could not be changed.	ServerMgrNew
1351	547	The entered ICA KeepAlive timeout value is invalid. Please enter a value between 1 and 3600 seconds.	ServerMgrNew
1360	550	The SpeedScreen settings could not be changed.	ServerMgrNew
1370	55A	Could not enumerate published applications for this server.	ServerMgrNew
1380	564	Error changing the Connect to Console setting.	ServerMgrNew
1600	640	A zone with the same name already exists!	IMACoreSettingsMgr
1601	641	A zone cannot be deleted until all servers have been removed from it!	IMACoreSettingsMgr
1602	642	A zone must contain at least one server!	IMACoreSettingsMgr
5556	15B4	An internal error occurred while loading default icons.	Ext.Widgets.IconChooser

Table A-3. MetaFrame Presentation Server Console Error Codes *(continued)*

Error Code (Decimal)	Error Code (Hex)	Error Message	Error Comes From
5650	1612	The data store is not available. Some features may not be available.	Ext.Framework.Tools
2147483659	8000000B	The operation to remove the server from farm has timed out, but it may have succeeded.	AdminUserMgr
2147483692	8000002C	The persistent store server cannot be removed.	AdminUserMgr
2148598021	80110105	The load evaluator name is already being used. Please use a different name.	LMSAdmin
2148598022	80110106	Cannot delete the default evaluator.	LMSAdmin
2148598023	80110107	The load evaluator is still in use. Please detach the load evaluator from any servers or applications before deleting.	LMSAdmin
2148598022	80110106	Cannot delete the default evaluator or load evaluators that are still in use. Please detach the load evaluators from any servers or applications before deleting.	LMSAdmin

Table A-3. MetaFrame Presentation Server Console Error Codes *(continued)*

Error Code (Decimal)	Error Code (Hex)	Error Message	Error Comes From
2148598023	80110107	At least one load evaluator could not be deleted because it is still in use. Please detach the load evaluators from any servers or applications before deleting.	LMSAdmin
Various	Various	At least one load evaluator could not be deleted.	LMSAdmin
2149318670	801C000E	The server is still reachable, and cannot be removed. It should be removed by uninstall program.	AdminUserMgr
3221553157	C0050005	Could not read application data from the Citrix server farm.	MetaFramePubAppMgr
3221553158	C0050006	Could not write application data to the Citrix server farm.	MetaFramePubAppMgr
3221553159	C0050007	Could not delete application data from the Citrix server farm.	MetaFramePubAppMgr
3221553162	C005000A	Display Name not specified.	MetaFramePubAppMgr
3221553163	C005000B	The Display Name already exists in this application folder.	MetaFramePubAppMgr
3221553166	C005000E	The Application Name cannot contain any of the following characters: \ / ; : . * ? = < > | [ ] ( ) ' "	MetaFramePubAppMgr

Table A-3. MetaFrame Presentation Server Console Error Codes *(continued)*

Error Code (Decimal)	Error Code (Hex)	Error Message	Error Comes From
3221553167	C005000F	The command line is required to publish an application. Enter the path and filename of the application's executable file in the Command Line box.	MetaFramePubAppMgr
3221553167	C005000F	The content address is required to publish a content. Enter the UNC or the URL address for the content.	MetaFramePubAppMgr
3221553170	C0050012	The window size specified is too small.	MetaFramePubAppMgr
3221553171	C0050013	The window size specified is too large.	MetaFramePubAppMgr
3221553173	C0050015	File paths cannot contain any of the following characters: / * ? " < > |	MetaFramePubAppMgr
3221553174	C0050016	The ICA filename you entered cannot be found. Use the Browse button to locate and select the ICA file.	MetaFramePubAppMgr
3221553175	C0050017	Unable to write the file to disk.	MetaFramePubAppMgr
3221553178	C005001A	The Display Name cannot contain any of the following characters: \ / ; : . * ? = < > | [ ] ( ) ' "	MetaFramePubAppMgr

Table A-3. MetaFrame Presentation Server Console Error Codes *(continued)*

Error Code (Decimal)	Error Code (Hex)	Error Message	Error Comes From
3221553180	C005001C	The application has a minimum required encryption level of: <level>. You cannot create an ICA file with an encryption level less than this.	MetaFramePubAppMgr
3221553181	C005001D	The application has a minimum audio requirement. You must specify an audio setting.	MetaFramePubAppMgr
3221553182	C005001E	You must enter a TCP/IP port between 1 and 65536.	MetaFramePubAppMgr
3221553182	C005001E	You must specify a server to get browsing information from.	MetaFramePubAppMgr
3221553186	C0050022	The Application Name may only have a maximum of 38 ANSI characters, or 19 Unicode characters.	MetaFramePubAppMgr
3221553187	C0050023	The selected application may not have been published because the request has timed out. If the published application does not appear in Citrix Management Console, please try again.	MetaFramePubAppMgr
3221553188	C0050024	The selected published application could not be copied because the data cannot be accessed from the data store.	MetaFramePubAppMgr

Table A-3.   MetaFrame Presentation Server Console Error Codes *(continued)*

Error Code (Decimal)	Error Code (Hex)	Error Message	Error Comes From
3221553189	C0050025	You cannot change the properties of an application published with an updated version of MetaFrame XP. To edit the properties, you must connect to a MetaFrame XP server with the latest service pack installed or install the latest service pack on all MetaFrame XP servers in your farm.	MetaFramePubAppMgr
3221553190	C0050026	The ICA file was not created because a server hosting the application did not respond. Please try again.	MetaFramePubAppMgr
3221553191	C0050027	The Application Name already exists in the server farm.	MetaFramePubAppMgr
3221553192	C0050028	Filename cannot exceed 255 characters.	MetaFramePubAppMgr
3222470657	C0130001	Failed to add Network Print Server <servername>.	PrinterMgr
3222470658	C0130002	The specified Network Print Server has already been added.	PrinterMgr
3222470659	C0130003	The specified Network Print Server could not be contacted or has no printers.	PrinterMgr
3222470660	C0130004	You must enter a username.	PrinterMgr

Table A-3. MetaFrame Presentation Server Console Error Codes *(continued)*

Error Code (Decimal)	Error Code (Hex)	Error Message	Error Comes From
3222470661	C0130005	Failed to delete Network Print Server *<servername>*.	PrinterMgr
3222470662	C0130006	Failed to refresh Network Print Server data for server *<servername>*.	PrinterMgr
3222470663	C0130007	Could not enumerate all printers.	PrinterMgr
3222470664	C0130008	Could not enumerate printers for server *<servername>*.	PrinterMgr
3222470665	C0130009	Could not enumerate all drivers.	PrinterMgr
3222470666	C013000A	Could not enumerate drivers for server *<servername>*.	PrinterMgr
3222470667	C013000B	Could not enumerate MetaFrame servers for this farm.	PrinterMgr
3222470668	C013000C	Could not enumerate servers that have print driver *<drivername>*.	PrinterMgr
3222470669	C013000D	Replication failed.	PrinterMgr
3222470670	C013000E	Replication from server *<servername>* failed.	PrinterMgr
3222470671	C013000F	The drivers you selected are for different platforms. When selecting multiple drivers, all drivers must be for the same platform.	PrinterMgr

Table A-3. MetaFrame Presentation Server Console Error Codes *(continued)*

Error Code (Decimal)	Error Code (Hex)	Error Message	Error Comes From
3222470672	C0130010	Could not enumerate operating system platforms.	PrinterMgr
3222470673	C0130011	The specified driver already exists in the Compatibility list.	PrinterMgr
3222470674	C0130012	Failed to set Compatibility list.	PrinterMgr
3222470675	C0130013	Could not enumerate Driver Mapping list.	PrinterMgr
3222470676	C0130014	Failed to set Driver Mapping list.	PrinterMgr
3222470677	C0130015	Could not enumerate bandwidth limits.	PrinterMgr
3222470678	C0130016	Failed to set bandwidth limits.	PrinterMgr
3222470680	C0130018	Could not enumerate users and groups configured for printer *<printername>*.	PrinterMgr
3222470681	C0130019	Could not enumerate all users and groups for specified domain.	PrinterMgr
3222470682	C013001A	Failed to set Autocreation settings for printer *<printername>*.	PrinterMgr
3222470684	C013001C	Failed to copy Autocreation settings from printer *<printername>*.	PrinterMgr
3222470685	C013001D	Could not enumerate Client Printer list.	PrinterMgr

Table A-3. MetaFrame Presentation Server Console Error Codes *(continued)*

Error Code (Decimal)	Error Code (Hex)	Error Message	Error Comes From
3222470686	C013001E	The specified client printer already exists in the list.	PrinterMgr
3222470687	C013001F	The specified port has already been assigned for this client.	PrinterMgr
3222470688	C0130020	Could not enumerate Autoreplication list.	PrinterMgr
3222470689	C0130021	Failed to set Autoreplication list.	PrinterMgr
3222470690	C0130022	Could not enumerate Compatibility list.	PrinterMgr
3222470691	C0130023	The specified client driver already exists in the Mapping list.	PrinterMgr
3222470692	C0130024	Could not enumerate domains.	PrinterMgr
3222470693	C0130025	Failed to set Client Printer list.	PrinterMgr
3222470694	C0130026	Failed to determine operating system platform for one or more servers in the farm. These servers cannot be used as destinations for printer driver replication actions.	PrinterMgr
3222470695	C0130027	The printer management system on the preferred server could not be contacted. You will not be able to make changes to printer-related data.	PrinterMgr

Table A-3.   MetaFrame Presentation Server Console Error Codes *(continued)*

Error Code (Decimal)	Error Code (Hex)	Error Message	Error Comes From
3222470696	C0130028	Could not enumerate servers with the print driver <drivername>.	PrinterMgr
3222470697	C0130029	The names of some users could not be obtained.	PrinterMgr
3222470698	C013002A	Could not get the platform for server <servername>.	PrinterMgr
3222470699	C013002B	Could not enumerate Network Print Servers.	PrinterMgr
3222470700	C013002C	Failed to get driver for printer <servername>.	PrinterMgr
3222470701	C013002D	The specified domain does not exist or does not trust the farm.	PrinterMgr
3222470704	C0130030	The specified driver has been marked incompatible with all server platforms in the farm.	PrinterMgr
3222470705	C0130031	Search failed.	PrinterMgr
3222503424	C0138000	An unknown error occurred.	PrinterMgr
3222503425	C0138001	General failure.	PrinterMgr
3222503426	C0138002	There is not enough memory to complete the operation.	PrinterMgr
3222503428	C0138004	There are not enough resources to complete the operation.	PrinterMgr
3222503429	C0138005	The item was not found.	PrinterMgr

Table A-3. MetaFrame Presentation Server Console Error Codes *(continued)*

Error Code (Decimal)	Error Code (Hex)	Error Message	Error Comes From
3222503430	C0138006	The operation timed out.	PrinterMgr
3222503431	C0138007	Enumeration failed.	PrinterMgr
3222503432	C0138008	Access is denied.	PrinterMgr
3222503433	C0138009	Network failure.	PrinterMgr
3222503434	C013800A	The destination could not be found.	PrinterMgr
3222503440	C0138010	The server could not be contacted.	PrinterMgr
3222503442	C0138012	Authentication failed.	PrinterMgr
3222503443	C0138013	The domain controller could not be contacted.	PrinterMgr
3222503444	C0138014	The item already exists.	PrinterMgr
3222503445	C0138015	The server is part of the farm.	PrinterMgr
3222503446	C0138016	The network server has already been added.	PrinterMgr
3222503447	C0138017	Could not read from event.	PrinterMgr
3222798336/ Various	C0180000/ Various	Could not enumerate the user accounts in this domain. There might be communication problems on the network.	UserEnumeration
3222798337	C0180001	Could not collect required user account information for some or all of the accounts from this domain. These users will not be added to Configured Accounts list.	UserEnumeration

Table A-3.   MetaFrame Presentation Server Console Error Codes *(continued)*

Error Code (Decimal)	Error Code (Hex)	Error Message	Error Comes From
3222798338	C0180002	The domain controller for this domain is not available.	UserEnumeration
3222798339	C0180003	One or more servers selected to host this application have failed to complete the initial startup sequence. The server(s) will not be available for publishing applications until the IMA service is restarted.	UserEnumeration
3222798340	C0180004	The accounts trusted by the selected servers could not be determined.	UserEnumeration
3222798341	C0180005	Could not enumerate domains.	UserEnumeration
Various	Various	Could not attach load evaluator to this server.	LMSAdmin
Various	Various	Could not create a new load evaluator.	LMSAdmin
Various	Various	Could not delete the load evaluator.	LMSAdmin
Various	Various	Could not get the list of servers attached to the application.	LMSAdmin
Various	Various	Could not modify the load evaluator.	LMSAdmin
Various	Various	The Citrix Management Console failed to remove the server.	AdminUserMgr

Table A-3.   MetaFrame Presentation Server Console Error Codes *(continued)*

Error Code (Decimal)	Error Code (Hex)	Error Message	Error Comes From
2301	8FD	An error occurred while retrieving information from Installation Manager. The information displayed may be incomplete. If the problem persists, contact Citrix Technical Support.	IMSMgr
	80240008	IM network browser failed.	IMSMgr
	80240002	Installer failed (usually ADF installer since MSI has its own error codes).	IMSMgr
	80240003	Logon to the network share account failed.	IMSMgr
	80240001	No network share point account is specified.	IMSMgr
	80240005	Package is in use and cannot be modified.	IMSMgr
	80240004	Package with the same name already exists.	IMSMgr
	80240006	The operation is not allowed; for example, a job cannot be modified after it is started.	IMSMgr
	80240007	The package file provided (when adding a package to the data store) is not a valid (MSI or ADF) package.	IMSMgr

Table A-3.   MetaFrame Presentation Server Console Error Codes *(continued)*

RESOURCE MANAGER BILLING ERROR CODES

Table A-4 lists the Resource Manager error codes returned from the Billing module.

Error Code	Error Message Returned	Cause/Solution
803a001	The Summary Database version information could not be found in the database. Billing reports will not be available.	Returned if either the Summary Database table SCHEMAVERSION contains no rows or there is no table (i.e., the Database Connection Server is pointing to a database that is not the Summary Database).
803a002	An error occurred while trying to enumerate user accounts in domain group, contained within a cost center. The billing report cannot be generated.	Returned if the Billing subsystem cannot enumerate a domain or local group in a cost center. This could fail because of not being able to contact a domain controller or insufficient permissions for local groups. More detailed information is written to the Database Connection Server's server log file.
803a004	An error occurred while generating the report.	Each time a report is generated, it is assigned a unique ID by the Billing subsystem. This error message will be displayed if this matches any ID already assigned to a report. The chances of this occurring are minimal.
803a005	An error occurred while generating the report.	The Billing subsystem limits the amount of report data to be retrieved by the Database Connection Server to 60,000 lines. This error message will be returned if the user is trying to generate a report that exceeds this limit. It is designed to prevent the IMA Service consuming excessive memory. To work around the problem, the user should narrow the reporting conditions or reduce the detail of the report.

Table A-4.   Resource Manager Billing Error Codes

Error Code	Error Message Returned	Cause/Solution
803a0013	An error occurred when trying to connect to the Summary Database.	Returned if the Billing subsystem cannot connect to the Summary Database—either the Database Connection Server configuration is incorrect or the subsystem cannot contact the Database Connection Server. More detailed information is written to the Database Connection Server's server log file.
803a0014	An error occurred when executing a database query.	Returned if any of the Billing Stored Procedures fail. More detailed information is returned to the Database Connection Server server log file. A possible cause could be a corrupted summary database schema.
803a0015	An error occurred while generating the report.	Returned if the Database Connection Server can not close the connection to the summary database after generating a billing report. More detailed information is written to the Database Connection Server log file.
803a0017	The version of the Summary Database is not compatible with this version of Resource Manager. Billing reports will not be available.	Returned if the schema is correct but the version in the Summary Database does not match that held in the subsystem. When a farm is upgraded, the schema version is updated. However, a user could see this problem if they were connecting an "old" farm (e.g., Feature Release 2) to a "new" Summary Database (e.g., Feature Release 3).
803a0018	The Summary Database DBMS type is not supported by Resource Manager. Billing reports will not be available.	Returned if the user is attempting to use a database that is not supported for the Summary Database (e.g., IBM DB2).

Table A-4.   Resource Manager Billing Error Codes *(continued)*

Error Code	Error Message Returned	Cause/Solution
803a0019	The fees that are used to calculate the costs in this Billing report have not been configured. Do you want to continue with the generation of the report?	Not an error message; more just a warning telling the user that they are attempting to generate a Billing report without having selected any of the configured fee profiles.
803a0020	The fees that will be used to calculate the costs in this Billing report were entered from a Management Console running in a different country. No currency conversion is performed. This may result in incorrect costs being calculated. Do you want to continue with the generation of the report?	Cause is as stated in message.
803a0021	An error occurred while generating the report.	Returned if the Reports subsystem has returned corrupted data to the Billing subsystem to be displayed.
803a0022	An error occurred retrieving the DBMS user credentials from the Database Connection Server. Billing reports will not be available.	Returned if the Database Connection Server is unable to provide the DSN connection details to the Billing subsystem via the Summary Database subsystem.
803f0001	The Billing HTML template file could not be found.	Returned if there is no template with which to create the Billing report.

Table A-4.   Resource Manager Billing Error Codes *(continued)*

GENERAL EVENT LOG WARNING AND ERROR MESSAGES

Table A-5 lists the Event log warning and error messages created in the Windows Server 2000 or 2003 Event Viewer by MetaFrame Presentation Server and its components.

Message ID	Type	Severity	Message Text
3584	System	Error	Failed to open system registry key with error %1.
3585	System	Error	Failed to initialize registrar component with error %1.
3586	System	Error	Failed to prepare the transport system for operation with error %1.
3587	System	Error	Incompatible WinSock version.
3588	System	Error	Failed to prepare the messaging system for operation with error %1.
3589	System	Error	Invalid FailedComponentId (%1).
3590	System	Error	Failed to prepare the plugin system with error %1.
3591	System	Error	Failed to initialize all components with error %1.
3592	System	Error	Failed to start transport with error %1.
3593	System	Error	Failed to create a new message port with error %1.
3594	System	Error	Failed to create an event queue with error %1.
3595	System	Error	Failed to load initial plugins with error %1.
3596	System	Error	Failed to unload initial plugin with error %1.
3597	System	Error	Failed to unload subsystems with error %2.
3598	System	Error	Failed to destroy system event queue with error %1.
3599	System	Error	Failed to stop transport with error %1.
3600	System	Error	Failed to stop system with error %1.
3601	System	Error	Failed to uninitialize system with error %1.
3602	System	Error	Failed to start system with error %1.
3603	System	Error	Failed to load plugin %1 with error %2.
3604	System	Error	Failed to initiate RPC for Remote Access Subsystem with error %1.

Table A-5.   Event Log Warning and Error Messages

Message ID	Type	Severity	Message Text
3605	System	Error	Failed to connect to the database. Error - %1: Increase the number of processes available to the database. See MetaFrame XP documentation for details.
3606	System	Error	The Citrix MetaFrame XP Server failed to connect to the data store. Error - %1: Invalid database username or password. Please make sure they are correct. If not, use **DSMAINT CONFIG** to change them.
3607	System	Error	Failed to connect to the database with error. Error - %1: The ACCESS .mdb file is missing.
3608	System	Error	The Citrix MetaFrame XP Server failed to connect to the data store. Error - %1: The database is down or there is a network failure.
3609	System	Error	The Citrix MetaFrame XP Server failed to connect to the data store. Error - %1: An unknown failure occurred while connecting to the database.
3610	System	Error	Configuration error: Failed to read the farm name out of the registry on a server configured to access the data store directly.
3611	System	Error	Configuration error: Failed to get the farm name from the data store proxy server with error %1. This server is configured to access the data store indirectly. The server specified as the data store proxy is not available. Verify that the data store proxy server is accessible and that the IMA service is started on it.
3612	System	Error	Configuration error: Failed to open IMA registry key.
3613	System	Error	96 hours have passed since last successful connection to the data store. This server will no longer accept connections until successful connection to the data store is established.

Table A-5. Event Log Warning and Error Messages *(continued)*

Message ID	Type	Severity	Message Text
3614	System	Warning	The Citrix MetaFrame XP Server failed to connect to the data store. Error - %1: Invalid database username or password. Please make sure they are correct. If not, use **DSMAINT CONFIG** to change them.
3615	System	Warning	The Citrix MetaFrame XP Server failed to connect to the data store. Error - %1: The database is down or there is a network failure.
3616	System	Warning	The Citrix MetaFrame XP Server failed to connect to the data store. Error - %1: An unknown failure occurred while connecting to the database.
3840	System	Error	Unable to bind to group context in data store. Group consistency check will not run. (Result: %1)
3841	System	Error	Unable to locate groups in data store at DN %1. Group consistency check will not run. (Result: %2)
3842	System	Error	Group Consistency Check: Group at DN %1 is missing the GroupMember Attribute.
3843	System	Error	Group Consistency Check: Group at DN %1 contained reference to an unknown object with type %3 and UID %2.
3844	System	Error	Group Consistency Check: Group at DN %3 contains an object with UID %1 and type %2. This object is missing the %4 attribute.
3845	System	Error	Group Consistency Check: Group at DN %3 contains an object with UID %1 and type %2. This object is missing the value for the %4 attribute.
3872	System	Error	Unable to bind to server contexts in data store. Server consistency check will not run. (Result: %1)

Table A-5.   Event Log Warning and Error Messages *(continued)*

Message ID	Type	Severity	Message Text
3873	System	Error	Server Consistency Check: Unable to locate host records in data store. The server host record consistency check will not run. (Result: %1)
3874	System	Error	Server Consistency Check: Unable to locate common server records in data store. The common server consistency check will not run. (Result: %1)
3875	System	Error	Server Consistency Check: Unable to locate MetaFrame Server records in data store. The MetaFrame server consistency check will not run. (Result: %1)
3876	System	Error	Server Consistency Check: Host record for HostName %2 at DN %1 references a Common Server record that cannot be found in the data store.
3877	System	Error	Server Consistency Check: Host record for HostName %2 at DN %1 references a Common Server record that has a HostName of %3. This mismatch is an error.
3878	System	Error	Server Consistency Check: Host record for HostName %2 at DN %1 references a Common Server record that cannot be found in the data store. (Result: %3)
3879	System	Error	Server Consistency Check: Common Server record for HostName %2 at DN %1 references a Host record that cannot be found in the data store.
3880	System	Error	Server Consistency Check: Common Server record for HostName %2 at DN %1 has a HostID of %3. The corresponding Host record has a HostID of %4. This mismatch is an error.

Table A-5.   Event Log Warning and Error Messages *(continued)*

Message ID	Type	Severity	Message Text
3881	System	Error	Server Consistency Check: Common Server record for HostName %2 at DN %1 references a Host record that cannot be found in the data store. (Result: %3)
3882	System	Error	Server Consistency Check: The Common Server record with HostName %1 at DN %2 is invalid. There is no registered server product for this record.
3883	System	Error	Server Consistency Check: The Common Server record with HostName %1 at DN %2 is invalid. The corresponding MetaFrame Server record cannot be accessed.
3884	System	Error	Server Consistency Check: The MetaFrame Server record with HostName %1 at DN %2 is invalid. The associated Common Server UID is not set.
3885	System	Error	Server Consistency Check: The MetaFrame Server record with HostName %1 at DN %2 is invalid. The associated Common Server record cannot be accessed.
3886	System	Error	Server Consistency Check: The MetaFrame Server record with HostName %1 at DN %2 may be invalid. The MetaFrame Server record HostID of %3 does not match the Common Server record HostID of %4.
3887	System	Error	Server Consistency Check: The MetaFrame Server record with HostName %1 at DN %2 is invalid. The associated Common Server record has a different HostName (%3).
3888	System	Error	Server Consistency Check: Unable to locate Load Manager for MetaFrame XP Server entry for HostName %1. (Result: %2)
3889	System	Error	Server Consistency Check: The MetaFrame Server record with HostName %1 at DN %2 may be invalid. The Load Manager for MetaFrame XP Server entry was not found.

Table A-5.   Event Log Warning and Error Messages *(continued)*

Message ID	Type	Severity	Message Text
3890	System	Error	Server Consistency Check: The MetaFrame Server record with HostName %1 at DN %2 is invalid. The associated Account Authority Server record was not found.
3904	System	Error	Unable to bind to application contexts in data store. Application consistency check will not run. (Result: %1)
3905	System	Error	Application Consistency Check: Unable to locate Common Application records in the data store. Common application consistency check will not run. (Result: %1)
3906	System	Error	Application Consistency Check: Unable to locate MetaFrame Application records in the data store. MetaFrame application consistency check will not run. (Result: %1)
3907	System	Error	Application Consistency Check: The Common Application record at DN %1 does not have a Friendly Name. (Result: %2)
3908	System	Error	Application Consistency Check: The Common Application record at DN %1 does not have a Browser Name. (Result: %2)
3909	System	Error	Application Consistency Check: The Common Application record with FriendlyName %1 at DN %2 does not have a specialized application UID. (Result: %3)
3910	System	Error	Application Consistency Check: The Common Application record with Friendly Name %1 at DN %2 references a MetaFrame Application record that cannot be accessed. (Result: %3)
3911	System	Error	Application Consistency Check: The Common Application record with Friendly Name %1 at DN %2 references a MetaFrame Application record. This record does not have a Friendly Name. (Result: %3)

Table A-5. Event Log Warning and Error Messages *(continued)*

Message ID	Type	Severity	Message Text
3912	System	Error	Application Consistency Check: The Common Application record with Friendly Name %1 at DN %2 references a MetaFrame Application record. This record does not have a Browser Name. (Result: %3)
3913	System	Error	Application Consistency Check: The Common Application record at DN %2 has a Friendly Name of %1. The corresponding MetaFrame Application record has a Friendly Name of %3. This mismatch is an error.
3914	System	Error	Application Consistency Check: The Common Application record at DN %2 has a Browser Name of %1. The corresponding MetaFrame Application record has a Browser Name of %3. This mismatch is an error.
3915	System	Error	Application Consistency Check: The MetaFrame Application record at DN %1 does not have a Friendly Name. (Result: %2)
3916	System	Error	Application Consistency Check: The MetaFrame Application record at DN %1 does not have a Browser Name. (Result: %2)
3917	System	Error	Application Consistency Check: The MetaFrame Application record with Friendly Name %1 at DN %2 does not have a common application UID. (Result: %3)
3918	System	Error	Application Consistency Check: The MetaFrame Application record with Friendly Name %1 at DN %2 references a Common Application record (UID %3) that cannot be accessed. (Result: %4)
3919	System	Error	Application Consistency Check: The MetaFrame Application record with Friendly Name %1 at DN %2 references a Common Application record. This record does not have a Friendly Name. (Result: %3)

Table A-5. Event Log Warning and Error Messages *(continued)*

Message ID	Type	Severity	Message Text
3920	System	Error	Application Consistency Check: The MetaFrame Application record with Friendly Name %1 at DN %2 references a Common Application record. This record does not have a Browser Name. (Result: %3)
3921	System	Error	Application Consistency Check: The MetaFrame Application record at DN %2 has a Friendly Name of %1. The corresponding Common Application record has a Friendly Name of %3. This mismatch is an error.
3922	System	Error	Application Consistency Check: The MetaFrame Application record at DN %2 has a Browser Name of %1. The corresponding Common Application record has a Browser Name of %3. This mismatch is an error.
3936	System	Error	Common Application cleanup, deleting record at DN <%1>
3937	System	Error	MetaFrame Application cleanup, deleting record at DN <%1>
3938	System	Error	MetaFrame Server cleanup, deleting record at DN <%1>
3939	System	Error	Common Server cleanup, deleting record at DN <%1>
3940	System	Error	Server Host Record cleanup, deleting record at DN <%1>
3952	System	Error	Unable to open Citrix Runtime registry key. Application terminated. (Status: %1)
3953	System	Error	Unable to read Neighborhood name from registry. Application terminated. (Status: %1)
3954	System	Error	Unable to initialize Data Store connection. This server must have a direct connection to the data store. Application terminated. (Result: %1)
3956	System	Error	Data Store Validation Utility. Version: %1.

Table A-5.   Event Log Warning and Error Messages *(continued)*

Message ID	Type	Severity	Message Text
3957	System	Error	Unable to initialize Event Log. Messages will be displayed on console only.
3958	System	Error	Some consistency checks were unsuccessful. Results below indicate the number of errors or -1 for test not run: Server Errors = %1, Application Errors = %2, Group Errors = %3.
3959	System	Error	All consistency checks were successful.
3960	System	Error	Some consistency checks were unsuccessful. Results below indicate the number of errors or -1 for test not run: Server Errors = %1, Application Errors = %2, Group Errors = %3.
3961	System	Error	The Data Collector is out of memory, and the Dynamic Store data might be out of sync. Please elect a new Data Collector and make sure you have enough memory on the new Data Collector.

Table A-5. Event Log Warning and Error Messages *(continued)*

APPENDIX B

Registered Citrix Ports

It is often helpful to know what ports are being utilized by software so that security and access can be configured, optimized, and maintained. Table B-1 lists the ports that MetaFrame Presentation Server and its components utilize.

Name	Number	Protocol	Description
ica	1494	TCP	ICA
ica	1494	UDP	<not used>
ica	0x85BB	IPX	ICA
ica	0x9010	SPX	ICA
icabrowser	1604	TCP	<not used>
icabrowser	1604	UDP	ICA Browser
icabrowser	0x85BA	IPX	ICA Browser
citrixima	2512	TCP	IMA (server to server)
citrixima	2512	UDP	<not used>
citrixadmin	2513	TCP	IMA (CMC to server)
citrixadmin	2513	UDP	<not used>
citriximaclient	2598	TCP	Common Gateway Protocol (Session Reliability)
citriximaclient	2598	UDP	<not used>
citrix-rtmp	2897	TCP	rtmp (Control) Video Frame
citrix-rtmp	2897	UDP	rtmp (Streaming Data) Video Frame
Citrix Systems	3845	MIB	Private Enterprise Number; used for SNMP MIB Object ID and Active Directory Schema Object IDs (OIDs)

Table B-1.   Registered Citrix Ports

APPENDIX C

Client Files, Folder Locations, and Registry Entries

The purpose of this appendix is to outline the various files, locations, and registry entries that are added to a system when MetaFrame Presentation Server Client for 32-bit Windows (Program Neighborhood Client), Web Client, and Program Neighborhood Agent are installed onto a client machine. This information is relevant only to a PC client (as apposed to a thin-client device).

CLIENT FILES, FOLDER LOCATIONS, AND REGISTRY ENTRIES FOR THE PROGRAM NEIGHBORHOOD CLIENT

This section outlines the various files, locations, and registry entries that are added to a system when the Program Neighborhood Client is installed onto a client machine.

The Program Neighborhood Client may be installed using one of the following packages:

▼ **ica32.exe**   A self-extracting executable, approximately 4.0MB in size (compressed).

▲ **ica32pkg.msi**   A Windows Installer package for use with Windows 2000 Active Directory Services or Microsoft Systems Management Server, approximately 3.1MB in size (compressed).

For more information on the Program Neighborhood Client software, see the Client for 32-bit Windows Administrator's Guide and the MetaFrame Presentation Server Administrator's Guide.

Regardless of which package is used, they both install the same files and registry entries.

NOTE: Some files and registry entries that are added/modified are specific to the installer program used. These files and registry entries will not be covered in this chapter.

Program Neighborhood Client Files

This section lists the folders, files, and other details added when the Program Neighborhood Client is installed (the locations provided are for a default installation).

New Folders Created

The following new folders are created upon installation of the Program Neighborhood Client:

%ProgramFiles%\Citrix\
%ProgramFiles%\Program Files\Citrix\ICA Client
%ProgramFiles%\Program Files\Citrix\ICA Client\Cache
%ProgramFiles%\Program Files\Citrix\ICA Client\Resource
%ProgramFiles%\Program Files\Citrix\ICA Client\Resource\EN

New Files Added into the Folders

Table C-1 lists the file and folder structure of the Program Neighborhood Client installation. The default base installation is in %ProgramFiles%\Citrix\ICA Client.

%ProgramFiles%\Citrix			
ICA CLIENT	DIR	%DATE%	6:06:15 P.M.
%ProgramFiles%\Citrix\ICA CLIENT			
CACHE	DIR	%DATE%	6:06:08 P.M.
RESOURCE	DIR	%DATE%	6:06:08 P.M.
acrdlg.dll	28.3 KB (28944 bytes)	2/21/2004	12:17:20 A.M.
adpcm.dll	32.3 KB (33040 bytes)	2/21/2004	12:17:20 A.M.
appsrv.ini	1.8 KB (1871 bytes)	%DATE%	6:06:20 P.M.
appsrv.src	1.7 KB (1738 bytes)	12/1/2003	10:40:04 P.M.
audcvtN.dll	32.3 KB (33040 bytes)	2/21/2004	12:17:20 A.M.
cgpcfg.dll	20.3 KB (20752 bytes)	2/21/2004	12:17:20 A.M.
CgpCore.dll	68.3 KB (69904 bytes)	2/21/2004	12:17:20 A.M.
concentr.cnt	0.0 KB (43 bytes)	1/12/2004	6:07:28 P.M.
concentr.dll	104.3 KB (106768 bytes)	2/21/2004	12:17:22 A.M.
CONCENTR.hlp	8.8 KB (9005 bytes)	1/15/2004	10:53:48 A.M.
ICAClObj.class	4.0 KB (4075 bytes)	2/21/2004	12:11:28 A.M.
icadlgn.dll	36.3 KB (37136 bytes)	2/21/2004	12:17:22 A.M.
icalogon.dll	44.3 KB (45328 bytes)	2/21/2004	12:17:22 A.M.
IICAClient.xpt	3.1 KB (3169 bytes)	2/21/2004	12:11:30 A.M.
License.txt	20.6 KB (21072 bytes)	1/14/2004	12:02:22 P.M.
Mfc30.dll	315.3 KB (322832 bytes)	10/23/2001	11:48:40 A.M.
migrateN.exe	52.3 KB (53520 bytes)	2/21/2004	12:16:10 A.M.
modem.ini	684.7 KB (701103 bytes)	12/1/2003	10:39:58 P.M.
modem.src	684.7 KB (701103 bytes)	12/1/2003	10:39:58 P.M.
modemN.dll	28.3 KB (28944 bytes)	2/21/2004	12:17:22 A.M.
module.ini	38.1 KB (38993 bytes)	%DATE%	6:06:21 P.M.
module.src	38.1 KB (38981 bytes)	12/1/2003	10:40:04 P.M.
msvcrt.dll	288.1 KB (295000 bytes)	2/7/2002	8:42:50 P.M.

Table C-1. File and Folder Structure of the Program Neighborhood Client Installation

%ProgramFiles%\Citrix			
neHttpN.dll	44.3 KB (45328 bytes)	2/21/2004	12:17:22 A.M.
neipxn.dll	28.3 KB (28944 bytes)	2/21/2004	12:17:22 A.M.
nenetbn.dll	28.3 KB (28944 bytes)	2/21/2004	12:17:22 A.M.
nenumn.dll	24.3 KB (24848 bytes)	2/21/2004	12:17:22 A.M.
netcpN.dll	32.3 KB (33040 bytes)	2/21/2004	12:17:22 A.M.
npicaN.dll	304.3 KB (311568 bytes)	2/21/2004	12:17:22 A.M.
nrhttpn.dll	44.3 KB (45328 bytes)	2/21/2004	12:17:22 A.M.
nripxN.dll	40.3 KB (41232 bytes)	2/21/2004	12:17:22 A.M.
nrnetbN.dll	40.3 KB (41232 bytes)	2/21/2004	12:17:22 A.M.
nrnetwN.dll	32.3 KB (33040 bytes)	2/21/2004	12:17:22 A.M.
nrtcpn.dll	40.3 KB (41232 bytes)	2/21/2004	12:17:22 A.M.
pcl4rast.dll	1.28 MB (1339664 bytes)	2/21/2004	12:17:22 A.M.
pdc128N.dll	76.3 KB (78096 bytes)	2/21/2004	12:17:22 A.M.
pdcompN.dll	28.3 KB (28944 bytes)	2/21/2004	12:17:22 A.M.
pdframeN.dll	28.3 KB (28944 bytes)	2/21/2004	12:17:22 A.M.
pdmodemN.dll	28.3 KB (28944 bytes)	2/21/2004	12:17:22 A.M.
pdreliN.dll	28.3 KB (28944 bytes)	2/21/2004	12:17:22 A.M.
pdtapiN.dll	52.3 KB (53520 bytes)	2/21/2004	12:17:22 A.M.
pn.exe	428.3 KB (438544 bytes)	2/21/2004	12:14:48 A.M.
pn.ini	0.4 KB (428 bytes)	12/1/2003	10:40:04 P.M.
pn.src	0.4 KB (428 bytes)	12/1/2003	10:40:04 P.M.
pnapin.dll	52.3 KB (53520 bytes)	2/21/2004	12:17:22 A.M.
pncachen.dll	108.3 KB (110864 bytes)	2/21/2004	12:17:22 A.M.
pndskint.dll	32.3 KB (33040 bytes)	2/21/2004	12:17:22 A.M.
pnipcn.dll	20.3 KB (20752 bytes)	2/21/2004	12:17:22 A.M.
pnsson.dll	36.3 KB (37136 bytes)	2/21/2004	12:17:22 A.M.
pnstub.exe	24.3 KB (24848 bytes)	2/21/2004	12:08:34 A.M.
progn.cnt	2.9 KB (3013 bytes)	1/22/2004	4:18:50 P.M.
PROGN.hlp	118.0 KB (120804 bytes)	1/30/2004	2:46:18 P.M.
ProxySup.ocx	72.3 KB (74000 bytes)	2/20/2004	11:56:42 P.M.
PScript.dll	24.3 KB (24848 bytes)	2/21/2004	12:17:22 A.M.
scriptN.dll	36.3 KB (37136 bytes)	2/21/2004	12:17:22 A.M.

Table C-1.   File and Folder Structure of the Program Neighborhood Client Installation *(continued)*

%ProgramFiles%\Citrix			
srcflter.dll	80.3 KB (82192 bytes)	2/21/2004	12:17:22 A.M.
sslsdk_b.dll	56.3 KB (57616 bytes)	2/21/2004	12:17:22 A.M.
ssoncom.exe	20.3 KB (20752 bytes)	2/21/2004	12:08:48 A.M.
ssonstub.dll	24.3 KB (24848 bytes)	2/21/2004	12:17:22 A.M.
ssonsvr.exe	16.3 KB (16656 bytes)	2/21/2004	12:08:54 A.M.
statuin.dll	32.3 KB (33040 bytes)	2/21/2004	12:17:22 A.M.
TcpPServ.dll	24.3 KB (24848 bytes)	2/21/2004	12:17:22 A.M.
tdcommN.dll	40.3 KB (41232 bytes)	2/21/2004	12:17:22 A.M.
tdnetbN.dll	40.3 KB (41232 bytes)	2/21/2004	12:17:22 A.M.
tdwsipxN.dll	44.3 KB (45328 bytes)	2/21/2004	12:17:22 A.M.
tdwsspxN.dll	44.3 KB (45328 bytes)	2/21/2004	12:17:22 A.M.
vdcamN.dll	36.3 KB (37136 bytes)	2/21/2004	12:17:22 A.M.
vdcmN.dll	40.3 KB (41232 bytes)	2/21/2004	12:17:22 A.M.
vdcom30N.dll	48.3 KB (49424 bytes)	2/21/2004	12:17:22 A.M.
vdcpm30N.dll	32.3 KB (33040 bytes)	2/21/2004	12:17:22 A.M.
vdfon30n.dll	48.3 KB (49424 bytes)	2/21/2004	12:17:22 A.M.
vdmmn.dll	40.3 KB (41232 bytes)	2/21/2004	12:17:22 A.M.
vdpnn.dll	24.3 KB (24848 bytes)	2/21/2004	12:17:22 A.M.
vdscardn.dll	36.3 KB (37136 bytes)	2/21/2004	12:17:22 A.M.
vdspmike.dll	24.3 KB (24848 bytes)	2/21/2004	12:17:22 A.M.
vdsspin.dll	28.3 KB (28944 bytes)	2/21/2004	12:17:22 A.M.
vdtw30n.dll	136.3 KB (139536 bytes)	2/21/2004	12:17:22 A.M.
vdzlcn.dll	88.3 KB (90384 bytes)	2/21/2004	12:17:22 A.M.
version.dat	0.0 KB (12 bytes)	2/21/2004	12:17:10 A.M.
wfclient.ini	0.5 KB (553 bytes)	%DATE%	6:06:20 P.M.
wfclient.src	0.5 KB (553 bytes)	2/20/2004	10:16:14 P.M.
wfcmoveN.exe	100.3 KB (102672 bytes)	2/21/2004	12:13:38 A.M.
wfcrun32.exe	236.3 KB (241936 bytes)	2/21/2004	12:13:34 A.M.
wfcwin32.log	0.1 KB (53 bytes)	%DATE%	6:06:23 P.M.
wfcwinn.dll	32.3 KB (33040 bytes)	2/21/2004	12:17:22 A.M.
Wfica.ocx	400.3 KB (409872 bytes)	2/21/2004	12:11:26 A.M.
wfica32.exe	756.3 KB (774416 bytes)	2/21/2004	12:12:44 A.M.

Table C-1.   File and Folder Structure of the Program Neighborhood Client Installation *(continued)*

%ProgramFiles%\Citrix			
%ProgramFiles%\Citrix\ICA CLIENT\CACHE			
%ProgramFiles%\Citrix\ICA CLIENT\RESOURCE			
EN	DIR	3/16/2004	6:06:11 P.M.
%ProgramFiles%\Citrix\ICA CLIENT\RESOURCE\EN			
acrdlgUI.dll	44.3 KB (45328 bytes)	2/20/2004	11:53:28 P.M.
concenUI.dll	100.3 KB (102672 bytes)	2/20/2004	11:53:34 P.M.
icadlgUI.dll	36.3 KB (37136 bytes)	2/20/2004	11:53:36 P.M.
icalogUI.dll	32.3 KB (33040 bytes)	2/20/2004	11:53:30 P.M.
migratUI.dll	20.3 KB (20752 bytes)	2/20/2004	11:53:22 P.M.
npicanUI.dll	40.3 KB (41232 bytes)	2/20/2004	11:52:52 P.M.
nrhttpUI.dll	44.3 KB (45328 bytes)	2/20/2004	11:52:40 P.M.
nripxnUI.dll	44.3 KB (45328 bytes)	2/20/2004	11:52:44 P.M.
nrnetbUI.dll	44.3 KB (45328 bytes)	2/20/2004	11:52:46 P.M.
nrnetwUI.dll	20.3 KB (20752 bytes)	2/20/2004	11:52:46 P.M.
nrtcpnUI.dll	44.3 KB (45328 bytes)	2/20/2004	11:52:48 P.M.
pnapinUI.dll	92.3 KB (94480 bytes)	2/20/2004	11:53:10 P.M.
pndskiUI.dll	20.3 KB (20752 bytes)	2/20/2004	11:53:08 P.M.
pnstubUI.dll	20.3 KB (20752 bytes)	2/20/2004	11:53:12 P.M.
pnUI.dll	644.3 KB (659728 bytes)	2/20/2004	11:53:42 P.M.
scriptUI.dll	20.3 KB (20752 bytes)	2/20/2004	11:52:56 P.M.
sslsdkUI.dll	24.3 KB (24848 bytes)	2/20/2004	11:53:32 P.M.
statuiUI.dll	24.3 KB (24848 bytes)	2/20/2004	11:54:04 P.M.
tdcommUI.dll	20.3 KB (20752 bytes)	2/20/2004	11:52:58 P.M.
tdnetbUI.dll	20.3 KB (20752 bytes)	2/20/2004	11:53:00 P.M.
tdwsipUI.dll	40.3 KB (41232 bytes)	2/20/2004	11:53:02 P.M.
tdwsspUI.dll	40.3 KB (41232 bytes)	2/20/2004	11:53:04 P.M.
vdcmnUI.dll	20.3 KB (20752 bytes)	2/20/2004	11:53:06 P.M.
vdzlcnUI.dll	20.3 KB (20752 bytes)	2/20/2004	11:53:14 P.M.
wfcmovUI.dll	20.3 KB (20752 bytes)	2/20/2004	11:53:44 P.M.
wfcrunUI.dll	76.3 KB (78096 bytes)	2/20/2004	11:53:46 P.M.
wfica3UI.dll	84.3 KB (86288 bytes)	2/20/2004	11:53:16 P.M.
wficaUI.dll	44.3 KB (45328 bytes)	2/20/2004	11:52:50 P.M.

Table C-1. File and Folder Structure of the Program Neighborhood Client Installation *(continued)*

First-Time Started Application Files

This section lists the file and folder directory structure that is created in the user profile after the application is started for the first time.

New Folder Locations

The following folders are created in the user profile after the client is run for the first time:

%USERPROFILE%\Application Data\ICAClient
%USERPROFILE%\Application Data\ICAClient\Cache
%USERPROFILE%\Application Data\ICAClient\Cache\ZLCache

Additional Files

The default base folder location for the Program Neighborhood Client user profile installation is %USERPROFILE%\Application Data\ICAClient. Table C-2 lists the file and directory structure.

Registry Entries for the Program Neighborhood Client

This section lists the registry keys that are added for the Program Neighborhood Client. These registry keys assume a default installation of the client.

```
Key Name: SOFTWARE\Citrix
Class Name: <NO CLASS>
Last Write Time: 3/16/2004 - 3:51 P.M.
```

%USERPROFILE%\Application Data\ICAClient			
CACHE	DIR	%DATE%	11:15:35 A.M.
APPSRV.INI	3.3 KB (3401 bytes)	%DATE%	11:20:19 A.M.
PN.INI	0.5 KB (513 bytes)	%DATE%	11:08:02 A.M.
UISTATE.INI	0.1 KB (109 bytes)	%DATE%	11:15:56 A.M.
WFCLIENT.INI	0.6 KB (577 bytes)	%DATE%	11:20:19 A.M.
WFCWIN32.LOG	0.2 KB (159 bytes)	%DATE%	11:15:56 A.M.
%USERPROFILE%\Application Data\ICAClient\CACHE			
ZLCACHE	DIR	%DATE%	11:15:35 A.M.
%USERPROFILE%\Application Data\ICAClient\CACHE\ZLCACHE			

Table C-2.   User Profile File and Directory Structure for the Program Neighborhood Client

```
Key Name: SOFTWARE\Citrix\CitrixCAB
Class Name: <NO CLASS>
Last Write Time: 3/16/2004 - 3:51 P.M.
Value 0
 Name: <NO NAME>
 Type: REG_SZ
 Data: 1

Key Name: SOFTWARE\Citrix\ICA Client
Class Name: <NO CLASS>
Last Write Time: 3/16/2004 - 3:51 P.M.
Value 0
 Name: MsiInstallDir
 Type: REG_SZ
 Data: C:\Program Files\Citrix\ICA Client\

Value 1
 Name: ProgramFolderName
 Type: REG_SZ
 Data: Citrix\MetaFrame Access Clients

 Key Name: SOFTWARE\Citrix\Install
Class Name: <NO CLASS>
Last Write Time: 3/16/2004 - 3:51 P.M.

Key Name: SOFTWARE\Citrix\Install\MUI
Class Name: <NO CLASS>
Last Write Time: 3/16/2004 - 3:51 P.M.

Key Name: SOFTWARE\Citrix\Install\MUI\Modules
Class Name: <NO CLASS>
Last Write Time: 3/16/2004 - 3:51 P.M.
Value 0
 Name: Module.1F7C76CE_0458_4E22_A908_E3F38F4E31BA
 Type: REG_SZ
 Data: en

Value 1
 Name: Module.4788A191_9E75_405B_866C_7B2FA459A38F
 Type: REG_SZ
 Data: en

Key Name: SOFTWARE\Citrix\Install\
{94F321B9-45B0-4125-970D-DE3D98CBCA1C}
Class Name: <NO CLASS>
```

```
Last Write Time: 3/16/2004 - 3:51 P.M.
Value 0
 Name: InstallLocation
 Type: REG_SZ
 Data: C:\Program Files\Citrix\ICA Client\

Key Name: SOFTWARE\Citrix\MUI
Class Name: <NO CLASS>
Last Write Time: 3/16/2004 - 3:51 P.M.
Value 0
 Name: ICA_DefaultLanguage
 Type: REG_SZ
 Data: en
```

WEB CLIENT PACKAGE

The Web Client can be installed using one of the following packages:

▼ **ica32t.exe**   A self-extracting executable, approximately 2.5MB in size, this package is significantly smaller than the other MetaFrame Presentation Clients. The smaller size allows quicker downloads and installation. You can configure the Web Client for silent user installation.

■ **Wficat.cab**   A Windows CAB file, approximately 2.2MB in size (compressed).

■ **Wficac.cab**   A Windows CAB file, approximately 1.3MB in size (compressed).

▲ **Wfica.cab**   A Windows CAB file, approximately 3.9MB in size (compressed).

For more information on the MetaFrame Presentation Server Client for 32-bit Windows software, see the *Client for 32-bit Windows Administrator's Guide* and the *MetaFrame Presentation Server Administrator's Guide*.

Both *Ica32t.exe* and *Wficat.cab* will install the same files and registry entries. The *Wfica.cab* file is the full Program Neighborhood Client. The *Wficac.cab* file will install a smaller client without encryption and UPD support.

Installed Folders and Files

This section lists the folders and files and other details that are added when the Web Client is installed. The locations provided are for a default installation.

New Folders Created

The following new folders are created during the installation:

```
%ProgramFiles%\Citrix\
%ProgramFiles%\Citrix\icaweb32
```

New Files Added into the Folders

Table C-3 lists the files and folders added to the base installation folder, %ProgramFiles%\Citrix\icaweb32, for the Web Client location.

%ProgramFiles%\Citrix\icaweb32			
acrdlg.dll	28.3 KB (28944 bytes)	2/21/2004	12:17:20 A.M.
adpcm.dll	32.3 KB (33040 bytes)	2/21/2004	12:17:20 A.M.
APPSRV.INI	1.7 KB (1738 bytes)	12/1/2003	10:40:04 P.M.
APPSRV.SRC	1.7 KB (1738 bytes)	12/1/2003	10:40:04 P.M.
audcvtn.dll	32.3 KB (33040 bytes)	2/21/2004	12:17:20 A.M.
cgpcfg.dll	20.3 KB (20752 bytes)	2/21/2004	12:17:20 A.M.
cgpcore.dll	68.3 KB (69904 bytes)	2/21/2004	12:17:20 A.M.
concentr.cnt	0.0 KB (43 bytes)	1/12/2004	6:07:28 P.M.
concentr.dll	104.3 KB (106768 bytes)	2/21/2004	12:17:22 A.M.
concentr.hlp	8.8 KB (9005 bytes)	1/15/2004	10:53:48 A.M.
ICAClobj.class	4.0 KB (4075 bytes)	2/21/2004	12:11:28 A.M.
icadlgn.dll	36.3 KB (37136 bytes)	2/21/2004	12:17:22 A.M.
icalogon.dll	44.3 KB (45328 bytes)	2/21/2004	12:17:22 A.M.
IICAClient.xpt	3.1 KB (3169 bytes)	2/21/2004	12:11:30 A.M.
mfc30.dll	315.3 KB (322832 bytes)	10/23/2001	11:48:40 A.M.
migraten.exe	52.3 KB (53520 bytes)	2/21/2004	12:16:10 A.M.
MODULE.INI	38.1 KB (39001 bytes)	2/21/2004	12:22:28 A.M.
MODULE.SRC	38.1 KB (39001 bytes)	2/21/2004	12:22:28 A.M.
msvcrt.dll	288.1 KB (295000 bytes)	2/7/2002	8:42:50 P.M.
netcpn.dll	32.3 KB (33040 bytes)	2/21/2004	12:17:22 A.M.
npican.dll	304.3 KB (311568 bytes)	2/21/2004	12:17:22 A.M.
nrhttpn.dll	44.3 KB (45328 bytes)	2/21/2004	12:17:22 A.M.
nrtcpn.dll	40.3 KB (41232 bytes)	2/21/2004	12:17:22 A.M.
pcl4rast.dll	1.28 MB (1339664 bytes)	2/21/2004	12:17:22 A.M.

Table C-3.   File and Directory Structure of the ICA Web Client Installation

%ProgramFiles%\Citrix\icaweb32			
pdc128N.dll	76.3 KB (78096 bytes)	2/21/2004	12:17:22 A.M.
pdcompN.dll	28.3 KB (28944 bytes)	2/21/2004	12:17:22 A.M.
ProxySup.ocx	72.3 KB (74000 bytes)	2/20/2004	11:56:42 P.M.
pscript.dll	24.3 KB (24848 bytes)	2/21/2004	12:17:22 A.M.
srcflter.dll	80.3 KB (82192 bytes)	2/21/2004	12:17:22 A.M.
sslsdk_b.dll	56.3 KB (57616 bytes)	2/21/2004	12:17:22 A.M.
statuin.dll	32.3 KB (33040 bytes)	2/21/2004	12:17:22 A.M.
tcppserv.dll	24.3 KB (24848 bytes)	2/21/2004	12:17:22 A.M.
uninst.inf	3.9 KB (3972 bytes)	%DATE%	4:19:49 P.M.
vdcamN.dll	36.3 KB (37136 bytes)	2/21/2004	12:17:22 A.M.
vdcmN.dll	40.3 KB (41232 bytes)	2/21/2004	12:17:22 A.M.
vdcom30n.dll	48.3 KB (49424 bytes)	2/21/2004	12:17:22 A.M.
vdcpm30n.dll	32.3 KB (33040 bytes)	2/21/2004	12:17:22 A.M.
vdfon30n.dll	48.3 KB (49424 bytes)	2/21/2004	12:17:22 A.M.
vdmmn.dll	40.3 KB (41232 bytes)	2/21/2004	12:17:22 A.M.
vdscardn.dll	36.3 KB (37136 bytes)	2/21/2004	12:17:22 A.M.
VDSSPIN.dll	28.3 KB (28944 bytes)	2/21/2004	12:17:22 A.M.
vdtw30n.dll	136.3 KB (139536 bytes)	2/21/2004	12:17:22 A.M.
vdzlcn.dll	88.3 KB (90384 bytes)	2/21/2004	12:17:22 A.M.
VERSION.DAT	0.0 KB (12 bytes)	2/21/2004	12:17:10 A.M.
WFCLIENT.INI	0.5 KB (553 bytes)	2/20/2004	10:16:14 P.M.
WFCLIENT.SRC	0.5 KB (553 bytes)	2/20/2004	10:16:14 P.M.
wfcmoven.exe	100.3 KB (102672 bytes)	2/21/2004	12:13:38 A.M.
wfcrun32.exe	236.3 KB (241936 bytes)	2/21/2004	12:13:34 A.M.
WFCSETUP.INI	0.1 KB (88 bytes)	12/1/2003	10:38:58 P.M.
wfcwinN.dll	32.3 KB (33040 bytes)	2/21/2004	12:17:22 A.M.
wfica.ocx	400.3 KB (409872 bytes)	2/21/2004	12:11:26 A.M.
wfica32.exe	756.3 KB (774416 bytes)	2/21/2004	12:12:44 A.M.

Table C-3.   File and Directory Structure of the ICA Web Client Installation *(continued)*

First-Time Started Application Files

This section lists the files and folders that are added to the user profile directory after the Web Client is started for the first time.

New Folder Locations

The Web Client creates the following directories after it is run for the first time:

```
%USERPROFILE%\Application Data\ICAClient
%USERPROFILE%\Application Data\ICAClient\Cache
%USERPROFILE%\Application Data\ICAClient\Cache\ZLCache
```

Additional Files

The default base folder location for the Web Client user profile installation is %USERPROFILE%\Application Data\ICAClient. Table C-4 lists the file and directory structure.

Registry Entries for the Web Client

This section lists the registry changes created from the installation of the Web Client. The following registry keys assume a default installation of the client:

```
Key Name: SOFTWARE\Citrix
Class Name: <NO CLASS>
Last Write Time: 3/16/2004 - 4:30 P.M.


Key Name: SOFTWARE\Citrix\CitrixCAB
Class Name: <NO CLASS>
Last Write Time: 3/16/2004 - 4:30 P.M.
Value 0
 Name: <NO NAME>
 Type: REG_SZ
 Data: 1


Key Name: SOFTWARE\Citrix\MUI
Class Name: <NO CLASS>
Last Write Time: 3/16/2004 - 4:30 P.M.
Value 0
 Name: ICA_DefaultLanguage
 Type: REG_SZ
 Data: en
```

	%USERPROFILE%\Application Data\ICAClient		
CACHE	DIR	%DATE%	11:50:17 A.M.
APPSRV.INI	1.9 KB (1957 bytes)	%DATE%	11:50:14 A.M.
UISTATE.INI	0.1 KB (109 bytes)	%DATE%	11:50:32 A.M.
WFCLIENT.INI	0.5 KB (553 bytes)	2/20/2004	10:16:14 P.M.
wfcwin32.log	0.2 KB (159 bytes)	%DATE%	11:50:32 A.M.
%USERPROFILE%\Application Data\ICAClient\CACHE			
ZLCACHE	DIR	%DATE%	11:50:17 A.M.
%USERPROFILE%\Application Data\ICAClient\CACHE\ZLCACHE			

Table C-4.   User Profile File and Directory Structure Installation for the Web Client

PROGRAM NEIGHBORHOOD AGENT PACKAGE

The Program Neighborhood Agent can be installed using **ica32a.exe**, a self-extracting executable, approximately 3.6MB in size. You can configure the ICA Win32 Program Neighborhood Agent for silent user installation.

For more information on the MetaFrame Presentation Server Client for 32-bit Windows software, see the *Client for 32-bit Windows Administrator's Guide* and the *MetaFrame Presentation Server Administrator's Guide*.

Installed Folders and Files

This section lists the folders and files added when the Program Neighborhood Agent is installed. The locations provided are based on a default installation.

New Folders Created

The following folders are created upon installation of the Program Neighborhood Agent Client:

    %ProgramFiles%\Citrix\
    %ProgramFiles%\Citrix\PNAgent
    %ProgramFiles%\Citrix\PNAgent\Cache
    %ProgramFiles%\Citrix\PNAgent\Resource
    %ProgramFiles%\Citrix\PNAgent\Resource\EN

New Files Added into the Folders

Table C-5 lists the file and directory structure that is created by the Program Neighborhood Agent in the base installation point, %ProgramFiles%\Citrix\PNAgent.

%ProgramFiles%\Citrix\PNAgent			
CACHE	DIR	%DATE%	5:18:37 P.M.
RESOURCE	DIR	%DATE%	5:18:23 P.M.
acrdlg.dll	28.3 KB (28944 bytes)	2/21/2004	12:17:20 A.M.
adpcm.dll	32.3 KB (33040 bytes)	2/21/2004	12:17:20 A.M.
appsrv.ini	1.9 KB (1937 bytes)	%DATE%	5:18:37 P.M.
audcvtN.dll	32.3 KB (33040 bytes)	2/21/2004	12:17:20 A.M.
cgpcfg.dll	20.3 KB (20752 bytes)	2/21/2004	12:17:20 A.M.
cgpcore.dll	68.3 KB (69904 bytes)	2/21/2004	12:17:20 A.M.
changeno.dat	0.0 KB (19 bytes)	2/20/2004	11:52:38 P.M.
concentr.cnt	0.0 KB (43 bytes)	1/12/2004	6:07:28 P.M.
concentr.dll	104.3 KB (106768 bytes)	2/21/2004	12:17:22 A.M.
CONCENTR.hlp	8.8 KB (9005 bytes)	1/15/2004	10:53:48 A.M.
dpihand.dll	32.3 KB (33040 bytes)	2/21/2004	12:17:22 A.M.
ICAClObj.class	4.0 KB (4075 bytes)	2/21/2004	12:11:28 A.M.
icadlgn.dll	36.3 KB (37136 bytes)	2/21/2004	12:17:22 A.M.
icalogon.dll	44.3 KB (45328 bytes)	2/21/2004	12:17:22 A.M.
IICAClient.xpt	3.1 KB (3169 bytes)	2/21/2004	12:11:30 A.M.
license.txt	20.6 KB (21072 bytes)	1/14/2004	12:02:22 P.M.
mfc30.dll	315.3 KB (322832 bytes)	10/23/2001	11:48:40 A.M.
migrateN.exe	52.3 KB (53520 bytes)	2/21/2004	12:16:10 A.M.
module.INI	38.1 KB (39002 bytes)	2/21/2004	12:27:20 A.M.
module.src	38.1 KB (38981 bytes)	12/1/2003	10:40:04 P.M.
msvcrt.dll	288.1 KB (295000 bytes)	2/7/2002	8:42:50 P.M.
npicaN.dll	304.3 KB (311568 bytes)	2/21/2004	12:17:22 A.M.
nrhttpn.dll	44.3 KB (45328 bytes)	2/21/2004	12:17:22 A.M.
nrtcpn.dll	40.3 KB (41232 bytes)	2/21/2004	12:17:22 A.M.
pcl4rast.dll	1.28 MB (1339664 bytes)	2/21/2004	12:17:22 A.M.
pdc128N.dll	76.3 KB (78096 bytes)	2/21/2004	12:17:22 A.M.

Table C-5.   Program Neighborhood Agent File and Directory Structure

%ProgramFiles%\Citrix\PNAgent			
pdcompN.dll	28.3 KB (28944 bytes)	2/21/2004	12:17:22 A.M.
pnagent.cnt	0.7 KB (722 bytes)	1/21/2004	11:15:08 A.M.
pnagent.exe	208.3 KB (213264 bytes)	2/21/2004	12:16:02 A.M.
pnagent.hlp	14.0 KB (14307 bytes)	2/10/2004	4:45:44 P.M.
ProxySup.ocx	72.3 KB (74000 bytes)	2/20/2004	11:56:42 P.M.
pscript.dll	24.3 KB (24848 bytes)	2/21/2004	12:17:22 A.M.
srcflter.dll	80.3 KB (82192 bytes)	2/21/2004	12:17:22 A.M.
sslpdo.dll	20.3 KB (20752 bytes)	2/21/2004	12:17:22 A.M.
sslsdk_b.dll	56.3 KB (57616 bytes)	2/21/2004	12:17:22 A.M.
statuin.dll	32.3 KB (33040 bytes)	2/21/2004	12:17:22 A.M.
tcppserv.dll	24.3 KB (24848 bytes)	2/21/2004	12:17:22 A.M.
vdcamN.dll	36.3 KB (37136 bytes)	2/21/2004	12:17:22 A.M.
vdcmN.dll	40.3 KB (41232 bytes)	2/21/2004	12:17:22 A.M.
vdcom30N.dll	48.3 KB (49424 bytes)	2/21/2004	12:17:22 A.M.
vdcpm30N.dll	32.3 KB (33040 bytes)	2/21/2004	12:17:22 A.M.
vdfon30n.dll	48.3 KB (49424 bytes)	2/21/2004	12:17:22 A.M.
vdmmn.dll	40.3 KB (41232 bytes)	2/21/2004	12:17:22 A.M.
vdscardn.dll	36.3 KB (37136 bytes)	2/21/2004	12:17:22 A.M.
vdspmike.dll	24.3 KB (24848 bytes)	2/21/2004	12:17:22 A.M.
VDSSPIN.dll	28.3 KB (28944 bytes)	2/21/2004	12:17:22 A.M.
vdtw30n.dll	136.3 KB (139536 bytes)	2/21/2004	12:17:22 A.M.
vdzlcn.dll	88.3 KB (90384 bytes)	2/21/2004	12:17:22 A.M.
version.dat	0.0 KB (12 bytes)	2/21/2004	12:17:10 A.M.
wfclient.ini	0.5 KB (553 bytes)	%DATE%	5:18:37 P.M.
wfclient.src	0.5 KB (553 bytes)	2/20/2004	10:16:14 P.M.
wfcmoveN.exe	100.3 KB (102672 bytes)	2/21/2004	12:13:38 A.M.
wfcrun32.exe	236.3 KB (241936 bytes)	2/21/2004	12:13:34 A.M.
wfcwinn.dll	32.3 KB (33040 bytes)	2/21/2004	12:17:22 A.M.
wfica.ocx	400.3 KB (409872 bytes)	2/21/2004	12:11:26 A.M.
wfica32.exe	756.3 KB (774416 bytes)	2/21/2004	12:23:34 A.M.
winsock1.dll	24.3 KB (24848 bytes)	2/21/2004	12:17:22 A.M.
winsock2.dll	24.3 KB (24848 bytes)	2/21/2004	12:17:22 A.M.

Table C-5.   Program Neighborhood Agent File and Directory Structure *(continued)*

%ProgramFiles%\Citrix\PNAgent			
%ProgramFiles%\Citrix\PNAgent\CACHE			
%ProgramFiles%\Citrix\PNAgent\RESOURCE			
EN	DIR	%DATE%	5:18:24 P.M.
%ProgramFiles%\Citrix\PNAgent\RESOURCE\EN			
acrdlgUI.dll	44.3 KB (45328 bytes)	2/20/2004	11:53:28 P.M.
concenUI.dll	100.3 KB (102672 bytes)	2/20/2004	11:53:34 P.M.
icadlgUI.dll	36.3 KB (37136 bytes)	2/20/2004	11:53:36 P.M.
icalogUI.dll	32.3 KB (33040 bytes)	2/20/2004	11:53:30 P.M.
migratUI.dll	20.3 KB (20752 bytes)	2/20/2004	11:53:22 P.M.
npicaNUI.dll	40.3 KB (41232 bytes)	2/20/2004	11:52:52 P.M.
nrhttpUI.dll	44.3 KB (45328 bytes)	2/20/2004	11:52:40 P.M.
nrtcpnUI.dll	44.3 KB (45328 bytes)	2/20/2004	11:52:48 P.M.
pnagenUI.dll	128.3 KB (131344 bytes)	2/20/2004	11:52:54 P.M.
sslsdkUI.dll	24.3 KB (24848 bytes)	2/20/2004	11:53:32 P.M.
statuiUI.dll	24.3 KB (24848 bytes)	2/20/2004	11:54:04 P.M.
vdcmNUI.dll	20.3 KB (20752 bytes)	2/20/2004	11:53:06 P.M.
vdzlcnUI.dll	20.3 KB (20752 bytes)	2/20/2004	11:53:14 P.M.
wfcmovUI.dll	20.3 KB (20752 bytes)	2/20/2004	11:53:44 P.M.
wfcrunUI.dll	76.3 KB (78096 bytes)	2/20/2004	11:53:46 P.M.
wfica3UI.dll	84.3 KB (86288 bytes)	2/20/2004	11:53:16 P.M.
WficaUI.dll	44.3 KB (45328 bytes)	2/20/2004	11:52:50 P.M.

Table C-5. Program Neighborhood Agent File and Directory Structure *(continued)*

First-Time Started Application Files

This section lists the files and folders added to the user profile directory after the application is started for the first time.

New Folder Locations

Table C-6 lists the file and directory structure for the Program Neighborhood Agent. The default base folder locations are

%USERPROFILE%\Application Data\ICAClient.
%USERPROFILE%\Application Data\Citrix
%USERPROFILE%\Application Data\ Citrix\PNAgent
%USERPROFILE%\Application Data\ Citrix\PNAgent\AppCache
%USERPROFILE%\Application Data\ Citrix\PNAgent\ResourceCache

%USERPROFILE%\Application Data\Citrix			
PNAGENT	DIR	%DATE%	11:33:51 A.M.
%USERPROFILE%\Application Data\Citrix\PNAGENT			
APPCACHE	DIR	%DATE%	11:33:45 A.M.
RESOURCECACHE	DIR	%DATE%	11:34:12 A.M.
%USERPROFILE%\Application Data\Citrix\PNAGENT\APPCACHE			
appdata.xml	2.8 KB (2844 bytes)	%DATE%	11:33:45 A.M.
%USERPROFILE%\Application Data\Citrix\PNAGENT\RESOURCECACHE			

Table C-6.   Program Neighborhood Agent Default User Profile File and Directory Structure

Registry Entries for the Program Neighborhood Agent

This section lists the registry entries for the Program Neighborhood Agent installation. These registry keys assume a default installation of the client.

```
Key Name: SOFTWARE\Citrix
Class Name: <NO CLASS>
Last Write Time: 3/16/2004 - 5:17 P.M.

Key Name: SOFTWARE\Citrix\Citrix Program Neighborhood Agent
Class Name: <NO CLASS>
Last Write Time: 3/16/2004 - 5:18 P.M.

Key Name: SOFTWARE\Citrix\Citrix Program Neighborhood Agent\1.00.000
Class Name: <NO CLASS>
Last Write Time: 3/16/2004 - 5:18 P.M.

Key Name: SOFTWARE\Citrix\CitrixCAB
Class Name: <NO CLASS>
Last Write Time: 3/16/2004 - 5:17 P.M.
Value 0
 Name: <NO NA.M. Type: REG_SZ
 Data: en

Key Name: SOFTWARE\Citrix\Program Neighborhood Agent
Class Name: <NO CLASS>
Last Write Time: 3/16/2004 - 5:18 P.M.
Value 0
 Name: Config Url
 Type: REG_SZ
 Data: <servername specified for Server Address during installation>
```

```
Value 1
 Name: DeleteBasedOnFilenamesOnly
 Type: REG_DWORD
 Data: 0

Value 2
 Name: DirectoryDepth
 Type: REG_DWORD
 Data: 0

Value 3
 Name: PersistentDesktopIcons
 Type: REG_DWORD
 Data: 0x1

Value 4
 Name: ProgramFolderName
 Type: REG_SZ
 Data: Citrix\MetaFrame Access Clients

Key Name: SOFTWARE\Citrix\Program Neighborhood Agent\Uninstall
Class Name: <NO CLASS>
Last Write Time: 3/16/2004 - 5:18 P.M.
Value 0
 Name: 0_desktop
 Type: REG_SZ
 Data: C:\Documents and Settings\Administrator\Desktop

Value 1
 Name: 0_IconName
 Type: REG_SZ
 Data: My Program Neighborhood Applications

Value 2
 Name: 0_programs
 Type: REG_SZ
 Data: C:\Documents and Settings\Administrator\Start Menu\Programs

Value 3
 Name: 0_RootFolder
 Type: REG_SZ
 Data:

Value 4
 Name: 0_RootFolder_root
 Type: REG_DWORD
 Data: 0x1
```

Value 5
 Name: 0_startmenu
 Type: REG_SZ
 Data: C:\Documents and Settings\Administrator\Start Menu

Value 6
 Name: Cache
 Type: REG_MULTI_SZ
 Data: C:\Documents and Settings\Administrator\Application Data

APPENDIX D

Citrix *e*Labs Testing Hardware

Table D-1 lists the hardware that was used in the Citrix *e*Labs for the MetaFrame Presentation Server testing referred to throughout this book.

Acer AcerPower Sd – PIV

Acer TravelMate C100

Acer TravelMate C110

Apple iMac

Apple Power MAC G4

Apple PowerBook G4

Cisco Wireless WAP

Cisco Aironet 350 Series wireless LAN adapter (802.11b)

Cisco LocalDirector 416

Cisco PIX 515 firewall appliance

Compaq Aero

Compaq Deskpro DPENM

Compaq Deskpro DPEND

Compaq DeskPro EN SFF

Compaq DL 320

Compaq DL 350

Compaq DL 360

Compaq DL 380

Compaq DL 580

Compaq iPaq

Compaq EVO T20

Compaq ML 330

Compaq Proliant BL20p

Compaq Proliant 1850R

Compaq Proliant 800

Compaq Proliant 8500R

Compaq StorageWorks FC-AL switch

Compaq StorageWorks RA4100

Table D-1.   Citrix eLabs Testing Hardware

Compaq StorageWorks MSA1000

Compaq TabletPC

Compaq TaskSmart N2400

DLink DWL-650+ wireless card (22MB)

Dell 1600SC

Dell 1750

Dell OptiPlex GX1

Dell OptiPlex Gxa

Dell PowerEdge 1400

Dell PowerEdge 1600SC

Dell PowerEdge 1655MC

Dell PowerEdge 1650

Dell PowerEdge 2650

Dell PowerEdge 6650

Dell Precision 220 machines

Dell Precision 340

Dell Precision 360

EMC Celerra SE

F5 BigIP 540 Load Balancer

Fujitsu LifeBook P Series

Fujitsu Stylistic 4100

Gateway ALR 7200

Hewlett-Packard Jornada

Hewlett-Packard LaserJet printers

Hewlett-Packard Netserver E60

Hewlett-Packard Netserver LXe Pro

Hewlett-Packard ProCurve switches

Hewlett-Packard TC4100

HHP USB barcode scanner

IBM 4600

IBM IntelliStation M-Series

Table D-1. Citrix *eLabs* Testing Hardware *(continued)*

IBM IntelliStation E-Series

IBM NetFinity 3000

IBM NetFinity 3500 M10

IBM NetFinity 3500 M20

IBM NetFinity 5500

IBM ThinkPad R32

IBM xSeries 335

Identix Biometric Login USB devices (fingerprint)

Intel 640T

Lucent Pipeline ISDN router

Nortel Networks Alteon Application Switch 2424

Packeteer AppVantage ASM-70

Packeteer PacketShaper 2500

Packeteer PacketShaper 4500

Panasonic PrivateID iris-scan

Precise Biometrics 100MC fingerprint readers (USB)

Rainbow CryptoSwift 200 SSL accelerator cards

Rainbow CryptoSwift 600 SSL accelerator cards

Shunra Storm

Sierra Wireless PCMCIA cards

Startek fingerprint reader (USB)

Sun Blade 150

Sun Ultra 5

Toshiba Portege 3500

ViewSonic Airpanel 100

Wyse Winterms WT9450, WT1200LE

Table D-1. Citrix *e*Labs Testing Hardware *(continued)*

Index

▼ E

S

INTERNATIONAL CONTACT INFORMATION

AUSTRALIA
McGraw-Hill Book Company
Australia Pty. Ltd.
TEL +61-2-9900-1800
FAX +61-2-9878-8881
http://www.mcgraw-hill.com.au
books-it_sydney@mcgraw-hill.com

CANADA
McGraw-Hill Ryerson Ltd.
TEL +905-430-5000
FAX +905-430-5020
http://www.mcgraw-hill.ca

GREECE, MIDDLE EAST, & AFRICA
(Excluding South Africa)
McGraw-Hill Hellas
TEL +30-210-6560-990
TEL +30-210-6560-993
TEL +30-210-6560-994
FAX +30-210-6545-525

MEXICO (Also serving Latin America)
McGraw-Hill Interamericana Editores
S.A. de C.V.
TEL +525-1500-5108
FAX +525-117-1589
http://www.mcgraw-hill.com.mx
carlos_ruiz@mcgraw-hill.com

SINGAPORE (Serving Asia)
McGraw-Hill Book Company
TEL +65-6863-1580
FAX +65-6862-3354
http://www.mcgraw-hill.com.sg
mghasia@mcgraw-hill.com

SOUTH AFRICA
McGraw-Hill South Africa
TEL +27-11-622-7512
FAX +27-11-622-9045
robyn_swanepoel@mcgraw-hill.com

SPAIN
McGraw-Hill/
Interamericana de España, S.A.U.
TEL +34-91-180-3000
FAX +34-91-372-8513
http://www.mcgraw-hill.es
professional@mcgraw-hill.es

UNITED KINGDOM, NORTHERN,
EASTERN, & CENTRAL EUROPE
McGraw-Hill Education Europe
TEL +44-1-628-502500
FAX +44-1-628-770224
http://www.mcgraw-hill.co.uk
emea_queries@mcgraw-hill.com

ALL OTHER INQUIRIES Contact:
McGraw-Hill/Osborne
TEL +1-510-420-7700
FAX +1-510-420-7703
http://www.osborne.com
omg_international@mcgraw-hill.com

99% of the *Fortune* 500 use Citrix.

Obviously, there's room for improvement.